Nearly the New World

To Sharon
with my best wishes,
Joanna

Advance praise for *Nearly the New World*

This book offers an unusual angle of vision on the tragic history of Jews in flight from Europe before and during the Second World War. Joanna Newman shows how British officials and West Indians, as well as refugees themselves, reacted to the forced emigration of victims of Nazi oppression. She tracks the miserable record of the colonial bureaucracy through a multitude of archives. For the first time, she exposes the scandal of deliberate under-utilization of available refugee camp facilities in Jamaica during the war. Throughout, she injects a human dimension with evidence from letters, memoirs and interviews. We learn how Jews disembarking in the West Indies were greeted with calypsos, some expressing sympathy at their plight, others resentment at their uninvited arrival. Admirably researched, deeply thoughtful and wonderfully readable, this book has a vital message for the worldwide humanitarian crisis of our own time, as a new generation of asylum seekers knocks desperately at our doors.

Bernard Wasserstein, University of Chicago

Joanna Newman's Nearly the New World *is a remarkable achievement. It is the first full study of Jewish refugee movements to the British Caribbean and for that alone it is of immense value. But the significance of this book is much greater. In the field of Holocaust studies it acts as a model, bringing together perspectives from the British imperial government, Jewish refugee organizations, local responses and the experiences of the refugees themselves. It is also a wonderful example of a historian creatively curating sources, ranging from Colonial Office minutes through to the rich resource of Trinidadian calypsos, to explore the history and memory of this neglected topic. For those in refugee studies it is also an important intervention with the persecuted at the forefront of her study. The author makes clear the connections between the refugees at sea in the Nazi era to find a place of safety and those on migrant boats today. This is a compelling story, beautifully told.*

Tony Kushner, Parkes Institute, University of Southampton and author of *Journeys from the Abyss: The Holocaust and Forced Migration from the 1880s to the Present* (2017)

Nearly the New World *is a richly researched book that addresses a key gap in the historiography of World War II—the forced migration of Jewish refugees to the British West Indies. It is a timely work that will make an invaluable contribution to the scholarly literature on Jewish refugees from the Nazis, Jews in colonial spaces and the Jewish Caribbean in particular.*

Sarah Phillips Casteel, Carleton University

NEARLY THE NEW WORLD

*The British West Indies and the Flight from Nazism,
1933–1945*

Joanna Newman

berghahn
NEW YORK · OXFORD
www.berghahnbooks.com

First published in 2019 by
Berghahn Books
www.berghahnbooks.com

Library of Congress Cataloging-in-Publication Data
A C.I.P. cataloging record is available from the Library of Congress
Library of Congress Cataloging in Publication Control Number:
2019026283

British Library Cataloguing in Publication Data
A catalogue record for this book is available from the British Library

ISBN 978-1-78920-333-2 hardback
ISBN 978-1-78920-649-4 paperback
ISBN 978-1-78920-334-9 ebook

Dedicated to my grandparents, Kurt and Lore Rockwell and
Lissi and Franz Newman.

In memory of the many known and unknown individuals who worked for
refugee organizations during the 1930s and 1940s, and gave their time,
energy and dedication to helping others.

For Bertrand, Eleonore, Jake, Ben, Matthew and Lucy.

Contents

Illustrations

Colour versions of several of the images in this book can be found on the publisher's website at www.berghahnbooks.com/title/NewmanNearly.

ACKNOWLEDGEMENTS

I wish to thank the following readers and friends for reviewing all or parts of this study, and for their invaluable help and advice: Professor Tony Kushner, Dr Lars Fischer, Professor Michael Berkowitz, Professor Adam Sutcliffe, Dr Julia Pascal, Professor Colin Riordan, Uwe Westphal, Matthew Reisz, Su Goldfish, Peggy Vance, Andrew Harrison, Caroline Pung, Oliver Urquart Irvine, Maria Balinska, and the anonymous peer reviewers for Berghahn Books. Their critique was immensely helpful in preparing this book. I would like to wholeheartedly thank my editor Chris Chappell, Soyolmaa Lkhagvadorj and Caroline Kuhtz at Berghahn Books for all their help, support and skilled guidance through the editorial process.

In particular, I would like to thank Professor Tony Kushner for his indefatigable support and advice and for reading several drafts and making key suggestions. Lars Fischer made an instrumental contribution to the editing of this book, including drawing my attention to many new sources of information, and to whom I am greatly indebted. I am deeply grateful to the University of Southampton for the Parkes Archival studentship, to the Institute of Commonwealth Studies, University of London, and to the American Jewish Archives in Cincinnati for a Fellowship in American Jewish Studies. I am also grateful to colleagues at King's College London, in particular the history department and to Professor Anthony Pereira, Professor Funmi Olonisakin and Professor Adam Sutcliffe. I am immensely sad that Professor John Klier and Professor David Cesarani, two scholars who have been so influential in the field of Jewish studies, and who offered me such valuable mentorship and encouragement, are no longer in this world. They are sorely missed but never forgotten. I am also grateful to Sue Ellis, my producer for the BBC Radio 4 Archive Hour that created the opportunity for me to visit Trinidad and Tobago and Jamaica, and to meet a number of the people whose stories are told in this book. I am also grateful to those people who took the trouble to answer my questions, share information and discuss their experiences with me, including Professor Bridget Brereton and Professor Gordon Rohlehr, Dr Luz Longworth, Dr Paulette Kerr and Jo-Ann

Granger from the University of the West Indies, Avril Belfon from the Trinidad and Tobago National Archives, Valerie Taylor and Judith Marchan, Abigail Lewis, Ray Funk, John Cowley, Ainsley Henriques, Arnold von der Porten, Professor Geoffrey Giles, William Kaczynski, Donah Farah, Lennox Honychurch, Aubrey Rose, Lore and Edward Schonbeck, Hans Stecher, Miriam Stanton and Professor Dr Fulberg-Stolberg, University of Hannover. Su Goldfish's film, *The Last Goldfish*, has been a great inspiration to me, and I am grateful to Su for sharing and providing permission to include much of her father Manfred's story in this book. I am also grateful to Su and Deborah for their warmth and hospitality in Sydney.

I thank the staff at the following libraries and archives for their helpful assistance in providing me with access to their materials: in Cincinnati, Kathy Spray, Kevin Profitt and staff at the American Jewish Archives; in New York, Dr Diane Spielmann and staff at the Leo Baeck Institute, staff at the American Jewish Joint Distribution Archives, the Jewish Theological Seminary, the New York Public Library, and the Yivo Archive; in Washington DC, Milton Gustafson and colleagues at the National Archives Washington, and to Ron Coleman and colleagues at the United States Holocaust Memorial Museum (USHMM); in London, staff at the British Library, particularly patient colleagues in the Newspaper Archive, to staff at the Institute for Advanced Legal Studies, University of London, the Institute for Historical Research, University of London, University College Library, the Wiener Library, and staff at the National Archives, Kew; at the University of Southampton, thanks to Karen Robson, Jenny Ruthven and Dr Chris Woolgar of the Parkes Library and University of Southampton Archive; in Trinidad, to staff at the St Augustine Campus, University of the West Indies, and at the National Archives of Trinidad and Tobago; and finally, in Jamaica, to staff at the Mona Campus, University of the West Indies.

I would like to thank my chair of the Association of Commonwealth Universities' Council, Professor Amit Chakma, for generously granting me study leave to complete this manuscript. I would also like to thank Eleanor Timms for keeping me mobile and optimistic at all times, even when walking was at its most problematic. To my niece Lucy Woolf, who asked me lots of questions about this book and who, alongside Bertrand, Eleonore, Jake, Ben and Matthew, is a constant source of joy and pride.

Finally, I wish to thank my parents and the Newman, Woolf and James families for their love and support and friendship.

Part I

INTRODUCTIONS

INTRODUCTION

On New Year's Day 1939, Manfred and Malka Goldfisch stepped ashore into the heat of a Trinidadian winter.[1] In Port of Spain it was 30 degrees centigrade and brilliant sunshine. Their journey to freedom had started two weeks earlier, as they left an ice-bound Hamburg to begin their lives as Jewish refugees in the Caribbean:

> On a cold day in Koenigsberg, [there was] nothing else left but to say goodbye to a few friends, and at the end of November we were ready to leave the now grey and wintry Baltic ... We boarded a train to Cologne to spend a last week with my parents, and then the sad moment of parting had to be faced. There were no tears, no sighs, only grim faces all round, when the whistle blew, and the Hamburg express started to pull out of the station ... The excitement of the imminent departure kept us awake, and it was almost morning before our eyes closed. At 7 am the desk [in the hotel] woke us as arranged, and an hour later a bus took us to the quay – the great adventure was about to begin. It was bitter cold ... The liner was to sail at noon, and icebreakers were busy keeping channels open so that departure would not be delayed. In spite of the biting cold I could not resist to go on deck to watch tugboats getting into position to pull the giant hulk into the stream. Then a shudder went through the ship as the powerful diesels down below started their run that would not stop for fourteen days and nights. I watched as, to the sound of grinding and crushing ice, the liner slowly edged away from the ice-covered concrete wall of the quay. A strip of black water appeared; we had lost contact with German soil. With long angry blasts of their sirens the tugs began to pull, and we were on our way.

Figure 0.1 Manfred Goldfish and Malka Goldfish (later Wagschal née Golding) a year before leaving Germany for Trinidad in 1937. From *The Last Goldfish*. Umbrella Entertainment, 2017. Screenshot. Published with permission.

Exactly a fortnight after the couple arrived, with mounting numbers of refugee arrivals, Trinidad, alongside other British colonies, placed a ban on the further admission of refugees from Europe. The Goldfisches had married just three months earlier, and immediately started to arrange for passports and look for places to which they might emigrate. After 'Kristallnacht', the Nazi pogrom on the night of 9/10 November 1938, with its thousands of arrests, the looting and destruction of Jewish homes and property, and the burning of synagogues across Germany, Manfred felt it too dangerous to remain. After a fruitless attempt to get visas for the United States through a relative there, in desperation they contacted shipping agents who sold them the last two tickets for a berth on the SS *Cordillera*, bound for Trinidad. It would cost Manfred almost all he had left in his bank account; but watching the 'still smouldering ruins' of one of the synagogues, he paid up. Saying goodbye to his parents in Hamburg, he did not register the full importance of the farewell. In a memoir written years later, he recalled: 'Gradually the figures of my dear parents Lina and Eugen Goldfisch faded into the steamy mist of the big railway junction and I had a feeling, almost a premonition, that I would never see them again'.[2] In 1942 his parents were deported to Theresienstadt where they both died, within a year of each other.

The Goldfisches' experience of escaping Nazi Germany is part of the much larger story of the plight of Jewish refugees fleeing Nazism, of whom, I have estimated, several thousand found sanctuary in British colonies in the Caribbean.[3] This book is called *Nearly the New World* because for most

Figure 0.2 View from the SS *Cordillera* (1938). From *The Last Goldfish*. Umbrella Entertainment, 2017. Screenshot. Published with permission.

refugees who found sanctuary, it was nearly, but not quite, the New World that they had hoped for. The British West Indies were a way station, a temporary destination that allowed them entry when the United States, much of South and Central America, the United Kingdom and Palestine had all become closed. For a small number, it became their home. This is the first comprehensive study of modern Jewish emigration to the British West Indies. It reveals how the histories of the Caribbean, of refugees, and of the Holocaust connect through the potential and actual involvement of the British West Indies as a refuge during the 1930s and the Second World War.

This book is also the first to provide a panoptic overview of the different waves of Jewish immigration to the British West Indies. It covers migration from Eastern Europe and Nazi Germany in the 1930s, to the wartime period when refugees crossed the Atlantic from southern France, Portugal and Spain, and Britain brought Jewish refugees to Caribbean colonies as in-transit refugees, internees or evacuees. It addresses the role of the West Indies as a refuge by exploring the actual reception of refugees, the impact on the West Indian economy, and the responses of a post-slavery society (still ruled within a colonial system where decisions on immigration, defence and security were made in Whitehall). As such, it also illuminates both accommodating and restrictive aspects of British immigration policy, as the British West Indies were part of the Crown Colony system of government.[4] Through researching the archives of the major Jewish aid organizations in the United States and Britain, including the American Jewish Joint Distribution Committee (JDC or 'Joint'), HICEM, the World Jewish Congress, the Central Council for German Jewry and the Chief Rabbi's Emergency Committee, I have unearthed new evidence of the crucial role these organizations played in aiding migration and supporting refugees. The themes in this book also have direct relevance to the refugee crisis of the early twenty-first century: the impact of refugees on island communities; the agency of refugee organizations; how competing priorities between government departments influence British refugee policy; refugee integration and acceptance in a post-slavery society; and the refugee experience itself.

Jeffrey Lesser's *Welcoming the Undesirables: Brazil and the Jewish Question* noted that historians have tended to 'lump all but the largest numerical communities into the category of "exotica", and thus not worthy of careful study'.[5] There has, in fact, been an increased focus on Jewish refugee migration to colonial and 'exotic' settings, most recently by Jennings' *Escape from Vichy* and Kaplan's *Dominican Haven*.[6] There have also been attempts to globalize Jewish studies by investigating transcultural and hemispheric American dimensions of Jewish experience, and by giving more emphasis to Sephardim; this study therefore adds an important new dimension to the Jewish Atlantic scholarship that has largely focused on the early modern period.[7] Caribbean studies itself has recently moved beyond an exclusive focus on African and South Asian diasporic presences to address other populations such as the Chinese and the Irish; however, the Jewish presence in the Caribbean and Jewish forms of creolization have been quite neglected by Caribbeanists, with the exception of some work on the early modern Dutch Caribbean. While there are interesting comparisons that can be drawn between the treatment of Jewish refugees in the French, Spanish and Dutch Caribbean, this study restricts itself to the British West Indies.[8] Also beyond scope of this study, but will remain for other scholars to explore, are the interesting comparisons to be made between the treatment of Jewish refugees and internees across the British Empire, where local conditions led to internment policies being carried out differently.

What happened to refugees in the 1930s has resonated in discourse about sanctuary ever since. In 2015, UN Human Rights Commissioner Zeid Ra'ad Al Hussein emphasized the dangers of turning away refugees from European shores, and compared the twenty-first century refugee situation to Europe in the summer of 1938, barely four months before Manfred and Malka Goldfisch left Germany for good. Recalling the Evian Conference, held in the French spa town of Evian les Bains in the July of 1938, Al Hussein criticized Britain and other European politicians for using dehumanizing language that, he claimed, 'has echoes of the pre-Second World War rhetoric with which the world effectively turned its back on German and Austrian Jews, and helped pave the way for the Holocaust'.[9] By the time of the Evian Conference, far-flung destinations such as Trinidad were becoming familiar in the lexicon of place names consulted by German Jewish families desperate to emigrate.[10] As strict immigration regulations were already in force around the world, opportunities for emigration became more limited, unless one had capital to invest, relatives or friends willing to provide guarantees, or employment offers. From being first regarded as obscure, destinations like Trinidad and Shanghai that did not require visas became the last chance for those still able to leave Nazi-occupied Europe. By that summer, the German Jewish mindset had also changed: after long believing that the antisemitic legislation and persecution introduced in 1933 would be reversed, by now the population of German Jewry who had not yet left had realized that emigration was the only viable response.

My father was a child refugee from Germany, and coming to Britain saved his life and that of his parents, brother and two grandmothers in 1937. Their entry rested on the serendipity of a British passport officer at Dover ignoring the fact that their entry permit was out of date by one day. They were among the approximately eighty thousand Jewish refugees admitted into Britain before the outbreak of war.[11] For those unable to enter the United States or Great Britain, these unlikely places of refuge across the British Colonial Empire, from Shanghai to Hong Kong, from Tanzania to Sierra Leone, from Trinidad to British Guiana, undoubtedly saved tens of thousands of lives but were clearly places of last resort for desperate refugees.[12]

I first became interested in this story when searching the Tate & Lyle Archive in Silver Town, London, for papers relating to the seventeenth-century Caribbean. I was researching the Jewish community in Barbados from the seventeenth to the nineteenth century, and found a file of correspondence about the internment of one Edward Schonbeck, a refugee chemist from Berlin working for WISCO (West Indies Sugar Company). A number of years later, when I began to research this book, I found files on his internment in the National Archives in the UK (TNA) and managed to contact him. He was the first refugee from the West Indies whom I met, and he told me his story sitting in the Mozart Cafe on the Upper West Side of New York. I subsequently presented an 'Archive Hour' broadcast for BBC Radio 4, 'A Caribbean Jerusalem', including interviews with former refugees and with some West Indians who remembered them in Trinidad and Jamaica. More recently, I have been in touch with a number of descendants, including Su Goldfish, the daughter of Manfred Goldfish, whose documentary, *The Last Goldfish*, was selected for the Sydney Film Festival in 2017.

Refugee narratives are threaded through this book. Using these sources extensively helps to tell a largely untold story, and fills in the gaps in the historiography and in collective memory. While official archives of organizations and governments tell much about the policies and decisions taken that materially impacted refugees and British West Indians, it is through their own voices that we can uncover the many conflicting stories of refugee survival and experience, of frustration and anguish, of pragmatism and adaptation. In contrast to more established narratives of refugee migration to countries such as the United States and Britain, many of these voices have not been heard before, and are part of the hidden history of Jewish migration to and from the Caribbean.[13] In Atina Grossmann's work on 'Asiatic' refugee migration, these stories of circuitous routes around the globe, like hers, 'render[s] the history of the Holocaust, its refugees and survivors, transnational and multidirectional in new ways'.[14]

This book takes a roughly chronological approach. In Chapter 1, I lay out the contextual drivers for the story to unfold. This includes an overview of how the Crown Colony system operated, of the political and economic changes in the British West Indies during the 1930s and 1940s, and of the formation and background to those Jewish refugee organizations that will be key players in this book. I start by discussing the anxiety expressed by the British Colonial Office from the 1920s about whether the Empire had sufficient immigration legislation to guard against unwanted migration. At this point, the unease was in Eastern Europe, where the world recession, alongside rising nationalism, had created the conditions whereby the Jewish population in particular was becoming increasingly impoverished and marginalized. Once the United States had instigated its hugely restrictive quota law of 1924, the most obvious emigration route had mainly closed.

From the 1920s, a steady accretion of legislation across the Americas and the Caribbean followed the United States' lead. During this period, a significant number of East European Jews, unable to enter the Americas, came to and made their homes in West Indian colonies, including Barbados, Trinidad, Jamaica, British Guiana, British Honduras and Dominica. They were more successful, in general, in putting down roots and establishing small businesses than the Jewish refugees from Nazism who followed. Although most were not interned, once war broke out they effectively became exiles, unable to go back to their country of origin.

The tensions that existed between Crown and colony are highlighted in this chapter, as the call for self-determination became ever louder across the British Empire. The British West Indies in 1933 was a colonial world, but the balance of power was shifting. While the Dominions (including South Africa, New Zealand, Canada and Australia) were viewed by Whitehall as 'grown up', colonial dependencies were viewed in a paternalistic way, and remained reliant on Whitehall for immigration, defence and security. And at the same time as right-wing nationalism was increasing and the refugee crisis in Europe deepening, metropolitan British concerns impacted on colonial ones, and refugee agencies began to see potential in spots around the globe that did not require visas to enter.

Chapter 2 focuses on the period between Hitler's accession to power and the year 1938, when the refugee crisis caused by Nazi Germany becomes an international crisis. It firstly focuses on British refugee policy. While not immune to the plight of refugees, instead of making changes to enable greater numbers to settle in Britain, the government's spotlight from 1933 onwards was placed on its colonies and Dominions to see whether they could provide temporary solutions. While the British government's stated policy in the 1930s was to demonstrate generosity towards refugees, official papers and memoranda show that, in reality, the Home Office, Foreign Office and Colonial Office all operated closed-door policies. One such note is emblematic of the British response: on 11 May 1938, Sir Cosmo Parkinson, the Permanent Under-Secretary of State for the Colonies, was clearly irritated with yet another request from the Foreign Office to find opportunities for refugees in the colonial empire. In an internal message, he wrote: 'People will find it hard to believe that in all the wide expanse of the colonial empire there is really no corner where some of these wretched victims of persecution could find shelter. However, this has been gone into before, and the conclusion reached is always the same'.[15]

Parkinson came to this conclusion in May 1938, two months before the Evian Conference. Despite the new urgency as Nazi persecution of the Jewish population had intensified, and German Jewish attempts to emigrate had dramatically increased, I will argue that the British government's position regarding immigration, both to Britain and its Empire, changed little. There was an abiding impasse between government departments due to the tension between their conflicting priorities, with the Colonial Office wishing to guard native populations against undesired large-scale migration, the Home Office resisting any relaxation in domestic regulations, and the Foreign Office increasingly concerned with preventing large-scale Jewish migration to Palestine. Partly to appease public opinion in response to the incontrovertible news of persecution in Germany, specifically following Kristallnacht, British policy did make a major exception. The government created block visa agreements that enabled some ten thousand unaccompanied refugee children, the 'Kindertransport', to come to Britain between 1938 and the outbreak of war.[16]

For the Colonial Office, protecting colonial territories from unwanted migration competed at times with the need to comply with Whitehall mandates. This led to a number of missed opportunities, and confused and contradictory messages being sent from Whitehall. On the one hand, governors regularly received circulars from the secretary of state for the colonies asking them to support opportunities for refugee settlement, but when tangible projects with local West Indian support were brought forward, Colonial Office civil servants actively discouraged colonial governors from sponsoring them. These included new refugee enterprises in a number of colonies with some start-up funding offered by the JDC, and an embroidery factory proposed for British Honduras. For the Home Office, any solution, however small, offered by the Colonial Office was permitted if it helped to draw attention away from their refusal to admit large numbers of adult refugees, increasingly desperate to leave Nazi Germany.

In Chapter 3, I explore how the first significant numbers of Jewish refugees from Nazism appeared in Caribbean colonies as a result of forced migration. Jewish aid agencies played a critical role in signposting Trinidad as one of the destinations that did not require visas. By the time the Goldfisches arrived, there were at least five hundred refugees crowded into temporary accommodation in Port of Spain, attempting to establish themselves.[17] While this was not as stark a situation as the incongruent sight of migrant tent cities on some Mediterranean islands in the early twenty-first century, and Trinidad was on a smaller scale, there were nevertheless very real local fears about the immigrants. These were expressed in observations about housing and health on the letters pages of the *Trinidad Guardian*, and in debates reported in the *Trinidad Hansard*. Interviews, photographs and letters found in the JDC, World Jewish Congress (WJC) and HICEM archives paint a rich picture of a new refugee community, finding its feet and beginning to contribute to the economy and culture. Businesses began to be established, including a hat factory, a cafe, a hairdressing salon, and dry goods stores. Refugees found local employment too, with one refugee becoming a fashion sketch artist for the *Trinidad Guardian*. Two organizations, the Jewish Association of Trinidad and the Jewish Refugee Society of Trinidad, were formed. Despite stark differences between East European and German Jewish refugees, the community overall started to put down roots in Caribbean soil – they sought permission to purchase a section of the graveyard in Port of Spain, rented a synagogue building, and created social activities, including a football club and a dramatic society.

For West Indians, refugees were viewed with ambivalence, reflective of a society undergoing profound change. Some twenty years earlier, a generation of British West Indians had served in the British West Indies Regiment (BWIR) during the First World War. Many came back to form new political parties and would become future leaders of independent Caribbean states. They returned to a society where the franchise still rested on property ownership, and labour and living conditions precipitated strikes and unrest. Most Caribbean societies were highly stratified, but also full of complex mixes of cultural and religious identities made over decades of transmigration between Europe, Africa, the Americas and the Caribbean. Since the nineteenth century, waves of immigrants – Syrian, Palestinian Arabs and Jews, Portuguese, South American, Chinese, German and Indian – had come to

Caribbean countries as indentured servants, for seasonal labour, to sell dry goods and peddle wares.

However, Jewish refugees, both from Eastern Europe and from Nazi Germany, arrived into a community where seasonal labour, both in the Caribbean and neighbouring countries, had dried up and poverty was widespread. While the refugee crisis and rise of Nazism and Fascism in Europe were writ large in daily headlines and syndicated articles in papers such as the *Daily Gleaner* in Jamaica, and the *Trinidad Guardian,* calypsos written at that time are evidence of the mixed responses of locals to the refugees. In addition to a number of calypsos about the situation in Europe and impending war, there were a number written on specific Jewish themes.[18] Some calypsonians greeted refugees with songs of resentment as another 'white' group of settlers competing for jobs and employment, while others expressed sympathy, their plight being compared with that of the slaves.[19] Charlie 'Gorilla' Grant's *Jews in the West Indies*, for example, starts with the question 'Tell me what you think of a dictator / Trampling the Jews like Adolph Hitler', and regarding the daily arrivals into Trinidad, he wrote the memorable line in the second stanza 'the way they are coming all of them, Will make Trinidad a New Jeresulem [*sic*]'.[20]

At the Trinidad Carnival of 1939 (see Figure 0.3), Michael Anthony, a local author, remembers that

> the city throbbed and jumped to two 'leggoes': *Don't give me the roast saltfish,* and *Matilda.* The roads were filled with tramping feet and the sound of bottle-and-spoon and 'tamboo-bamboo'. During the two hectic days the spectators lived in a fantasy land of Midnight Robbers, fierce Red Indians, marauding Arabians, sailors on shore leave, and beasts of the forests and of the night.[21]

As throngs of Trinidadians and recent arrivals lined up along the crowded streets to watch the processions and be part of the melee of the 1939 Carnival, it is possible they may have heard some of the calypsos on Jewish themes being performed.

In May 1939, the infamous journey of the SS *St Louis* became symbolic of the plight of Jewish refugees. It left Hamburg for Havana, Cuba, and on board were 937 passengers, mostly fleeing Nazi Germany. Cuba refused to honour the valid landing permits, and instead, despite much negotiation with other Latin American countries and the United States, the ship turned back to Germany. At the last minute, Britain, France and Belgium admitted the passengers. As I will show in Chapter 4, it was by no means the only journey where the outcome was partially dependent on Jewish Refugee Organizations (JROs) negotiating with governments and providing financial guarantees for the refugees. Not only have the Evian Conference and the

Figure 0.3 Image of Carnival. Photograph by Hans Stecher. By kind permission of Hans Stecher.

voyage of the *St Louis* often been cited as examples of propaganda coups for Nazi Germany, they also serve as potent symbols of the powerlessness of refugee bodies. Despite being well organized and, to some extent in the early 1930s, well funded, many JROs were powerless to influence Allied or Nazi policies towards Jews and other persecuted groups, whilst remaining, as they had to, the ipso facto main negotiators and financial guarantors for refugees who found themselves on ships 'bound for nowhere'.[22] The American Jewish Joint Distribution Committee named these ships 'Floating No Man's Lands' as they sailed from pillar to post, their refugee cargo refused entry in each port. Journeys like those of the SS *Caribia*, the SS *Koenigstein*, the SS *Alsina* and the SS *Winnipeg* all involved refugee agencies.[23]

As journeys across the Atlantic became more dangerous for refugees, often on board unseaworthy vessels, in crowded conditions, without valid papers, the role of the JROs became evermore critical, negotiating safe passage and temporary shelter, providing maintenance for refugees dependent on aid, and guaranteeing post-war refugee remigration. In Chapters 3 and 4, using the archives of Jewish refugee agencies, their role is brought to life in the moral dilemmas they faced in light of massive humanitarian disaster. In exploring the issues facing these American-Jewish and Anglo-Jewish agencies, which were mainly funded by public philanthropy, there are direct parallels with dilemmas facing aid organizations today. For example, in February 1939, the JDC called for a meeting to discuss:

[a] question of important policy which important [*sic*] Jewish organizations must consider together. We [are] in [a] great quandary although [the] judgement [of] many members [of] our committee and offices is that with continuous similar dumping of shiploads [of refugees] we have no alternative but to refuse financial help. Important question in principle [to] be canvassed with other organizations to determine decision re these passengers and [the] future.[24]

In 2019, non-governmental organizations (NGOs) continue to rescue people from unseaworthy boats in the Mediterranean, and help them to sanctuary, even when they know that they are on board because of a trade in people smuggling. By continuing to help, they know that they may encourage more illegal trafficking. By refusing assistance, they know these migrants or refugees may drown. It is an impossible dilemma, but from the perspective of an aid organization there is only one humanitarian answer: to rescue refugees from peril. That is the answer that Jewish agencies gave time and time again during the refugee crisis of the 1930s, and against the backdrop of the Holocaust in the 1940s, even when their funding and energies became dissipated and exhausted.

With the onset of war, refugees of an enemy nationality were classified as 'enemy aliens' and interned. Chapter 5 demonstrates how detainment disrupted nascent new beginnings for the refugees. In Trinidad and Jamaica, conditions and length of stay in internment camps varied. In general, conditions were relatively humane. However, for some, psychologically, it was agonizing to be in an internment camp, with its attendant inaction and isolation, as knowledge grew about the war and the unprecedented massacres against Jews within occupied Europe. In addition, in Jamaica, some Jewish refugees were incarcerated for long periods with pro-Nazi Germans and Italians. From 1939, refugees on board ships temporarily docking in Caribbean ports, en route to further destinations, were taken from the ships and moved to internment camps. Those whose visas were renewable or valid were kept for a short period; those whose visas were not acceptable were kept far longer, sometimes for the duration of the war.

Until the outbreak of war, the Colonial Office had been successful in protecting its colonies from any schemes, including most of those involving refugees, that they felt might disadvantage local populations. However, as a result of shifting wartime priorities, these arguments no longer held sway over metropolitan ones. This is evidenced in the summer of 1940, with the decision to build 'Gibraltar Camp' – at speed, and at great cost – in Jamaica. Gibraltar was of military and strategic importance to Britain, and in April of that year it had been agreed to evacuate the entire civilian population to French Morocco. This failed with the fall of France, and eventually the majority of these evacuees went to Britain, where it was planned that they would be moved on to Jamaica. Subsequently, in October 1940, a group of 1,104 Gibraltarians arrived in Jamaica. In 1941, a new use was found for the largely unused parts of the camp. The sole escape route from occupied Europe at that time was through Spain and Portugal. A large community of refugees, amongst them stateless Jewish refugees, had managed to cross the mountain ranges of Spain and Portugal and had gathered in Lisbon. These two neutral powers made it plain to Allied forces that they would only allow their vitally important escape routes to be kept open if they removed the bottleneck of refugees staying in the port city. Hence the SS *Serpa Pinto* sailed from Lisbon to Jamaica on 24 January 1942 with 152 Polish Jewish refugees on board. The Polish government in exile was involved with the British in this arrangement, but it was the JDC that shouldered the financial costs. Over the next few years, small groups of Allied nationals, including Jewish refugees, continued to be brought from Spain and Portugal to Gibraltar Camp. Alongside the Gibraltarians, there was a constantly shifting Jewish population which, at its height, numbered about five hundred.[25] It is a heretofore largely unknown scandal, which this book uncovers, that the camp remained underoccupied, and its capacity deliberately reduced after receiving enquiries from the High Commissioner for Refugees, Sir Herbert Emerson. These enquiries came shortly after the Allied Declaration of 17 December 1942, when Britain and the United States announced that Germany was carrying out the deliberate extermination of the Jewish population of Europe. I will argue that, despite this knowledge, attempts to bring further refugees to safety in Gibraltar Camp were stalled throughout the war years. The context for the camp's woeful underuse will be shown to be down to Colonial Office intransigence, fear of chartering ships across the Atlantic, particularly during the U-boat war, and a reluctance to bring refugees to Jamaica unless they or JROs could guarantee their remigration after the war.

Fourteen-year-old refugee Hans Stecher arrived in Trinidad in 1938, and his memoir, written in his later years, evokes his sense of adventure, landing in 'a tropical country', which was 'a dream come true'; however, he remembers that for his parents, 'everything was strange and unfamiliar and somewhat frightening'.[26] Fred Mann, in his account of life as a teenager at Gibraltar Camp in Jamaica, evokes the sense of adventure but also the boredom they experienced as youths, which was in contrast to the despair that many of the Polish evacuees of military age felt, who were desperate to leave the camp and join the Allied fighting forces.[27] In so many cases of refugee testimony, those who were young at the time could see much of the experience as an adventure, while older refugees were less able to adjust to new circumstances, and were perhaps more aware of the dangers they had left and those that might still face them if the Allies lost the war.

Individual accounts tell us much about the experience of being a refugee. In the Epilogue I will explore these accounts, of adapting to challenging circumstances, and of the hope of the majority to continue their journeys to places of permanent refuge, often with established Jewish communities such as in the United States, Canada, South America, South Africa and Palestine. But a few made successful lives in the Caribbean. Hans Stecher's business grew from the initial watch shop that his father set up before internment, to the ten luxury goods shops in Trinidad that bear his name today. Manfred Goldfisch worked for Emory Cook Records, eventually becoming the manager of Cook Caribbean. Henry Altman, born in Lublin, Poland, emigrated to Barbados in 1932 and became successful in business, and in the 1970s was instrumental in restoring the Sephardic synagogue, now included on the circuit of Jewish heritage tours to the Caribbean.

There is a complex set of connections to Caribbean and Jewish history, from the Sephardic diaspora of the fifteenth century, to nineteenth-century immigration from Europe and the Middle East, to refugees from Nazism in the 1930s, to the present day. In a recent study of post-colonial literature, Sarah Casteel studies the influence of Jewish identity and presence on West Indian novelists and poets.[28] Casteel writes about a contemporary Caribbean where Jewish life is fading, and the twentieth-century refugee episode remains a story largely untold. The British West Indies was, in the 1930s, on the periphery in discussions about refuge, and during the Holocaust on the very margins of what was discussed in relation to rescue, but it nevertheless offered sanctuary and opportunities, some of which resulted in lives being saved, some of which were missed. This book seeks to understand rather than cast blame, drawing heavily on the range of Caribbean, Allied, and refugee perspectives to demonstrate the context in which the British West Indies became involved in the refugee crisis of the 1930s and the question of rescue in the 1940s.

Notes

1. Unpublished manuscript by Manfred Goldfish in author's possession. At some point Goldfisch anglicized his name to Goldfish. Therefore, a mixture of Goldfish and Goldfisch has been used throughout the book. For the full text, see Chapter 3.
2. Ibid., 2.
3. I estimate that approximately five thousand European refugees came to the British West Indies. It is difficult to give a precise figure of Jewish refugees as they were counted under nationalities, not their religion. From listing those dependent on aid from the American Jewish Joint Distribution Committee (JDC), and from internment camps and Gibraltar Camp records in Jamaica, it would be reasonable to assume a maximum at any one time of three thousand Jewish refugees amongst the five thousand overall, including all

British West Indian colonies. Most recently, an estimate of between 5,530 and 6,730 European refugees to British West Indian colonies has been published by Christian Cwik and Verene Muth: 'European Refugees in the Wider Caribbean in the Context of World War II', in Karen E. Eccles and Debbie McCollin (eds), *World War II and the Caribbean* (Jamaica: University of West Indies Press, 2017), 255.

4. For the most comprehensive study of British policy towards Jewish refugees, see Louise London's *Whitehall and the Jews 1933–1948: British Immigration Policy and the Holocaust* (Cambridge: Cambridge University Press, 2000). See also Ari J. Sherman's *Island Refuge: Britain and Refugees from the Third Reich 1933–1939* (London: Elek, 1973); this was followed shortly afterwards by Bernard Wasserstein's *Britain and the Jews of Europe, 1939–1945* (originally published in Oxford 1979; edition used here 2nd revised edition, Leicester: Leicester University Press, 1999). All include British policy towards its colonial empire.

5. Jeffrey Lesser, *Welcoming the Undesirables: Brazil and the Jewish Question* (Berkeley: University of California Press, 1995), XV.

6. Eric Jennings, *Escape from Vichy: The Refugee Exodus to the French Caribbean* (Cambridge, MA: Harvard University Press, 2018). Marion A. Kaplan, *Dominican Haven: The Jewish Refugee Settlement in Sosúa, 1940–1945* (New York: Museum of Jewish Heritage – A Living Memorial to the Holocaust, 2008).

7. See Jonathan Schorsch's *Jews and Blacks in the Early Modern World* (New York: Cambridge University Press, 2004); Laura Arnold Leibman, *Messianism, Secrecy and Mysticism: A New Interpretation of Early American Jewish Life* (London: Vallentine Mitchell, 2013); Jane S. Gerber (ed.), *The Jews in the Caribbean* (Oxford: The Littman Library of Jewish Civilization, 2014); and in literature, see Sarah Phillips Casteel, *Calypso Jews: Jewishness in the Caribbean Literary Imagination* (New York: Columbia University Press, 2016).

8. For the Dutch West Indies, see Oscar E. Lansen, 'Victims of Circumstance: Jewish Enemy Nationals in the Dutch West Indies 1938–1947', *Holocaust and Genocide Studies* 13(3) (1991), 441–42. For the French West Indies, see Eric Jennings, *Escape from Vichy: The Refugee Exodus to the French Caribbean* (Cambridge, MA: Harvard University Press, 2018).

9. https://www.theguardian.com/global-development/2015/oct/14/refugee-rhetoric-echoes-1938-summit-before-holocaust-un-official-warns (last accessed 28 July 2018).

10. There were a number of publications, like the PHILO-Atlas: *Handbuch für die jüdische Auswanderung*, printed in 1938 and listing immigration requirements around the world, which was made available to Jews seeking information on emigration. However, in Steven Robins, *Letters of Stone: From Nazi Germany to South Africa* (Cape Town: Penguin, 2016), it is touching to see how places like Trinidad inhabit private correspondence between families. Robins describes a letter written to his father, already in exile in South Africa, from his grandmother on 20 January 1939, in which she has clearly looked up Trinidad and refers to 'Trinidad being blocked' shortly after the Ordinance was enacted (see pp. 152–53).

11. See London, *Whitehall and the Jews*, 12.

12. Paul Bartrop (ed.), *False Havens: The British Empire and the Holocaust* (Lanham, MD: University Press of America, 1995), discusses the difficulties of estimating Jewish refugee numbers as official estimates would count refugees under their nationality; see 'The British Colonial Empire and Jewish Refugees during the Holocaust Period: An Overview', *False Havens*, 1–15. For an estimate of figures across the Caribbean, see Cwik and Muth, 'European Refugees', 253.

13. See Eureka Henrich, 'Mobility, Migration and Modern Memory', in Anna Maerker, Simon Sleight and Adam Sutcliffe (eds), *History, Memory and Public Life: The Past in the Present* (Oxford: Routledge, 2018). Henrich looks at the way that migration is memori-

alized in public displays and museums. The dominant narrative of redemption and gratitude leaves little room for a more nuanced historical treatment of the refugee experience,
as related by raw memoirs.

14. Atina Grossmann, 'Remapping Relief and Rescue: Flight, Displacement, and
    International Aid for Jewish Refugees during World War II', *New German Critique* 117,
    39(3), (2012), 79. See also the bibliography for an extensive list of refugee memoirs,
    mainly to the Caribbean, but I have included some to other parts of the British Empire,
    for example to Mauritius and Rhodesia.

15. Sir Cosmo Parkinson, Permanent Under-Secretary of State for the Colonies, inter-
    nal Colonial Office memorandum, 11 May 1938, TNA (The National Archives) CO
    323/1605/2.

16. See London, *Whitehall and the Jews*, chapters 5 and 6, pp. 97–169.

17. I have estimated that in the previous month, December 1938, there were approxi-
    mately 200 East European Jews in Trinidad. By March 1940, the refugee population was
    counted as 585, including 366 recorded under the Aliens Registration Order 1939. See
    Edgar Pereira to Charles Leibman, Refugee Economic Corporation, NY, 12 December
    1938, #1047, JDC and Supt. W.E. Rumbelow, 'Refugees in Trinidad and Tobago',
    Security Office Report, 1 March 1940, TNA CO 323/1799/2.

18. For example, see typescripts of the following calypsos in Colonial Secretary Office
    (C.S.O.) files Reference Numbers: C.S.O. No. 41126 Pts. I, II and III dated 1939 to
    1941. Courtesy of the National Archives of Trinidad and Tobago: *Hitler Demands* by
    Growler, *The Horrors of War*, *The World Needs Peace* and *European Situation* by Atilla, *The
    League of Nations* by Executor, *Neville Chamberlain* by Radio.

19. See Chapter 3 for a discussion on calypsos.

20. *Jews in the West Indies* by Gorilla. Typescript of calypso in C.S.O. files. Reference
    Numbers: C.S.O. No. 41126 Pts. I, II and III dated 1939 to 1941. Courtesy of the
    National Archives of Trinidad and Tobago. None of the calypsos on Jewish themes
    were ever recorded according to the Decca Catalogue in the National Archives; see
    also https://www.bear-family.com/various-history-calypso-1938-1940-10-cd.html (last
    accessed 8 May 2019).

21. Michael Anthony, *The Making of Port-of-Spain*, Vol. 1, Key Caribbean Publications,
    National Cultural Council of Trinidad and Tobago, 1978, 200.

22. This report by Cecilia Razovsky is an unpublished typescript found in the JDC archive:
    Report by Cecilia Razovsky, National Coordinating Committee, 'Bound for Nowhere:
    Disorganized Panic Migration', 9 February 1939, JDC, File 1059. The National
    Coordinating Committee was established in 1934 by the American Jewish Joint
    Distribution Committee (JDC), to maintain close links with the Intergovernmental
    High Commission for Refugees established at the League of Nations in 1933 to deal
    with the problem of Jewish refugees from Nazi Germany. The NCC's main function
    was to coordinate the relief work of affiliated private refugee agencies in the US. The
    financial support of the NCC came mainly from the JDC. For more on the National
    Coordinating Committee (NCC) see *Guide to the Records of the National Refugee Service,
    1934–1952, (bulk 1939–1946), RG 248*, processed by Zosa Szajkowski and micro-
    filmed in 1971; microfilm inventory prepared by Yermiyahu Ahron Taub in 1998;
    finding aid compiled and encoded by Violet Lutz in 2013. http://digifindingaids.cjh.
    org/?pID=1865416 (last accessed 30 April 2019).

23. Eric Jennings has written about the involvement of the French Caribbean in the journeys
    of the SS *Alsina* and SS *Winnipeg* in his history of refugee migration to that area; see
    Jennings, *Escape from Vichy*.

24. Telegram, JDC Office NY to JDC Office Paris, 28 February 1939, JDC File 1059.
25. This estimate is discussed in the book, and may well be an underestimate. The firm figure of Jewish refugees dependent on JDC aid at its height is five hundred.
26. Unpublished manuscript by Hans Stecher, in author's possession.
27. Fred Mann, *A Drastic Turn of Destiny* (Toronto, ON: Azrieli Foundation, 2009).
28. Casteel, *Calypso Jews*.

Chapter 1

THE CONTEXTUAL DRIVERS

The British West Indies, the Colonial Office and Jewish
Refugee Organizations

The Jews from Nazi Germany (and later from Nazi-dominated Europe) who
sought refuge in the West Indies in the 1930s and 1940s were by no means
the first Jews to turn up on those shores. As Jonathan Israel has pointed out,
Sephardi Jews from northern Europe played 'a key role' in the 'vast triangular,
transatlantic conflict' involving the Portuguese, Spanish and Dutch in the
period between 1640 – when Portugal seceded from Spain – and 1668 –
when Spain accepted Portugal's independence. In this conflict, Jews played 'a
political and economic role, the dimensions of which have not ... been fully
appreciated'.[1]

After 1645, when Catholic Portuguese planters began a sustained insur-
rection against Dutch Brazil, and especially following the eventual fall of the
heartland of Sephardi settlement in Dutch Brazil in and around Recife in
1654, significant numbers of Jews – at its height, the Jewish population of
Dutch Brazil is estimated at 1,450 – resettled across the Caribbean.[2] Some
three hundred Sephardim joined the expeditionary force sent from Holland
to defend Dutch Brazil.

As the sugar economy replaced small plantations, Jewish merchants and
traders became part of the slave and sugar economies of the Protestant-
held Dutch and British colonies. Mainly occupied in selling dry goods, they
formed 1–3 per cent of the white settler populations in Barbados and Jamaica
in the mid seventeenth century.[3]

Best known among the early modern Jewish communities of the Caribbean
is that of Curaçao. Its new synagogue, built in 1730–32 in Willemstad, the

island's capital, was 'one of the largest buildings in the Caribbean and by far the most imposing synagogue in the Western hemisphere until well into the nineteenth century'. For many years, Curaçao's Jewish community was 'without doubt the "mother" community of the Caribbean, indeed [of] all the Americas'.[4]

Yet Jewish settlement and trade became crucial for Barbados too from the mid to late 1640s onwards, and by 1681 the island's Jewish population was estimated at 260,[5] rising to some 300 in 1690, and a peak of 400–500 by 1750, amounting to about 3 per cent of the white population.[6] While the Navigation Act of 1651 sought to force the English colonies in the Caribbean to trade exclusively with England and use only English ships, the Sephardi trade networks continued to gravitate around Holland and Zeeland. Yet they were too important to the Commonwealth for the authorities to have any genuine interest in enforcing the Navigation Act. Indeed, Jonathan Israel has suggested that one of the main reasons for Cromwell's willingness to consider the readmission of Jews to England in the 1650s sprang from the need for 'the Barbados–Amsterdam circuit to be camouflaged and dressed up to look like trade between England and Barbados. Officially, the Barbados Sephardim … had to appear to be agents of merchants … residing in London, and this was facilitated by the post-1656 Readmission'.[7]

None too surprisingly perhaps, given the advantage that familial networks across the Spanish, Dutch and British empires brought, Jews were by no means universally popular in the British West Indies and were soon targeted by conventional complaints about their supposed economic preponder-ance. As early as 1661, one English merchant lamented that the governor of Barbados consistently 'countenanced Jews, who have become very numer-ous and engrossed the greatest part of the trade of the island, to the great discouragement of English merchants'.[8] In marked contrast to Cromwell and his successors, who seem to have paid little attention to such complaints, the civil servants in the Colonial Office of the 1930s and 1940s were, as we will see, rather more amenable to the misgivings of the West Indian population about any further potential influx of new immigrants and refugees, Jewish or otherwise.

In the meantime, given their continued heavy dependence on the once mighty Dutch trading system, its waning in the eighteenth century also massively weakened the position of the Sephardi traders not only in the Dutch but also in the British West Indies.[9] Moreover, by the mid nineteenth century, as the West Indian sugar economy (on which more in a moment) declined in importance, large numbers of European settlers from the West Indies, Jews included, emigrated to the United States and other destinations. By the 1930s, with the exception of Jamaica and Curaçao, the Sephardi Jewish communities in the Caribbean had been seriously diminished by emigration, intermarriage and conversion. According to the *American Jewish Year Book* for 1938/39, the Jewish populations of Jamaica and British Guiana stood at about 2,000 each (figures were given for 1935 and 1925 respectively), that of Dutch Guiana (Surinam) at slightly over 1,000 (1936), and that of Curaçao at 566 (1929).[10] Neither Barbados nor Trinidad even featured in the year book's statistics. Indeed, by 1932, of the original congregation in Barbados, only two brothers remained.[11] As Wilfred Samuel noted in 1935:

> The Barbados Synagogue still stands, but in a dismantled state. Some years back it was sold for use as a Law Library, but in the spring of 1935 was still unoccupied. The tombstones which surround it are undisturbed – save by the encroachment of tropical vegetation. The last of the Barbados Jews, Edmund Isaac Baeza ... died on the 6th June, 1934, in his eightieth year (*Times*, 12th June, 1934). Some time previously the Spanish and Portuguese Jews' Synagogue in London had taken over the possessions of the Island congregation.[12]

The British West Indies

The British West Indies, a collective term for the British territories in the Caribbean, comprised at the time a group of mainland and island colonies stretching from British Honduras (now Belize), situated on the east coast of Central America, to British Guiana (now Guyana) on the South American coast. The islands stretched across some three thousand miles, but the two mainland colonies had the greatest land mass. Of the colonized islands, Jamaica is the largest with 4,411 square miles, followed by Trinidad with 1,856 square miles; at the opposite end of the scale, Barbados and Grenada are each less than 200, and islands such as St Kitts and Nevis less than 100 square miles.[13] Given the large distances between the colonies and their diverse histories of colonization, it is difficult to talk of a homogeneous West Indian identity.[14] Successive European powers colonized the Caribbean during the seventeenth, eighteenth and nineteenth centuries, transplanting political and legal systems, language and cultural practices from their respective European metropolis.

Each island had a different history of colonization: for example, whilst there was a continual British presence on Barbados from 1627 onwards, Trinidad remained under Spanish ownership until its capture by the British in 1797. The effects of European settlement decimated and dispersed indigenous populations. Indeed, it has been suggested that 'the destruction of the native people was more complete in the Caribbean than anywhere else in America'.[15] Migration, both forced and voluntary, has thus been a crucial characteristic of the Caribbean since the early modern period.

As agriculture in the West Indies moved from smallholdings to sugar plantations in the course of the seventeenth century, thousands of West Africans were brought to Caribbean colonies as slaves. This shift fundamentally changed the demographic and economic make-up of the islands, as sugar plantations demanded land and labour-intensive methods for their cultivation. Barbados is an illustrative case in point. In 1645, the average holding on the island comprised less than ten acres, while a total of 100,000 arable acres were being worked. Of the estimated 18,000 white men in Barbados, 11,000 were proprietors of small landholdings. The slave population stood at an estimated 5,680. By 1667, by contrast, ten-acre holdings had disappeared and were replaced by plantations of between 200 and 1,000 acres, held by 745 plantation owners. Over the same two decades, the slave population had grown to 82,023.[16]

Following the abolition of slavery in 1833, large numbers of indentured labourers – the majority from India, but also significant numbers of Chinese and Portuguese labourers (the latter from Madeira) – migrated to the West Indies to replace freed slaves on sugar and other agricultural plantations. They also settled in Jamaica, Grenada, St Lucia, St Kitts and St Vincent, but the largest numbers of immigrants were absorbed by Trinidad and British Guiana.[17] In the course of the second half of the long nineteenth century, more than half a million (536,310) immigrants came to the British West Indies, mainly as indentured labourers. By far the largest share came from India (429,623 between 1838 and 1918), followed by immigrants from Madeira (40,971 between 1838 and 1881), Africa (39,332 between 1834 and 1867) and China (17,904 between 1853 and 1884).[18] According to the census returns for Trinidad between 1871 and 1921, recent immigrants from outside the British West Indies consistently made up more than one-third of the population.[19]

By 1931, however, this figure had decreased to one-quarter, and large-scale immigration to the West Indies had ceased.[20] Indeed, by the end of the nineteenth century, with the cane sugar industry in decline due to competition from beet sugar grown in Europe, immigration began to be replaced by emigration, both seasonal and permanent, to South and North America, and other areas in the Caribbean, as well as to Asia and Europe.

The First World War had a fundamental impact on the lives of West Indians. Firstly, during the war, the West Indian economy enjoyed a brief boom as the availability of European beet sugar declined. Sugar production increased and a period of prosperity ensued. Secondly, over 15,000 men, including some 400 officers, served in the British West Indies Regiment during the war. Whilst many were introduced to the egalitarian and socialist

ideals of the British Labour Party, they were also exposed to 'the most appalling racism at the hands of those whose war they were fighting, and their
bitterness fuelled a period of unrest'.[21] Abroad, many were able to see more
clearly the need for change in their own society, and returned to the West
Indies with demands for better social, political and economic conditions.
Those returning from work in South and North America also brought back
to the West Indies ideas for trades union organizations and the need to
safeguard the rights of working men and women. The interwar years thus
saw the future intellectuals, writers and leaders of the West Indian colonies
become involved in movements for constitutional, economic and social
reforms.

In the 1930s and 1940s, economic factors and considerations of class,
race and ethnicity continued to constrain social mobility in the West Indies.
The ethnic composition of the population in each colony varied depending
on its economic history. Census data were collected according to the following categories: White, Black, East Indian, Syrian or other Asiatic, Chinese,
Mixed or Coloured (including Chinese-Creole and Indian-Creole), and Race
Not Stated. It should be noted that all of these were inherently problematic
categories.[22] In British Guiana and Trinidad, East Indians constituted a large
percentage (35 and 43.5 per cent respectively) of the population. In Jamaica,
by contrast, which was more typical of other British West Indian colonies,
they made up only 2.1 per cent of the population, and were one among
a number of minorities including Jews, Lebanese (generally referred to as
Syrians) and Portuguese.[23]

The dominant religion in the British West Indies was Christianity. In
former French or Spanish colonies, a strong Catholic tradition often prevailed,
but elsewhere Protestantism (in both established and dissenting guises) took
centre stage. In territories with East Indian minorities, Hinduism and Islam
also played a prominent role. According to the census of 1931, of the population in Trinidad, 24.6 per cent declared their adherence to the Church of
England and 22.5 per cent their affiliation to dissenting Protestant denomi-
nations. No fewer than 22.8 per cent categorized themselves as Hindus, and
another 5.2 per cent as Muslims.[24]

Of the overall population of some 2.5 million in 1936, more than 90 per
cent formed a working class comprising urban and rural labourers, peasant
proprietors of smallholdings, and artisans.[25] Of these 90 per cent, the majority was black or East Indian. This majority was affected to a considerable
degree by illiteracy and unemployment.[26] According to census data for 1946,
in Trinidad 50.44 per cent of East Indians were illiterate (compared to 22.5
per cent of Trinidadians in general).[27] This resulted in no small part from the
fact that children were regularly withdrawn from school early in order to help
their parents farm the family's smallholding.

Primary and secondary education was delivered in most colonies, sometimes to a high standard; but overall, provision was inadequate and the majority of children attended only to primary level, and even then attendance was poor. It has been estimated that in Jamaica, 'as late as the 1930s, only one out of every eighty children of school age received secondary schooling'.[28] For those who did manage to remain in secondary education, no university existed in the West Indies, and competition for the one annual scholarship to study abroad – an 'escape-hatch from the colonial prison' – was fierce.[29]

Race was an important factor in limiting social mobility. Whilst there were 'coloured' West Indians in all classes, black West Indians almost inevitably belonged to the working class.[30] The upper class comprised British officials, white landowners, and a few wealthy coloured and/or long-established colonial families. The upper middle class consisted of those whose education and background enabled them to take professional positions, and comprised white and coloured West Indians. The majority of clerical and civil service employees, self-employed small businessmen, and skilled artisans, as well as some peasant proprietors and elementary schoolteachers, belonged to the lower middle class. It too consisted almost entirely of white and coloured West Indians, and only a small percentage of black West Indians.

Alongside racial distinctions, minority ethnic identities had some influence on social mobility. Ethnic minorities tended to belong to an 'urban and commercial bourgeoisie' comprising pedlars, shopkeepers and owners of small businesses.[31] Although partially acculturated, it has been suggested that these groups enjoyed an advantage in that their alien status allowed them to form a 'distinct class of professionals and merchant capitalists in West Indian life: the Chinese grocery and merchandise families; the Indian family dynasties of professional practitioners like the Luckhoos in Guyana ... the Portuguese business families in Guyana ... the Jewish-Jamaican business magnates'.[32]

Against this backdrop, there are striking similarities between the East European Jews and the Syrian (Lebanese) immigrants who came to the West Indies between the late nineteenth century and the 1930s. Both groups came en route to or from South or North America, and both groups made their living peddling or selling dry goods. There were in fact Jews among the Syrian immigrants, and in Jamaica they became influential members of the Jewish community, and of Jamaican society more generally. One prominent example is the Matalon family. Joseph Matalon arrived in Jamaica from Syria in the 1920s and entered the drygoods business. After the Second World War, the family attained both economic and political power in Jamaica.[33] There was also some level of cooperation between Chinese, Syrians and Jews involved in trading in Jamaica, though from the 1930s onwards a division of labour seems to have been established and Syrians largely monopolized the retail drygoods trade whilst Jews concentrated more on wholesaling.[34] In Trinidad, by contrast, and rather more characteristically of colonial society, Syrian and Jewish merchants competed for trade.

Whatever the possible benefits of their marginal status, the minority groups nevertheless did undergo some degree of 'creolization', of acculturation into a stratified West Indian society, though often this was principally an elite concern.[35] Gordon Lewis has suggested that Jews were socially integrated into Jamaican society to a far greater degree than, for instance, the Chinese.[36] Yet Jewish acculturation, like that of the other minorities, was in fact an uneven process. There can be little doubt that the Jewish community of Jamaica was tolerated rather than genuinely accepted. It was as politicians, landowners, newspaper editors and in various professional capacities that *individual* Jews found acceptance within Jamaican society – but the status of Jamaican Jewry was more precarious, and it was in steady decline.

Lewis has also suggested that the process of 'creolization' was one in which minorities were compelled to give up their distinct identities in order to achieve some measure of integration, leading, in the case of the Jewish community, to a 'general attenuation of Jewish faith and tradition'.[37] Yet this assumption has been questioned by Carol Holzberg, who has demonstrated that until at least the 1970s, Jews in Jamaica remained a distinct group.[38] That Jews, in any historical context, responded to assimilationist pressures by actually relinquishing their identity has lost credibility among scholars of Jewish history. Rather, many would argue that responses were based on forming new, composite identities that combined what they considered the best both of their own tradition and that of the society in whose midst they lived.

Confronted with immigrants from ethnic minorities arriving in the nineteenth century, Creoles themselves were no strangers to prejudice and stereotyping that often corresponded to the categories deployed to impose legal restrictions on immigrants. On Lewis's account, it was widely held among West Indians that the

> Asiatic has an innate capacity, the Negro an innate incapacity, for business; that the one is the 'economic man' with all of the petty-bourgeois acquisitive instincts, the other the spendthrift of the well-known West Indian Creole 'personality image'. Sometimes too, the stereotypes, inevitably, contradicted each other: so, at times, the Oriental is blamed because he is 'clannish' and 'won't mix'; at other times, he is criticised for his 'aggressive' intrusion into areas where he 'doesn't belong'.[39]

As noted, in the 1920s the generation of West Indians who had experienced the First World War, represented by a newly emergent coloured and black professional middle class, began to articulate demands for constitutional change. Representative government associations were formed in several colonies, and members of these associations lobbied Parliament. This political pressure for change led to the inauguration of several government commissions and the publication of several official reports.

The first of these was a report published in 1922 by Churchill's Under-Secretary of State in the Colonial Office, Edward Wood, following a visit to the region.[40] Deeply sceptical about the idea of introducing genuinely representative government to the colonies, given what he considered the 'backward and politically undeveloped' nature of much of the population, Wood sought to 'reconcile the need for political control in the interest of metropolitan and local white investors and the demands of the middle class', noting 'that the middle class had been exposed to wartime "democratic sentiment" and the broadening effect of foreign travel'. His recommendation that elected members should gradually replace nominated members as the majority in the colonial legislatures, but that the secretary of state should maintain ultimate authority through the use of the governor's veto, was thus 'a deliberate act to co-opt the educated middle class'.[41] His recommendations were eventually accepted, and new Acts of Parliament were passed affecting the Leeward Islands, Virgin Islands, Dominica, Trinidad, Grenada, St Lucia and St Vincent. In 1925, Trinidad changed from a wholly nominated legislature to one in which half of the members were directly elected.[42] We will return to this issue in the following section.

Since the Royal Commission to Inquire into the Public Revenues, Expenditure, Debts, and Liabilities of the Islands of Jamaica, Grenada, St Vincent, Tobago, and St Lucia, and the Leeward Islands of 1882 had published its recommendations in 1884, the Colonial Office had been committed to bringing the British West Indies together in some form of federal structure, principally because it hoped that this would help to save administrative costs. Wood too reiterated the case for a federation, but also noted that none of the populations in the region seemed to have any appetite for such a solution.[43] The issue was raised again with the then colonial secretary, Lord Passfield (Sidney Webb), in 1929, who, in March 1931, established a Closer Union Commission, consisting of the former governor general of New Zealand, Sir Charles Ferguson, and the governor of the Bahamas, Sir Charles Orr. Only the governors in the region were informed of this mission, and it was clear from the outset that the commission would not recommend any substantive broadening of the franchise. In response to this top-down mission, labour leaders and other activists, foremost among them Arthur Cipriani and Theophilus Marryshow, convened the Dominica Conference, which took place in Roseau (Dominica) in October/November 1932. Its calls for a federation and extension of the franchise were much more ambitious than those of the commission, which duly reported in 1933 that 'we are definitely opposed to the grant of universal adult suffrage until the present standard of education in the islands has greatly advanced'.[44] The introduction of the Crown Colony system, which will be discussed in the next section, was an attempt by the Colonial Office to counter such demands with gradual reforms.

A Royal Commission to survey developments in the British West Indies in 1938–39, the Moyne Commission, found that the reforms of the 1920s and 1930s had in fact made little difference to the political climate. Nominated and co-opted members still held the majority in legislative assemblies and were principally representatives of local business interests. The franchise was based on high property and income thresholds, and excluded the majority of the population. Hence, even those who were elected represented only a small, privileged section of West Indian society. The Moyne Commission found that in 1938 only 6.6 per cent of the population in Trinidad, and 3.3 per cent of the population in Barbados, were eligible to vote.[45] With the exception of Jamaica, where a new constitution created a bicameral legislature with a fully elected lower house in November 1944, the British West Indies had to wait for substantive democratization until after the war.

While campaigns for constitutional reforms were largely a preserve of the middle class, the working class and peasantry too were politicized in the 1920s and 1930s, largely through engagement in the emergent trades union movement. Indeed, developments between 1935 and the outbreak of war have been characterized as 'nothing short of a political revolution', as issues such as slum clearance, extension of the franchise, land settlement and social services were 'forced onto parliamentary timetables'.[46]

The Great Depression affected the West Indies badly, creating yet more unemployment and leading to overpopulation as opportunities for seasonal employment and migration elsewhere decreased. During the 1930s, a wave of strikes and political unrest spread throughout the region. In July 1934, some fifteen thousand sugar workers struck in Trinidad, followed later that year by agricultural workers in British Honduras. In 1935, strikes occurred amongst sugar and oil workers in St Kitts, Jamaica, British Guiana and St Vincent. This unrest was provoked by wage cuts, increased taxation and general political dissatisfaction with the nature of colonial rule. In 1937 and 1938, workers in the sugar, oil and water industries struck again in Trinidad, Barbados and Jamaica.[47]

The Colonial Office met this unrest in two ways. In the first instance, it put down strikes and other forms of unrest with force and mass arrests, which only created further resentment. But, as we saw, it also initiated the Moyne Commission to investigate conditions in the West Indies and make recommendations for change. Many in the Colonial Office evidently sympathized with the causes of those involved in the unrest. Yet the need to appease an intransigent block of colonial capitalists implacably opposed to change, while at the same time pacifying a large and increasingly militant workforce and guarding British oil and security interests in the region, presented them with a considerable dilemma.[48]

With the strikes came a new political consciousness, and various organizations, along with a new generation of political leaders, sprung up with the aim of representing the West Indian masses and forcing a change in working conditions onto the political agenda. To name just one example, in Trinidad, the already mentioned Arthur Cipriani, who had fought in the First World War as a captain in the British West Indies Regiment, founded the Trinidad Workingmen's Association on his return, which was later renamed the Trinidad Labour Party. In 1936, this association comprised 125,000 workers, peasants and small business owners. Yet however popular and respected he was in the colony, on the Legislative Council, to which he had been elected in 1925, Cipriani was sidelined and could do little more than complain about, rather than actually influence, policy. Focusing on the Trinidadian oil workers' strikes of 1937, C.L.R. James has suggested that

> had Cipriani been the man he was ten years earlier, self-government, federation and economic regeneration ... could have been initiated then. But the old warrior was nearly seventy. He flinched at the mass upheavals which he more than anyone else had prepared, and the opportunity was lost. But he had destroyed a legend, and established once and for all that the West Indian people were ready to follow the most advanced theories of an uncompromising leadership.[49]

A new type of labour leader, rather more radical than Cipriani, was Tubal Uriah 'Buzz' Butler, who represented sections of the workforce in the oil industry. In 1936, he founded the British Empire Workers' and Citizens' Home Rule Party. A loose alliance evolved between Cipriani, Sarran (Ramsaran L.) Teelucksingh, Timothy Roodal and Adrian C. Rienzi, all of whom sat in Trinidad's Legislative Assembly. Roodal, though a propertied oil magnate, mobilized support from the Indian working class and played a prominent role in the Workingmen's Association. They all opposed the nomination of non-elected members to the Legislative Assembly.[50]

In Barbados, Grantley Adams formed the Barbados Progressive League, known as the 'First Party of the Barefoot Man'. It sought to organize trades union activity and ran candidates in local elections. In Jamaica, Norman W. Manley founded the People's National Party in 1938. From 1942 onwards, it faced competition from the Jamaica Labour Party, established by Manley's cousin, Alexander Bustamante, following his release from internment.

Other West Indians participated in movements abroad that supported the cause of fundamental change in the West Indies, of which the original Universal Negro Improvement Association, founded by Marcus Garvey in

Jamaica in August 1914, was an important forerunner. Although founded in Jamaica, it was after Garvey's move to New York in 1916 that it really took off and 'put the cat among the pigeons' of the existing 'Negro' organizations in the United States. The organization's pioneering role was not diminished by the fact that it never recovered from Garvey's imprisonment for fraud and his deportation to Jamaica following his pardon by President Coolidge in 1927. The Universal Negro Improvement Association propagated the return of black Africans to Africa, but Garvey's own political consciousness was really rooted in the problems of West Indian identity. In the words of C.L.R. James,

> [Garvey] never set foot in Africa. He spoke no African language. His conceptions of Africa seemed to be a West Indian island and West Indian people multiplied a thousand times over. But Garvey managed to convey to Negroes everywhere (and to the rest of the world) his passionate belief that Africa was the home of a civilization [that] had once been great and would be great again. When you bear in mind the slenderness of his resources, the vast material forces and the pervading social conceptions [that] automatically sought to destroy him, his achievement remains one of the propagandistic miracles of this century.[51]

Garveyism was an important inspiration, not least for the revival of African religions and revivalist cults in the West Indies and for the Rastafari movement in Jamaica, which contributed to the creation of a West Indian identity predicated on the notion of the West Indians as a people in exile. This was a motif that, as we will see, also surfaced in some of the calypsos created in response to the influx of Jewish refugees from 1938 onwards.

James himself, together with George Padmore, established the International African Service Bureau in London in 1937, which called for a declaration of rights for the West Indian peoples, and for universal suffrage. In July 1940, the West Indies National Emergency Council was established in New York and issued the 'Declaration of Rights of the West Indian Peoples to Self-Government and Self-Determination'. Provoking 'a mindset of "reds under the bed" and "Niggers in the pile" among officialdom of the North Atlantic Colonial Powers', the black political activists involved in these various movements were subject to increasing surveillance in Europe and the United States.[52]

Yet demands for greater autonomy did not necessarily militate against a strong sense of connection with Britain, which many continued to view as the 'mother country'. Take the example of Connie (Constance) Mark, née MacDonald. Bousquet and Douglas present her as an example of the 'contradiction between the rebellious and loyal sides' that could coexist in attitudes towards Britain. Mark, who died in 2007, had been born in Kingston in

1923. Of her four grandparents, one was Scottish, one an Indian who had come from Calcutta as an indentured labourer, one was half-Lebanese, and one Jamaican-born. She was educated privately, at Wolmer's Girls' School. In 1943, aged 19, she joined the Auxiliary Territorial Service (ATS) in Jamaica, and worked as a medical secretary at the British military hospital for ten years. Her exemplary service notwithstanding, she also had a rebellious streak. When called upon by an English officer to take on the role of charwoman, she flatly refused. She later sued for equal pay and became a campaigner, inter alia, for the appropriate recognition of Caribbean servicewomen's achievements as well as the Mary Seacole Memorial Association. Mark explained:

> We were taught since before we came out of our mother's womb that we were British. We were taught that England was our mother country. And if your mother had a problem you had to help her. Do you think I could go into my house and say anything against the royal family? We were taught that the King and everybody loved you because you are their subjects. And so we didn't have any bitterness.[53]

James also commented on the lack of bitterness amongst West Indian writers and intellectuals who were struggling to evoke new forms of West Indian identity. In *The Black Jacobins*, he wrote that 'the West Indian writers have discovered the West Indies and West Indians, a people of the middle of our disturbed century, concerned with the discovery of themselves, determined to discover themselves, but without hatred or malice against the foreigner, even the bitter imperialist past'.[54]

During the Second World War more than five thousand West Indians served in the Royal Air Force, many more enlisted in Canada and the United States, and the majority of local defence forces in the Caribbean were made up of West Indians who had volunteered.[55] Generally, they saw 'Britain's fight as a fight to defend not only the United Kingdom, but also their own islands, from German occupation'.[56]

The Great Depression had a considerable impact on the British West Indies. The West Indian sugar industry again found itself in crisis. Since the majority of the West Indian population was dependent on wages from sugar estates, unemployment soared. In addition, seasonal migration, a source of employment for many West Indians, also ended as the recession hit industry in the Panama Canal Zone, Venezuela, Cuba and other neighbouring countries. Because of the high unemployment, measures were taken to curb the influx of immigrants looking for work. Cuba began to repatriate workers, and British colonies began to adopt similar policies. Consequently, in the early 1930s, the colonial governments in the British West Indies, with considerable popular support, looked to the Colonial Office to help them prevent further migration to the Caribbean.

British Colonial Policy and the West Indies

The willingness of the civil servants in the Colonial Office of the 1930s and 1940s to listen to West Indian concerns about further immigration was owed not least to increasing British sensitivity with regard to its record as a colonial power. Britain was aware of continued criticism from the United States over its protectionist policies towards the Empire that were embodied in the Ottawa Agreement signed in 1932 between Britain and the Dominions.

In the course of the 1920s, the Dominion States – Canada, Australia, New Zealand and South Africa – had gradually attained independence from Britain, ratified in the Treaty of Westminster in 1931. These countries, much as their legislative and executive systems were modelled closely on the British parliamentary system, now had equal status with Britain and maintained their own policies and governments. The colonial empire, however, remained under British jurisdiction. Whereas the progression of the Dominions to equal status with Britain was seen as a natural development, the attitude towards the colonial empire was entirely different.

Writing in his journal shortly after the Second World War, Sir John Shuckburgh, who had been Deputy Permanent Under-Secretary at the Colonial Office from 1933 to 1942, summarized the prevalent attitude of the government towards its colonies and the Dominions:

The broad distinction between the Dominions on the one hand and the Colonial Empire on the other was obvious enough. The Colonial Empire was inhabited, so far as concerned the vast majority of its population, by people of non-European descent. Leaving aside the Mediterranean area, it contained scarcely any territory within any of its categories where the European element predominated, or indeed formed more than a small minority of inhabitants. In the Dominions, on the other hand, the European element was everywhere the all-important factor, and in two at least of them the great majority of them were not only of pure European stock but traced their origin back to ancestors born in the British Isles. Only in the Union of South Africa was the white population still outnumbered by the original coloured inhabitants. The development of the Dominions had proceeded on the lines of homogeneous European communities, with inherited instincts of self-government and self-development. Their progress towards full nationhood, finally achieved in 1926 and confirmed by the Statute of Westminster (1931), had been natural and inevitable. The Colonial Empire presented an entirely different picture. There the Imperial power had had to deal with large numbers of people with habits, traditions and outlooks upon life wholly alien to its own, and with people necessarily lacking the political instincts and practical experience which more advanced communities had acquired by a slow process of development.[57]

As far as the Colonial Office was concerned, the British West Indies clearly fell into the latter category and, with the exception of Barbados, they were therefore governed in accordance with the Crown Colony system.

The Crown Colony System

In most cases, the Crown Colony system supplanted earlier representative systems that had been installed by European colonialists during the seventeenth and eighteenth centuries. The previous system had vested power in a legislative House of Assembly, elected by the small minority of freeholders included in the franchise, which was based on property ownership. With the abolition of slavery in the mid nineteenth century, and a growing white and coloured middle class thus excluded from representation, the Colonial Office favoured a new system of government – one that would give direct control to the Crown and thus wrest power from the now in fact highly unrepresentative House of Assembly.

Under Crown Colony government, power was effectively exercised by the Colonial Office through the medium of the governor, who was appointed by the Crown. From the perspective of Whitehall, this new system was more efficient, as it replaced elected representatives by a government and council entirely composed of civil servants and members nominated by the governor. Yet it was also welcomed by the colonial elites as a way of preventing an elected majority of non-white West Indians from taking over colonial government. Sir Alan Burns, governor of British Honduras from 1934 to 1940, later recalled how many in the ruling elite had come to favour the new system:

> Gradually, as the white population grew smaller and the number of coloured electors increased, the planters saw the danger of the coloured element securing a majority in the House of Assembly. Much as they disliked control from Downing Street through the Governor, they disliked still more the possibility of a coloured legislature, manned by the descendants of their former slaves.

Conversely, Burns explained, 'the British government was also anxious to secure control of legislature, by which means alone it would be possible to pass the legislation necessary to secure the social reforms which were the logical results of emancipation'. Even so, ultimately the 'abandonment of old constitutions and [the] substitution of Crown Colony government was not forced upon the West Indian colonies: it was the deliberate act of the white citizens of these colonies, who alone, in practice, controlled the political machine of those days'.[58]

The exact composition of the executive and legislative branches of government varied in each Crown Colony, but broadly speaking the governor controlled the absolute majority in both the executive, which was composed of the governor and his council, appointed by the Crown, and the Legislative Assembly, which consisted of ex officio, nominated and elected members. After the First World War, pressure for constitutional change from within the West Indies led the Colonial Office to favour a policy that sought to replace nominated members with representatives elected on a wider franchise.

In order to maintain stability while nevertheless moving forward with legislative reform, change was to be introduced gradually. New constitutions were enacted in several West Indian islands to increase the number of elected representatives in the legislative assemblies. British Guiana's new constitution of 1928, for example, allowed for her Legislative Council to include a majority of elected representatives. Yet the new constitutions in the Leeward and Windward Isles (1936), Trinidad (1941) and Jamaica (1944) came with the caveat that the governor was given 'emergency powers', which in effect gave him the power to veto any legislation if the secretary of state for the colonies agreed.

According to Burns, the governors were able to push through legislation, however unpopular. 'In the Crown Colonies', he wrote, 'the Governor had only to satisfy the Secretary of State on any point of policy or development'.[59] Yet Bernard Poole has argued that in practice the governors were prevented from exercising their 'arbitrary power ... by the known unpopularity of such action and the force of public opinion in the colonies'.[60] This notion is borne out by the account offered in his memoirs by Sir Cosmo Parkinson, who was the Permanent Under-Secretary of State in the Colonial Office from 1938 to 1942:

> It is sometimes supposed that the Secretary of State administers colonial territories. That is a complete misunderstanding of the position. Colonies are administered by colonial governments; that is the constitutional position and that is the factual position. But the Secretary of State is responsible to Parliament for colonial administration and all that happens in the colonies: and if anyone doubts the interest now taken in Parliament, let him look through the weekly questions which it falls to the Secretary of State to answer in the House, ranging over the whole field of colonial administration. Consequently, the Secretary of State must be kept fully informed of events in all the colonies. It is not a case of interference from headquarters; indeed, during the war more authority has been devolved upon colonial governors in various respects, but there is a limit to what is practicable in the way of devolution.[61]

Even though power ultimately rested with the Crown, then, exercising colonial rule from Whitehall required something of a balancing act. As a general rule, the elected members in the legislative assemblies, drawn from a small minority of the plantocracy, needed to be placated. Yet on occasion they also had to be resisted in order to advance reforms that would gradually afford the majority of the colonial population a voice in colonial affairs. The governors tended to be receptive to opinion emanating from the colony, and instinctively wary of enacting laws or reforms likely to cause widespread opposition or resistance.

From the West Indian perspective, the Crown Colony system had both positive and negative implications. On the one hand, it was seen to perpetuate colonial rule by denying the majority of the population active participation in the political decision-making process. On the other hand, it was welcomed as a form of government able to implement reforms without being unduly fettered by the vested interests of the colonial elites.[62] In practice, then, the Crown Colony system enabled local legislatures to formulate policies and laws, which would be enacted provided they gained the sanction of the Crown, as represented by the secretary of state for the colonies and the governor.

While the governor was appointed by the Crown to be its representative in the colony, the role of the secretary of state for the colonies was more bifurcated. On the one hand, he was the Crown's representative in the colonial empire where the supreme authority was his, even though his powers varied according to the constitutions of the individual territories. On the other hand, he was answerable to Parliament for the actions of the Colonial Office. As its head, he was responsible for ensuring that British imperial policy was being carried out satisfactorily, and for representing colonial concerns over that policy to Parliament. John Lee and Martin Petter have nicely captured the secretary of state's tricky position between royal prerogative and parliamentary scrutiny. Their account is therefore worth quoting at some length:

> The Secretary of State legitimised the action of colonial governments by signifying the Crown's approval. All the powers of the Colonial Office stemmed from the basic constitutional fact that the colonies were subject to the Crown, not to the British Parliament. The relationships between the Crown and the colonies lay largely within the scope of the royal prerogative. The reference of business to the House of Commons was often a matter of courtesy …
>
> The Secretary of State had the doubtful privilege of being held responsible to Parliament for what ultimately happened in the colonies without always having adequate power to effect his wishes. Throughout most of the dependent Empire the principal authority in each territory was its Governor. He was constrained in the exercise of his duties by prerogative instruments. Governors were empowered by letters patent which, although they had the force of statute, were normally supplemented by Royal Instructions in order to establish that the form of laws to be administered in each territory might include some

expression of local custom. The constitution of a colony, which determined how local laws were made, was only amended by Order in Council. The technical standing of the Secretary of State rested on his entitlement to intervene in any matter of administration which fell within the Governor's authority, and to consider all forms of legislation passed by the territorial legislature, if such existed.[63]

Yet while Parliament played no role in approving legislation emanating from colonial territories, in certain key areas, such as matters of defence, the Westminster government could readily disregard colonial concerns. This was the case, for instance, in the context of the Anglo-American Destroyer Base Agreement of 1940, which was finalized at the highest levels and against opposition from the Colonial Office and the Trinidadian governor.[64]

The Colonial Office

The bulk of the responsibility for ensuring that Crown policy was carried out in the Empire was borne by the Colonial Office, which was separated from the Dominions Office in 1925 to form its own government department. Reflecting a new emphasis on development and welfare in the colonial empire, from the late 1920s onwards the Colonial Office was reorganized to include area-based and thematically focused departments. In the late 1930s, it comprised the General and Defence Division, the Personnel Division and the Economics Division, as well as area-based departments for the Middle East, the West Indies, the Far East, Ceylon and Mauritius, the Gold Coast and the Mediterranean, Nigeria, East Africa, and Tanganyika and Somaliland. In addition, permanent advisers on development in the fields of medicine, agriculture, labour and law were appointed.

The creation of area-based divisions notwithstanding, general questions relating specifically to the West Indies were discussed across different departments. For example, questions regarding aliens, nationality and naturalization, immigration and emigration in the West Indies were the concern of the General and Defence Division as well as the West Indian department. Whereas the Colonial Office was responsible for administering immigration controls in colonial territories, crossovers occurred with the responsibilities of other departments, such as the Treaty Department of the Foreign Office, who were responsible for passport controls, procedural aspects of international agreements, passport and visa questions, nationality, naturalization and deportation.

Although the Foreign Office generally took the lead in foreign affairs, during the Second World War the Colonial Office became involved in major policy areas such as supply and production, and the provision of manpower for the armed forces.[65] At certain junctures, the Foreign and Colonial Offices disagreed over the implementation of policy – particularly over matters relating to refugees in areas administered by the Colonial Office. This found its clearest expression in connection with Palestine, where the Middle East department of the Colonial Office and the Refugee Section of the Foreign Office clashed frequently over interpretation of government policy.[66]

Since the secretary of state for the colonies was responsible to Parliament, which might well be committed to policies that went against concerns formulated in the colonies, the Colonial Office acted as conduit between colonial governments and other central government departments, such as the Home Office and Foreign Office. Consequently, it facilitated an important form of two-way traffic. On the one hand, it implemented policy directives from London; on the other hand, it informed and advised Westminster and Whitehall about policy initiatives suggested by the governors and colonial legislatures.

One of the key questions for our examination of the role played by the Colonial Office in the context of Jewish flight and immigration to the British West Indies in the 1930s and 1940s, therefore, is whether this two-way relationship led to divided loyalties in the Colonial Office. Did the officials of the Colonial Office, when any conflicts arose, generally seek to prioritize the interests of the colonies or those of the British government?

Britain's Interests in the Caribbean

That the British West Indies remained Crown colonies for the time being did not rule out the goal of incremental progression towards self-determination for these territories too. During the 1930s, both the Conservative and Labour parties were in favour of a gradual move towards some form of self-rule for Britain's colonies.[67] However, given Parliament's limited influence on colonial policy, it ultimately paid little attention to colonial matters prior to the widespread labour unrest in the West Indies in the mid-1930s, which focused its attention.

In response to the strikes and riots, the British government showed greater interest in colonial problems and, in 1938, appointed the Moyne Commission. It was chaired by Baron Moyne (Walter Guinness), a close associate of Churchill's who would go on to serve as colonial secretary in 1941–42 before being sent to Cairo, where he was assassinated by radical Revisionist Zionists in November 1944. Among the other eleven members of the commission were: Mary Blacklock, an expert in tropical medicine; the distinguished social reformer, Dame Rachel Crowdy; and Sir Walter Citrine, the secretary general of the Trade Union Congress (TUC) and president of the International Federation of Trade Unions. While in the West Indies, the members of the commission travelled and resided on Moyne's private yacht, the *Rosaura*.

The Moyne Commission published a summary of its findings in December 1939, advocating wide-ranging changes to improve working conditions, an adjustment of legislative structures, and the establishment of a fund for development projects in the West Indies.[68] In July 1940, the Colonial Development and Welfare Act followed. Providing the sum of £5 million annually over ten years for the social and economic development of the colonial territories, it clearly demonstrated the importance that Britain placed on supporting her colonial empire.

It has rightly been suggested that the Moyne Commission and the Colonial Development and Welfare Act were both initiated, at least in part, in response to domestic and international criticism of British colonial policy. Conditions in the West Indies were, after all, well known to the Colonial Office. But the establishment of a prestigious Royal Commission had considerable propaganda value. It indicated the strength of Britain's interest in, and commitment to, the West Indies at a time when her record as a colonial power was under attack from Italy, Germany and, to a lesser extent, the United States.[69]

More importantly, though, this reiteration of Britain's attentiveness to the West Indies was directed not only at US criticism of British imperial policy, but also at the increasing involvement of the United States in West Indian affairs, and it reflected British concerns over the sovereignty of the islands and other colonial possessions more generally. At the outbreak of war in September 1939, the government was aware of much pro-Nazi feeling in neighbouring South American countries, which expressed itself in various hostile threats regarding the sovereignty of West Indian and other colonial territories. In July 1940, just as the Colonial Development and Welfare Act came into force, several South American foreign ministers gathered in Havana to discuss the repercussions of the war in Europe for European Caribbean possessions.

They debated their reaction to the Allied occupation of the Dutch West Indies, planned and executed by French and British troops following the German invasion of the Netherlands in May 1940, the future of the Vichy-held French West Indies following the German victory over France, and what would happen if Germany won the war. The conference made plans for a 'pan-American' trusteeship to occupy key European territories in the Western hemisphere and the Caribbean in order to pre-empt the danger of an Axis occupation of islands close to the American continent.

In Fitz Baptiste's account, the Havana Conference was seen by some South American governments as a 'green light' to pursue their own territorial agendas. Venezuela, for example, upset at the Allied occupation of Aruba and Curaçao, hoped the conference would adopt resolutions to grant it sovereignty over Trinidad, while Argentina laid claim to Belize and the Falkland Islands. Argentina therefore backed a petition by the Jamaican Progressive League of New York for full self-determination for Jamaica, but at the same time, given its own claims, refused to accord the same option for the Falkland Islands.[70]

The British government's increased and demonstrative interest in the West Indies was designed to send a clear signal not only to competing powers with Caribbean aspirations, but also to the populations and local authorities in their West Indian territories. Clearly, Britain did not intend to relinquish sovereignty over the islands to either the Pan-American trusteeship, as suggested by the Havana Conference, or the United States, whose influence in the region had grown considerably as a result of the Lend–Lease Agreement and the subsequent establishment of American bases on several West Indian islands.

Yet the most important motive underlying this commitment sprang from the importance of the region and its products – especially crude and refined oils – for both Britain and the United States. In 1936, crude oil from Trinidad's oilfields accounted for 62.8 per cent of the Empire's production, and refined oil fuels were manufactured under contract to the Air Ministry and Admiralty. Conditions for workers in the oil companies precipitated widespread strikes in 1937. The decision of the secretary of state for the colonies to support many of the workers' claims stemmed from an early realization of the significance of Trinidad's oil production for Britain if she were cut off from other supplies.[71] Britain's dependence on the Caribbean indeed increased during the war. In 1942, when Britain needed four tankers of oil per day, the majority came from the oilfields of Trinidad, Venezuela and Aruba.[72] Similarly, as food became scarce, Britain increasingly depended, especially for the nutrition of her children, on the Caribbean for exports such as sugar and concentrated orange juice from Jamaica, British Honduras and Trinidad.[73]

Its supplies apart, the Caribbean was also of strategic significance, rendering its defence vital to Britain and the United States. Situated centrally in the New World, much of the merchant shipping carrying goods to and from Europe needed to pass through or close to Caribbean waters and shipping lanes. The expansion of the US aircraft industry, for instance, hinged crucially on a ready supply of bauxite from the Guianas.[74] The British government hoped that Germany would not risk provoking the United States by attacking the region.[75] Even so, when war broke out, an Allied patrol was established to protect the region's sea lanes and oil-producing territories from German attack.[76]

The Colonial Office viewed American activity in the Caribbean with suspicion, but their concerns were overruled as agreement on US involvement and influence in the region was reached at the highest levels of government.[77] In the event, the more optimistic assessment – namely, that greater US involvement in the Caribbean would aid the region's defence – proved correct once war broke out, and the 'neutrality' of the United States in the Caribbean was understandably questioned by the Axis powers.

In summary, while legally entitled to exercise direct legislative control over the West Indian colonies, the Colonial Office had a number of weighty reasons for wanting to avoid any measures that might alienate the colonial populations and institutions. Crucially for our discussion here, in the 1930s and 1940s, permitting immigration on any substantial scale to the British West Indies would have been a measure suited like few others to do just that.

Immigration to the British West Indies, and British Immigration Policy

Migration, often involuntary, had been a more or less constant feature of life in the Caribbean for centuries, but had more or less been brought to a halt by 1930. In 1931, a statement prepared by the Colonial Office mapped out the immigration restrictions in force in the colonial empire. Generally, legislation existed in all non-self-governing British colonies, protectorates and mandated territories to prohibit the entry of aliens unless they complied with certain conditions: immigrants needed to be in possession of a valid visa and passport; criminals, individuals 'of bad character', paupers and those suffering from certain diseases were barred; and immigrants needed to possess adequate means to fund their own repatriation should they fail to make a living in the territory. In fulfilment of this last condition, many territories demanded a deposit or proof of a certain amount of capital before entry was allowed.[78]

Due, however, to the patchwork nature of legislation in the colonial territories, there were many exceptions, particularly in the West Indies, where no colony stipulated exactly the same requirements as any other. In most cases, draft legislation concerning immigration was proposed by the colonies concerned, where it would be discussed by the legislature and governor. It was then passed on to the Colonial Office for comment and approval. Once the colonial secretary had approved the proposal, the bill could become law. Occasionally, the Colonial Office, in consultation with the colonial secretary, would suggest legislation to one of the governors, which would then become law if the relevant Legislative Assembly approved the proposal.

In 1931, only Jamaica, the Leeward Islands, Trinidad and the Windward Islands required immigrants to show passports, and none of the West Indian colonies required visas. All of them demanded certain sums as deposits, and excluded immigrants on the standard grounds indicated earlier (criminality, extreme poverty, etc.). Non-British citizens generally had to pay a higher deposit than their British counterparts. For example, British immigrants to British Guiana were required to pay a minimum deposit of $24, but for immigrants who were not British subjects, the minimum deposit was $96. In order to be admitted to the Bahamas, an immigrant had to provide a certificate of good character and a valid medical certificate. Immigrants wishing to settle in Jamaica had to pass a literacy test or deposit £100 with an immigration official.[79] This test, introduced in 1919, followed the United States, who two years earlier had begun to limit immigration by adding a literacy test to the Immigration Statutes.[80]

In November 1931, the Foreign Office alerted the Colonial Office to a letter from Captain Maurice Jeffes, their passport control officer in France. Jeffes wrote that he had received 'a number of enquiries as to the conditions for entering Bermuda, Trinidad and other Islands, emanating from Russians, Poles, Palestinians and others of the immigrant type'. He felt that attention was turning to British West Indian possessions 'in view of the embargo on immigration, which has recently been extended to most of those countries formerly easy of access'. He had been advising applicants that it was unlikely they would find a welcome unless they were in a position to support themselves and their dependants, Jeffes explained, and asked for guidance.[81]

In response, the Colonial Office began to debate whether immigration regulations in the colonial empire should be changed, particularly in the West Indies. 'If the hungry multitudes of Central Europe' were to gain the impression that the West Indies offered easy entry and might function as an intermediate stop for subsequent immigration to the United States, a memorandum suggested,

> you might get a general invasion of Poles and heaven knows what! … Barbados, Windwards and Leewards are danger spots because of lack of restrictions. We have a fairly difficult problem in many of these places with existing over-population and prospects of returned emigrants from Central and South America. I doubt if there is any serious danger of a flood of Bohunks, but we may as well be on our guard.[82]

It was decided that Jeffes should 'continue his present practice in the case of Eastern Europeans or Asiatics attempting to emigrate to British Colonies', and that the West Indian department should be asked to consider tightening up immigration laws in the colonies.[83]

The General Department of the Colonial Office prepared a draft reply for the Foreign Office, listing existing requirements. It advised that the colonial secretary was considering whether immigration regulations should be tightened. In the interim, the foreign secretary, Sir John Simon, was informed that 'in present conditions it is most undesirable that aliens from Central Europe should endeavour to emigrate to, and establish themselves in, these Colonies'.[84] The Foreign Office was asked to advise passport control officers to 'do everything possible to discourage emigration to the West Indies'. This Colonial Office advice laid the foundation for all future responses to enquiries about refugee settlement in the West Indies. In the course of the 1930s, as the plight of the refugees fleeing Nazi persecution escalated and despite mounting pressure from other government departments and from outside agencies, it remained the same.

From 1931 onwards, a series of laws were enacted in the West Indies to curb immigration by tightening up the rather lax regime. By 1933 passports were required in all West Indian colonies with the exception of the Bahamas, though even now only Jamaica and British Honduras demanded visas.[85] The principal means deployed to restrict unwanted immigration was an increase in the amount required as a deposit on entry, which was designed to target specific groups. Syrians (Lebanese) and Chinese immigrants were singled out by colonial governments as 'undesirable immigrants' because they were seen to compete against West Indians in certain sectors of the economy, particularly in trade and dry goods.

In Trinidad, an immigration committee, which advocated setting a deposit of $50, identified 'two outstanding classes of aliens, whose advent to the colony and methods of gaining a livelihood had attracted most attention of recent years … the Chinese and Syrians'. The report also found that there were persons of alien race amongst immigrants of British nationality – Chinese from Hong Kong, and Palestinians from TransJordan – whose entry to the colony was also to be discouraged.[86] This trend certainly did not go unnoticed. Indeed, when legislation was enacted in Jamaica with the specific intention of preventing further Chinese immigration to the colony, the Chinese chargé d'affaires lodged an official complaint with the Colonial Office.[87]

Yet despite the accretion of various immigration ordinances in the early 1930s, the West Indies, alongside other colonial territories, remained relatively open to immigrants with sufficient means. Whilst governors in some dependencies had the power to prevent the entry of any alien who fell under the broad definition of 'undesirable immigrant', that definition excluded those possessing sufficient means for a deposit or a guarantee, and/or a passport and/or a visa.[88]

Moreover, both Britain and the United States had concurrently enacted anti-immigration legislation of their own to curb the mass movement of refugees and migrants leaving Eastern Europe.[89] Jeffes was quite right in assuming that, as entry into the United States become increasingly difficult, the Caribbean, along with a number of Central and South American states, would be of increasing interest to migrants hoping that migration there, given the region's proximity to the United States, might prove a good stepping stone towards eventual immigration to the US.[90]

In January 1933 – the month in which the Nazis came into government in Germany – an internal Colonial Office review stated that the feared flood of East European immigrants to the West Indies had not materialized, and the head of the West Indian department in the Colonial Office, Harold Beckett, noted that no more had been heard on this matter from Maurice Jeffes (or from any other passport control officer). Yet, even though the matter of immigration controls was not pressing, Beckett maintained that new legislation was needed to protect the West Indies from 'undesirable immigrants'.[91] While the measures subsequently taken to curtail immigration to the West Indies yet further were in no way connected, or meant as a response, to the refugee crisis that had been unleashed by Nazi terror and persecution, they were to take on crucial import for Jewish refugees trying to flee the Nazis.

Several hundred immigrants from Eastern Europe, many of them Jewish, did in fact settle in the British West Indies in the early 1930s, especially in Barbados, Jamaica and Trinidad. It is not without irony, and in marked contrast to the situation in Britain where several hundred East European Jewish immigrants would have been seen as a huge problem, that the British government, its own scaremongering notwithstanding, obviously failed to take any great notice of this. This is presumably because these immigrants met the entry requirements, quickly found an economic niche (mainly as pedlars), required no public assistance and took care of their own. Yet the government's fear of these very immigrants whose actual existence failed to register with them, precipitated a tightening up of immigration rules. These rules would block the way not only for further Jewish immigration from Eastern Europe but also for refugees from Nazi Germany (a distinction that obviously became obsolete after the German conquests in Eastern Europe from 1939 onwards). This, then, was the backdrop against which the efforts of Jewish migrants, refugees and refugee organizations would be played out from 1933 onwards.

Jewish Refugee Organizations and Their Development Prior to 1933

While the anti-Jewish policies the National Socialists implemented from 1933 onwards would present Jewish refugee organizations with an unprecedented challenge, they had certainly gathered ample experience in assisting Jewish migration by the early 1930s, though they differed in their assumptions about how best to make the political case for Jewish immigration in the countries best suited to offer Jewish refugees shelter.

Tzedakah (charity) is one of the core tenets of Judaism, and Jews can look back on a long history of mutual support. Given the dispersal and continuous migration of Jews, both voluntary and involuntary, such mutual support often transcended the remit of individual communities. The Hallukah system, by which diaspora Jewish communities supported indigent Jews in Palestine throughout the early modern period and prior to the emergence of Zionism, demonstrates that there has long been a significant transnational dimension to the exercising of *tzedakah*.

Even so, as many of the Jewish communities in Western and Central Europe gained full civil and political rights, the majority of the world's Jewish population remained in economic poverty and subject to persistent bouts of legal and popular antisemitism.[92] Emancipated Jews faced new challenges in defining their relationship to Jews elsewhere, and a novel 'transnational assistance system' emerged. It is now widely accepted that the 'symbolic turning point' in this regard was the Damascus Affair of 1840,[93] a blood libel eventually quashed by substantial campaigning on the part of Western Europe's Jewry. This campaign 'marked the symbolic birth of a public Jewish sphere that transcended national and imperial borders'.[94]

It has often been suggested that such efforts created a conflict of loyalty between newly emancipated Jews' attachment to their countries of residence, on the one hand, and their sense of solidarity with Jews elsewhere in the world, on the other. Whilst antisemites would certainly seek to portray Jewish solidarity that transcended national boundaries in such terms, it seems clear that for most Jews who actively participated in international philanthropic organizations, 'the relationship between the national and the transnational spheres, between national and Jewish belonging, was not a priori a relationship of conflict but rather dialectical'.[95]

It was as proud citizens of their respective countries that emancipated Jews established organizations to represent their concerns at home and abroad, such as the Alliance Israélite Universelle (AIU) in France (1860); the Anglo-Jewish Association (AJA) in Britain (1871), which established its own Joint Foreign Committee in 1878; the Israelitische Allianz in Austria-Hungary (1873); the Central-Verein deutscher Staatsbürger jüdischen Glaubens (Central Association of German Citizens of the Jewish Faith) in 1893, followed, in 1901, by the Hilfsverein der deutschen Juden (Aid Association of German Jewry); and in the United States, the American Jewish Committee in 1906 and, in 1917, the American Jewish Congress, created as an alternative body to represent the growing numbers of Jewish immigrants from Eastern Europe who felt unrepresented in the American Jewish Committee. In contrast to the American Jewish Committee, the American Jewish Congress was Zionist in orientation, and in 1936 it sponsored the creation of the World Jewish Congress (WJC).[96] Prior to the First World War, both organizations left most diplomatic activity on behalf of European Jewry to the AIU and the AJA.

This increase in international Jewish cooperation had been accelerated in particular by the mass exodus of Jews from Eastern Europe, especially from 1880 onwards, and stemmed from two contradictory impulses: the rise in confidence and stature of Western Jewry, and their simultaneous anxiety about the impact of political antisemitism in Western Europe. Genuine concern aside, emancipated Jewish communities viewed with some trepidation the impact that a sustained and highly visible stream of impoverished Jewish migrants through Central and Western Europe would have on the acceptance they enjoyed as increasingly acculturated Jews within their respective non-Jewish majority societies.[97] It was therefore considered crucial to ensure, firstly, that Jewish migrants under no circumstances became a burden to the non-Jewish authorities, and secondly, that their visibility was diminished as far as possible. These efforts dovetailed in part with efforts to improve Jews' living standards in their current locations, which might render migration unnecessary in the first place but could also ensure that potential Jewish migrants were 'improved' before turning up in Europe's less 'backward' regions.[98]

It was also as a result of this international Jewish cooperation that Jews were able to maintain an 'unofficial' and 'shadowy international presence', allowing them to plead for the recognition of Jewish interests at 'every major meeting of the European state system between the Congress of Vienna (1815) and the negotiations ending World War I at Versailles (1919)'.[99] That said, Jewish organizations by no means automatically agreed on what those Jewish interests might be in any given case. The Versailles Conference is an obvious case in point. Many East European Jewish representatives pressed for recognition of Jewish national and cultural autonomy, while West European organizations such as the Anglo-Jewish Association and Alliance Israélite Universelle, in accordance with Western patterns of emancipation, pressed for legal equality between Jews and non-Jews, and rejected calls for the recognition of Jews as a national minority.[100]

Of the more than 2.5 million Jews who left Eastern Europe during the period of mass migration between 1881 and 1914, most travelled overseas to the American continent, but significant numbers of Jewish migrants nevertheless remained in Western and Central Europe. In keeping with the desire to prevent large numbers of immigrants from settling in Germany, France and Britain – the countries through which East European Jewish migrants mainly travelled – organizations were formed specifically to aid their emigration to destinations further afield and to facilitate emigration directly from the migrants' original points of departure.

For this latter purpose, organizations such as the Jewish Colonization Association (ICA), founded in Paris in 1891 by Baron Maurice von Hirsch, established vocational training schemes in agriculture and trades throughout Eastern Europe, and attempted to direct young Jews to farming colonies established by the association.[101] Various organizations set up agencies and local committees in a number of East and West European ports and major cities to aid the flow of migrants leaving Eastern Europe for Western destinations, principally the United States.[102] In Germany, the transit country through which the majority of immigrants travelled, the Hilfsverein der Deutschen Juden assisted East European Jews. Its chief objective was to aid their passage through Germany in collaboration with Jewish and non-Jewish agencies in Russia, Europe, the United States and Palestine. The organization gave financial and practical help, obtained visas and tickets, and received remittances on behalf of migrants from their families in the United States.[103]

In turn, agencies and organizations concerned with the reception of immigrants were formed in countries of immigration. In Britain, the Anglo-Jewish elites were appalled by the highly visible religious customs, dress and mode of behaviour of recently arrived East European Jews. At a time of increasing poverty, unemployment and industrial crisis, Jewish immigrants were often the targets of public antipathy, and the established Jewish bodies, such as the Anglo-Jewish Association and the Board of Guardians, responded by setting a high priority on projects to 'anglicize' immigrants as well as to encourage the onward migration of many of the recently arrived. Thus, in 1891, to give one rather topical example, the Board of Guardians set up the Russian-Jewish Committee. Its objective was to repatriate to Russia immigrants who were not 'authentic' refugees but had come on economic grounds. It has been estimated that some fifty thousand Jews were in fact repatriated to Russia.[104]

In the United States, American Jewry responded by forming a number of organizations. One of the most important was the Hebrew Sheltering and Immigrant Aid Society (HIAS), which emerged in 1909 from a merger of the Hebrew and Immigrant Aid Society and the Hebrew Sheltering House Association. Its remit was to provide shelter and help for newly arrived immigrants. In Mark Wischnitzer's account, at the turn of the century some 140 Jewish organizations were engaged in assisting migration and promoting colonization opportunities.[105]

At the end of the First World War, American Jewish organizations became more actively involved in European affairs. War-torn and uprooted Jewish communities in Eastern Europe now contributed to a huge refugee crisis as large numbers fled the effects of civil war and pogroms following the October Revolution. In October 1921, Fridtjof Nansen, recently appointed by the League of Nations as its high commissioner for refugees, estimated that there were approximately two hundred thousand Jewish refugees in Eastern and Central Europe.[106] The refugee crisis was further exacerbated as new nation states expelled displaced Jews and other minorities at the same time as countries of immigration erected barriers to prevent their admission.

In response, HIAS expanded its links with emigration agencies and established its own offices in Eastern Europe, and thus became actively involved in aiding immigration to the United States. In addition, in 1914, the American Jewish Joint Distribution Committee (JDC), generally known simply as 'the Joint', was formed to dispense funds collected by American Jewry for refugee agencies in Europe. During the war, it initially worked alongside Hoover's American Relief Administration. After the war, the Joint began to fund and initiate longer-term rehabilitation projects, such as vocational schools and training institutes. In 1922, it attempted to change the nature of its overseas help from relief work to rehabilitation, but as economic and political circumstances remained harsh, it in fact continued to spend most of its income stopping the most important gaps and sending relief to prevent starvation.[107]

In 1921, the United States limited annual immigration to 3 per cent of the number of co-nationals already resident in the country, and in 1924 this number was reduced to 2 per cent. This slashed the annual influx of Jewish immigrants from an average of 100,000 prior to the restrictions to 10,092 in 1924/25.[108] With the exception of France, which, for the most part, welcomed immigrants because of the huge death toll during the war,[109] most European and South American countries and the British Empire followed the lead of the United States and initiated restrictions and quota laws designed to prevent large-scale immigration from Eastern Europe. As emigration on a massive scale was no longer possible, Jewish organizations focused on Eastern Europe, intensifying reconstruction and beginning settlement projects there. Migrants were also directed to agricultural settlements in South American states.[110]

Yet agricultural colonies offered only a limited solution, and were really only suited to the young and the fit. This was also the case in Palestine. The Jewish Agency, established in 1920, established training institutions allowing potential emigrants to acquire agricultural skills or learn a trade (while also teaching them Hebrew and Jewish history) in various cities across Eastern Europe. Yet conditions in Palestine in the 1920s were harsh, and Zionist groups were themselves ambivalent about encouraging refugee, rather than immigrant, migration to Palestine. Whilst economic and political conditions stimulated emigration there, as one of the few places that encouraged settlement at the time, the level of remigration from Palestine reached 43 per cent in 1923.[111]

Politically, Jewish organizations were divided over what policies to follow regarding aid and migration in this increasingly restrictionist climate. On the whole, Western Jewish leaders were reluctant to engage in activity likely to stimulate emigration from Eastern Europe, and felt a responsibility to ensure that immigration restrictions were not ignored. Indeed, many Jewish policy makers feared that aid directed to East European bodies would be used to fund emigration to Western countries.[112] Instead, they focused on assistance to established projects, such as the training schools and emergency relief projects set up by their own bodies operating in Eastern Europe.

The Joint was established by the German Jewish elite. It was modelled on well-established Western Jewish organizations like the Alliance Israélite Universelle (AIU), and shared many of the same ideals as the American Jewish Committee. In Yehuda Bauer's memorable formulation, the Joint and the American Jewish Committee were 'in many ways ... merely different organizational expressions of the same elite'.[113] The AIU aside, its most obvious partners were the Hilfsverein and the Jewish Colonization Association (ICA). HIAS, by contrast, itself shaped by Jews of East European origin, was in favour of strengthening the role of East European Jewish organizations in determining the further course of migration assistance and relief work.[114]

The different approaches towards issues of migration were drawn out at two conferences held by Jewish organizations in 1921. Both were attempts to coordinate activities by founding a single emigration body, and both failed to create unity because of differences over policy and objectives concerning the politics of aid, distribution of funds, and migration. In June 1921, the ICA convened a conference in Brussels to suggest that all future emigration activities should come under their control, but dissent prevented the conference from adopting the idea. Objections centred around two issues, the distribution of aid and attitudes towards emigration from Eastern Europe. Whereas Western organizations wanted to concentrate on providing aid in Eastern Europe, East European organizations were more interested in getting help for their own projects, and in finding avenues for emigration. Western organizations called for selective emigration, arguing that despite 'desperate appeals' from Jews to leave Europe, only those 'fit for overseas migration should be aided'.[115] HIAS was far more sympathetic to the cause of the East European delegates at the conference than the other established Western bodies. Indeed, Lucien Wolf, acting as the British representative of the ICA, accused HIAS of stimulating migration to the United States, and being involved in the trafficking of illegal visas.[116]

In October 1921, HIAS called a second migration conference in Prague. It resulted in the establishment of the United Committee for Jewish Migration, 'EmigDirect'. From its inception, EmigDirect focused predominantly on East European priorities. It worked through locally established committees affiliated with the organization, and established a complex loan system (kassas) in Eastern Europe to enable emigrants to fund their own emigration.

Although EmigDirect was established as an umbrella organization, the Joint, the Hilfsverein, the AIU and the ICA in fact refused closer involvement with it because they feared that association with HIAS and EmigDirect would discredit their own activities. HIAS was certainly viewed with suspicion by the authorities. State Department officials suspected the organization of stimulating migration at a time when quotas were being introduced, and accused it of sending migrants to South American states with the express purpose of enabling them to reapply from there for entry to the United States. As one official from the US Labor Department wrote to Stephen Wise in January 1924: 'The Department of Labor looks with disfavor upon any expenditure incurred by the HIAS on immigration to countries contiguous to the United States. The Department of Labor designates this as "assisted immigration" with a view of eventually landing those immigrants in the United States, who would otherwise come under the purview of the rule of inadmissibility.'[117] Yet HIAS continued to support East European emigration bodies, insisting that this was the only way of offering 'the prospect of an emigration route that might at least lead there [to the USA] eventually, in spite of the drastic new restrictions'.[118]

In 1927, ideological differences were, to some extent, put aside when ICA, HIAS and EmigDirect formed a permanent migration and aid organization, HICEM. It is not clear how or why the ICA and HIAS managed to overcome their different attitudes to migration, but this may have been the result of successful collaboration in the United Evacuation Committee, formed in 1925 to help to evacuate Jews stranded in European ports.[119] The arrangement was initially valid for three years but the new arrangement evidently satisfied the participating organizations sufficiently for it to be made permanent in 1930.[120] HICEM specialized in the organization of emigration from the original point of departure, through local committees and processed immigration into the United States. All local migration branches of the three organizations (ICA, HIAS, EmigDirect) and the European transit committees became branches of HICEM. The ICA covered 40 per cent and HIAS 60 per cent of the expenses. HICEM established offices and bureaus of information in thirty-two countries and helped to organize local committees to aid emigration.

Even so, differences remained, not only in political orientation but also in political practice. Whilst HIAS, the Liberal Immigration League and similar organizations held mass meetings and published petitions to further their cause, the American Jewish Committee and the Joint preferred lobbying in Washington and exerting political pressure by more subtle means.[121] These differences would continue to overshadow the organizations' decision-making processes and collaboration in the 1930s and 1940s, as the ascendancy of National Socialism in Germany and its subsequent European conquests presented the Jewish relief and migration organizations with a truly unprecedented challenge.

Notes

1. Jonathan Israel, *Diasporas within a Diaspora: Jews, Crypto-Jews and the World Maritime Empires (1540–1740)* (Leiden: Brill, 2002), 355.
2. Ibid., 367, 375.
3. Joanna Westphal, 'Jews in a Colonial Society: The Jewish Community of Barbados 1654–1833' (unpublished master's thesis, University College London, 1993), 8. For a more general overview of Jewish involvement in the transatlantic slave trade of the seventeenth century, see Schorsch, *Jews and Blacks*, and Stephen Fortune, *Merchants and Jews: The Struggle for British West Indian Commerce, 1650–1750* (Gainesville: University of Florida, 1984).
4. Israel, *Diasporas within a Diaspora*, 520.
5. Ibid., 396–97; Wilfred S. Samuel, 'A Review of the Jewish Colonists in Barbados in the Year 1680', in *Transactions of the Jewish Historical Society of England, Vol. 13* (1932–1935), 13.
6. Mordechai Arbell, *The Jewish Nation of the Caribbean: The Spanish–Portuguese Jewish Settlement in the Caribbean and the Guianas* (Jerusalem: Geffen, 2002), 199; Fortune, *Merchants and Jews*, 40.
7. Israel, *Diasporas within a Diaspora*, 403.
8. Cited in ibid., 397.
9. Ibid., 531. See also Holly Snyder, 'English Markets, Jewish Merchants, and Atlantic Endeavors: Jews and the Making of British Transatlantic Commercial Culture, 1650–1800', in Richard Kagan and Philip Morgan (eds), *Atlantic Diasporas: Jews, Conversos, and Crypto-Jews in the Age of Mercantilism 1500–1800* (Baltimore, MD: Johns Hopkins University Press, 2009), 55.
10. *American Jewish Year Book* 40 (5699/1938–39), 545.
11. Malcolm Stern and Bernard Postal, *Jews in the West Indies* (New York: American Airlines Guide, n.d.), 11.
12. Samuel, 'Review', 48.
13. Morley Ayearst, *The British West Indies: The Search for Self Government* (London: George Allen & Unwin, 1960), 11.
14. Yet it has also been argued that the degree of insularity that exists, and the lack of a sense of 'West Indian nationhood' is a result not of geography, but of British colonial policy, which ensured that the avenues of communication ran between each individual island and London rather than between the islands themselves. See Gordon Lewis, *The Growth of the Modern West Indies* (London: MacGibbon & Kee, 1968), 18.
15. Philip Sherlock explains this with the fact that 'the islands were comparatively small. There was nowhere for the Arawaks and Caribs to go'. See Philip Sherlock, *West Indies* (London: Thames & Hudson, 1966), 17. For a description of the Spanish conquest of West Indian islands and their subsequent treatment of Indian Caribs and Arawaks, see Eric Williams, *From Columbus to Castro* (London: André Deutsch, 1970), 30–34. In Williams's memorable words, the Spanish conquistadors 'first … fell on their knees, and then they fell on the aborigines' (ibid., 30). In 1492, a population of between 200,000 and 300,000 Indians lived in Hispaniola (to become the Dominican

Republic). By 1548 their number had decreased to some 500, living in two villages. Thousands of Caribbean Indians were also deported to Spain, forming the first slave movements from, rather than to, the Caribbean. In 1938, a Royal Commission focusing on the British West Indies counted some 14,000 Mayas and 5,000 Caribs in British Guiana. See West India Royal Commission Report (London: HMSO, 1940), 403.

16. Williams, *Columbus to Castro*, 104, 112; Fortune, *Merchants and Jews*, 58. Fortune's estimates of the slave population, drawing on Colonial Office files, are markedly lower than those of Williams. Fortune estimates the slave population to have stood at 20,000 in 1655 and 33,000 in 1673. Even so, this still illustrates a massive increase, compared to a slave population of less than 6,000 in 1645. For a recent critique of Williams's figures, see K. Morgan, *Slavery, Atlantic Trade and the British Economy, 1660–1800*, New Studies in Economic and Social History (Cambridge: Cambridge University Press, 2001).

17. Hewan Craig explains this with the fact that the native populations were small in these two territories relative to the amount of fertile and underdeveloped land. Hewan Craig, *The Legislative Council of Trinidad and Tobago* (London: Faber & Faber, 1952), 3–4.

18. George W. Roberts and Joycelin Byrne, 'Summary Statistics on Indenture and Associated Migration Affecting the West Indies, 1834–1918', *Population Studies* 20(1) (1966), 127 (Table 1); Walton Look Lai, *Indentured Labor, Caribbean Sugar: Chinese and Indian Migrants to the British West Indies, 1838–1918* (Baltimore, MD: Johns Hopkins Press, 1993), 276 (Table 5).

19. Look Lai, *Indentured Labor*, 302 (Table 32).

20. Ibid.

21. Ben Bousquet and Colin Douglas, *West Indian Women at War: British Racism in World War II* (London: Lawrence & Wishart, 1991), 31; Ayearst, *British West Indies*, 33.

22. See Carol S. Holzberg, *Minorities and Power in a Black Society: The Jewish Community of Jamaica* (Lanham, MD: NorthSouth Books, 1987), xvii–xxx.

23. Craig, *Legislative Council*, 4. These figures are based on census data from 1946.

24. Ibid., 111.

25. Moyne Commission Report, 9. As the commission itself conceded, this figure was an estimate based on census figures from 1921, suggesting a considerable margin of error.

26. See Ayearst, *British West Indies*, 56.

27. Craig, *Legislative Council*, 5.

28. Sherlock, *West Indies*, 129.

29. Lewis, *Growth of the Modern West Indies*, 87.

30. Ayearst has defined the word 'coloured' in its West Indian context as meaning 'a person of mixed European and non-white ancestry … The mixture may include Indian or Chinese as well as Negro forbears' (Ayearst, *British West Indies*, 56).

31. Craig, *Legislative Council*, 4.

32. Lewis, *Growth of the Modern West Indies*, 38. See also Robin Cohen, *Global Diasporas: An Introduction* (London: UCL Press, 1997), 101.

33. Holzberg, *Minorities and Power*, 203–5.

34. Ibid., 127.

35. Lewis, *Growth of the Modern West Indies*, 38.

36. Ibid., 39.

37. Ibid.

38. Holzberg, *Minorities and Power*, 7.

39. Lewis, *Growth of the Modern West Indies*, 42.

40. West Indies. Report by the Honourable E.F.L. Wood, MP, on his visit to the West Indies and British Guiana. December 1921 – February 1922 (London: HMSO, 1922). Wood became the subsequent Viceroy of India, and would take over as foreign secretary from Eden in February 1938.

41. Howard Johnson, 'The British Caribbean from Demobilization to Constitutional Decolonization', in Judith Brown and Wm Roger Louis (eds), *The Oxford History of the British Empire, Vol. 4: The Twentieth Century* (New York: Oxford University Press, 1999), 602.

42. See Ayearst, *British West Indies*, 35–37.

43. Amanda Sives, 'Dwelling Separately: The Federation of the West Indies and the Challenge of Insularity', in Emilian Kavalski and Magdalena Żółkoś (eds), *Defunct Federalisms: Critical Perspectives on Federal Failure* (Aldershot: Ashgate, 2008), 18.

44. West Indies. Report of the Closer Union Commission. Secret. CP 171 (33), The National Archives, London (hereafter TNA) CO 318/411/11, 21. The document has now been declassified.

45. Moyne Commission Report, 379–80.

46. Bousquet and Douglas, *West Indian Women at War*, 43.

47. Ibid., 34–36.

48. On the sympathies of the governor of Trinidad, Sir Murchison Fletcher, for the demands of the striking oil workers, see Craig, *Legislative Council*, 127–35. See also Howard Johnson, 'Oil, Imperial Policy and the Trinidad Disturbances, 1937', *Journal of Imperial and Commonwealth History* 4(1) (1975), 32–35.

49. C.L.R. James, *The Black Jacobins: Toussaint L'Ouverture and the San Domingo Revolution*, 2nd edn (New York: Vintage, 1989), 404.

50. Craig, *Legislative Council*, 86–89.

51. James, *Black Jacobins*, 396.

52. Fitz Baptiste, 'Caribbean Decolonisation Caught between the Manchester Principles and the Cold War'. Presentation at conference on 'Africa in the World: The 1845 Pan-African Congress and its Aftermath', Manchester, 13–15 October 1995, 3–5.

53. Quoted in Bousquet and Douglas, *West Indian Women at War*, 47. See also https://www.theguardian.com/news/2007/jun/16/guardianobituaries.obituaries (last accessed 9 May 2019).

54. James, *Black Jacobins*, 417.

55. Oliver Marshall (ed.), *The Caribbean at War: 'British West Indians' in World War II* (London: The North Kensington Archive at The Notting Dale Urban Studies Centre, 1992), 22.

56. Bousquet and Douglas, *West Indian Women at War*, 116.

57. John Shuckburgh, 'Colonial Civil History of the War', Vol. 1. Unpublished typescript (London: Institute of Commonwealth Studies Library), 6.

58. Alan Burns, *Colonial Civil Servant* (London: George Allen & Unwin, 1949), 263.

59. Burns, *Colonial Civil Servant*, 266.

60. Bernard L. Poole, *The Caribbean Commission: Background of Cooperation in the West Indies* (Columbia: University of South Carolina Press, 1951), 59.

61. Cosmo Parkinson, *The Colonial Office Within* (London: Faber & Faber, 1947), 63.

62. Poole, *The Caribbean Commission*, 60.

63. John M. Lee and Martin Petter, *The Colonial Office, War, and Development Policy: Organisation and the Planning of a Metropolitan Initiative, 1939–1945* (London: Maurice Temple Smith, 1982), 14.

64. Ibid., 50.

65. For a detailed account of this development, see ibid., 25–67.
66. The clashes between departments of the Foreign and Colonial Offices regarding government policy in Palestine are recounted in Ronald Zweig, *Britain and Palestine during the Second World War* (Woodbridge, UK: Boydell, 1986).
67. Morley Ayearst has argued that the British West Indies had as good a case – in terms of good literacy levels, education and the existence of an educated middle class – as India and Ceylon in seeking self-government. Yet as long as such colonies were unable to pay their own way, consideration of self-government was postponed. See Ayearst, *British West Indies*, 68. For the Labour Party's position on the West Indies, see Neal R. Malmsten, 'The British Labour Party and the West Indies, 1918–1939', *Journal of Imperial and Commonwealth History* 5(2) (1977), 173–205.
68. The conclusions of the Moyne Commission were ready in December 1939, and a short summary of the commission's recommendations was issued in 1940. The report was not published in full until 1945 'in order to prevent its possible use as Nazi propaganda'. The main recommendations of the Moyne Commission were accepted, but funds were to come from the general Development and Welfare Act, and no separate West Indian welfare fund was established. By the end of 1944, some £1.5 million had been spent, and total grants of £7.5 million had been approved. See Poole, *The Caribbean Commission*, 147, 152.
69. Which, as already indicated, is not to say that the full publication of its results was considered opportune. Indeed, it has been argued that it was postponed not only to avoid its exploitation by the Nazis but also because of Chamberlain's concern regarding American criticism over Britain's role in the West Indies. See Lee and Petter, *The Colonial Office*, 39. According to Howard Johnson, 'traditional American hostility to the British Empire' was heightened by the preferential tariffs agreed in 1932 between Britain and the Dominions in Ottawa, which effectively excluded American entrepreneurs from the markets of the British Empire. See Howard Johnson, 'The Political Uses of Commissions of Enquiry (1): The Imperial–Colonial West Indies Context, The Forster and Moyne Commissions', *Social and Economic Studies* 27(3) (1978), 276, note 22.
70. See Fitz Baptiste, *War, Cooperation and Conflict: The European Possessions in the Caribbean 1939–1945* (New York: Greenwood, 1988), 43–45.
71. See Johnson, 'The Political Uses of Commissions of Enquiry', 258.
72. Gaylord T.M. Kelshall, *The U-Boat War in the Caribbean* (Annapolis, MD: Naval Institute Press, 1994), 13.
73. See Sir Harold Mitchell, *Europe in the Caribbean* (Edinburgh and London: W. and R. Chambers, 1963), 35.
74. Kelshall, *U-Boat War*, 18.
75. Since the region was of such importance, there had been government support to increase defence spending there, but treasury objections and the pragmatic instinct that America would protect its own interests by guarding the waters around the Caribbean ensured that regional defence was left mainly to the Americans. On Baptiste's reading, Britain's plans for the defence of the Caribbean were scaled down because it was assumed that the US would have a direct interest in the security of the Caribbean, and that the Germans would not want to provoke the United States into the war by attacking the Caribbean. See Baptiste, *War, Cooperation and Conflict*, 9.
76. The oilfields of Venezuela, Curaçao, Aruba and Trinidad were also important to the Germans. In 1938, 44 per cent of their oil imports came from there. A special Allied Oil Protection Force was deployed in September 1939 to protect this area (ibid.).

77. For an account of the general disapproval of the Colonial Office, and the opposition of Trinidad's governor to United States involvement in the West Indies, and specifically the bases agreement, see Lee and Petter, *The Colonial Office*, 50, 105.
78. 'Statement Showing the Immigration Restrictions in force in British non-self-governing Colonies, Protectorates and Mandated Territories administered under the authority of His Majesty's Government in the United Kingdom', undated, but almost certainly written in 1931, TNA CO 318/412/4 – hereafter, 'Statement Showing the Immigration Restrictions'.
79. Ibid. See also J. Simmens, internal memorandum on immigration requirements to the West Indian colonies, 1 March 1933, TNA CO 318/412/4. To give an indication of the order of magnitude: in 1931, the median weekly earnings of an industrial worker in Britain stood at about £2.60, and thus £100 would have been equal to roughly 38 weeks' (or nine months') wages. Ian Gazely, 'Manual Work and Pay, 1900–70', in Nicholas Crafts, Ian Gazely and Andrew Newell (eds), *Work and Pay in Twentieth-Century Britain* (New York: Oxford University Press, 2007), 68, Table 3.9.
80. See Mark Wischnitzer, *To Dwell In Safety: The Story of Jewish Migration since 1800* (Philadelphia: JPS, 1948), 142. On Roger Daniels's account, the test itself had little impact on immigration into the United States though. See Roger Daniels, 'American Refugee Policy in Historical Perspective', in Jarrell C. Jackman and Carla M. Borden (eds), *The Muses Flee Hitler: Cultural Transfer and Adaptation 1930–1945* (Washington, DC: Smithsonian, 1983), 64.
81. Under-Secretary of State for Foreign Affairs to Under-Secretary of State for the Colonies, 7 November 1931, enclosing letter from Maurice Jeffes, Passport Control Officer, France, to Major Herbert E. Spencer, Passport Control Department, Foreign Office, 5 November 1931, TNA CO 318/412/4.
82. Gerard Clauson to Harold Beckett, internal memorandum, Colonial Office, 4 December 1931, TNA CO 318/412/4. 'Bohunk' was a derogatory term for people of Central European descent, especially Bohemians and Hungarians.
83. Ibid.
84. Roland V. Vernon, Colonial Office, to Under-Secretary of State, Foreign Office, 8 December 1931, TNA CO 318/412/4.
85. In 1931, Trinidad enacted an ordinance requiring a valid passport and deposit of £50. Jamaica enacted an ordinance requiring both a valid passport and a visa. In 1932, Barbados passed an act requiring aliens to possess valid passports, and British Honduras asked for visas and passports. See TNA CO 318/412/4; CO 323/1604/3; CO 323/412/4. For details on the Barbados Passport Act, see summary of replies to Circular of 11 August 1938, TNA CO 323/1604/3, and Laws of Barbados, Vol. III, Part IV, Session 1932–1933, Barbados, 1933, Institute for Advanced Legal Studies (henceforth IALS), University of London.
86. Cutting from the *Port of Spain Gazette*, 21 May 1931, included in the American Vice Consul's Report on Immigration to Trinidad to the Secretary of State, Washington, 27 May 1931. National Archives Washington (hereafter NARA), Record Group 59, Decimal File 1930–39, Box number 6222, file no. 844G.55/4.
87. TNA CO 351 Registers, 86135/31. Again in 1934, a law, Number 32 of 1933, the Aliens Admission and Deportation Regulation, which was enacted on 24 January 1934, was sent by the Colonial Office to the Foreign Office, who were instructed to inform consular offices not to grant visas to persons of Chinese or Syrian origin without prior reference to the Jamaican government. TNA CO 351 Registers, Acting Governor to Secretary of State for the Colonies, 27 April 1934, file 36431/34 (destroyed).

88. The Barbados Passport Act of 1932 is a case in point. It repealed the Aliens Restriction Act of 1916 and gave the governor wide powers to prevent the landing 'of all immigrants bar those able to assist the economic development of the colony, and temporary visitors'. It also made the production of passports mandatory. It thus went further than the regulations of any other colony (Barbados Passport Act 1932, Laws of Barbados, Vol. III, Part IV, Session 1932–1933, Barbados, 1933, IALS). Most, like the British Honduras Undesirable Immigrants Ordinance of 1932, gave governors the power to ban those categorized as 'undesirable immigrants': indigents, paupers, criminals, the sick, and those without passports and/or visas. The governor of British Honduras was, however, able to admit such 'undesirable' immigrants if they deposited the sum of $100, had a valid engagement in the colony, or gave a security of $100 (Ordinance No. 18 of 1932, Ordinances of British Honduras Passed in the Year 1932, Belize, 1933, IALS).

89. Immigration statutes introduced in 1921 and 1924 transformed immigration policy in the United States, drastically limiting annual immigration to a quota system that militated against the entry of East European immigrants. In Britain, the 1905 Aliens Act was the first attempt to restrict immigration. This was followed by the Aliens Restriction and Aliens Restriction (Amendment) Act introduced in 1914 and amended in 1919, which only allowed the entry of immigrants at the discretion of immigration officers. Laws in West Indian colonies appear to have been introduced only after alien restrictions were introduced in Britain and the United States. The 1909 Paupers Prevention Act in Barbados, for instance, was replaced in 1916 by the Aliens Restriction Act, which in turn was supplanted by the 1932 Passports Act. Jamaica introduced its first Immigration Restriction Law in 1919, enacting a Control of Aliens Law in 1920 and a Passport Law in 1925. In 1933, the Aliens Admission and Deportation Regulation Law replaced the 1920 Law controlling the admission of aliens. Trinidad's first immigration ordinance relating to aliens was passed in 1924 and amended in 1926 (Laws of Barbados, British Guiana Ordinances, Ordinances of British Honduras, Laws of Jamaica, Ordinances Passed by the Legislative Council of Trinidad and Tobago, published annually, IALS).

90. See Haim Avni, 'Patterns of Jewish Leadership in Latin America during the Holocaust', in Randolph Braham (ed.), *Jewish Leadership during the Nazi Era: Patterns of Behavior in the Free World* (New York: Social Science Monographs, 1985), 89.

91. Harold Beckett, Colonial Office memorandum, 12 January 1933, TNA CO 318/412/4.

92. Before the First World War, the largest Jewish populations, comprising about 5.6 million Jews, lived in the Russian Empire.

93. Tobias Brinkmann, 'The Road from Damascus: Transnational Jewish Philanthropic Organizations and the Jewish Mass Migration from Eastern Europe, 1840–1914', in Davide Rodrigo, Bernhard Struck and Jakob Vogel (eds), *Shaping the Transnational Sphere: Experts, Networks and Issues from the 1840s to the 1930s* (New York: Berghahn Books, 2015), 147. The significance of the Damascus Affair was thrown sharply into relief by the late Jonathan Frankel in *The Damascus Affair: 'Ritual Murder', Politics, and the Jews in 1840* (New York: Cambridge University Press, 1997).

94. Brinkmann, 'Road from Damascus', 147.

95. Ibid., 155.

96. On the establishment of the WJC and its activities during the Shoah, see Zohar Segev, *The World Jewish Congress during the Holocaust: Between Activism and Restraint* (Berlin: de Gruyter, 2014).

97. On the issue of transmigration, see Tobias Brinkmann, 'Strangers in the City: Transmigration from Eastern Europe and its Impact on Berlin and Hamburg 1880– 1914', *Journal of Migration History* 2 (2016), 223–46.
98. Brinkmann, 'Road from Damascus', 155.
99. Henry Feingold, *Bearing Witness: How America and Its Jews Responded to the Holocaust* (Syracuse, NY: Syracuse University Press, 1995), 34.
100. Louis Marshall, representing the American Jewish Congress, took a more nuanced stance. He insisted that, as Western Jews, 'we must be careful not to permit ourselves to judge what is most desirable for the people who live in Eastern Europe by the standards which prevail on Fifth Avenue'. See Ronald Sanders, *Shores of Refuge: A Hundred Years of Jewish Emigration* (New York: Holt, 1988), 348.
101. The original purpose of the ICA was to encourage Russian Jews to colonize over a million acres acquired by the organization in Argentina. Although its intention was to settle some twenty-five thousand Russian Jews there, the actual numbers were small since the United States remained the main target for immigration. In 1896 the ICA widened its remit to aid emigration to countries other than Argentina, and opened branches throughout Eastern Europe. It also introduced a loan system, which enabled immigrants to fund their own emigration. See Theodore Norman, *An Outstretched Arm: A History of the Jewish Colonization Association* (London: Routledge & Kegan Paul, 1985); Sanders, *Shores of Refuge*, 150–51; Avni, 'Patterns of Jewish Leadership', 88. Avni claims that prior to the First World War, some 20 per cent of Jewish immigrants to Argentina remigrated, whereas only 7.14 per cent of Jewish immigrants to the United States did so.
102. According to Mark Wischnitzer, between 1901 and 1925, 86 per cent of all Jewish migrants entered the United States, 7.1 per cent went to Argentina and Brazil, 0.9 per cent to other countries in the Americas and 3.6 per cent to Palestine. Wischnitzer, *To Dwell in Safety*, 295.
103. Wischnitzer estimated that between 1905 and 1914, the peak period of Jewish migration, 700,000 East European Jews travelled to German ports to embark for Western destinations. The Hilfsverein helped 210,771 of them (ibid., 115).
104. See David Feldman, *Englishmen and Jews: Social Relations and Political Culture, 1840– 1914* (New Haven, CT: Yale University Press, 1994).
105. Wischnitzer, *To Dwell in Safety*, 297, cited in Valery Bazarov, 'HIAS and HICEM in the System of Jewish Relief Organisations in Europe, 1933–31', *East European Jewish Affairs* 39(1) (2009), 70.
106. See Michael Marrus, *The Unwanted: European Refugees in the Twentieth Century* (New York: Oxford University Press, 1985), 64.
107. Zosa Szajkowski, 'Private and Organized American Jewish Overseas Relief (1914– 1938)', *American Jewish Historical Quarterly* 57(1) (1967), 63.
108. See Wischnitzer, *To Dwell in Safety*, 151, 154; idem, *Visas to Freedom: The History of HIAS* (Cleveland, OH: World Publication Co., 1956), 25, 111. The reduction of 1924 left some 8,000 Jews with US immigration visas stranded in European ports. See Zosa Szajkowski, 'Private American Jewish Overseas Relief: 1919–1938: Problems and Attempted Solutions', *American Jewish Historical Quarterly* 57(3) (1968), 337.
109. Marrus, *The Unwanted*, 113.
110. The Bund (General Jewish Labour Bund), the oldest and largest Jewish socialist party in Eastern Europe, set up a labour emigration bureau, sending migrants mainly to France and Argentina, and published a weekly column on emigration possibilities. In 1924, the Joint established the AgroJoint, which founded 112 colonies in the Ukraine

and 105 in Crimea, and, together with the Jewish Colonization Association (ICA), set up the American Joint Reconstruction Foundation to carry out economic reconstruction in Eastern and Central Europe. By 1928 the AgroJoint had settled at least sixty thousand Jews in its settlements (Marrus, *The Unwanted*, 118). The ICA started directing refugees to agricultural settlement projects in South America, and set up reception committees in Argentina, Canada, Chile, Bolivia and Mexico. The subcommittees set up in countries of reception not only assisted newly arrived immigrants but also provided intelligence on prospects for further immigration.

111. Ibid., 115–17.
112. See Szajkowski, 'Private and Organized', 235.
113. Yehuda Bauer, *American Jewry and the Holocaust: The American Jewish Joint Distribution Committee, 1939–1945* (Jerusalem: Institute of Contemporary Jewry / Detroit: Wayne State University Press, 1981), 22.
114. Szajkowski, 'Private and Organized', 233–34.
115. Wischnitzer, *To Dwell in Safety*, 148.
116. Szajkowski, 'Private and Organized', 233.
117. Ibid., 231.
118. Sanders, *Shores of Refuge*, 392.
119. Wischnitzer, *Visas to Freedom*, 122–23. On the United Evacuation Committee, see idem, *To Dwell in Safety*, 155–56.
120. Bazarov, 'HIAS and HICEM', 71.
121. Sjakowski, 'Private and Organized', 217.

Part II

Confronting the Need for Refuge

Chapter 2

JEWS SEEKING REFUGE, 1933–1938

When the National Socialists came to power in Germany in 1933, the German Jewish community numbered an estimated 525,000, equivalent to less than 0.8 per cent of the German population at the time. The total number of German Jews, including those who were no longer affiliated with the Jewish religious community but would nevertheless fall foul of Nazi anti-Jewish legislation, has been estimated at 867,000, equivalent to less than 1.3 per cent of the population.[1] Germany's Jewish population was in 'sharp demographic decline', as the number of deaths far outweighed the number of births.[2] Fewer than a quarter of Germany's Jews were aged between six and twenty-five, compared to more than a third of the German population as a whole (according to the census of 1925).[3] The majority of Jews were concentrated in urban centres, with just under half the entire Jewish population living in six major German cities.[4] Although Jews were well represented amongst the upper social classes, the majority belonged to the lower middle and working class. Of those Jews who worked (among them, 27 per cent of Jewish women),[5] over half were self-employed, and there was a strong concentration in trade and commerce.[6]

The Evolution of Nazi Anti-Jewish Policy

In the minds of convinced National Socialists there was no doubt that they could only secure for Germany the future she deserved if that future was one without Jews. As is well known, the National Socialists' answer to the question of how this might best be achieved evolved gradually in the course of the 1930s and early 1940s until, in the autumn of 1941, the decision was made to proceed to systematic genocide;[7] but in the first instance, the regime set out, step by step, to exclude the Jews from German society and drive them out of the country.

Nazi policy on Jewish emigration has been characterized as haphazard and chaotic.[8] As Marion Kaplan has pointed out, the direction and systematic nature of Nazi anti-Jewish policy 'appeared obvious to those who had suffered it only in retrospect', but Germany's Jews 'confronted a growing menace bewilderingly embedded in life as they had known it'.[9] Nazi leaders followed policies that at times encouraged mobs to terrorize and assault Jewish citizens without fear of prosecution, and at other times relocated violence and terror away from the public gaze.[10] To complicate matters further, as Wolf Gruner has demonstrated, 'mayors and local officials often devised proscriptive measures years ahead of the state regulations, or went far beyond instructions from above in order to discriminate socially, politically and culturally against the Jewish population'.[11] It was, then, a programme of 'creeping persecution' by legislative means that gradually stripped the Jews of their rights in Germany.[12] In 1933, most Jews were excluded from the civil service, and those Jews naturalized during the Weimar period had their citizenship revoked. In 1935, the Nuremberg Laws effectively stripped Jews of their nationality, and articulated the physical separation of German Jews from non-Jews through a series of racial interdicts.

Not least, given the somewhat uneven evolution of Nazi anti-Jewish policy, German Jews were confused, and they disagreed amongst one another regarding the most appropriate response. Herbert Strauss has pointed out in his study of attitudes articulated and reflected in the German Jewish press that many initially 'hoped that Jewish propaganda tactics might influence Nazi policies'. Consequently, emigration was not at first a primary concern.[13] *C.V.-Zeitung*, the weekly paper of the Centralverein deutscher Staatsbürger jüdischen Glaubens – Germany's foremost mainstream Jewish association – argued that anti-Jewish persecution was bound to become less severe once the new regime had settled down, and it therefore openly opposed Nazi pressure to emigrate.

Emigration was not advocated by Jewish organizations until after the introduction of the Nuremberg Laws in 1935, when institutionalized oppression increased. A number of new periodicals focusing on emigration were then founded, and the major Jewish papers also began to devote more space on their front pages to practical issues regarding emigration, foreign currency information and reports on life in foreign countries. Of particular interest, as Strauss noted, were reports from those who had already left and were able to elucidate the conditions in their countries of immigration, and provide up-to-date information on admission regulations there.[14]

The actual numbers of Jewish refugees from Germany did not reflect this shift in emphasis and vacillated quite considerably between 1933 and 1938. According to Strauss, 37,000 Jews fled Germany in 1933 in response to the initial brutality, loss of employment, and for political asylum. But from 1934 to July 1938 emigration took place at a steadier and lower rate, as various factors prevented a mass exodus. Only 21,000 Jews left in 1935; 25,000 in 1936; and 23,000 in 1937.[15]

Both internal and external factors played a role in this development. Internal factors included a belief that the regime would improve, political opposition to leaving Germany, an unwillingness to become uprooted, and family concerns such as reluctance to take children out of their schools.[16] Among the external factors were the difficulties involved in leaving Germany and finding places to which to emigrate. Given that the demographic profile of German Jewry was an ageing population with a concentration in trade and commerce, German Jews were hardly likely to be welcomed with open arms, whether in other European countries, their overseas territories or elsewhere overseas. Palestine, as long as it remained open to Jewish immigration, was an obvious exception, but it sought an influx of Jews who were young and fit or who could invest substantial capital in the Yishuv (the Jewish settlement there). Roughly half of the Jews living in Germany were able to save themselves by leaving Germany after 1933, including more than 80 per cent of those aged 24 or under. Some 18,000 unaccompanied minors were sent to safety by their desperate parents between 1934 and 1939.[17]

As a general rule, immigration regulations stipulated the need for financial self-sufficiency, family connections and/or definite offers of employment. As discussed in the previous chapter, the worldwide depression and economic insecurity led to harsh restrictions being imposed on entry to most countries in the Western hemisphere for those not meeting these criteria. For those Jews who owned capital and property in Germany, the conditions imposed on Jews leaving the Reich also acted as an impediment to emigration. Apart from the Haavara scheme, which allowed the transfer of capital to Palestine, the flight tax ensured that individuals leaving Germany could only take a small amount of foreign currency from the country.[18] Jewish emigrants lost between 30 and 50 per cent of their capital when leaving between 1933 and 1937, and 60 to 100 per cent between 1937 and 1939.[19]

Even so, initially most refugees leaving Nazi Germany were able to meet the immigration requirements of their destinations. With the acceleration of persecutory measures against Jews in Germany and its annexed territories, emigration became more difficult as few countries were willing to lower the hurdles. Instead, most maintained restrictive policies built on the belief that an influx of refugees would exacerbate domestic problems of unemployment and recession, and, moreover, would fan public antisemitic hostility towards native Jewish communities and new immigrants alike. Another underlying concern for many governments was that unless a firm line on immigration was maintained, antisemitic regimes, such as those in Germany, Poland and Romania, would infer that the liberal democracies could, and would, absorb their unwanted Jewish populations.

Estimates of the number of Jews leaving Germany prior to the outbreak of war in 1939 need to be treated with caution. The number who managed to emigrate under their own steam is almost impossible to estimate, and the organizations who assisted Jewish refugees, depending on the context, could have good reasons either to inflate or deflate the numbers.[20] Bearing this in mind, it would seem that some 150,000 Jews – roughly 28 per cent of the religiously affiliated, and 17 per cent of the total German Jewish population – emigrated between January 1933 and July 1938. They were able to enter various countries by satisfying the existing immigration conditions; and as the 1930s progressed, overseas destinations overtook European countries and Palestine. By the end of 1937, more than 60 per cent of émigrés were going overseas, with 15 per cent to Palestine, and 25 per cent to Europe. Of the overseas countries, the United States was the foremost destination, followed by Argentina and Brazil.

From 1937, Jewish emigration became a primary Nazi objective as more pragmatic forces in the Nazi hierarchy, who had emphasized the need for orderly emigration and for the continuation of Jewish involvement with the German economy, lost influence. Policy was now designed to speed up the Jews' emigration whilst retaining their assets. This policy systematically turned the Jews who were leaving into penniless refugees.[21] Whilst Nazi policy had evolved gradually in Germany, its implementation in Austria, following its annexation in March 1938, was swift and brutal. The *Anschluss* of Austria brought an additional two hundred thousand Jews into the Greater German Reich – 'cancelling out the reduction of German Jews by recent emigration'[22] – and immediately in April 1938, a Central Office for Jewish Emigration was established in Vienna under Eichmann. The British Home Office, determined to stem the flow of refugees attempting to leave the now Greater German Reich, responded by introducing visa requirements for German and Austrian passport holders.[23]

Unprecedented Challenges: The Jewish Refugee Organizations

For the most current information and advice on emigration, German Jews hoping to leave consulted the offices and publications of Jewish organizations specializing in emigration. Either through direct contact with offices and agencies, or in the pages of annual reports and publications, detailed information on conditions throughout the world was made available.[24]

As we saw, by 1933 Jewish philanthropic organizations had been evolving and operating for the best part of a century. They had been dispensing advice and information through emigration and relief organizations linked to local committees throughout Europe, the Americas and the Far East for several decades, and had developed considerable expertise in providing aid to impoverished communities in Eastern Europe and in facilitating emigration to the West. Already increasingly constrained by the limits on migration enacted in the 1920s and early 1930s outlined in the previous chapter, these constraints now massively aggravated the refugee crisis caused by Nazi anti-Jewish policy. More so than ever before, Jewish relief organizations found themselves between a rock and a hard place. As Chaim Weizmann put it when summing up the situation for the Palestine Royal Commission in 1936: 'For six million Jews in Eastern and Central Europe the world is divided between states in which it is not possible for Jews to live, and others which prevent them from entering their boundaries'.[25] The existing Jewish refugee bodies were now forced to shift their principal focus from Eastern Europe to Nazi Germany, and new organizations were set up with the specific brief of dealing with the migration of German Jewish refugees.

The most active domestic agency concerned with Jewish emigration from Germany was the Hilfsverein, part of the Reichsvertretung der Deutschen Juden, which was created as a coordinating agency for the various German Jewish bodies involved in emigration, social work and vocational training. It published regular reports and correspondence from German-Jewish immigrants on conditions in countries of immigration. It worked alongside the Palästinaamt, the office of the Jewish agency for Palestine in Germany. In addition, the Reichsvertretung represented German Jewry in negotiations with Nazi authorities, and acted as an intermediary for funds sent from overseas Jewish organizations.[26] It was required to rename itself the Reichsvertretung der Juden in Deutschland – the representative body not of German Jewry but of the Jews in Germany – in 1935.

In the United States, the National Coordinating Committee for Aid to Refugees and Emigrants Coming from Germany (National Coordinating Committee) was set up in 1934. It was affiliated with the Joint, the American Jewish Committee, the American Jewish Congress and HIAS, and renamed the National Refugee Service in 1939. In Britain, the Jewish Refugees Committee (JRC) was formed in March 1933 and the Council of German Jewry (CGJ), founded in 1936 to organize a programme of permanent emigration overseas, had representatives on its board from Jewish organizations in Britain, the United States and Germany.[27] The British section remained dominant in policy making and was the funding body of the Jewish Refugees

Committee. In 1939, it was renamed the Central Council for Jewish Refugees. Its council was based at Woburn House in central London.

Anglo-Jewish refugee groups were far more involved with the process of securing the admission of refugees than American Jewry. Louise London has shown that a degree of trust developed between the Home Office and Jewish bodies in this matter, not least because both parties ultimately agreed on the role Britain should play regarding the refugees. Both saw Britain as a place of temporary refuge and agreed on the need to be selective in identifying 'desirable immigrants'. Indeed, in London's account, refugee organizations 'performed much of the work of screening refugees to assess which of them were desirable immigrants'.[28] They also concurred in the initial assumption that only a small proportion of refugees from Nazi Germany would want to settle in Britain. It was for this reason that the Anglo-Jewish community felt confident in offering their guarantee, in 1933, that the admission of Jewish refugees would require no public funding – a guarantee that was no longer tenable from 1938 onwards.[29]

Given their access to more substantial funds, American Jewry became the main financiers of aid and migration activities in Europe. The Joint was the largest Jewish relief organization and contributed to the budgets of other American aid organizations such as HIAS, but also gave directly to overseas organizations such as the Hilfsverein. HIAS, in turn, used funds from the Joint to cover part of the budget of HICEM, which received funding directly from the Joint too, and from the Jewish Colonization Association and the British Section of the Council for German Jewry.[30] The Joint engaged in fundraising of its own but also received money collected by the United Jewish Appeal, which divided its funds for overseas initiatives between the Joint and the American Palestine Campaign.[31] From 1935 the Joint avoided transferring dollars into Nazi Germany. Instead, money was donated to the budgets of other organizations, and a transfer system was devised that benefited both emigrants and local committees. Emigrants would pay the costs of their journey to a local migration agency, such as the Hilfsverein or a HICEM branch, in local currency. Once they arrived at their destination, the Joint would then reimburse them in dollars.[32] By September 1939, the funds of the European Jewish relief organizations were either depleted or absorbed by assistance to Jewish refugees in Europe, and the support of overseas migration became totally dependent on funding from the United States.[33]

Broadly speaking, three problems occupied Jewish organizations during the 1930s: lack of funds, lack of influence, and a lack of unity. Firstly, the lack of funds: due to the Great Depression, Jewish organizations found it difficult to persuade donors to prioritize foreign aid over domestic issues. In the United States in particular, many felt that charity should be directed towards poor Jewish communities at home.[34] This rendered the redistribution of funds between Eastern Europe and Nazi Germany all the more difficult.[35] Its total income of $24.4 million between 1929 and 1939 notwithstanding, the Joint's funds for overseas work remained limited, and by 1939 it was running a loss of $1.9 million.[36]

Secondly, then as now, the effectiveness of refugee organizations was seriously curtailed by their lack of political power. They were repeatedly called upon to finance, investigate or approve plans conceived by intergovernmental committees and organizations. Yet Jewish social workers and policy makers, although consulted, had no official status on these committees or in these intergovernmental organizations. The Joint and the Jewish Colonization Association did enjoy fuller representation on the Advisory Committee of the High Commissioner for Refugees (Jewish and Other) from Germany, yet the powers of the commissioner were severely limited by political considerations, rendering the office highly ineffectual in its dealings with Nazi Germany. Separated from the League of Nations' headquarters, it had no power to intervene in Germany, limiting its remit to refugees who had already left. In 1935, James McDonald resigned as commissioner after two years in post, stating publicly that the organization lacked political and economic teeth in dealing with Germany, and that the unwillingness of Western countries to alter immigration restrictions prevented the organization from achieving any of its goals. 'Where domestic policies threaten the demoralization and exile of hundreds of thousands of human beings, considerations of diplomatic correctness must yield to those of common humanity', he wrote in his letter of resignation, which was published as a pamphlet that also included 'an Annex containing an analysis of the measures in Germany against "Non-Aryans", and their effects in creating refugees'.[37] It was high time for a 'friendly but firm intercession' with Germany.[38] McDonald's successor, Sir Neill Malcolm, who held the position until 1938, fared little better.

Thirdly, the relevant Jewish organizations were divided over how to address the problem. As already indicated, organizations closely linked to established Jewish communities in the West tended to prefer a non-political line, whilst those whose roots lay in Eastern Europe often chose a more confrontational way to achieve their objectives. For instance, the American Jewish Committee and B'nai B'rith opposed the boycott of German goods planned by the American Jewish Congress, arguing that overt action was too provocative and would endanger the safety of German Jewry. Instead, they sought to apply pressure on their own government to intercede with the Nazi regime. Those supporting the boycott, in turn, felt that the Haavara scheme facilitating the transfer of capital to Palestine undermined the effectiveness of the boycott.[39]

Many Anglo-Jewish groups favoured forms of back-door diplomacy, seeking to influence policy through unofficial high-level meetings whilst maintaining a non-partisan appearance in public. This attitude is exemplified by the following response from Leonard Montefiore, a scion of Anglo-Jewry's high nobility who played a key role in the Jewish relief work of the 1930s, to Chief Rabbi Hertz, commenting on a proposed series of protest meetings:

> All German Jews I have been in contact with say protest meetings at this juncture can do no good but only harm. In view of that I feel I must resist all attempts to stampede us into meetings, wild speeches, etc. Wise and Co. are too obsessed with applauding crowds to judge of their actions. … It seems to me that we play into their extremist hands by holding or organizing protest meetings à la Stephen Wise.[40]

Montefiore's letter ended with the following postscript: 'Bernhard Kahn [of the Joint] said to me: "Wir sind Geiseln in Deutschland" [We are hostages in Germany], hostages, for every insult and attack on Hitler, we shall surely suffer. I believe it to be true'.[41]

Similarly, efforts by the American Jewish Congress in the early 1930s to initiate concerted Jewish action failed, as organizations in the Americas, Germany, Britain and France feared that supporting calls to form a 'United Jewry' would fan antisemitic feelings at home. Yet the American Jewish Congress persisted, and played a key role in facilitating the foundation of the World Jewish Congress (WJC) in Geneva in 1936. The WJC was clearly predicated on the notion of Jewish national identity, and was designed, in the words of Nahum Goldmann, its first chairman, as a rebuke to 'the perspective of the AJC [American Jewish Committee] and its elitist counterparts in England, France and Germany, which feared that any international organisation would engender more antisemitism'.[42] These differences resurfaced, as we will see, at the Evian Conference in July 1938, and again during the war.

British Government Responses to the Evolving Refugee Crisis

Between January 1933 and the outbreak of war in September 1939, some eighty thousand refugees were admitted to Britain, many on a temporary basis pending remigration elsewhere.[43] Up to the November Pogrom of 1938, they had been shown no special consideration as refugees and had to satisfy the existing immigration criteria, which demanded that immigrants could either support themselves or had to have an individual or institutional guarantor. From late 1938 to September 1939, refugees were able to enter on block visas.

Given the background discussed in the previous chapter, it is perhaps not surprising that the Colonial Office ruled out the possibility that migration to the colonial empire might help to solve the refugee crisis that was unfolding in Nazi Germany. While the admission of Jewish refugees to the colonial empire was, in principle, an attractive option for some British policy makers, a range of factors played a decisive role in the success or failure of any plans to this effect. These included not only the conditions in the colonial territories and opinions of colonial legislatures, but also the willingness of the government to fund such ventures. The extent to which the colonial empire might serve as a destination for Jewish refugees thus became the issue of protracted debate within government.

At the first meeting of the appropriately named Cabinet Committee on Aliens Restrictions to discuss the option of Jewish refugees being admitted to Britain in April 1933, the representative of the Colonial Office stated in no uncertain terms that, as far as the refugees' potential subsequent remigration was concerned, there was no realistic possibility of settling refugees in the colonies, though the Colonial Office did anticipate that Jews might find refuge in Palestine at relatively short notice.[44] Given that both the government and Jewish organizations assumed at this time that Palestine would play an important role in solving the Jewish refugee problem, the insistence that there should be no space for Jewish refugees anywhere in the colonial empire was met with less incredulity at the time than it would be later. Officially, neither the Cabinet Committee on Aliens Restrictions nor the Cabinet as a whole discussed further the fate of the Jewish refugees until 1938.[45]

In the meantime, the Colonial Office and British immigration officials abroad received numerous queries from potential immigrants seeking information about conditions in various colonial dependencies – including Cyprus, Tanganyika, Kenya, Northern Rhodesia and the British West Indies. In response to all these enquiries, refugees were sent a standard reply, listing the entry requirements for each colony and advising that immigrants were extremely unlikely to be able to earn a living there, even if they did possess a certain amount of capital. Potential emigrants were further advised not to proceed without first contacting the governor of the colony concerned.[46]

The Colonial Office's insistence on the impossibility of offering refuge in the colonial empire was motivated in part by the fruitless investigations undertaken in 1933 and 1934 to gauge the possibility of accommodating Assyrian refugees.[47] Following a request from the League of Nations, the Foreign Office had put repeated pressure on the Colonial Office to explore whether some ten thousand Assyrian refugees who had been forced to flee Iraq could be allowed to settle in Cyprus, East Africa, Ceylon, Mauritius, Seychelles, Tanganyika, Northern Rhodesia, British Guiana, Nyasaland or Uganda. The Colonial Office repeatedly dismissed this initiative as impractical and was reluctant to antagonize the colonial governors by requiring them to respond to suggestions that it in any case deemed unrealistic. The Foreign Office nevertheless pressurized the Colonial Office into sending out several circulars on the matter. As one rather peevish Colonial Office minute noted, 'the Foreign Office are still not satisfied that the Colonial Office knows enough about the Colonial Empire to be able to express an opinion on this matter without consulting Colonial Governments'.[48]

While individuals received only a generic response, listing existing immigration regulations, the Colonial Office felt compelled to respond to requests from organizations credited (often with considerable paranoia) with influence in a more proactive manner. In March 1934, for instance, Leonard Montefiore, acting on behalf of the German Jewish Emigration Council (GJEC), sent the Colonial Office a list of refugees with professional qualifications in nursing, biochemistry and medicine, asking whether employment could be found for them in the colonial empire.[49] At first, officials were unwilling to circulate the list to the governors. As Sir John Shuckburgh noted:

> It is very unlikely that any of the Governors concerned will respond favourably, and the majority of them will probably not thank us for putting them to what they may well regard as unnecessary trouble. On the other hand, the Jews are very persistent in matters of this kind, and have powerful means (as we know to our cost) of exercising political pressure. I doubt whether it would be wise to refuse even to make enquiry.[50]

Senior Colonial Office officials discussed Montefiore's request and agreed to send it as a 'demi-official' circular to colonial governors in the West Indies, the East African Territories, Ceylon, The Straits Settlement, Mauritius, Hong Kong and Fiji. The majority of West Indian governors who received the circular maintained that they were unable to help. The governor of Jamaica, Sir Arthur Jeef, used the occasion to report that the local branch of the British Medical Association was pursuing a bill to prevent the admission of refugee doctors to the colony.[51]

The governor of the Bahamas, Sir Charles Dundas, noted that, 'as a consequence of past policy', there were 'very few Jews in the Bahamas'. He expressly pointed to an 'antisemitic bias' that existed in the colony. The tourist business was the Bahamas' principal source of revenue, he noted, and the winter visitors were mainly 'Americans of the better class, whose antipathy to all Jews is a bye word in their own country'. Local residents were inclined to adopt the same attitude towards the 'Hebrew people'. Acknowledging that Montefiore had enquired specifically about openings for qualified nurses, biochemists and doctors, the governor argued that it would be unwise to discriminate between the 'professional and labouring-class Jew, as to admit the former would render it difficult to exclude the latter, who are regarded as undesirable'.[52]

The colonial secretary in British Guiana, Sir Crawford Douglas-Jones, writing on behalf of the governor, likewise maintained that there was little space for individual refugees in the colony. Yet he went on to inform the Colonial Office that he had been approached by an American Zionist organization interested in purchasing land in the Rupunini district for an agricultural settlement for German Jewish refugees. Douglas-Jones indicated that the colonial government was likely to look favourably on the possibility of allowing German Jews with sufficient funds to form an agricultural colony, and asked for guidance from the secretary of state for the colonies.[53] In response, a consensus emerged in the Colonial Office that 'as regards Jews, British Guiana must (so long as there is a chance for Assyrians) be treated as *not* providing a possible opening', and Douglas-Jones was informed that priority should be given to settling Assyrian refugees in the Rupunini district.[54] Once the Assyrian scheme had fallen through, Colonial Office personnel began to look more favourably on the possibility of Jewish settlement in British Guiana, though no practical consequences followed and the department as a whole remained firm in its stance, arguing that there 'would be little scope for the exiled intellectuals and town dwellers who form such a large proportion of these refugees' to succeed as agricultural settlers.[55]

In 1935, the Colonial Office was again approached on behalf of the League of Nations and asked to investigate possible openings for refugees in the colonial empire.[56] The League of Nations was seeking accommodation for Jewish, Assyrian, Turkish, Armenian, Russian and Saar refugees. The Colonial Office was asked to provide a draft reply for the foreign secretary, Sir Samuel Hoare, to send to the secretary general of the League of Nations. Given their experience with the enquiries launched on behalf of Montefiore the year before, Colonial Office officials, discussing their response, rejected the idea of circularizing the governors again. While any refugee with sufficient funds could actually secure entry into most British overseas dependencies fairly easily at the time, the Colonial Office placed the emphasis of the draft on the difficulties involved in migrating to the colonial empire, and stressed that no colony would assist or admit destitute refugees.

As Hoare informed the League of Nations, there 'appears to be no present prospect of settlement in British overseas dependencies of refugees who are without definite prospects of employment or means of subsistence'. While 'any refugee, who has definite prospects of employment or means of subsistence, should[,] … subject to compliance with the regulations enforced in the territory in question, have no difficulty in securing admission to any of those dependencies', Hoare continued, positions in these territories were ordinarily filled with British personnel.[57]

Aware that this response might raise eyebrows, Shuckburgh alerted his immediate superior, Sir John Maffey, to the contents of Hoare's letter, warning that the colonial secretary should be notified in case of adverse comment. Shuckburgh wrote:

> The proposed reply amounts to a *non possumus*, so far as the Colonial Empire is concerned. I do not say that it is not the right answer: but it may expose us to some criticism abroad, where people are slow to believe that, in all our vast overseas possessions, we could not if we choose find a corner in which to settle some of these unfortunate refugees. I confess that foreign incredulity on the point seems to me not wholly unreasonable; but our experience over the Assyrians showed that the practical difficulties are almost insuperable, and I agree that it would serve no useful purpose to circularize Colonial Governments again.[58]

As before, the fact that Britain had not yet curtailed immigration to Palestine may have allowed the Colonial Office's intransigence to escape closer scrutiny. By the time Palestine was closed off as a viable alternative, the department had shifted its principal line of defence to the issue of over-population and overcrowding in some of the West Indian colonies, arguing consistently that if space could be found, priority should be given to the internal resettlement or remigration of West Indians currently stranded in Latin or South America, rather than bringing even more migrants to the British West Indies.

In principle, then, the Colonial Office was only too happy to support colonial governments' demands for harsher immigration controls. Between 1933 and 1936, ordinances were enacted in British Honduras, British Guiana, the Bahamas, Barbados, Jamaica and Trinidad, which gave governors further powers to restrict or in some cases ban the entry of indigent aliens. In British Honduras, the Destitutes Act of 1936 stated that aliens could land only with the approval of the governor and on payment of a deposit of $100. Similarly, new legislation in Trinidad gave the governor wide-ranging powers, and introduced a three-tier system of deposits. Anyone from within the British West Indies wishing to enter Trinidad would have to pay $100, anyone from Europe, the Americas and the North Atlantic $250, and anyone from elsewhere $500.[59]

Against the background of widespread economic depression, this legislation was principally designed to prevent workers from migrating to the Caribbean, and it specifically targeted Chinese and Syrian (Lebanese) immigrants. This is clear, for example, from advice sought by the governor of Jamaica from the Colonial Office on the possibility of drafting new legislation to prevent the entry of Chinese to Jamaica, and his subsequent proposal, in 1938, to amend the Aliens Law.[60] The following year, the governor advised the colonial secretary that all alien Chinese would be barred from entering Jamaica unless they were either tourists or had been granted special permission by the government.[61]

Yet legislation to achieve this goal required the approval of the colonial secretary. In order to avoid diplomatic repercussions and international criticism of its policies, the Colonial Office would not condone legislation that specifically targeted certain groups of immigrants. Consequently, immigration could only be restricted by legislating 'general powers' to control it. In this respect, the Immigration Restriction Ordinance of 1936 in Trinidad went further than any other legislation in the British West Indies. Although Syrian and Chinese immigrants were not explicitly mentioned, the deposits introduced by the ordinance made the underlying purpose clear enough. As the governor, Sir Murchison Fletcher, remarked in a confidential communication with the Colonial Office, it was 'frankly designed for the purpose of preventing entry into the Colony, and aimed more particularly at Chinese and Syrians, against whom the labour leaders can readily incense public opinion. The deposits required of immigrants are much in excess of the cost of passages back to the country of origin'.[62] To achieve this goal without being seen to discriminate specifically against potential Syrian or Chinese immigrants, the ordinance granted the governor the power to temporarily extend the definition of 'prohibited immigrants' to cover virtually any individual or group of persons by special Order in Council.[63] These sorts of sweeping powers, then, were by no means introduced specifically with Jewish refugees from Europe in mind. Once enacted, however, they obviously proved a considerable hurdle for them too.

In 1937, the Colonial Office yet again found itself under pressure from the Foreign Office following repeated reminders from the Office of the High Commissioner for Refugees from Germany to the Foreign Office regarding its commitment to investigate possibilities for the admission of refugees to the colonial empire. At the Session of the Assembly of the League of Nations in Geneva in September 1937, the high commissioner, Sir Neill Malcolm, noted critically that since immigration restrictions were being enforced in many countries, no progress had been made towards the resettlement of refugees.[64] To make things worse, immigration to Palestine was now being restricted.

It was in 1936 that Britain began to change her policy over Jewish immigration to Palestine. Arab unrest resulted in the appointment of a Commission of Inquiry, announced by the Colonial Office on 18 May 1936. The Peel Commission report, published in July 1937, recommended the partition of Palestine and the creation of a separate Jewish state. Yet by this time, the number of certificates permitting immigration to Palestine had been reduced to a trickle. Only the number of 'A' certificates, linked to the possession of significant capital, remained unchanged.[65]

Against its own better judgement, the Colonial Office bowed to the pressure from the Foreign Office and sent an official circular to sixteen colonial governments, including those of all the West Indian colonies. 'As you know', the circular addressed the governors,

> the position of the Jews in Germany and elsewhere in Europe has rapidly deteriorated during the last four years. It has caused great anxiety to the League of Nations, which decided in 1936 that a High Commissioner should be appointed for the purpose of liquidating so far as possible the problem of refugees coming from Germany, and that, as regards emigration, and final settlement, his duties should include the encouragement of initiative on the part of private organizations, and giving such initiative support by negotiations with the Governments of the countries of refuge, and if necessary, arranging to have definite plans for colonization and emigration studied on the spot in agreement with the Governments concerned.

The circular then went on to explain that the high commissioner 'recently called upon [Colonial Secretary] Mr Ormsby Gore and asked [for] his assistance in bringing this part of his task to the attention of any Colonial Government in which possibilities might exist for certain of these refugees to settle and make a living'.[66] The governors were asked whether opportunities existed for refugees bringing with them capital of between £500 and £600. Enclosed was a list, compiled by the Jewish Refugee Committee in London, of Jewish refugees with specific occupations.[67] Responses to the circular were slow in coming, and in the meantime, preparations began for the Evian Conference, initiated by President Roosevelt in March 1938.

In February 1938, Britain signed a League of Nations Convention in Geneva that was designed to extend the rights of refugees made stateless by Germany and Austria. The convention became virtually meaningless, as objections by various signatories – including Britain – exempted them from altering existing immigration controls.[68] When the convention was signed, the British colonial empire was excluded from it on the grounds that there had been insufficient time to consult colonial governments over any objections they might have had. Hence, in August 1938, a circular was sent to the colonies which included the text of the convention and asked whether it needed to be amended.[69] In response, most colonies agreed to the convention with the proviso that the exemptions Britain had secured for herself should also apply to them, so that they would retain individual control over the entry of any alien refugees.

Barbados, however, went a step further and refused to sign the convention, arguing that it would otherwise have to amend its 1932 Passport Control Act, which ran counter to the spirit of the convention. The colonial legislature wished 'to continue its policy of keeping out all immigrants other than those with considerable funds, and to make entry of refugees in any case dependent on the possession of a travel document entitling the holder to return to the country of issue of the travel document'. Indeed, 'even to allow refugees temporarily to reside in the colony while making arrangements for permanent residence elsewhere would cause difficulty as the local Immigration Laws do not provide for temporary permits, and a person given permission to land could not be compelled to leave'.[70] Needless to say, the 1932 Passport Control Act had most certainly not been drafted with a possible influx of Jewish refugees from Germany in mind. Yet now that Germany was not only forcing more and more Jews to emigrate but also compelling them to sign commitments never to return, they too fell foul of regulations enacted with quite different groups of immigrants in mind.

As the National Socialists proceeded to force the matter of Jewish emigration from 1937 onwards, and especially following the *Anschluss* of Austria in March 1938, the British government introduced additional restrictive measures to prevent the anticipated increased influx of Jewish refugees. On 28 April 1938, the Foreign Office issued a circular informing consular officials that Austrian passport holders now needed visas to enter Britain, and that the same requirement would be introduced for refugees with German passports from 21 May. As far as the colonial empire was concerned, the circular stated that:

> It is not proposed at this stage to issue any special detailed instructions regarding colonies, but in any case in which there is doubt whether the applicant will be in possession of adequate means on his arrival in a colony, or as to his readmission to German or Austrian territory, or in any case of doubt, visas should not be granted without prior reference to the authorities in the territory concerned.[71]

Given that the new visa requirements did not apply to many of Britain's colonial territories, the circular failed to provide sufficient clarity for the passport control officers confronted on a daily basis with the refugee crisis. Consular offices in Europe were besieged by thousands of enquiries from refugees, and organizations acting on their behalf, asking for information regarding areas in the British Empire that might take individuals or groups of refugees.

A case in point is the inquiry sent by the passport control officer in Vienna, Captain Thomas Kendrick, to the Foreign Office on 26 April 1938.[72] As Kendrick's superior, the consul general in Vienna, Donald St Clair Gainer, reported to Alexander Hutcheon of the Foreign Office, on 2 August, that Kendrick's 'staff are so overwrought that they will burst into tears at the slightest provocation and every means must be found of easing their burden'.[73] In April 1938, Kendrick wrote to the Foreign Office asking for guidance concerning the policy to be adopted regarding the emigration of Jews to various parts of the colonial empire. He wished to draw to the attention of the Foreign Office the 'desperate situation of the Jews in this country'. He explained that 'large numbers of Jews are now trying to obtain permission to proceed [to parts of the British Empire] ... and we are now endeavouring to discourage such people from making the attempt until we are in possession of more detailed instructions. It is certain, however, that many are already on their way there'.[74] He asked how many settlers each part of the colonial empire would be prepared to consider, what qualifications were needed, and whether Jews would be accepted in significant numbers anywhere.

The Foreign Office passed Kendrick's query on to the Colonial Office, who, on 21 May, sent a response to the Foreign Office for distribution to passport control officers throughout Europe. For individual applications, it reiterated the basic requirements for entry to colonial dependencies, stating that, provided applicants complied with existing immigration regulations, there were no restrictions on entry. However, immigrants would need to demonstrate either the possession of substantive means or definite prospects of employment. On the possibility of settling groups of Jews in the colonial empire, the circular stated that although enquiries were proceeding, no suitable area for such a project had yet been identified.

Turning to refugees with qualifications, the Colonial Office's circular informed the Foreign Office that recent enquiries made with colonial governors had yielded negative results, and that 'with the exception of one or two possible openings for individuals with special qualifications, there is no prospect for such refugees in these territories'. The circular ended with the advice that '[Colonial Secretary] Mr MacDonald regrets that he sees no alternative to instructing the British Passport Control Officer in Vienna that he should strongly discourage Jewish refugees from attempting to go to any of the Colonial Dependencies unless they have definite offers of employment'.[75]

As already mentioned in the Introduction, Sir Cosmo Parkinson, the Permanent Under-Secretary of State for the Colonies, noted that the response

in effect says that we can do nothing. I am afraid that no other reply is possible; but, regarded as a response to such an appeal, it is not one of which we can feel particularly proud, or which will bring us any credit in the eyes of the world. People will find it hard to believe that in all the wide expanse of the colonial Empire there is really no corner where some of these wretched victims of persecution could find shelter. However, this has been gone into before, and the conclusion reached is always the same.[76]

On a similar note, he wrote to the Parliamentary Under-Secretary of State in the department, Lord (Basil) Dufferin, that

> it is all very well for the British Passport Control Officer in Vienna to write as he does: everyone here will have sympathy with the wretched Jews in Austria, and everyone would like to help them. But, while doubtless there will be a good deal of pressure, it is not specially for His Majesty's Government to find homes for Jewish refugees.[77]

In a nutshell: 'it is better to be as brutal as the draft than to hold out false hopes'.[78]

The Evian Conference

Roosevelt's initial invitation to the Evian Conference called for the formation of a 'special committee' to meet in the summer of 1938 and discuss measures to alleviate the refugee crisis. The invitation was not greeted with any great enthusiasm in the Foreign Office where it was considered an ill-conceived idea. The proposal came with two caveats that indeed gave few grounds for optimism: firstly, 'no country would be expected or asked to receive a greater number of emigrants than is permitted by its existing legislation', and secondly, 'any financing of the emergency emigration ... would be undertaken by private organisations'.[79]

In order to prepare the British delegation for the conference, an interdepartmental meeting was held at the Foreign Office to discuss and incorporate the demands of the relevant government departments. The Home Office insisted that the conference should not infringe on its sovereignty over immigration controls, and signalled that whilst it was willing to review its admissions procedures, it would not change existing legislation. The Foreign Office feared that publicity surrounding the conference might encourage some East European countries to accelerate antisemitic attacks and expel their Jewish populations with the expectation that Western governments would financially aid their resettlement, thereby exacerbating the refugee crisis.[80]

On the other hand, the Foreign Office was 'deeply concerned with avoiding any action which might be regarded by America as a rebuff'.[81] Indeed, Louise London has pointed out that the American proposal for the conference was greeted by the Foreign Office as an opportunity to strengthen Anglo-American bonds at a time of impending war, and welcomed as a sign from the United States that its isolationist stance towards Europe might be changing.[82]

Given this objective, both the Foreign Office and the Home Office hoped for a positive response from the Dominions Office and Colonial Office. Whilst it was agreed by all departments that no concessions regarding policy in Palestine should be made, it was considered highly desirable that at the conference Britain should be able to offer some space, somewhere, in the British Empire as a refuge. Roger Makins, the Foreign Office lead on Jewish refugees, suggested in no uncertain terms that the US administration presumably expected Britain to make a substantive contribution towards a solution of the refugee crisis.[83]

Since the Foreign Office already feared that the conference was unlikely to offer any genuine solutions, given America's vagueness over its objectives and American and British constraints over immigration control and Palestine, it was considered important that the British government could offer 'something' in the British Empire as a way of escaping blame if no other positive results were achieved. The Foreign Office hoped that Britain might offer facilities for the settlement of refugees in some British colonial territory, lease land at a peppercorn rent, or support some scheme to finance emigration through an international loan. Although these suggestions would have entailed a reversal of the British policy that ruled out any funding of refugee projects, there would be two advantages to this approach: firstly, the immigration pressure on Palestine would be alleviated, and secondly, Britain would be seen to take a lead in solving the refugee problem.

In the months leading up to the Evian Conference in July 1938, the Colonial Office thus found itself under increasing pressure to offer some sort of settlement option in the colonial empire. This pressure came not only from government departments. Whilst preparations for the conference continued, individuals and refugee organizations sent volumes of correspondence to the Colonial Office, suggesting various settlement schemes for refugees. Suggestions ranged from the ludicrous to the credible, but all would founder on government determination not to provide financial assistance, local and Colonial Office opposition, or a lack of refugee organization funds. The decision not to fund refugee initiatives came under increasing attack. On 23 May 1938, the impassioned campaigner and independent MP for the Combined English Universities, Eleanor Rathbone, attacked government policy in the House of Commons, asking why no space in the Empire could be made available to refugees.[84]

At the first meeting to discuss the British delegation's instructions, held at the Foreign Office on 28 March, John Hibbert claimed that:

So far as the British Empire is concerned, the position was exceedingly difficult. The Colonial Empire would have to be ruled out so far as any kind of mass immigration was concerned, as had been clearly shown during the investigations into the possibility of re-settling the Assyrians. Apart from Gibraltar, Malta and Cyprus, the Colonial Empire lay almost entirely in the tropics and at present supported a population of 55 million natives compared with 55 thousand Europeans. It might be possible to absorb a few professional men, but that was all. It must also be remembered that there was considerable anti-Jewish feeling in some areas.[85]

Just as the Colonial Office was firming up its position, it was inconvenienced by a proposal from the governor of British Honduras, Sir Alan Burns, to settle twenty-five refugee families from Germany on private land, funded by an American Jewish organization. 'I should welcome such immigrants', Burns wrote, 'and I see no objection other than difficulty of repatriation if for any reason this should be necessary. I should be grateful for your advice.'[86] The Colonial Office decided to try and kick the proposal into the long grass by sending Burns a lengthy reply, asking detailed questions about the organization, and more importantly, requesting that he ascertain how refugees could be repatriated if the scheme was not successful.[87] On 10 May, Burns replied positively to nine of the questions raised by Sir Cosmo Parkinson, though he found it impossible to ascertain what prospects of further migration from British Honduras there might be for the refugees if required.[88] Following this positive and therefore highly inopportune response, John Hibbert advised Parkinson the following day that this potential scheme should not be disclosed to the Foreign Office, neither in response to Kendrick's inquiry from Vienna, nor in the context of the preparations for the Evian Conference.[89] 'If we pass the information on to Vienna', Hibbert wrote, 'there will be a rush of Austrian refugees, some possibly of a very undesirable type.'[90]

As the Evian Conference drew closer and instructions had to be drafted, Hibbert asked for a final decision from Parkinson as to whether the British Honduras scheme should be mentioned at the conference. Since the twenty-five Jewish families who would be settled in British Honduras, should the scheme be successful, 'may prove the forerunners of a considerable invasion', the issue needed to be decided 'as a matter of policy'. Hibbert explained:

> Personally I do not think this should be done. We have not told the Foreign Office anything about this scheme to settle 25 Jewish families on private land in British Honduras. The Governor has indicated that there is room elsewhere in the colony for a substantial number of West Indian migrants, and the possibility of settling some of the surplus population of such colonies as Jamaica and Barbados is apparently under consideration in the West Indian Department. In these circumstances it seems to me that we ought to consider our own people first and to let the question of settling German Jewish refugees take second place.[91]

In response, Hibbert was informed by MacDonald's principal private secretary, Gerald Creasy, that no decision could be taken regarding British Honduras until the department had received responses from the Middle East

Department regarding future immigration to Palestine, and from officials investigating possible settlement areas in Northern Rhodesia.[92]

From the Colonial Office's point of view, there was another complication. As one official noted,

> It would be extremely difficult on general lines to defend Jewish immigration to the West Indies when we are about to discourage Jamaica and Trinidad from allowing the entry of Chinese and Syrians into these Islands on the grounds that they would compete unfairly with the already unemployed West Indian population. The Bahamas, like Bermuda, is very strict and jumpy over immigration questions, while the old established Spanish Jews in Jamaica is not too popular as it is [sic].[93]

As the instructions for Evian had to be finalized, Creasy too advised MacDonald that 'if there are any areas in the West Indies or neighbouring colonies suitable for settlement, we ought, in the present circumstances, to reserve them for possible migration from Barbados or other overpopulated West Indian Islands'.[94] In the event, the Colonial Office informed the Foreign Office:

> It is desirable that the question of any possibilities of Jewish immigration into the West Indian Colonies or the adjacent territories, namely, British Guiana and British Honduras, should be excluded from the discussions. One of the causes of the numerous recent disturbances is overpopulation, and if suitable schemes can be devised for settlement in that area, prior consideration must be given to the needs of the surplus population of the more overcrowded West Indian Islands. This is a matter which will come within the purview of the proposed Royal Commission on the West Indies.[95]

Under mounting pressure, the Colonial Office eventually looked into possibilities for the settlement of refugees in Northern Rhodesia, Kenya and Tanganyika but categorically ruled out any mention of either the British West Indies or Palestine. Not least, this raised the question of why areas previously deemed unsuitable for the resettlement of Assyrian refugees should now be appropriate as a destination for Jewish refugees. As Sir Cosmo Parkinson noted,

> if the Secretary of State for the Colonies should suggest the possibility of finding a settlement place for Jews in Northern Rhodesia, someone may turn round and say that if there is room for Jews then there is room for Assyrians, and as you know, there are many critics of Government here who maintain that it is an absolute duty of the British Government to find a home for the Assyrians.[96]

On 3 June, an official letter from the Foreign Office informed the Colonial Office of an interdepartmental meeting to discuss the proposals. Regarding the position of the colonial empire, it urged the Colonial Office to consider that:

> The United Kingdom Delegation will further require to be in a position to state the contribution which His Majesty's Government are prepared to make to the solution of the problem, both in respect of the United Kingdom and in respect of the Colonial Empire. [Foreign Secretary] Lord Halifax considers that the instructions given to the Delegation on this point should be as full and detailed as possible, and should represent a generous and constructive contribution, more particularly in respect of the colonies.[97]

At the meeting, held on 8 June at the Foreign Office, the Colonial Office again stated that few opportunities existed in the colonies, possibly barring options currently under exploration in Northern Rhodesia, Kenya and Tanganyika. The Colonial Office 'regarded these three territories as offering the least unhopeful prospect for the admission of a certain number of refugees'. Whilst 'it may be possible to deal with individual cases, the colonies were not in a position to make a serious contribution to [solving] the problem'.[98]

The following day Lord Halifax wrote a personal letter to Malcolm MacDonald and again urged the Colonial Office to 'consider very seriously whether the Colonial Empire can offer more extended facilities for the entry of refugees than it has been possible to give hitherto'. MacDonald replied a few days later, confirming that at the interdepartmental meeting on 8 June the Colonial Office representative had stated the department's position. 'There are serious difficulties in the way of any large-scale settlement in the Colonies', he added, 'and I cannot hold out any hope that the Colonial Empire will be able to contribute much to the settlement of the problem.' However, responses from Northern Rhodesia, Tanganyika and Kenya were still forthcoming and would hopefully be submitted before the conference.[99]

On 13 June, the Colonial Office received the skeleton draft of instructions that the Home Office and Foreign Office intended to give to the British delegation. It was now up to the Colonial Office to complete the draft with their instructions.[100] On 30 June, amended instructions to the British delegation were transmitted to the Foreign Office. Their contents were bleak. Neither Palestine nor the West Indies should be mentioned as possible locations. Only two territories potentially merited further consideration, Northern Rhodesia and Kenya; but since investigations were still ongoing regarding Northern Rhodesia, it was 'highly desirable that as little as possible should be said on this subject by the United Kingdom Delegate, in order that false hopes may not be aroused and that embarrassing publicity may be avoided. The same considerations apply to information supplied by the Governor of Kenya'. The note also stated that neither of these two colonial governments, nor any other colonial government, was in a position to contribute financially towards the settlement or upkeep of any German Jewish refugees.[101] The generic list of entry requirements for individual migrants was attached for circulation.

In the event, neither Britain nor the United States took the lead at the Evian Conference, and the outcome was modest in the extreme. Most notably, it saw the establishment of the Intergovernmental Committee for Refugees (IGCR), whose remit ranged more widely than that of existing intergovernmental refugee organizations such as the League of Nations' High Commissioner. It was designed to be a permanent body with the immediate aim of negotiating with Germany and reception countries to facilitate an orderly emigration from Germany and Austria. The IGCR would work alongside the President's Advisory Committee on Political Refugees (PACPR), which was founded by Roosevelt in April 1938 to advise the administration on refugee policy and coordinate the work of private refugee organizations in the United States. It was chaired by the former High Commissioner for Refugees, James McDonald, and George L. Warren, who had previously worked for the Red Cross and the International Migration Service, serving as its executive secretary. Its status was quasi-official although it received no government funding, and most of its modest budget was covered by the Joint. The committee's main focus was on the settlement of refugees in agricultural colonies in remote areas. In Michael Marrus's memorable formulation, 'the ebullient Franklin Delano Roosevelt entertained a series of frequently exotic resettlement ideas', which the PACPR, in turn, pursued, and Jewish refugee organizations, consequently, were compelled to explore and debate, frequently at great length and cost, even though most of these schemes hardly seemed viable from the outset.[102] Among these, once again, was British Guiana, an option suggested and examined time and again, not least by the Freeland League for Jewish Territorial Colonization.

Adler-Rudel has argued that the Jewish relief organizations were 'not free from blame' for the vague nature of deliberations at Evian, suggesting that a joint plan submitted in advance might have had a more formative influence on the discussions at the conference.[103] Yet others have argued that the relief organizations' failure to call for the mass evacuation of entire Jewish populations in Central and Eastern Europe demonstrates their lack of political foresight.[104] The World Jewish Congress had called for one joint memorandum to be submitted by all relevant Jewish organizations, yet the already outlined disagreements over the relative merits of back-door diplomacy and public activism got in the way. Numerous organizations, including the Council for German Jewry, again expressed the fear that any suggestion of there being such a thing as a united 'international Jewry' would play into the hands of the antisemites.[105]

Consequently, Jewish organizations submitted a number of memoranda to the conference. They tended to fall into four categories, calling, firstly, for a reversal of British immigration policy in Palestine to allow unrestricted migration there; secondly, for Western countries to relax immigration restrictions; thirdly, for areas of settlement for Jewish refugees outside Palestine; and, finally, for Western governments to bring more political pressure to bear on Germany to alleviate persecution rather than facilitate emigration.[106]

The Committee for Jews in Germany, the Jewish Colonization Association, HICEM, the Joint and the Jewish Agency addressed the conference with a joint memorandum. It stressed that measures needed to be taken to alleviate the suffering of Jews in Eastern Europe as well as Nazi Germany; that emigration could not realistically be organized on a large scale unless Germany was put under serious pressure to allow the transfer of Jewish assets abroad; and that private resources were already strained to the limit and so governments now had to step up and offer financial support to emigration plans.[107]

The Reichsvertretung also prepared a memorandum for the conference. It needs to be read, as Adler-Rudel has pointed out, bearing in mind the organization's vulnerable status, situated as it was in the lion's den. The Reichsvertretung too considered mass evacuation an impossibility, arguing: 'Obviously, a certain proportion of the Jewish population of Germany will have to stay in Germany, as, for lack of suitable employment abroad, reasons of age, health, or a financial or personal nature, they are not yet ready or can never expect to be able to emigrate from Germany'.[108] Cautious in tone, the Reichsvertretung emphasized that whereas before 'emigration was primarily a problem to be answered according to the qualities of the individual involved, conditions have lately undergone a steady change so that it is now almost exclusively a question of using all possibilities to immigrate'. However, the document stressed that emigration would have to be gradual and planned. The refugees could only be absorbed successfully in the countries of immigration over a period of years.[109]

Several commentators have argued that the multiple representations at the Evian Conference created a 'ridiculous spectacle' and may have contributed to the lack of a positive outcome.[110] Yet it was not the lack of unity amongst Jewish organizations that turned the conference into the 'humiliating' and 'ridiculous' spectacle, as it has been described by most witnesses and historians; rather, it was the way in which Jewish organizations were sidelined at the conference. Evian clearly demonstrated the extent to which private relief organizations lacked the requisite power to influence refugee policies. The initiative for the conference had come as a surprise to these organizations and they had not been given any formal status, even though the United States had made it clear from the outset that it was they who would have to finance any proposal developed at the conference. Instead, they were invited to give evidence to a subcommittee, which heard twenty-four representations, mostly from Jewish bodies. On Adler-Rudel's account:

> The hearing was a humiliating procedure. Nobody was prepared for it, neither the members of the Committee, nor the representatives of the various organizations who had to queue up at the door of the meeting room to be called in, one after the other, to face the eleven members of the Sub-Committee, to whom they were supposed to tell their tale within ten minutes at the most.[111]

Most historians have viewed the Evian Conference as a failure, and an important signal to Nazi Germany that no country was willing to admit large numbers of Jewish refugees. Many have assumed that the conference was a cynical exercise in going through the motions with no intent of finding a solution. Then again, it can also be seen as a genuine attempt to bring together the relevant parties and lay the groundwork for more far-reaching forms of collaboration. To do so, sensitive issues had to be avoided, allowing everyone around the table to be confident that the desired solution to the refugee crisis would not inevitably militate against their sovereignty over immigration or other interests or concerns, or require a financial commitment. Against the backdrop of the Great Depression, widespread unemployment and domestic anti-alienism, the demand for laxer immigration controls was a big ask, and as unrest in Palestine increased and war loomed, British reluctance to alienate Arab opinion in the Middle East cannot be dismissed as wholly unreasonable.

Viewed from the perspective of the Colonial Office, the Evian Conference was a success. No reference was made to the West Indian colonies, and Palestine was not mentioned until the last day when, in response to repeated criticism, the British representative, Lord Winterton, justified restrictions on Jewish entry as a 'temporary' measure justified by the 'acute' problems in the region.[112] In the statement read out on admission to colonial dependencies, the line regarding individual entry was reiterated and mention was made of 'the question of the admission of a limited number of refugees into certain East African territories', which was still being investigated.[113] This generated a fair amount of post-conference publicity, and any publicity concerning potential refugee destinations other than Palestine was beneficial. No decisions had been taken, and any financial undertakings would have to be borne by private bodies. When Winterton's report on the conference was discussed in Cabinet, the Colonial Secretary thanked him for 'the skill with which he had looked after the colonial interests involved at Evian'.[114]

Whatever the intentions and aspirations may have been at the conference, subsequent developments clearly showed that it had been a failure. The hope attached to the British statement regarding the possible admission to colonial territories is an obvious case in point. It in any case never envisaged more than the potential settlement of a few hundred Jewish refugees either in Kenya or Northern Rhodesia. The offer was soon shown to be illusory. In September 1938, the Foreign Office asked on behalf of the IGCR for more information about the possibilities in the colonies mentioned at the conference in Evian. In response, the Colonial Office clarified that few existed, though the option that some 150 refugees could perhaps be settled in Kenya was still under investigation. An intervention from Lord Winterton did not sway the Colonial Office. The content of the Colonial Office's response was considered 'most unhelpful' in the Foreign Office, so much so that it was recommended not to relay the response to the IGCR since it would only highlight 'the tiny contribution of the Colonies to the refugee problem'.[115]

The IGCR did not relent, however, and continued to pester the British government for information on its contribution to the solution of the refugee crisis, past, present and future. Possibly in an attempt to avoid further criticism, the Colonial Office sent a circular to colonial governors in October 1938, asking them to give information on the numbers of German and Austrian refugees who had entered their territories – firstly, between 1933 and 1938, and secondly, during the six-month period ending in March 1938. The governors were informed that the purpose of this exercise was to give the British representative at the IGCR information on 'the contribution *already* [emphasis added] made by the various parts of the British Empire towards the solution of the problem'.[116] That the focus of the Colonial Office at this juncture was directed firmly towards those refugees who had already obtained refuge in the colonial empire, rather than those who might still do so in future, seems telling in the extreme.

Jewish Immigration to the British West Indies

There was a limited but significant number of East European Jews fleeing from increasing persecution and economic deprivation who settled in the British West Indies in the early to mid-1930s. As the immiseration of Central and East European Jewry gathered pace, emigration was an option for many; and given that the United States had drastically reduced its intake of new immigrants, East European emigrants focused increasingly on Palestine and South and Central America. Many emigrants indeed saw Mexico, Cuba and various South American destinations as a halfway point from which they could later reapply for entry to the United States.[117] Ships en route to or from these destinations frequently made stops in West Indian ports. Migrants on board who wished to remain had little difficulty in satisfying existing immigration controls in the West Indian colonies, given that they required no visas. Consequently, communities of East European Jews began to settle in British Honduras, British Guiana, Dutch Guiana, Curaçao, the Windward and Leeward Islands, and especially in Barbados and Trinidad.

These East European Jews generally established trading networks and peddled wares, often moving from one colony to another. They used their entry deposit, which was refundable after one year, as initial collateral to purchase goods on credit from wholesale merchants.[118] Manfred Goldfisch later recalled one such case, demonstrating that by the time of his arrival – along with numerous other refugees – on 1 January 1939, this had become a well-established practice. Within days, while the others had barely begun to find their bearings, 'two young men from Romania' had already left the temporary accommodation provided for the refugees.

> They had used their receipts from the immigration department for their security deposits and used them as a collateral for the purchase of goods. They had purchased a stock of textiles which they had cut into dress and suit lengths. They intended to offer them to the families in the sugar-growing areas where agricultural labour was deplorably still very poorly paid. They asked for a down payment and then visited their customers every week to collect small sums until the item was paid off. They had just returned from their first trip in their 12-year-old Ford 'T', which they had purchased for $10, but by the time they had paid for repairs, licence fees and tax, the cost was about $120 – still a sizable investment when funds are limited.
>
> However, their first effort was a great success – they had sold nearly all their stock and collected enough cash to buy more. So encouraged, they were leaving us to set up headquarters in one of the small country towns where most of their customers lived.[119]

Complaints about the unwelcome competition from Jewish businesses notwithstanding, it is well worth noting that Jewish pedlars supplied customers who, for whatever reason, would have found it difficult to buy their goods from established shops, and for many of their customers they provided what the long-standing journalist and editor of the *Trinidad Guardian*, Arthur Ince, has described as 'a new type of credit, affordable credit'.[120]

Some of the refugees were able to open stores in towns and villages, and began to send for relatives from Europe. Henry Altman, originally from Lublin, was on his way to Venezuela with his family in 1932 when their boat docked in Barbados en route and they decided to stay. He gave the following account of the growth of the Jewish community in Barbados, where a further thirty Jewish families had settled by 1934:

> We had family come over, we had friends, and also people from other islands came to Barbados, from Curaçao, some people from Guatemala, and in no

time we had our nice community … Most came from Poland, a few from Romania, who actually went to Trinidad. Trinidad had a larger community than ours of new immigrants, but somehow they never made their homes there or established themselves, they had no roots. But we found roots here.[121]

The pattern of settlement in Trinidad was similar. In 1932, there were initially only ten Jews in Trinidad, all established in business. Yet 'about forty Jews arrived from Romania' that year, 'all of whom immediately became peddlers and were all able to support themselves and families. Some of them soon established small businesses and created no trouble of any kind'.[122] The Averbouck family from Poland came to Trinidad the following year and established a synagogue in a room in their home.[123] According to Lorna Yufe, there were some ten Jewish families in Port of Spain, the capital of Trinidad, when she arrived there with her family in 1936. They had previously emigrated from Poland to Honduras but had found conditions there difficult and so moved on to Trinidad, where they established a store in Port of Spain.[124]

By 1938, the community had grown to over two hundred families. When Edgar Pereira (on whom more shortly) contacted the Refugee Economic Corporation, an affiliate of the Joint, in November 1938 to seek assistance in dealing with the new influx of Jewish refugees, he described the situation as follows:

> I believe I am the only Trinidad-born Jew in this colony, and up to last year I was not aware that there were more than fifteen or twenty Jews in this island, but now we have considerably over two hundred families. A good portion of these are Romanians who make their living by peddling, whilst others have established dress stores, clothing factories, etc., and their economic position is improving rapidly.[125]

Given that the established Caribbean Jewish communities belonged to the Sephardi tradition, the new East European Jewish immigrants created their own institutions to reflect their different cultural, linguistic and religious background. In Trinidad, where no established Caribbean Jewish community existed, East European Jews formed a Hebrew Aid Society in 1937. The following year it was renamed the Jewish Association of Trinidad (JAT), which may have been a reflection of its integrationist aspirations. For its president, Edgar Pereira, its purpose was to look after 'every aspect of Jewish life in this colony'.[126]

Pereira was the son of Jews from Curaçao who had settled in Trinidad in 1873. Anthony de Verteuil, former principal of St Mary's College, 'one of T&T's most avid and prolific historians',[127] gives the following account of Pereira's contested status:

Edgar Pereira, the Jews' perennial advocate ... was very ill. A doctor had declared him to be in an advanced stage of leprosy and he had to be quarantined. He lived in a house outside Tunapuna, and his wife lived nearby and attended to him each day until his death.

Edgar Pereira had claimed to be the first Jew born in Trinidad – which the Jews he helped did not believe. They described him as 'sickly and irascible, if not downright peculiar', and even his Jewish roots and his motives were questioned by his fellow Jews. We may well ask, what drove the man to cast in his lot for the Jews, to fight for the Jews at huge personal cost to himself?

He corresponded almost obsessively with the Jewish aid organizations in Britain and the US, begging for assistance. His office in downtown Port of Spain was often the first stop for desperate refugees seeking advice and assistance. He single-handedly negotiated the entry of seventy-nine immediate family members of refugees already on the island.

It was only after his death that the Jews began to claim him as their own and recognize his altogether extraordinary work for them.[128]

De Verteuil cites two evidently apocryphal narratives designed to underscore the notion that Pereira was a religious Jew at the time of his death, yet then reveals that he in fact received a Catholic burial.

Whether through his own fault or not, Pereira was definitely a divisive figure. As Friedrich Borchardt and David Glick wrote, when the Joint sent them to Trinidad early in 1939 to assess the situation, Edgar Pereira was

the only native-born Jew on the island; [he was] blind, crippled and a very difficult man to deal with because of his tragic physical disabilities. He has been extremely helpful in giving advice and council [sic] to the newcomers and is held in high esteem by the German and Austrian group. On the other hand, he is in great disfavor with the Polish and Roumanian groups who have as their champion a Dr. Pulver and an American Jew named Girion. Although one would be justified in expecting 450 new arrivals from persecuted lands to work in harmony in a new land of freedom, it is sad to relate that they have split wide into two very hostile groups.[129]

It is evident that, as the conflict escalated, 'both sides resorted to name-calling'.[130] Whatever the truth may be, and Pereira is certainly deserving of greater scholarly attention, if only credible source material could be found, there can be no doubt that he indeed played a crucial role in assisting, and negotiating on behalf of, Jewish refugees from 1938 onwards.

Yet Jewish refugees from Germany did not in fact begin to arrive in the British West Indies in any significant numbers until the panic migration of 1938–39. Although potential emigrants from Nazi Germany inundated British consulates and the Colonial Office with enquiries about conditions in British colonial dependencies, the number of enquiries received far outstripped the number of refugees who actually emigrated there. Knowledge about the region was sparse, and the refugee organizations did not encourage emigration to the West Indies, though they were clearly aware of the entry requirements stipulated by the British colonial dependencies.[131]

The Hilfsverein, the most active agency concerned with Jewish emigration from Germany, published regular reports and correspondence from German-Jewish immigrants on conditions in countries of immigration. Yet even their special report on South America, first published in 1936 and reprinted unchanged in 1939, did not mention the West Indies.[132] Only in 1938 did it begin to play an active role in sending emigrants to West Indian destinations. The table of refugee destinations in the annual report of the Reichsvertretung (under whose auspices the Hilfsverein functioned) for 1938 included twenty-one sponsored emigrants for 1937 and 1938 who had gone to the West Indies (though it is unclear whether any of them went specifically to the British West Indies). Since only those emigrants who had received assistance from the Hilfsverein were included in the list, it is also unclear how many emigrants the organization may have directed to West Indian destinations altogether.[133]

Tourism was still an elite activity in the 1930s, and cruise ships to the Caribbean were the preserve of the very rich. For most Europeans, the Caribbean was a remote colonial backwater. Although a significant number of British West Indians had fought in the First World War, as yet very few had emigrated to Europe, and only a tiny number of Europeans would ever have met somebody from the British West Indies.

Even so, some Jewish emigrants from Nazi Germany did settle in the West Indies prior to the panic migration of 1938–39, often because they had been forced to remigrate from their initial country of refuge. Ernest Schönbeck/ Edward Schonbeck is a case in point. A qualified chemical engineer from Berlin, he had emigrated from Germany to London in 1933. Since he was unable to secure a work permit in Britain, he initially joined his family who had emigrated to Holland but was then offered a position with the British Sugar Corporation in Columbia, where he worked until 1935, when he was admitted to the Imperial College of Tropical Agriculture in Trinidad. In 1937 he moved to Jamaica where he obtained a position with the West India Sugar Corporation (WISCO).

Although the Jamaican Legislature tried to prevent immigrants from entering the medical profession in the colony, Jewish refugees were occasionally able to work as medics. The best-known example is Dr Hans Stamm, who had trained in Giessen and Tübingen and was amongst the first wave of German Jewish refugees to emigrate from Germany in 1933. He initially moved to London where he was joined by his wife. Presumably because he had been unable to find work in London, he accepted an invitation to work as an assistant doctor in a Quaker project in Jamaica.[134]

It is very difficult to arrive at any reliable figures for the number of Jewish refugees from Greater Germany who did arrive in the British West Indies prior to the panic migration of 1938–39. The colonial dependencies had been asked in October 1938 to provide information on the number of individuals of German and Austrian nationality who had settled in their territories in the five years prior to, and the six-month period ending on, 31 March 1938. The Colonial Office had also asked how many of these could be classified as 'refugees unable to return to their countries of origin'.[135] The responses from the colonial governors indicated that only 350 Germans and Austrians had been admitted to the colonial empire. Of this number, just over a third had entered West Indian colonies, most of them Trinidad.[136] Of this third, 127 were classified as refugees who were unable to return.

There are, however, several problems with these numbers. Firstly, in most cases, figures had not previously been collated to match the rubrics laid out by the circular. In Trinidad, for example, all Europeans were classified together, so the share of refugees among the total number of Europeans could only be estimated. The figures provided by the governor were predicated on the assumption that of 116 Europeans who had entered the colony in the twelve months leading up to 31 March 1938, 23 had been refugees. For the six-month period from 1 April to 30 September 1938, on the other hand, the number of refugees who were unable to return was estimated to have been 97 out of a total of 136 Europeans arriving in Trinidad. Similarly, the governor of Jamaica informed the Colonial Office that aliens were not registered in the colony, and so the figures he could supply were largely guess-work and almost certainly represented an underestimate. Nor did the figures include immigrants who had arrived because they had received an offer of employment, or who had simply fulfilled the existing immigration criteria and were consequently not included in the refugee statistics. Yet whatever the precise numbers may have been, they were about to be dwarfed by the numbers of Jewish refugees arriving or seeking entry once panic migration set in as Nazi anti-Jewish policy escalated in the course of 1938.

Notes

1. See Herbert Strauss, 'Jewish Emigration from Germany: Nazi Policies and Jewish Responses (I)', in *Leo Baeck Institute Year Book, Vol. 25* (1980), 316–18.
2. Ibid., 319–20.

3. Marion Kaplan, *Between Dignity and Despair: Jewish Life in Nazi Germany* (New York: Oxford University Press, 1998), 94; Statistisches Jahrbuch für das Deutsche Reich vol. 49 (1930), 14.
4. Strauss, 'Jewish Emigration (I)', 323.
5. Kaplan, *Dignity and Despair*, 11.
6. Ibid., 324–25. See also Leni Yahil, *The Holocaust: The Fate of European Jewry* (New York: Oxford University Press, 1990), 22.
7. See Christopher R. Browning, *The Origins of the Final Solution: The Evolution of Nazi Jewish Policy, September 1939–March 1942. With contributions by Jürgen Matthäus* (London: Heinemann, 2004).
8. Like much of the existing literature, the following account draws extensively on Strauss, 'Jewish Emigration (I)', and idem, 'Jewish Emigration from Germany: Nazi Policies and Jewish Responses (II)', in *Leo Baeck Institute Year Book, Vol. 26* (1981), 343–409. Strauss himself relied, inter alia, on Arthur Prinz, 'The Role of the Gestapo in Obstructing and Promoting Jewish Emigration', *Yad Vashem Studies* 2 (1958), 205–18; Werner Rosenstock, 'Exodus 1933–1939: A Survey of Jewish Emigration from Germany', in *Leo Baeck Institute Year Book, Vol. 1* (1956), 373–90; Wischnitzer, *To Dwell in Safety*.
9. Kaplan, *Dignity and Despair*, 15, 3.
10. Widespread violent attacks against Jews following the Jewish boycott announced in April 1933, for instance, were quickly discouraged by Nazi authorities and replaced by legislative persecution. An estimated ten thousand Jewish emigrants who fled Germany in 1933 had returned by early 1935 (Kaplan, *Dignity and Despair*, 73), partly because they were unable to secure a living in neighbouring countries, and partly because of the apparent cessation of anti-Jewish violence in Germany. In fact, the level of violence and brutality varied greatly from one location to another. Strauss noted that violence was always organized, and that pogrom-style brutality and attacks of a spontaneous nature were uncommon in Nazi Germany. In reality, 'the passivity of broad strata of the population in Germany remained a constant throughout the period of persecution'. Strauss, 'Jewish Emigration (I)', 331.
11. Wolf Gruner, 'Local Initiatives, Central Coordination: German Municipal Administration and the Holocaust', in Gerald D. Feldman and Wolfgang Seibel (eds), *Networks of Nazi Persecution: Bureaucracy, Business, and the Organization of the Holocaust* (New York: Berghahn Books, 2005), 269.
12. Strauss, 'Jewish Emigration (I)', 331.
13. Herbert A. Strauss, 'Jewish Attitudes in the Jewish Press', in idem (ed.), *Jewish Immigrants of the Nazi Period in the USA. Vol. 6: Essays on the History, Persecution and Emigration of German Jews* (New York: Saur, 1987), 110. Between 1930 and 1933, 130 Jewish periodicals, newspapers and weeklies were published in Germany. Between 1933 and 1938 the major periodicals, which wielded the most influence and were most widely read, were the *C.V.-Zeitung*, the *Jüdische Rundschau*, the *Israelitisches Familienblatt*, and the *Gemeindeblatt Berlin*. After January 1933, Jewish periodicals operated under censorship, but continued to appear until November 1938. Many German Jewish periodicals of the nineteenth and early twentieth centuries have been digitized and are now available at http://sammlungen.ub.uni-frankfurt.de/cm/nav/index (last accessed 17 June 2019).
14. Ibid., 113.
15. Strauss, 'Jewish Emigration (I)', 330.
16. Ibid., 328.

17. Kaplan, *Dignity and Despair*, 132, 116.
18. Although currency controls had already been introduced prior to 1933, the Nazi regime substantially increased the flight tax. See Wischnitzer, *To Dwell in Safety*, 190. For a fuller account see Avraham Barkai, 'Self-Help in the Dilemma: "To Leave or to Stay?"' and 'In a Ghetto without Walls', in Michael A. Meyer (ed.), *German-Jewish History in Modern Times, Vol. 4, Renewal and Destruction 1918–1945* (New York: Columbia University Press, Leo Baeck Institute, 1998), 318–30 and 346–50.
19. Kaplan, *Dignity and Despair*, 71.
20. Rosenstock, 'Exodus', 373–77.
21. Yahil, *The Holocaust*, 105.
22. Kaplan, *Dignity and Despair*, 119.
23. See Sherman, *Island Refuge*, 88; London, *Whitehall and the Jews*, Chapter 4.
24. Keen to encourage Jewish emigration, the regime too compiled detailed information on immigration conditions. One example of this is the report of 13 September 1936 on entry to British colonies (presumably) by SS Oberscharführer Herbert Hagen, though it is unknown whether this report was made available to refugee organizations. John Mendelsohn and Donald S. Detwiler (eds), *The Holocaust: Selected Documents in Eighteen Volumes. Vol. 5: Jewish Emigration from 1933 to the Evian Conference of 1938* (New York: Garland, 1982), Document 4, p. 51.
25. Chaim Weizmann, 'Statement made before the Palestine Royal Commission in Jerusalem, 25 November 1936', in Meyer Weisgal (ed.), *Chaim Weizmann: Statesman, Scientist, Builder of the Jewish Commonwealth* (New York: Dial Press, 1944), 304; cited in Abraham Margaliot, 'The Problem of the Rescue of German Jewry During the Years 1933–1939: The Reasons for the Delay in their Emigration from the Third Reich', in Yisrael Gutman and Efraim Zuroff (eds), *Rescue Attempts during the Holocaust: Proceedings of the Second Yad Vashem International Historical Conference, Jerusalem, 8–11 April 1974* (Jerusalem: Yad Vashem, 1977), 245–65; reprint in Michael Marrus (ed.), *The Nazi Holocaust: Historical Articles on the Destruction of European Jews, Vol. 2. Pt. 6: The Victims of the Holocaust* (Westport, CT: Meckler, 1989), 571.
26. Strauss, 'Jewish Refugees (II)', 394.
27. The JRC was renamed the German Jewish Aid Committee (CJAC) in January 1938 but reverted to its original name in 1940. Its American members included the banker Felix Warburg (until his death in 1937) and Paul Baerwald of the Joint, Charles Liebman of the Refugee Economic Corporation, and the Reform rabbi and Zionist leader Stephen Wise. Its British members included: Sir Herbert Samuel, the former high commissioner for Palestine and home secretary; Viscount Bearsted (Walter Samuel), the head of Shell and an opponent of Jewish nationalism and member of the Jewish Fellowship; Simon Marks, the head of Marks & Spencer; Chaim Weizmann for the Jewish Agency; and Sir Osmond Goldschmidt for the Jewish Colonial Association and Central British Fund for German Jewry.
28. London, *Whitehall and the Jews*, 54.
29. Ibid., 26, 29–30, 60.
30. 'Aid to Jews Overseas. Report of the AJJDC for the Year 1937' (New York: JDC, 1938), 20.
31. Zosa Szajkowski, 'Budgeting American Jewish Overseas Relief (1919–1939)', *American Jewish Historical Quarterly* 59(1) (1970), 88.
32. Bauer, *American Jewry*, 27.
33. Marrus, *The Unwanted*, 183.
34. Szajkowski, 'Budgeting', 83–85; Bauer, *American Jewry*, 15.

35. Szajkowski, 'Budgeting', 98–101.
36. Marrus, *The Unwanted*, 183; Bauer, *American Jewry*, 24.
37. Letter of Resignation of James G. McDonald, High Commissioner for Refugees (Jewish and Other) from Germany. Addressed to the Secretary General of the League of Nations (London: Headley, 1935), x.
38. Ibid., ix.
39. See Richard A. Hawkins, 'Samuel Untermyer and the Boycott of Nazi Germany, 1933–1938', *American Jewish History* 93(1) (2007), 21–50. On the crucial role of the Women's Division of the American Jewish Congress in campaigning for the boycott, see Rona Sheramy, '"There are Times When Silence Is a Sin": The Women's Division of the American Jewish Congress and the Anti-Nazi Boycott', *American Jewish History* 89(1) (2001), 105–21.
40. Leonard Montefiore to Chief Rabbi Hertz, 23 March 1933, Anglo-Jewish Archives, University of Southampton (hereafter AJA), MS177, 114/3.
41. Ibid.
42. Nahum Goldmann, *The Autobiography of Nahum Goldmann* (London: Weidenfeld & Nicolson, 1970), 144.
43. London, *Whitehall and the Jews*, 10.
44. Ibid., 9, 38.
45. Ibid., 31.
46. See TNA CO 323/1271/2 (30812/1A).
47. The Assyrians were Christians (descendants of the Nestorian Church) who had lived in the Ottoman Empire, inhabiting roughly the same area as the Kurds. The victims of persecution and atrocities committed by the Ottoman regime early in the First World War, they sided with the Entente. Following Russia's withdrawal from the war, they were left stranded at the mercy of the Turks, which led to a mass exodus. Many subsequently found themselves in northern Iraq where they aligned themselves closely with the British mandatory power, inter alia helping the British to put down the Arab Revolt of 1920 and Kurdish uprisings in the north of the country. This hardly made them popular with the Arab majority in Iraq. The Turks had no intention of letting them return, the Kurds resisted any suggestion that they should share territory with them, and the Iraqi government squarely denied them the right to settle collectively in northern Iraq. Following the end of the British Mandate in 1932, violence ensued, and many of the Assyrians fled to Syria. Against this backdrop, the League of Nations was desperately trying to find alternative settlement areas for the Assyrian refugees, yet to no avail. See David Omissi, 'Britain, the Assyrians and the Iraq Levies, 1919–1932', *Journal of Imperial and Commonwealth History* 17(3) (1989), 301–22.
48. J. John Paskin, Colonial Office memorandum, 23 July 1934, TNA CO 323/1296/13.
49. Leonard Montefiore, German Jewish Emigration Council, to the Colonial Office, 2 March 1934, TNA CO 323/1271/1.
50. Sir John Shuckburgh, Colonial Office memorandum to Sir John Maffey, 10 March 1934, TNA CO 323/1271/1.
51. Sir Arthur Jeef, Governor of Jamaica, to Sir John Maffey, Permanent Under-Secretary in the Colonial Office, 30 April 1934; Colonial Office memorandum by Roland V. Vernon (undated), TNA CO 323/1271/1.
52. Sir Charles Dundas, Governor of the Bahamas, to Sir John Maffey, Permanent Under-Secretary in the Colonial Office, 20 April 1934, TNA CO 323/1271/1.
53. Colonial Secretary of British Guiana, Sir Crawford D. Douglas-Jones, to Sir John Maffey of the Colonial Office, 6 June 1934, TNA CO 323/1271/1; 323/1296/13.

54. J. John Paskin, Colonial Office memorandum, 13 March 1934, TNA CO 323/1271/1; Colonial Office to Sir Crawford Douglas-Jones, 11 July 1934, TNA CO 323/1271/1.
55. See Sir John Maffey to Sir Cosmo Parkinson, 22 May 1935; Minute by Jasper St John Rootham, 31 May 1935, TNA CO 323/1345/6.
56. For the background to this request, see 'Work of the Inter-Governmental Advisory Commission for Refugees – Seventh Session March 1935', TNA CO 323/1347/8.
57. Sir Samuel Hoare to the Secretary General of the League of Nations, Geneva, 29 November 1935, TNA CO 323/1347/8.
58. Sir John Shuckburgh to Sir John Maffey, 20 September 1935, TNA CO 323/1347/8.
59. See TNA CO 318/440/5; CO 123/376/6.
60. See TNA CO 351, Registers, 68637/35 (destroyed), 68637/36, and 68637/38.
61. See TNA CO 351 Registers, 68637/39.
62. Cited in Tony Martin, 'Jews to Trinidad', *Journal of Caribbean History* 28(2) (1994), 250.
63. See Immigration (Restriction) Ordinance, No. 4 of 1936, Ordinances Passed by the Legislative Council of Trinidad and Tobago during the Year 1936. Trinidad, 1937. IALS.
64. Sherman, *Island Refuge*, 80–82.
65. Strauss, 'Jewish Emigration (II)', 353.
66. Circular, December 1937, TNA CO 323/1605/2.
67. Ibid.
68. Sherman, *Island Refuge*, 81–84; London, *Whitehall and the Jews*, 83–84.
69. Extract from Official Report, Intergovernmental Conference for the Adoption of Legal Status of Refugees from Germany, 27 April 1939, TNA CO 323/1604/2.
70. Summary of replies to Circular of 11 August 1938, undated, TNA CO 323/1604/3. Since Barbados was not a Crown Colony, the legislature was not compelled to sign the convention.
71. Circular S.12994, Passport Control Department, Foreign Office, 28 April 1938, TNA CO 323/1603/3.
72. Following the *Anschluss*, Kendrick apparently issued permits liberally to Jewish emigrants, enabling thousands to escape until he was arrested and expelled in August 1938 in connection with his activities for MI6. See Helen Fry, *Spymaster: The Secret Life of Kendrick* (London: Marranos, 2014).
73. TNA FO 372/3284, T 10774/3272/378, cited in Sherman, *Island Refuge*, 134.
74. Kendrick, PCO Vienna to Foreign Office, 26 April 1938, passed on to the Colonial Office, 4 May 1938; see TNA CO 323/1605/2.
75. F.J. Howard of the Colonial Office to the Foreign Office, 21 May 1938, TNA CO 323/1603/1.
76. Cosmo Parkinson, internal Colonial Office memorandum, 11 May 1938, TNA CO 323/1605/2.
77. Cosmo Parkinson to Lord Dufferin, 16 May 1938, TNA CO 323/1605/2.
78. Office minutes (unsigned), TNA CO 323/1605/2.
79. Memoranda communicated by the United States Embassy on 24 March and 6 April 1938, TNA CO 323/1605/2.
80. See Sherman, *Island Refuge*, 101. Poland, for instance, had, since 1936, been considering a large-scale – and mainly forced – settlement plan for Polish Jews in Madagascar. See Leni Yahil, 'Madagascar: Phantom of a Solution for the Jewish Question', in Bela Vago and George L. Mosse (eds), *Jews and Non-Jews in Eastern Europe, 1918–1945* (New York: Wiley, 1974), 315–34.

81. John G. Hibbert, Memorandum on Foreign Office meeting to discuss the American proposal, 28 March 1938, TNA CO 323/1605/2.
82. London, *Whitehall and the Jews*, 86.
83. Sherman, *Island Refuge*, 103.
84. HC Deb (23 May 1938) Series 5, Vol. 336, cc 834–36. Available at http://hansard.millbanksystems.com/sittings/1938/may/23 (last accessed 23 April 2017).
85. Note from John Hibbert on the approach to take at the interdepartmental meeting, 25 March 1938; Revised Record of interdepartmental meeting, Foreign Office, 28 March 1938, both TNA CO 323/1605/2.
86. Governor of British Honduras to the Secretary of State for the Colonies, telegram no. 37, 4 April 1938, TNA CO 323/1603/1.
87. Sir Cosmo Parkinson to Sir Alan Burns, 22 April 1938, TNA CO 323/1603/1.
88. Sir Alan Burns to Sir Cosmo Parkinson, 10 May 1938, TNA CO 323/1603/1.
89. John Hibbert, note to Sir Cosmo Parkinson, 11 May 1938, TNA CO 323/1605/2.
90. John Hibbert to Sir Cosmo Parkinson, internal memorandum, 13 May 1938, TNA CO 323/1605/2.
91. John Hibbert, memorandum for Sir Cosmo Parkinson on preparations for the Evian Conference, 23 June 1938, TNA CO 123/370/2.
92. Gerald Creasy, Memorandum, 24 June 1936, TNA CO 123/370/2.
93. [Author's signature illegible], Memorandum to Sir Cosmo Parkinson, 24 June 1938, TNA CO 123/370/2.
94. Gerald Creasy to Malcolm MacDonald, 30 June 1936, TNA CO 123/370/2.
95. Note for Evian Conference, 30 June 1938, TNA CO 323/1603/1.
96. Sir Cosmo Parkinson to Sir Hubert Young, Governor of Northern Rhodesia, 19 May 1938, TNA CO 323/1603/1. The cause of the Assyrians enjoyed some popular support because of their prominent role in the Iraq Levies. It was felt by some that, having depended on their support while holding the Iraq Mandate, the British had betrayed them when relinquishing the Mandate.
97. Under-Secretary of State, Foreign Office, to Under-Secretary of State, Colonial Office, 3 June 1938, TNA CO 323/1605/2.
98. Record of an interdepartmental meeting held at the Foreign Office on 8 June 1938 for circulation to the representatives of the departments for amendment or approval, TNA CO 323/1605/2.
99. Viscount Halifax to Malcolm MacDonald, 9 June 1938; Malcolm MacDonald to Viscount Halifax, 14 June 1938, TNA CO 323/1605/2.
100. Foreign Office to Colonial Office, 13 June 1938, TNA CO 323/1605/2.
101. John A. Calder, Colonial Office, to the Under-Secretary of State, Foreign Office, enclosing 'Note for Evian Conference', 30 June 1938, TNA CO 323/1603/1.
102. Marrus, *The Unwanted*, 187.
103. Salomon Adler-Rudel, 'The Evian Conference on the Refugee Question', in *Leo Baeck Institute Year Book Vol. 13* (1968), 255
104. See Margaliot, 'The Problem of the Rescue', 567. Strauss argues against this view in 'Jewish Emigration (II)', 390.
105. Geoffrey Alderman, *Modern British Jewry* (Oxford: Clarendon, 1992), 281.
106. Ibid., 256–57.
107. Council for German Jewry, 'Evian Conference – Concerning Political Refugees: Memorandum of Certain Jewish Organisations Concerned with the Refugees from Germany and Austria' (London: n.p., [1938]).
108. See Adler-Rudel, 'Evian Conference', Appendix 1, 264.

109. Ibid.
110. For this view see, for example, Avi Becker, 'Diplomacy without Sovereignty: The World Jewish Congress Rescue Activities', and Monty Penkower, 'Dr. Nahum Goldmann and the Policy of International Jewish Organizations', both in Selwyn Ilan Troen and Benjamin Pinkus (eds), *Organizing Rescue: National Jewish Solidarity in the Modern Period* (London: Frank Cass, 1992), 351 and 148–49 respectively.
111. Adler-Rudel, 'Evian Conference', 255.
112. See Sherman, *Island Refuge*, 116.
113. Ibid.
114. Ibid., 121.
115. Ibid., 135.
116. Circular from Malcolm MacDonald, 7 October 1938, TNA CO 323/1602/17.
117. Avni, 'Patterns of Jewish Leadership', 89.
118. Donna Farah, 'The Jewish Community in Trinidad, 1930s–70s', unpublished Caribbean Studies Project (Kingston, Jamaica: University of the West Indies, 1991), 8.
119. Unpublished typescript, courtesy of Su Goldfish.
120. Joanna Newman, 'A Caribbean Jerusalem', Radio 4, 11 August 2001.
121. Interview with Henry Altman by the author, 28 August 1990, Bridgetown, Barbados (transcript in my possession).
122. Friedrich Borchardt and David Glick, Report to the Joint on Trinidad, 22 March 1939, JDC, File 1047.
123. Feature on Jewish settlement in Trinidad during the 1930s, and interview with Mrs Averbouck, in *Sunday Guardian* (Trinidad), 10 December 1989.
124. See Lorna Yufe, 'History of the Jews in Trinidad', unpublished typescript in my possession; Martin, 'Jews to Trinidad', 248.
125. Edgar Pereira to Charles Liebman, Refugee Economic Corporation, New York, 12 December 1938, JDC, File 1047.
126. Ibid.
127. *Trinidad Guardian*, 1 March 2015, http://www.guardian.co.tt/lifestyle/2015-02-28/no-letting. Interestingly, this report, despite including a long list of his publications, makes no mention of de Verteuil's 2014 publication on Trinidadian Jewry (last accessed 29 April 2019).
128. Anthony de Verteuil, *Edward Lanza Joseph and the Jews in Trinidad* (Port of Spain: Litho Press, 2014), 169–70.
129. Friedrich Borchardt and David Glick, Report to the Joint on Trinidad, 22 March 1939, JDC, File 1047.
130. Alisa Siegel, 'An Unintended Haven: The Jews of Trinidad, 1937 to 2003', PhD thesis, University of Toronto, 2003, 82.
131. This is evident, for example, from a report on conditions in British Guiana compiled by Anglo HICEM and published by the Jewish Refugee Committee in 1935. It stated that anyone with a deposit of £50 would gain entry, and gave the address of the representative of 'British Jewry' in the colony. Economic conditions were promising, British Guiana was becoming prosperous and possibilities in trade and commerce appeared favourable. Specifically, some sugar factories, 'in which a number of German refugees might be absorbed', could be acquired at reasonable terms. See 'Summary of Information on emigration possibilities collected by the Anglo-Hicem, German Jewish Emigration Council, London, 31 December 1934', Jewish Refugees Committee, report of work March 1933–January 1935, pp. 11, 31, Wiener Library Book Section, Microfilm collection S49–S146, reel S123, Leo Baeck Institute New York (hereafter LBI NY).

132. Hilfsverein der Juden in Deutschland [Jewish Aid in Germany] (ed.), *Jüdische Auswanderung: Korrespondenzblatt über Auswanderungs- und Siedlungswesen* (Berlin: Schmoller & Gordon, [September] 1936, 1939).

133. Arbeitsbericht der Reichsvertretung der Juden in Deutschland für das Jahr 1938 (Berlin, 1939), 53.

134. Gertrud Aub Buscher, 'Obituary of Dr Hans Stamm' (in the author's possession). Aub Buscher – the daughter of Rudolf Aub, whom we will meet later – is Stamm's daughter-in-law.

135. Malcolm MacDonald, Colonial Office Circular, 7 October 1938, TNA CO 323/1602/17.

136. See TNA CO 323/1602/17.

Chapter 3

PANIC MIGRATION

The British West Indies and the Refugee Crisis of 1938–1939

The year 1938 saw a dramatic escalation of Nazi anti-Jewish policy. The regime not only shifted its focus squarely towards forced emigration; it also introduced legislation that robbed emigrants of virtually all their capital and rendered them stateless, thus turning them into the paradigmatic 'undesirable refugees': penniless and with no option of return. Of the roughly thirty thousand men arrested and taken to concentration camps during the pogrom of November 1938, most were released on the explicit condition that they and their families leave Greater Germany immediately.

Many officials of the Hilfsverein, including the subsequent historian of German Jewish emigration, Arthur Prinz, who worked for the Hilfsverein from 1933 to 1939, were also arrested during the pogrom. On Prinz's account, regional offices of the Hilfsverein had 'their typewriters ... thrown out of the windows, files torn up and furniture smashed; a very effective form of promoting emigration'. Based on the notion that 'no holds were barred in an emergency', thousands now travelled to South America on tourist visas; many emigrants procured false papers and bought foreign passports – 'the most diverse passports were being traded on the black market' – in order to emigrate illegally.[1]

Whilst the emphasis of Prinz's account lies on the role of individual emigrants in purchasing illegal or invalid travel documents at this juncture, Strauss and Marrus have both stressed the involvement of refugee organizations in this process. According to Strauss:

Organizations in aid of emigration, frequently under Gestapo pressure, chartered ships and sent groups of persecuted refugees abroad with visas that were acquired through questionable channels, or with no immigrant visas at all, hoping that overseas governments would waive regulations, or [that] aid organizations, relatives or friends would be on hand to set things straight.[2]

To be sure, following the November Pogrom, the public outcry over persecutory measures in Germany led to increased pressure on Western governments to act, resulting in concessions both in Britain and America. Britain admitted some forty thousand refugees between November 1938 and the outbreak of war, mainly on 'block visa' agreements, which led to a streamlining of procedures and the admittance of large groups of Jewish refugee children.[3] Yet this still left significant numbers of Jewish refugees with nowhere to go. As already indicated, both individual refugees and relief organizations, in their desperate need to find a way out, now became less discriminating in their choice of possible destinations and prospects. It was at this juncture that a number of previously rather unattractive colonial territories – including the British West Indies – for all the difficulties that they presented as sites of immigration, began to receive rather more serious consideration.

The Colonial Office was only too aware of this increased interest. By the time the governors had sent in their returns in response to the circular sent out in October 1938 to inquire about the number of previously admitted Jewish refugees, the figures had already, as John Hibbert noted, become

> more or less valueless, because we know for a fact that since the Grynszpan business and the rabid anti-Semitic [*sic*] drive in Germany [that] followed it, many hundreds of Jews have enquired regarding the possibility of entering one or other of the Colonies, and that a considerable number have actually got in – for example, into territories such as Trinidad and, I believe, Kenya.[4]

The Jewish refugee organizations were now forced, yet again, to alter their course dramatically. Having initially argued against mass emigration in 1933, by 1935 they had begun to accept that Nazi anti-Jewish policy would lead to the emigration of a substantial number of Jews. As Nazi persecution continued to intensify, they recognized that the bulk of German Jewry would most likely have to leave eventually. The refugee crisis forced onto the international agenda by the Nazis in the course of 1938 now confronted the refugee organizations with what the Joint soon began to call 'panic migration'.[5]

Consequently, refugee organizations felt compelled to help refugees gain access (both legally and 'illegally') to any country they could. Against this backdrop, some of them also began to advocate certain West Indian colonies, such as Trinidad, as a destination for Jewish refugees from Greater Germany. All the while they were effectively fighting with their hands tied behind their backs, as the responsibility they were expected to take on continued to outstrip by far any influence they had on the conditions under which they laboured. Governments responded to the refugee crisis by tightening up immigration regulations yet further. Hundreds of refugees eventually boarded ships across the Atlantic. Most were without the necessary documents to allow them entry. As we will see in the next chapter, many were temporarily left stranded at sea while the refugee organizations desperately negotiated to gain their access more or less anywhere to avert the threat of their being forcibly returned to Greater Germany.

The Joint in New York registered in December 1938 that the Hilfsverein and HICEM were sending significant numbers of refugees to Trinidad.[6] In response, the National Coordinating Committee in New York, the Joint and other organizations circulated information on the immigration requirements in the West Indies to their European counterparts based on the regular updates they received from Edgar Pereira.[7]

Trinidad's new-found significance as a refugee destination was threefold. Firstly, it served as a transit station for refugees from which they hoped to be able to reapply for visas to the United States and other more desirable destinations. Secondly, it served as a temporary destination for 'change of status' cases – that is, refugees who had sought permanent entry to another destination on transit visas or illegally, and who, in order to regularize their status, needed to leave their desired destination and reapply for entry from elsewhere. Thirdly, its entry requirements were, for the time being, fairly surmountable.

In December 1938, the Coordinating Committee explained the procedure to their European partners in a memorandum:

> Firstly, cooperating agencies had to notify the National Coordinating Committee of details of the refugees. The National Coordinating Committee would then notify the Harbour Master in Trinidad and obtain landing certificates. This certificate would be forwarded to the passenger, who would present it to the steamship company at the port of embarkation. The cash deposit of $265 should be paid at the port of embarkation, but in cases where American relatives were supplying the money, other arrangements could be made.[8]

The memorandum also noted that, 'while there are few restrictions now for admission to Trinidad, it is feared that there may be radical changes within the next two months, and therefore we urge that persons wishing to immigrate do so immediately'.[9]

New Restrictions on Immigration

Once the refugee organizations began sending Jewish refugees to the British West Indies in earnest in 1938, Trinidad was the first colony to seek a specific ban on refugee immigration. At the time, Trinidad required no visas and the relatively modest deposit was paid either by the refugees themselves or by an organization on their behalf. The Colonial Office had contacted the acting governor, Alfred W. Seymour, in December 1938 to inform him that the number of inquiries about Trinidad had increased dramatically, and that he should expect 'a considerable influx of individual immigrants in December'.[10]

On 12 December 1938, Edgar Pereira informed Charles Liebman of the Refugee Economic Corporation in New York that 'each European steamer brings in between twenty and thirty [refugees], nearly all of whom bring only sufficient funds to last them only [sic] a few weeks'.[11] In January 1939, the Jewish Association of Trinidad (JAT) outlined their difficulties to the National Coordinating Committee:

> The situation is very serious for the Jews here. The 1st of January arrived 85 Jews with the SS Cordillera, and with the SS Columbia we have expected more but only 80 arrived. We have settled them temporarily in a Sailors' Club, for our Home from 19 Marli Street [the JAT's Jewish Centre] is crowded. If the number of the Jews still increase with the arrival of every ship the situation will be impossible.[12]

The JAT was in a difficult position. Most of the refugees arriving in Trinidad from December 1938 onwards were penniless. Unlike the earlier East European arrivals, many were professionals who would be unable to find work in Trinidad. The JAT had to find housing and clothing for these refugees and counsel them. The more refugees who arrived in Trinidad unable to support themselves, the greater the risk that the colonial authorities would bar further immigration. And still each day brought new lists from Jewish organizations in Paris and Berlin, and from HICEM, with the details of further passengers on their way to Trinidad.

Many of the male refugees who now arrived had been released from concentration camps in Germany and Austria on the condition that they leave immediately, and so they had no choice but to grasp the first opportunity they could to emigrate.[13] The Markreich family is a case in point. Max Markreich had been a lay leader in the Jewish community in the north-west German city of Bremen since 1927. He had appealed to the Chief Rabbi's Religious Emergency Council (CRREC) to help him and his family emigrate to Britain, but in vain. Since he was not a rabbi, the council referred him to

Woburn House. Yet apparently the Central Council for Jewish Refugees could not help him either. Taken to Sachsenhausen concentration camp in suburban Berlin in November 1938, he was only released when he had managed to purchase a ticket for Trinidad. He arrived in the colony in December 1938 with his youngest daughter, Irene. His wife, Hänne (Johanna) Markreich, née Behrens, and elder daughter, Maria Theresa, were able to join them a few months later. The Markreichs' son, Wilhelm Ludwig, had emigrated to Italy in 1934 where he studied at the universities of Perugia and Genoa; he was able to remigrate to Honduras in 1938, and from there to the United States in 1940.[14]

In January 1939, the governor of Trinidad, Sir Hubert Winthrop Young, informed the Colonial Office that he wished to take action under the 1936 Immigration Ordinance by initiating an Order in Council to prohibit refugee immigration for a six-month period. He justified this intention with the steady flow of refugees into the colony, mainly directed there by refugee organizations aware of the lack of visa requirements. He reported that the arrival of a Red Star liner, chartered by a Jewish organization, with some 297 refugees on board was expected in the same week that 461 Jews had already arrived. He was aware of two further steamers on their way to Trinidad, the Hamburg Amerika line's *Caribia* and the *Königstein*, which had been chartered specifically to bring 300 refugees to Trinidad. The colony could not possibly absorb further refugees, hence the need for a six-month ban on further immigration.[15]

The colonial secretary acknowledged that these were 'special circumstances' and therefore approved the ban. It took effect on 15 January 1939 and would remain in force until further notice. In a defensive memorandum that only served to highlight the contradictions in the legislation, the Colonial Office noted: 'Although there had been no suggestion that the Order should discriminate in terms against refugees from particular countries, the term "alien refugees" has been defined to mean refugees from certain named countries', namely, Germany, Hungary, Czechoslovakia, Poland, Lithuania, Romania and Italy, plus the regions of Danzig and Memel. Only refugees who had set sail before 15 January would still be admitted to the colony.[16]

On 10 January 1939, the imminent new rules were communicated to the British ambassador in Berlin, who was instructed to notify immediately all shipping agencies, refugee organizations and British consular officers.[17] The Foreign Office was also informed of the new regulations in Trinidad and forthcoming similar legislation in other West Indian colonies, and asked to warn consular and passport control officers of the new situation.

In the Foreign Office, the sense prevailed that the new legislation would be insufficient to prevent a further influx of refugees. On 28 February, William Dunlop wrote to Hilton Poynton of the Colonial Office that, unless visa requirements were introduced, British officials would be powerless to prevent refugees from purchasing, or shipping companies from selling, tickets for passages to the West Indies, 'restrictive legislation' notwithstanding:

> The persons concerned make a point of finding out which colonies they can reach without being subject to any sort of control in the country from which they are being ejected, and the shipping companies are encouraging them to book passages. Naturally neither the refugees nor the shipping companies are going to consult British officials abroad if they think in the one case that they will be dissuaded or prevented from travelling, and in the other that they will lose their prospective customers. In the circumstances we are not disposed to pass on information about these restrictive regulations to Consular and Passport Control Officers unless we can at the same time say that travellers to the colonies concerned will, in future, require to obtain a visa as a preliminary requirement for their intended journey.[18]

In his response, Ponyton agreed that the introduction of visas was desirable in principle but argued that without keeping consular officials up to date, refugees who were refused admission would have justifiable grounds to complain against the Foreign Office for withholding current information, which would only 'make it more difficult for the Colonial authorities to consider the immigrants' case impartially'.[19] The matter of visa requirements for the Empire more generally was in fact being deliberated upon in the Colonial Office, but it did not come to fruition, presumably because attention was focused elsewhere once the war began.

Pereira and Pulver kept the Joint up to date on the imminent ban on further immigration. On Pereira's account, the ban had been issued on 'economic grounds', and the authorities had signalled that it would be reconsidered when the refugees who had already arrived had managed to settle into occupations in the colony.[20] Pereira also reported to Cecilia Razovsky that he had been informed by the Hamburg Amerika line of the fact that similar bans were being enacted in other West Indian colonies.[21]

On Siegel's account, Pereira was convinced that the Jewish Association of Trinidad was simply not making enough of an effort to try to avert the ban on the entry of further refugees to the colony. Hence, while the JAT remained 'unwilling to confront the Colonial Secretary, Edgar Pereira leapfrogged the Jewish Association and marched up to the Governor's office and pleaded the case of the German Jews on his own'.[22] Another explanation may be that only Pereira, as an English speaker, could communicate effectively with the colonial authorities in a manner that commanded sufficient respect.

Just after the ban on further immigration came into force, the secretary of the JAT, Dr Pulver, described the situation to Razovsky as follows:

There are four categories of Jews. The first category comprises the native Jews. But this category is formed only of about 3 or 4 Jews. The second category is formed of these [*sic*] Jews who arrived here in 1937 and 1938. The majority are Rumanians and Poles, and are pedlars. Some have little stores. They live only from the business that they do, and have financed their assistance of the German refugees. Their number is between 150 [and] 170. The third category are the first refugees who arrived from Germany about the middle of 1938. There almost [are] a hundred of them who have settled in small business, jobs, etc. The fourth category is most unfortunate. They are the refugees who arrived here in great numbers in the last few months. Their situation is desperate. They are unemployed and are scarcely possible [*sic*] to get employment here.[23]

Despite the initial assurances that the ban in Trinidad would be temporary, the acting governor, Sir John Huggins, wrote to the JAT on 3 March 1939 to reiterate that, 'in view of the influx of refugees from Central European countries, it has become necessary on economic grounds to prohibit further immigration to the colony' from the countries from which the Jewish refugees were trying to flee.[24] This suggested that the ban was there to stay. The National Coordination Committee and the Joint immediately sent this information to refugee agencies in European ports, informing them that no further refugees should be sent to Caribbean destinations.

As soon as the intention of the colonial government in Trinidad to prevent the immigration of further refugees was communicated to consulates and refugee organizations in Europe, applications to other West Indian colonies increased dramatically. The governors of British Guiana, British Honduras, Barbados, the Leeward Islands and Jamaica all contacted the secretary of state for the colonies in the course of January 1939 to inform him that they had received increased numbers of applications to enter their colonies, and wished to enact legislation similar to that introduced in Trinidad.[25] These requests posed problems for the Colonial Office, given that it needed to strike a balance between its determination to protect the West Indies from a large influx of refugees, and the need to pay heed to policy directives from London that discouraged the introduction of legislation, which could be seen as discriminatory.

As early as December 1938, Malcolm MacDonald, the colonial secretary, had reminded the colonies in a circular of the 'desperate' situation of the Jews in Greater Germany. Referring to the work of the Intergovernmental Committee formed after the Evian Conference, MacDonald explained that he was 'anxious that the Colonial Empire should play its part in furnishing a contribution towards the solution of this grave and most urgent problem'. To be sure, the West Indies were in a difficult position, but they should nevertheless at least consider the admission of suitably qualified individuals and give 'sympathetic consideration' to any schemes of organized settlement.

The colonial governments should not relax their immigration regulations specifically to facilitate the immigration of foreign refugees, MacDonald explained, but he did 'greatly deprecate the introduction of any restrictions expressly designed to render the entry of refugees from Germany more difficult'.[26]

In the course of January 1939, officials in the Colonial Office discussed how best to respond to the colonial requests to enact more restrictive legislation whilst not acting against the spirit of the December circular. The head of the West Indian department, Harold Beckett, noted that 'the Circular certainly deprecates the introduction of legislation expressly designed to render the entry of refugees from Germany more difficult, but it does not follow that there is the same objection to a general tightening up of immigration restriction in Colonies [that] have overpopulation and unemployment problems'.[27]

There was general agreement that the legislation enacted in Trinidad was unsatisfactory, leaving the Colonial Office open to accusations of discrimination. While MacDonald had approved the Trinidad ban because it was, to his mind, justified by the large numbers of refugees who had already entered the colony, he was unwilling to allow other colonies to exclude specific groups by introducing new legislation. Existing legislation had already provoked protest from the Chinese and Indian governments over the level of the deposits required of their nationals. Given the international attention focused on Britain's part in solving the refugee crisis, specific legislation barring refugees would only provoke further criticism from refugee bodies and foreign governments.

Consequently, the governor of British Honduras, William Johnston, ran into trouble when he sent draft legislation for approval. The draft stipulated that the deposit required to enter would rise to $1,000; that no 'alien who is a native, or who has been ordinarily resident, in any part of Europe' would hitherto be able to enter; and that other aliens would only be allowed in if, on top of paying the deposit, they undertook not to take up employment in any sector other than agriculture.[28] The Colonial Office rejected the proposal on the grounds that the governor already had sufficient existing powers to bar immigrants. MacDonald had been advised on 30 March 1939 by one of his officials, Kenneth Robinson, that it 'would be very difficult to rebut charges of national or racial discrimination, and we should certainly, I think, get protests from the Chinese, and above all the Government of India, if the clause was used in the manner suggested'.[29] On 7 April 1939, MacDonald informed the governor of British Honduras that, much as he appreciated that the proposal was based on the recent Trinidadian legislation, it would expose the government to a 'charge of discrimination against nationals of particular countries', and that, 'as far as there are refugees with reasonable funds and agricultural experience, it is agreed that it is desirable that they should be admitted'.[30]

Against this backdrop, between February and June 1939 new ordinances extending the general discretion of the governor to curtail immigration were introduced in British Guiana, Barbados and British Honduras. In September, Trinidad amended its legislation and also adopted the clause granting the governor 'absolute discretion' in prohibiting the entry of aliens.[31]

Exemptions

As we will see, the *Trinidad Guardian* generally supported the call for harsher immigration controls. Yet once the ban came into force on 15 January 1939, the paper adopted a more conciliatory tone and promptly reminded its readers that the governor also had the power to exempt individuals from the ban. Surely, the paper commented, special permits would be granted to spouses and other close relatives of aliens already resident in Trinidad. While insisting that 'the underlying motive – that is, to safeguard the Colony against a new economic problem – must be adhered to', the paper expressed its hope that the colonial administration would be 'wise and merciful in considering applications for exemption'.[32]

In this respect at least, Pereira's efforts, whether on his own initiative or on the behest of the Jewish Association of Trinidad, were not entirely without success, and some concessions were made. As Pereira informed Razovsky on 16 January, refugees were expected to arrive on the *Cottica* on 18 January, and others were not far behind on the *Pericles*, the *De La Salle*, the *Amazon*, and the *Horn*.[33] In the course of a complex series of negotiations, he was able to obtain permission for refugees whose landing permits had been issued prior to the ban on 15 January to land in Trinidad, and the refugees on board the *Cottica* were able to enter the colony.[34] In April 1939, Dr Ulrich Schächter of the JAT reported to the National Coordinating Committee: 'We are now permitted to bring over from Europe those relatives who are parents or children under 16 years of age; also those who are engaged to be married to those already in Trinidad and who are willing to be married within one year of arrival here'.[35]

There was some precedent for the admission of close relatives follow-ing a general ban on further immigration. Male Chinese had been denied admission to Jamaica since 1935, yet spouses, children and fiancées were still allowed to join those Chinese already living in the colony until the summer of 1939.[36] Late in December 1938, the Trinidadian Executive Council initially agreed that the cases of relatives of refugees already resident in the colony should be examined on a case-by-case basis.[37] In February

1939, it determined general principles for this process. Consular officers in overseas territories were authorized to issue landing permits automatically to spouses and to children aged under sixteen. When it came to parents or older children, their cases had to be submitted to the Legislative Assembly for individual consideration.[38]

Under this scheme, between January and September 1939 the Executive Council agreed to exempt 105 parents and other relatives of refugees already in Trinidad from the ban, and granted them permits to enter the colony, though it is unclear how many were actually able to take advantage of this.[39] As late as June 1939, relatives of refugees already in Trinidad were still arriving.[40] When the war started in September, all previously issued permits were rescinded. We definitely do know that at least some of the 38 parents of refugees already resident in the colony who were granted permits on 28 June 1939 did make it to Trinidad, since they have left traces there. This list included Paul Bley, Josefine Koffler Bley and Siegfried Beer.

Another group of 41 parents whom the governor, Sir Hubert Winthrop Young, agreed to admit to Trinidad in the autumn of 1939, were less fortunate.[41] First the Colonial Office 'concocted a host of excuses' to try to keep them at bay.[42] 'Every "mouth" of which Germany is relieved', John Shuckburgh wrote to Sir Cosmo Parkinson,

> helps, *pro tanto*, to increase her power of withstanding our blockade. It has also to be remembered that the Jews are past masters in the art of 'asking for more'. If we make them this concession in Trinidad it is pretty certain that they will come back sooner or later and ask for some similar concession elsewhere. We shall have established a further precedent against ourselves, and in consequence may find it the more difficult to resist any renewed appeal. All this tells again the action suggested.[43]

In the end, though, the Colonial Office grudgingly approved Young's proposal, at which point the Foreign Office began to stonewall. John E.M. Carvell, the former British consul in Munich who had been recalled to the Foreign Office in London at the beginning of the war, wrote to John Hibbert in the Colonial Office:

> It occurs to us that, as the Government of Trinidad seems to be in the mood to receive refugees, this might be an opportunity of disposing of some of the 50,000 refugees in this country whose maintenance was discussed at a meeting of the War Cabinet Sub Committee on Refugees ... at which your Secretary of State was in the chair.[44]

While waiting for a decision, Norman Bentwich of the Council for German Jewry tried to press the case of one couple in the group of 41,

Heinrich and Flora Grün, the parents of Edgar Gruen who worked for the Jewish Refugee Society (on which more later in this chapter) in Trinidad. While the other parents were still in Germany, the Grüns were in Yugoslavia and were thus the only couple on the list who could actually have left without further complications, had they received a visa. Bentwich suggested that they be dealt with separately, yet to no avail.[45]

Eventually, the Foreign Office agreed to issue visas to the 41 parents, provided the governor expressly affirmed his initial offer. As Hibbert wrote to Harold Beckett and Carvell, he 'secretly hoped the Governor would turn down this proposal'. He was surely not alone in thinking this would be the optimum solution. Yet Young did not budge.[46] On 6 April 1940, the admission of the 41 parents was finally approved, though it took several weeks for the Jewish refugee organizations to be informed of this decision. The approval was given on the understanding that the Jewish Refugee Society would cover the maintenance for all those among the 41 parents who required assistance. In late April, the JRS urgently contacted the Joint, asking them to guarantee these costs; but the Joint refused, explaining that they could simply not afford to do so. Soon after, the Germans invaded the Netherlands, blocking the originally envisaged exit route, and then France, precipitating the end of the Phoney War and a blanket ban on all further entry permits by the governor. The same officials who had thwarted the plan at every stage 'now oozed sympathy for the refugees' plight'.[47] 'It is unfortunate for these 41 elderly Jews that their chance of escape should be barred at the last moment', John Shuckburgh wrote to Cosmo Parkinson on 28 May, 'but they are not the only people in the world who are suffering from misfortune at the present time.'[48] John Hibbert explained:

> It is my duty to adopt as sympathetic an attitude as possible in regard to refugees from the Nazi regime, and I must say that the Governor's revised decision seems, prima facie, very bad luck on these unfortunate parents. Nevertheless, I fully realise that the claims of security must come first … I, therefore, with some reluctance, feel that we must accept the Governor's decision.[49]

Even now, Bentwich would not relent, and continued to pursue the case of the Grüns. He was able to persuade the Colonial Office that had the Grüns already managed to obtain visas, theirs would not be revoked. At the same time the Foreign Office 'was under strict instructions not to grant the Grüns visas should they subsequently show up at the British Consulate in Belgrade'.[50] One can only assume that the Grüns had not secured visas prior to the deadline and that they did not come to Trinidad.

The British Guiana Refugee Commission

As the plight of the refugees grew increasingly desperate, the Jewish organizations were determined to leave no stone unturned, and sought to place the possibility of settling refugees in British Guiana on the agenda once again. In February 1939, an Anglo-American commission, the British Guiana Refugee Commission, sponsored mainly by American Jewish organizations, set off to British Guiana to investigate options for the settlement of Jewish refugees there. It submitted its report to the Foreign Office in April, recommending an initial settlement of some 3,000 to 5,000 young people over a period of two years at a cost of $3 million.[51] Yet in July, Lord Winterton informed the High Commissioner for Refugees and Director of the Intergovernmental Committee on Refugees, the former governor of the Punjab, Sir Herbert Emerson, that the British government had at no point intended to permit the settlement of large numbers of Jewish refugees in British Guiana. It would, though, allow scattered groups of '50 here and 50 there interspersed throughout the territory' to settle.[52]

Before publishing the findings of the British Guiana Refugee Commission, the Colonial Office consulted the Moyne Commission. On 5 May, the latter expressed its 'grave misgivings':

> Even on the most favourable view the undertaking is likely … to need continuing financial support. If any large part of a subsidy was provided from British funds, there would be legitimate grounds for complaint from the people of the overcrowded island of Barbados and from those natives of British West Indian islands who are now destitute in Cuba and Central America. If on the other hand the experiment is unsuccessful and the settlers are unable even to supply their own needs of food, the grave problem will arise of finding means of support for an alien population or of providing them with an alternative place for settlement.[53]

On 9 May, MacDonald reported these views to a special meeting of the Cabinet Committee on Refugees, not without adding yet another argument against the scheme. If refugee settlers became British subjects, he pointed out, they 'would acquire the right to migrate into the United Kingdom if they wished'.[54]

The Foreign Office, however, keen to deflect any criticism of the massive restriction on Jewish immigration proposed by the White Paper on Palestine that it was in the process of publishing, nevertheless welcomed the report of the British Guiana Refugee Commission. On 12 May – five days before the White Paper on Palestine was introduced in the House of Commons – the government issued a statement on the commission's findings to the House; it was in writing, since Chamberlain was 'anxious not to encroach upon the time allotted for the Military Training Bill'. The government's response sounded extremely positive, although the declaration did warn that 'any prospect of large-scale settlement, which they hope may prove possible, must depend largely on the possibility of industrial development', which would require 'further inquiries'.[55]

When the British Guiana Refugee Commission's report was discussed in the House on 15 May, attention focused principally on the question of how realistic it was to expect the entire project to be privately funded. The Conservative MP, Ian Hannah, asked the government whether it would, 'in view of the promising prospects of refugee settlement in British Guiana', consider providing a loan guarantee to cover the costs as suggested by the commission. MacDonald, standing in for Chamberlain, clarified that 'His Majesty's Government will help and co-operate in other ways'. The Labour MP, Philip Noel-Baker, an academic and disarmaments specialist intimately involved with the work of the League of Nations and later the United Nations, who would go on to win the Nobel Peace Prize in 1959, questioned the government's commitment. 'In view of the speculative nature of the hopes in which the Commission indulge', he asked whether the government would 'refrain from stimulating too great hopes in this enterprise, having regard to the urgent and desperate condition of hundreds of thousands of refugees in Germany now'. Rather disingenuously, given the Colonial Office's actual stonewalling against all settlement projects for Jewish refugees in the colonial empire, MacDonald responded that, 'in view of the urgent need, which we fully appreciate, I hope that Hon. Members of the Opposition will not discourage unduly the hopes that can be centred in British Guiana. With regard to the general question, the House may rest assured that we shall keep in close touch with refugee and other authorities on the matter, and will endeavour to do whatever is strictly practicable'.[56]

The scheme was never realized. Since adequate funding for the project was not forthcoming from American refugee organizations or private sources, the British government considered retracting its offer of land in July 1939, and further debate was overtaken by the onset of war.[57] On 18 October 1939, Lord Winterton explained at an IGCR conference, on behalf of the British government, that 'private organisations sponsoring this scheme were unable to proceed with the proposed two-year experimental settlement owing to the outbreak of war, and it must therefore be regarded as indefinitely suspended'.[58]

Given the government's refusal to even underwrite, never mind fund, the costs of the project, and the Colonial Office's persistent opposition to any such undertaking, the scheme was, as Sherman has argued, neither realistic nor practical, and was thus effectively doomed from the outset. Even so, it remains a lost opportunity, given that the settlement might well have benefited not only Jewish refugees but also the colony – an argument to which contemporaries were by no means entirely oblivious.

Walter Citrine, for instance, in his capacity as one of the members of the Moyne Commission, explained in a note sent to the colonial secretary under separate cover on 8 May that, much as he understood some of his colleagues' reservations, 'the proposed Jewish experiment' could provide 'a valuable guide' for future resettlement plans 'for the overcrowded population of some parts of the West Indies'. Consequently, he was 'reluctant to oppose the recommendation of the Refugee Commission that an experimental settlement should be established in British Guiana', and felt that the proposal was 'justified'.[59]

In the Foreign Office, meanwhile, Roger Makins, while noting that 'the offer of British Guiana … is largely an illusory one, and this must inevitably become apparent in due course', explained in the very same memorandum that the scheme would be beneficial, and not only in diverting attention from Palestine:

> Lastly, though this may be thought to be mainly a Colonial Office point, we shall be increasing the prosperity of the Empire. I have suggested … that it might also be open to HM Government to assist in the development of a territory or settlement by making loans from the colonial development fund for road making, railway building, etc. We appear therefore in a position to make an offer which may turn out to be a major stroke of policy, but we are being held up by the opposition of a handful of settlers.[60]

Although the Joint participated in the British Guiana Refugee Commission's investigations in February 1939, it had serious reservations not only about the specific site in British Guiana but also about the extent to which any of the various 'exotic' destinations discussed at one time or another could genuinely contribute to a solution of the refugee crisis.[61] Yet the Jewish refugee organizations were in a double bind: on the one hand, they advised against spending time and money investigating schemes they felt were neither viable nor practical; but on the other hand, given how few possibly suitable options there were and how desperate the situation of the refugees was, they had little choice but to become involved in any scheme that might conceivably come to fruition.

In April 1939, the Joint discussed the failure of a settlement project in French Guiana. One of the members of the British Guiana Refugee Commission, Dr Joseph Rosen, reported that 'somebody from France got people to French Guiana and inside of two weeks the people either ran away, got into trouble or got others into trouble'. Cecilia Razovsky responded to Rosen's report as follows:

> There isn't a day that we don't get letters from committees in all parts of the country insisting that we put Jews on the land, and they are very indignant because we seem to pass over these suggestions, as though we never heard of them and write a cold reply to their enthusiasm. ... It seems to me that a statement worked out by the JDC, emphasizing exactly what Dr. Rosen has said today, would be very helpful in educating the Jewish population in the United States. They say they don't want them in the cities. Put them on the land.[62]

Another concern was shared by government officials in the Colonial Office and some (though by no means all) campaigners and organizations pursuing possible refugee destinations in the colonial empire, who worried about the implications of settling European refugees in territories with a predominantly black population. The Freeland League for Jewish Territorial Colonization, for instance, having explored options in a number of territories, including British colonies such as British Guiana and Tanganyika, concluded that Kimberley in Western Australia – an extremely inhospitable territory that has seen barely any settlement to this day – was the preferred option.[63] Any proposal for settlement in Africa, they argued,

> overlooks the fact that Africa differs widely, in almost every condition pertaining to mass-settlements, from those countries into which European civilisation has been successfully introduced in modern times, such as North America, Australia and New Zealand. These were transformed into white men's lands mainly because the immigrants encountered only sparse native populations which could either be absorbed by the newcomers or disappeared in contact with European customs and institutions.[64]

For a short while there was nevertheless a plan to facilitate the settlement of significant numbers of Jews in Trinidad by cultivating swamp land on the island. Edgar Pereira initiated the scheme, and he convinced Norman Bentwich of the Council for German Jewry of its merit. It was then approved by the Joint, the Chief Rabbi's Religious Emergency Council and the Colonial Office, but was abandoned at the outbreak of war.[65] As Chaim Weizmann put it following the November Pogrom of 1938, 'all the fancy territorialist projects are useless. It is merely dangling false hopes before the eyes of a tortured people'.[66]

Jewish Refugees in Trinidad

Given that the refugee organizations had not previously focused on the British West Indies as a possible refugee destination, nor even circulated meaningful information on the Caribbean as an option, most of the new refugees had virtually no idea what to expect. The following account by the journalist, Ernst Otto Fischer, formerly of the Viennese *Kronen-Zeitung*, published in the *Trinidad Guardian* in December 1938, gives a sense of what was known, even this late in the day, about the West Indies as a possible destination:

> It is extraordinary how little is known of the West Indies in Central Europe. And when I left my native land for Trinidad I did not know what I would find; and it is most peculiar that [during] my stay in London, which lasted three months before coming on to Trinidad, I got less information there than I secured in Vienna, and that was very little ... [A]lthough I visited many places for information, such as the Colonial Office and the West Indian Committee, there was little about this island to be got ... I can say I received much more help from the shipping office ... The more I see of this beautiful Island, the more I am enchanted. Before arrival here I was very much afraid I would not be able to settle down in Trinidad ... [but we now] feel that we have come to a home which will be to us a haven of rest and peace, not only for our travel-worn bodies but also for our wounded souls.[67]

Manfred Goldfish, in his recollection of events, similarly referred to Trinidad as 'a country which only two weeks ago was only a blot of colour print on a map to us ... We knew little or nothing of our destination, and the agent was no help either'.[68]

Figure 3.1 The Tauscher family, recently arrived, pose with a Trinidadian family. Photograph 79548, courtesy of the U.S. Holocaust Memorial Museum.

Figure 3.2 The Tauscher family pose outside in Trinidad where they arrived as refugees. Photograph 75938, courtesy of the U.S. Holocaust Memorial Museum.

While most East European Jews, even those arriving late in 1938, continued to be successful in the dry goods trade and peddling, refugees from Germany and Austria found it much harder to adjust to their new surroundings. Even so, despite arriving penniless, some German and Austrian Jews did succeed in establishing businesses or adapting their occupations. As the *Trinidad Guardian* admiringly reported:

> Even in Trinidad there are a number of Jewish professional men and women, lawyers, doctors, a university teacher, journalists of good standing, artists ... who have found a home here, creating a situation similar to that existing in Paris, London and New York, where, following the mass emigration of White Russians, Princes, Grand Dukes and countesses could be found washing dishes. One of the physicians, a lady doctor is now a midwife, another turned chemist and a third one is a foreman in a local factory. A famous master-builder of Vienna is now looking for any kind of work. His wife makes a living by tailoring. A lawyer has become a canvasser, another a floor-walker, while a third one is going to open a jewellers' store on Frederick Street.[69]

The 'situations wanted' adverts in the *Trinidad Guardian* illustrated the professional profile of many of the Jewish refugees from Greater Germany:

A first-class European Dressmaker, just arrived from Europe, looking for employment.
European lady seeks work as secretary or stenotypist. English, French and German translated.
Young Viennese Gentleman seeks work of any kind.
Piano lessons by expert European musician.[70]

Borchardt and Glick, in their report to the Joint, judged the prospects of the refugees with relative optimism.

The island is sound economically. Business is good, the natives are employed and spend liberally what they make. It is our belief that even though the German and Austrian Jews are not yet absorbed into the economic life, with some help this can be accomplished and the community of Jews will become self-supporting. There appears to be a good possibility for the large majority of those not yet employed to find or to create work for themselves.[71]

Borchardt and Glick recommended that a loan fund of $10,000 be established to provide loans to individual Jewish refugees to allow them to establish small businesses. In the event, the Joint decided to create a fund of $2,000. By May 1940 – when the Phoney War ended and internment cut short these efforts – fourteen new entrepreneurs had borrowed a total of $1,800 from the fund to set up their businesses, which included the manufacture of upholstered furniture, shirts and pyjamas, a boarding house and a restaurant, the manufacture of sausages, and an (expanded) photographic business.[72] The loans were secured by the landing deposits of $250, and the Joint hoped that a successful scheme would allow for a cut in the monthly subsidy sent by the Joint to Trinidad to support indigent refugees. Other refugees were able to find employment in existing local businesses or as pedlars, or managed to establish businesses under their own steam, such as Siegel and Karlsbad's Ladies Hat Factory and the Stechers' short-lived initial business in Port of Spain.

Borchardt and Glick's optimism in the spring of 1939 notwithstanding, the state of the labour market deteriorated as did relations between refugees from Nazi Germany and those from Eastern Europe. Like the East European immigrants before them, the refugees from Germany and Austria who came to the British West Indies tended to establish their own institutions. For the most part, the Sephardi, East European and Central European refugees and their organizations cooperated. Yet in Trinidad, as large numbers of destitute refugees arrived, the strain of supporting and aiding these refugees exposed the emerging community to divisions, which they were unable to overcome. In April 1939, the German and Austrian Jews formed their own Jewish Refugee Society (JRS) because they felt that the Jewish Association of Trinidad (JAT) focused too much on the interests of the East European Jewish immigrants.

Borchardt and Glick attempted to prevent this schism, but to no avail. In the report they submitted to the Joint in New York in March, they described the hostility that had developed between Polish and Romanian Jews, on the one hand, and German and Austrian refugees, on the other. One problem was the German and Austrian refugees' attachment to Pereira, whom the Polish and Romanian Jews despised. Yet given that Pereira, as already indicated, could communicate well in English and was the 'only Jew with access' who was 'welcomed at the Colonial Office', the JAT had little choice but to continue their association with him. Pereira's engagement notwithstanding, Austrian and German refugees felt that they were not represented in the JAT, and that the funds provided by the Joint were not being distributed fairly. In short, the JAT had 'split wide into two very hostile groups'.[73] Borchardt and Glick therefore initiated the formation of an eleven-member committee incorporating Jews from both Eastern and Central Europe, but as they reported:

> A general assembly was called of all the Jews on the island, and about 400 were present. The names of the men on the proposed committee were read, and after an hour of decent discussion the meeting broke into bedlam, and from the floor a committee of eleven was elected composed only of Romanian and Polish Jews.[74]

In response to this outcome, the Jewish Refugee Society of Trinidad was formed on 14 April 1939. It elected Pereira as its president. As Herbert Philip, the secretary of the new society, explained to Cecilia Razovsky, 'the German and Austrian refugees resident here found that it had become absolutely necessary to establish a body [that] could look after their interests, and be representative of their opinions and their needs'.[75] The JRS stressed that it would not discriminate between applicants for loans or assistance, and that 'adherence is made to the principle laid down at the inaugural meeting that our interpretation of the "world-refugee" is any Jew, irrespective of nationality, who may be in need'.[76]

Initially, the Joint funding continued to run solely through the JAT, and Pereira attended the association's meetings when the distribution of the funds was discussed. Yet there was 'general dissatisfaction amongst the refugees from Germany and Austria that funds intended for their assistance should be administered by a committee [that] is absolutely unrepresentative of this section of the Jewish community'.[77] Having received Borchardt and Glick's report, the Joint began to transmit funds directly to the Jewish Refugee Society as well.[78]

Figure 3.3 The site of Duke Street Synagogue, as shown to the author by Hans Stecher in 2001. Photograph by the author.

Ostensibly, these two organizations, the Jewish Association of Trinidad and the Jewish Refugee Society, were formed with distinct aims in mind. The JAT was meant to serve as a permanent body to provide for the cultural and social needs of the community, whereas the purpose of the JRS was to represent and administer aid to refugees. Yet these aims changed with the views and attitudes of the refugees themselves. Both organizations came to mirror the fluctuating and contested nature of a Jewish community in transition, making and remaking itself, but never quite overcoming its internal divisions despite being encouraged to do so both from within and without.

At first glance, one might conclude that the more established East European Jews, with communities in San Fernando and Port of Spain, were more interested in creating a permanent Jewish community in Trinidad, while Jews from Germany and Austria were principally interested in remigrating. Indeed, some saw it this way at the time. Edgar Pereira, for instance, wrote to Cecilia Razovsky in May 1939 that whilst the JRS was principally concerned with practical matters revolving around refugee admittance and settlement, the JAT's focus was on establishing Jewish institutions, such as a synagogue, club, library and other cultural concerns.[79]

The US consul in Trinidad, Claude H. Hall, Jr., painted a similar picture in a report to the secretary of state in Washington, DC on 15 January 1939 – the day the ban on further immigration to Trinidad came into force.

Boatloads of refugees were continuing to arrive, mostly without funds, Hall explained, and 'more than half of the refugees entering Trinidad intend to proceed to the United States, and immediately upon arrival make application at the Consulate for immigration visas under the German, or occasionally, Polish quotas'.[80]

Yet a survey undertaken by the Religious Committee of the JAT shows a more complex picture. Whilst only ten completed questionnaires have been preserved, the replies submitted suggest that it was not only East European refugees who saw a future in Trinidad. The Religious Committee was established in March 1939 by Max Markreich, who had been a lay leader of the Jewish community in Bremen. Although part of the JAT, the Religious Committee saw itself as semi-independent, and it focused on the provision of religious services and education for Trinidad Jewry. The questionnaire was publicized on 1 May 1939 and was designed with two goals in mind: firstly, to gather statistical information to help to answer enquiries from refugee committees abroad; and secondly, to establish the religious and social needs and expectations of Trinidad Jewry. As Markreich conceded, 'only [a] few forms have been filled out. It is very difficult to find an agreement. Even the parents of the children liable to going to Jewish education don't return the forms (with one exception)'.[81]

Of the ten male respondents whose completed forms have survived, seven included their wives' responses on the forms, so the sample encompasses seventeen adults. Two respondents also included details of their children. Nine of the ten male respondents had arrived between November 1938 and January 1939, the tenth had come to Jamaica from Poland in the early 1930s and moved to Trinidad in 1935. Eight were from Germany and Austria, and two came from Poland. Asked whether they wished to remain in Trinidad or remigrate, five stated that they wished to remain, one did not respond, and four stated that they wished to remigrate. In other words, in this particular (admittedly very small) sample, not only did the two Polish respondents wish to remain but so too did three respondents from Germany and Austria. Asked whether they wished to take part in religious services, five responded positively, four left the answer blank, and one crossed out all questions relating to religious practice.

The questionnaire also indicated the diversity of religious traditions that those refugees who were still religious and practising represented: traditional East European orthodoxy, German Reform and German neo-orthodoxy. A number of organizations were established under the umbrella of the Religious Committee. Markreich established the neo-orthodox Bethausverein (lit. bet hamidrash association) Agudas Achim, which claimed seventy-three members. Associations of this kind had been set up in Germany and Austria, mainly by orthodox Jews reacting against the reform movement. They were usually located in small (often private) houses, where services could be held. The statutes of Agudas Achim stated that it was a 'union of Jews for the purpose of creating and preservation of a Synagogue, Jewish cemetery and religious lessons, as well as cultivation of all other matters concerning religious rites'.[82] Weekly services were organized for Friday evenings and Saturday mornings, and a teacher, Mr Ottenhooser, began to give religious instruction to some of the children. These initiatives hardly suggest a community intent, before all else, on moving on.

Given the diversity in religious experience and traditions amongst refugee members of the committee, the Religious Committee found it difficult to determine what type of congregation they wished to establish. It therefore entered into correspondence with a number of Jewish organizations in Britain and the United States to seek advice. In April 1939, the committee approached the World Union for Progressive Judaism (WUPJ) with a view

Figure 3.4 Jewish Dramatic Group, Trinidad and Tobago, 1943. Front row: Gizi Feiner, unknown, Nunia Sadovnik. Second row: Yasha Medvejer, unknown, Aron Szydlowicz, Biba Schecter, Samuel Oszslack, Ronea Rabinovitch, Moye Zonensein, Thora Yufe, Lorna Yufe, unknown. Third row: Buze Schechter, Leo Katz, Golda (Gusta) Zonensein, Salo Gross, Bubi Schneider, Willy Turkenwiez. Back row: Mr. Bialogorodsky, Idel Rabinovitch, Moishe Steinbok, Egon Huth, Reynold Strasberg, unknown, Michael Strasberg. Names provided by Libby Ellyn's mother, Lorna Yufe, and Zeno Strasberg. By kind permission of Hans Stecher.

to establishing a Jewish congregation, reporting that the JAT was planning to build a synagogue and employ a Hebrew teacher for the children. The chair of the JAT explained that some immigrants intended to go to the United States, and were waiting in Trinidad for their visa numbers, but 'a great number will stay in Trinidad. Therefore, it is in the Jewish interest to erect here a new point of support for Judaism and to make a Jewish covenant for all Jews of the old and new immigration'.[83]

Lily Montagu of the WUPJ suggested in response that since Trinidadian Jewry clearly seemed to be traditional in religious orientation, the association should contact orthodox congregations for assistance.[84] The JAT thereupon clarified that scarcely 10 per cent of the congregants were orthodox, with the majority progressive, although this might well have resulted from the lack of orthodox provision rather than personal inclination towards reform or progressive Judaism. 'It is not possible at all to live ritual here because there is no "Schechita". Everybody is working on Shabbath to make livelihood [sic]'.[85] The WUPJ then offered to send a German-trained rabbi who spoke English, provided the congregants established a progressive congregation that would cover the salary of the rabbi after the first year. Since the prospects of the congregation were too insecure to be able to offer financial guarantees, the JAT turned down this offer.[86]

The original assumption that liberal Judaism, of the British variety, was not appropriate for the Trinidad community was confirmed, when the WUPJ sent the JAT a prayer book used by the liberal synagogues in England, publications of the Jewish Religious Union and a copy of the Prayer for the Royal Family used on Sabbaths and the Day of Atonement. The JAT wrote to the WUPJ that 'we shall make use of the prayer for the Royal Family, but we are sorry to say that the contents of the prayer book do not correspond with the mentality of our friends in any way, who also being liberal would never appreciate such a profound change of our old prayer-orders'.[87] In her reply, Lily Montagu expressed understanding and stressed the diversity of liberal congregations. Despite some confusion about the type of liberal Judaism that the community would accept, the WUPJ upheld its offer to send a suitable rabbi, provided the congregation could cover the salary after a year, and continued to uphold this offer after the war had begun.[88]

In April 1939, the JAT was contacted by Alexander Burnstein of the Committee on Refugee Jewish Ministers in New York to inform the association that the committee had received 'a pathetic and urgent request for a rabbi and schochet for Trinidad. Some of these refugees are observant and religious-minded, and complain of the woeful lack of rabbinic guidance and leadership, and appeal to me to send them someone to take charge of the religious and spiritual affairs of the community'. It was unlikely that rabbis who were already in the United States could be persuaded to serve the congregation in Trinidad, but the committee was in touch with a significant number of qualified rabbis who were still in Germany and Czechoslovakia, one of whom would surely welcome the chance to go to Trinidad.[89] Yet as Max Markreich informed Burnstein on 19 May, the JAT had in the meantime secured the assistance of the Chief Rabbi's Religious Emergency Council (CRREC) to resolve this question.[90]

The CRREC had suggested in March 1939 that they send a German rabbi to Trinidad.[91] The prospective candidate was Leo Trepp, who had studied at the Rabbinical Seminary in Berlin, held a doctorate in philosophy and had been the rabbi of the Jewish congregation in Oldenburg. Trepp was among those arrested during the November Pogrom and sent to Sachsenhausen. When the chief rabbi secured a one-year visa for him, Trepp was released on condition that he leave Germany within a fortnight. He was one of a group of forty-seven refugee rabbis and their families whom the CRREC had managed to bring to Britain, either on temporary permits or with visas, on the understanding that their maintenance would be guaranteed by the CRREC and that they would be placed outside Britain.[92] Yet this plan too came to nothing, perhaps for financial reasons or because the war had begun.[93] When US troops came to Trinidad during the war, the Jewish army chaplain, Rabbi Sydney Ungar, began to officiate at joint services for the soldiers and refugees.[94]

While the Religious Committee was a committee of the Jewish Association of Trinidad, its status was not uncontroversial. For the committee, none too surprisingly, catering for the religious and spiritual needs of the community was the highest priority. The JAT, on the other hand, tended to look at the committee as one among many. When Markreich requested funds from the association to provide religious schooling for thirty of the community's children in March 1939, he was informed that funds were not available and that religious provision in any case did not fall within the JAT's remit.[95] Similarly, when the Religious Committee suggested in November 1939 that the JAT and the Jewish Refugee Society should be replaced by a single Hebrew congregation, which would be in a better position to meet the religious needs of Trinidad's Jews, it was informed in no uncertain terms that it was only one of the association's committees, and no more important than others, such as the Social Committee.[96]

When a synagogue and community centre was established in Port of Spain in a rented house at 114 Duke Street (see Figure 3.3), many presumably perceived of the Jewish community as united and self-confident. The fact that the JAT contacted the *Trinidad Guardian* in 1939 to request that the way in which Jewish services were announced in the religious section of the paper be corrected, would have reinforced this perception. Previously, Jewish services had been listed in small print beneath the Christian Science rubric. 'We are neither a part of the Christian Science nor of any other Church', the

Figure 3.5 Group photograph of about fifty children with their Hebrew and Jewish religion and history teacher Fanny Lapscher in Port of Spain. By kind permission of Hans Stecher.

JAT pointed out, 'but – as the oldest and original of all these churches – quite independent. Here in Trinidad we came as the last, and therefore we would be obliged to you, if you place our HEBREW CONGREGATION at the end of your list, to compose the types in the same size as the other headings.'[97]

In September 1939, the community's request to purchase land for a Jewish cemetery was turned down by the authorities. As the *Trinidad Guardian* reported, the proposal met with 'strong opposition' from some city councillors. Councillor Gormandy argued that 'there should be no segregation because there could be no question of nationality after death'. Councillor Albert Gomes – the former editor of the pioneering but short-lived magazine, *The Beacon*, who now wrote for the *Trinidad Guardian* and would go on to become the city's deputy mayor and Trinidad's first chief minister in the 1950s before emigrating to Britain in 1962 – argued that, 'if they were permitting a fetish in one case they would have to allow it in all cases'. When the mayor asked Councillor Richards if he was making a 'Hitler speech', given his objection to the Jewish cemetery, Richards replied that he was 'making a Christian speech. I am speaking of the Fatherhood of God and the brotherhood of man. In the eyes of God we are all children of God. But the

Figure 3.6 Photograph of Chuma Averboukh, President of Trinidad's Women's International Zionist Organisation (WIZO), on left at back of picture. Photo taken in the Averboukh's Park Street business place. By kind permission of Hans Stecher.

Jews cannot come here and dictate to us what we can do'.[98] In light of this opposition, the Jewish Association of Trinidad wrote to the council to clarify that their request 'was NOT made with the wish to separate ourselves from our fellow men. It was made in order to comply with the rules laid down by religion; and religious rules are beyond our power to adjust at will'.[99] In late October 1939, a compromise was reached and 250 graves were reserved for Jewish burials in a special section of the cemetery at Mucurapo.[100] When Eva Gandelman was buried there on 31 May 1940, the *Trinidad Guardian* reported on the funeral as a landmark for the colony under the heading, 'Trinidad has first Jewish funeral'.[101]

Councillor Richards also led the opposition to a request in March 1940 for permission to engage a shochet to provide kosher meat. Richards argued that foreigners should not have the right to impose their own rules but should adapt to those of the host country. When the mayor stated that Jews were asking for a privilege already accorded to Muslims, Richards replied that the Muslims in the colony were British citizens. In the event, only one councillor voted to grant permission. To laughs in the chamber, he was taunted by Richards for being 'pro-Nazi'.

Even following the arrival of Rabbi Ungar, the community continued to face considerable hurdles. In May 1943, Claude Hall complained to the colonial secretary that he was being prevented from marrying Jewish soldiers in the colony.[102] To the Department of War in Washington it seemed clear that this was

> discriminatory and definitely adversely affects the morale of our troops. It is also inconsistent with the thesis that the United Nations are fighting for religious freedom as well as other objections ... The continuation of this situation, if known, will undoubtedly have a more or less adverse influence upon the Jewish element in our nation, thereby affecting in some degree at least the amicable relations between the Colonial Government of Trinidad and our own Government.[103]

Yet for all that non-Jews readily tarred all Jews in Trinidad with the same brush, the relationship between Central and East European Jews remained problematic as their visions for the character of the Jewish community in Trinidad continued to differ. The notion often propagated by the Jewish Association of Trinidad was that they represented the Jews who wished to remain in Trinidad, while the Jewish Refugee Society was only concerned with those who planned to remigrate. Yet this really was a gross oversimplification. In fact, many of the controversies, be they about the use of German or Yiddish, or the relative importance of religious and secular activities, ran not only between Central and East European Jews but also within each group. The war heightened anxieties all around as the community felt external pressure to conform.

None too surprisingly, the youngsters among the refugees tended to find it the easiest to adapt to their new environment. As Hans Stecher, who, as mentioned in the Introduction, arrived on the island in October 1938 as a teenager, and whom we will meet several more times, later explained, his reaction was rather different from that

> of mature people like my parents; to them everything was strange and unfamiliar and somewhat frightening. To me as a boy a tropical country was like a dream come true. We all read Karl May avidly, the great adventure writer, and coming to the New World, to the Americas, was a great adventure to me, and coming to a tropical island so beautiful with people of all colours and religions ... it was all a dream come true.[104]

Helen Breger, whom we will meet again as Helen Hammermann later in this chapter, similarly recalled that, on arriving in Trinidad, 'my family seemed stunned, but I felt a secret exhilaration as in an adventure'.[105]

Stecher was not the only former refugee to refer to Karl May in this context. So too did Fred (Manfred) Mann, whom we will meet again among the Polish Jewish Refugees in Gibraltar Camp. 'We were all fascinated with the writing of the German "Indian" writer Karl May', he later wrote.

In his seventy years he had never actually met a real 'Red' Indian, but his writings seemed authentic to us. He wrote some seventy books, of which the most widely read is probably the novel *Winnetou*, the story of an Indian chief and his white friend 'Old Shatterhand'. Reading it made us participants in the life in the West of the great land America. We heard our parents speak of moving to America, and we would visualize encountering Karl May's Indian there.[106]

The Reception of the Jewish Refugees

The British West Indies had attracted limited attention among German Jewish refugees and refugee organizations prior to the November Pogrom of 1938. In fact, the actual arrival of Jewish immigrants from Eastern Europe in the Caribbean drew relatively little comment from the West Indian public prior to the refugee crisis of 1938–39, and this despite the fact that newspaper readers in the region certainly knew, or at least could have known, what was happening to the Jews in Europe.

The Trinidadian Legislative Assembly and Colonial Government

Reservations about the influx of East European Jewish immigrants were first aired in Trinidad's Legislative Assembly in the spring of 1938. On 1 April 1938, Adrian Rienzi asked the colonial government whether its 'attention has been drawn to the resentment and dissatisfaction expressed in the local press in connection with the proposed settlement of Jews in Trinidad', and whether it could reassure the people that it would advise the Colonial Office that 'whilst capital would be welcome in Trinidad, it is undesirable to encourage Jews or immigrants of any other race seeking professional, technical or any other kind of employment settling in the colony?'[107] Three weeks later, Timothy Roodal wanted to know how the colonial administration had responded to the Colonial Office's circular of December 1937 enquiring about possibilities for the settlement of refugees.[108] The following month, on 20 May 1938, Arthur Cipriani tabled a motion establishing the 'broad principle of putting the shutters of immigration up against all nationals whether Jew or Gentile, Englishman, Frenchman or Dutchman, and even our West Indian friends'.[109] Cipriani spoke at length, declaring:

> I hold out this to my friends the merchants, and I want to tell my friends the Frederick Street merchants that those who have guaranteed or undertaken to this Government to employ Jews or any other nationals and to dismiss the local men have another guess coming. We will use, Sir, the perfectly English method of boycott of those merchants, and I say it in this Council so that they will not be kept in the dark.[110]

He went on to give a specific example of what he considered unfair competition:

> Now, Sir, I have in my hands – I am an expert on this and my friends on the other side will allow that I know as much about khaki cloth as anybody in this House, and a good deal more because I have worn it all my life, and it has been usual in the past and recent past to pay around $5 to $6 for a suit of khaki, I have always paid that – I have here in my hands an advertisement: 'European Tailoring Establishment'. God help the European. 'Khaki, best Stockport, $3; White Drill 2-piece suit' – my friends of the 3-piece will suffer – '$3'.
>
> Now, Sir, this can only be brought about by the sweating of the working man. I have consulted several tailors here and they have all agreed that a suit of Stockport Khaki made for $3 can only be made by sweating the workers. And I hope my friend the working man will try to continue paying $5 and $6 for his khaki rather than stoop to paying $2 and $3. ... The working man must aspire to earn wages to pay that $5 and not to pay $3 for a suit of khaki and aspire to earn wages $2 or $3 less, and for that reason I am sure that it will be doing this Colony a great deal of harm by allowing the immigration as it is at the present

Figure 3.7 Exterior view of the watch store belonging to Erich Tauscher, a Jewish refugee in Trinidad. Tauscher re-established his enterprise on 77 W. 46 St (corner of Sixth Avenue) in New York, advertising himself as being 'fr. Wien u Trinidad' (adverts in *Aufbau* vol. 39, no. 39 [24 September 1948] and no. 41 [8 October 1948]). Photograph 75945, courtesy of the U.S. Holocaust Memorial Museum.

moment to be increased or stretched, regardless whatever of any deposit, in this country. We are just simply saying this, we have no room for the outsider, we have no work and no jobs to give him, therefore he is not welcome.

If on the other hand the British Government in their great generosity and for Imperial reasons my friend Lord Halifax shed his crocodile tears or the Prime Minister juggling with a jig-saw puzzle to find the missing pieces for Fascist civilization choose to send Jewish refugees to Trinidad, all well and good. Let them foot the bill; but I, Sir, will object, and I know I will have the support of all right-thinking people in this country, to any of these nationals from mid-Europe.[111]

In September 1938, the findings of an Immigration Restriction Committee were put before the Executive Council in Trinidad. It found that since 1928 annual immigration had consistently outstripped emigration – the overhang reaching 1,412 by 1937 – and argued that this was an important factor in explaining unemployment in the colony. In 1937, 435 aliens (as opposed to immigrants from elsewhere in the West Indies and the British Empire) entered Trinidad, most of them from the United States and China. The total number of immigrants coming from unspecific other locations, including Jewish refugees, was 67.[112] A White Paper followed in December 1938, proposing protectionist measures to ensure that no immigrants should be allowed to replace local residents in skilled or unskilled employment. The authors of the White Paper distinguished between alien immigrants, on the one hand, and those from other West Indian colonies and elsewhere in the British Empire, on the other. Whilst recommending stringent immigration controls, they specified that 'special treatment' should be given to British subjects, relatives of those living in Trinidad, those of independent means and those with special training or professional skills currently not available in the colony. In an attempt to pre-empt criticism, the committee stated that:

This Colony, is part of a group of Colonies which are closely linked both geographically and racially, and are bound by economic and sentimental ties. There are those who think that little, if any, restriction should be placed on the movement of British West Indians within the West Indies, and that the individual Colonies should not attempt to raise artificial barriers against one another. There is much to be said for this point of view. Nevertheless, in the absence of political federation, this Colony must, we feel, insist on the right to protect its own labour market, to conserve its standard of living and to control the increase by immigration of its population.[113]

The Trinidad Guardian and Sunday Guardian

Given the reporting of the *Trinidad Guardian*, the members of the Legislative Assembly and the colonial government certainly knew, or at least could have known, just what the Jews in Greater Germany were actually up against, and there can be no doubt that the decision actively to curtail immigration was taken in relatively full knowledge of, and as a direct response to, the refugee crisis the Nazis had unleashed. Then again, one eyewitness account, published in September 1938, offers a particularly good example for the ambivalences that characterized this reporting. Its author noted that the antisemitic mood in Germany was 'pretty terrifying' but also reported that 'around Berlin you can still see Jews behaving as ostentatiously as that type of Jew does in every other city in the world'. The author then went on to present, with considerable empathy, the case of a former law student who had been imprisoned in a concentration camp. 'His morale is broken', he related, 'and the expression in his eyes is that of a wounded being who is still suffering, whose spirit requires careful and kindly treatment so that he may be induced to take interest in life once more.' On 30 October 1938, the *Sunday Guardian* published an article under the heading, 'Hitler sees Aryan race as superior to Jews, Negroes, Chinese and French'. It was accompanied by a photograph of Paul Robeson. 'Even such cultured men of colour', the caption read, 'are despised in the Reich'.[114]

The drawing of connections between the current Jewish plight and that of West Indians whose ancestors had been enslaved was a trope that also featured, as we will see at the end of this chapter, in some of the calypsos created in response to the refugee crisis. While well meaning, it was also seen as a two-edged sword by some. Kurt Kersten, for instance, was a prolific radical historian and writer who had been widely published in the Münzenberg press. He continued to play a prominent role in the émigré press, after he had emigrated via Prague and Paris to Martinique, later to become occupied by the Vichy Regime. Kersten reasoned in an unpublished manuscript on antisemitism in the West Indies that 'the coloured man cannot conceive of the martyrdom of the Jewish people. Even if he could, it would be a moot question how he would react to it because he would be overwhelmed by the memory of his own past, and harassed by the mortifications and insults of the present'.[115]

Once panic migration set in, the local press in the West Indian colonies began to speculate rather more intensely about the role that Britain expected them to take in helping to solve the Jewish refugee crisis; and the increase of Jewish immigration to Trinidad rendered the issue all the more topical. In most of the British West Indies the issue was to remain a matter of speculation, given that, between January and September 1939, they responded to the situation in Trinidad by introducing measures to pre-empt the immigration of Jewish refugees on a similar scale. Only in Trinidad were the debates about immigration predicated on actual experience with a significant number of Jewish refugees, many of whom would stay until the end of the war – and some of whom, in fact, settled in Trinidad for good.

The onset of panic migration following the November Pogrom certainly turned the Jewish refugees into the object of headline news, and the initial response to their arrival was one of panic. Many reports spoke of overcrowding in Jewish houses and the health risk that this supposedly posed to the general population. When the Trinidadian Executive Council decided on 6 January 1939 to seek permission from the secretary of state for the colonies to prohibit further emigration to Trinidad, it cited the effect of the refugees on 'housing accommodation, employment and health conditions' as grounds for their decision.[116]

Having been robbed of virtually all their financial resources by the Nazis, many of the refugees arriving in Port of Spain had indeed been rendered penniless by the costs of the voyage and the deposit required to secure their entry. The Jewish Association of Trinidad rented a number of houses to accommodate them. As the Joint reported, having looked into the authorities' decision to seek a ban on further immigration:

> A Committee of Jews is renting housing accommodation and has seriously accentuated the already acute housing situation. Certain local inhabitants have been dispossessed. There is a serious overcrowding among the refugees, and the director of medical services states that the conditions under which they are living constitute a grave danger to the public health.[117]

Yet, whilst it is true that the presence of Jewish refugees exacerbated the pre-existing housing shortage, the language in which the debate about overcrowding took place suggests that the issue was also being used to provoke hostility towards the refugees. In June 1939, a report from the chief medical officer to the Port of Spain City Council found that in fact no serious overcrowding was occurring in Jewish homes. On his account, 'there would be six or eight or ten people coming off the boat and staying at the house for two days or so and then going to another place. I could not satisfy myself that there was any overcrowding'.[118]

The Jewish Refugee Society and the Jewish Association of Trinidad both sought to allay public fears about the effect of Jewish immigration in statements submitted to the *Trinidad Guardian*. Both organizations made the point that no Jewish refugees would become public charges, that their organizations were receiving money from Jewish charities abroad, and that efforts were being made to facilitate the establishment by Jewish refugees of businesses that would benefit the local population. The JRS, moreover, went as far as expressing its approval of a ban on further immigration, stating that they had advised refugee organizations abroad not to send further refugees to Trinidad since it could no longer absorb them.[119]

There was certainly no doubt in the minds of those responsible for the *Trinidad Guardian* that something needed to be done. On 20 November

1938, the *Sunday Guardian* used its front page to inform its readers that '200 Jew Refugees Entered Trinidad in Six Months'. The article beneath the headline argued that existing immigration controls were insufficient, and claimed that the British government was encouraging Jewish migration to Trinidad. The harbourmaster of Port of Spain had confirmed, the report went on, that, 'as long as these people made the necessary deposit, they could not be debarred from entering the colony due to the decision of the British government to help them by letting them enter the colonies'. The article was accompanied by an editorial, printed alongside it, under the heading, 'Germany at Bay'. The editorial argued that the persecution of Jews in Germany was unlikely to continue. Now that Germany had succeeded in annexing Austria and the Sudetenland, stability and peace would return to Europe. Consequently, the increase in refugee numbers resulting from the November Pogrom was a transient phenomenon. Not only was Trinidad in no position to admit any more refugees, there was also no real need to do so. Hence the call for tighter immigration restrictions was entirely justified, given the prospect of 'an uncontrolled influx of immigrants'. To be sure, there was

> every reason to believe that the Jew makes a good citizen, [but] we do not need more traders in Trinidad, nor should we welcome competition with workers whether in the 'white collar' or manual class. ... On the other hand, an immigrant possessing capital which he proposes to put into productive industrial enterprise to develop the Colony's resources and afford employment, would be welcome.

Paradoxically, despite the paper's determination to downplay the situation that Jewish refugees faced, it did force the *Trinidad Guardian* to draw its readers' attention to the November Pogrom and the unfolding refugee crisis. The paper noted with some concern that humanitarian concerns seemed to be gaining primacy among the British public. 'The Mother Country has been turning its eyes about the Empire in the hope of finding spots where Jews can be conveniently placed', it noted. Against the backdrop of the renewed interest in British Guiana as a possible refugee destination, the *Trinidad Guardian* called for reassurance:

> We should like to be assured that no representations have been or will be made which may give the impression in the United Kingdom that there is a prospect of settling Jewish or any other immigrants here. Trinidad does not suffer from under-population, and deeply as we appreciate the nature of the call which the refugee problem makes upon the humanities, it is clearly impossible for us to offer aid. Any unwise action would not contribute towards order and stability but would simply create new embarrassments.[120]

Two days earlier, the *Trinidad Guardian* had cited the British Guiana-based *Daily Argosy*. The latter had reported that local opinion was 'vigorously opposed' to Jewish settlement there. 'In addition to sincere, humanitarian motives', the *Daily Argosy* reasoned, 'Britain will support Jewish immigration into her colonial Empire for two reasons: first, less than a thousandth part of the colonial population is white; second, the absorption of German Jews might strengthen the opposition to Germany's colonial claims [regarding Tanganyika, South Africa, Cameroon and Togoland]'.[121]

Harold Persaud, who later served as cabinet secretary in Cheddi Jagan's government in British Guiana in the early 1960s, recalled that as vice president of his school's debating society he had put forward a motion in favour of Jewish immigration, saying that 'they're a great race' and suggesting how beneficial it would be 'if we could have people like Einstein and that sort'. Yet the teacher who supervised the debate had responded that, much as he had 'listened to Persaud's speech with a great deal of interest … the people you're going to get here are not Einsteins and that sort!' On Persaud's account, as 'racial problems became more pronounced, more overt, then people began to say they didn't want another European race to come to Guyana to lord over the local population [*sic*]'.[122]

Similar concerns were reflected in a letter Marcus Garvey wrote, on behalf of his organization, the Universal Negro Improvement Association, to the colonial secretary, Malcolm MacDonald, on 22 November 1938. Referring to possible plans to support the settlement of Jewish refugees in Tanganyika, Kenya or British Guiana, Garvey wrote:

> I am seriously protesting on behalf of the natives, to whom these countries belong, against the attempt to complicate their national and future existence … Without any prejudice toward the Jew, nor any desire to in any way do anything that would now or henceforth obstruct him … the introduction into these Colonies and Mandated Territories of large numbers of alien races will only tend to create an extreme dissatisfaction among the natives, who may be considered up to the present, as haven't expressed themselves on any such desire as may be intended by the British Government and politicians.

'Rather than be shifted from place to place, all over the world, to create other problems in other ages', Garvey argued, Jews should put their backs into creating a country of their own, 'to which they have moral and legal rights'.[123]

The *Trinidad Guardian*'s coverage of the discussion on British Guiana as a refugee destination was occasionally ambiguous, presumably because deflecting attention from Trinidad onto British Guiana was better than nothing, yet at the same time it undermined the contention that there was simply no capacity to admit refugees to the British West Indies in general. Thus the paper reported on 23 November 1938 that 'British Guiana welcomes Jews', explaining that the 'proposal to settle Jewish refugees in British Guiana was warmly welcomed here [i.e. in Georgetown, British Guiana] in newspapers'. This was so because 'it has long been recognized that lack of population is the chief obstacle in the way of British Guiana's development, and though the feeling that the West Indies always have first claim is known, neither British Guiana nor the West Indies is financially able to make large-scale settlement'.[124] Clearly, the *Trinidad Guardian* took it for granted that Jewish relief organizations would cover the costs of Jewish settlement in British Guiana, suggesting that it had dramatically overestimated the funds available to Jewish organizations. As we saw, it was precisely the lack of such funding that would lead the British government to consider retracting its offer of land in British Guiana in July 1939.

In February 1939, the paper presented the prospects of the British Guiana scheme in rather darker colours, using as its heading a quotation attributed to a local refugee: 'The Jews may not be able to pioneer in British Guiana jungle'. The colonial administration in British Guiana, the paper now suggested, was willing to allow the refugees to 'occupy their spare rooms in the yard' but did 'not want their visitors to walk into the hall, eat in the dining room, [or] sleep in their bedrooms'. Against this backdrop, the *Trinidad Guardian* decided to ask Ernst Otto Fischer – who, as a journalist, it was reasoned, could offer 'a more general point of view' than other refugees – for his opinion. Fischer argued that British Guiana was far from suitable for the settlement of Jewish refugees, given her climate, the challenge of turning city dwellers into 'Jungle pioneers', and the time and money that would be required to render the project a success. The Jewish refugees from Greater Germany needed immediate refuge, not settlement options that it would take years to establish.[125]

Once the scheme had been suspended following the outbreak of war, the *Trinidad Guardian* commented that the Jewish refugees would have to 'possess their souls in patience' now, concluding with the prognosis that 'the urge to help the Jewish people who have been driven from their homes and divested of all they owned will be the greater after the war, by reason for the loyalty so many of them are showing in this time of distress'.[126]

Public opinion in Trinidad seems to have been torn between satisfaction that the other West Indian colonies were following suit in barring further Jewish refugees, on the one hand, and dissatisfaction that Trinidad had supposedly become the 'sole refuge' for them, on the other.[127] Reporting on the situation in Jamaica, the *Port of Spain Gazette* explained to its readers:

> It is known that a good many European refugees desire to come to Jamaica, not as visitors but to reside here, some in the hope of obtaining positions in the Colony. Scores of them have applied to the Government for permits

upon which they could apply at steamship offices to come this way; but there is reason to believe that their applications have been refused. Not even one permit has been granted, the official view being that there is no room in Jamaica for immigrants whose air is to seek a living here. All things being equal, opportunities in respect of employment must be reserved for Jamaicans.[128]

On the same day, the *Sunday Guardian* quoted one refugee whom it had asked about his reasons for coming to Trinidad. 'It was the only place he could come without any trouble', he had responded. 'Most places, he said, refuse to admit refugees at all. Other places, such as Australia, issue permits of entry, but these often take as long as two years to procure'. The article went on to describe the difficulties Jewish refugees from Greater Germany faced in bringing money with them, emphasizing that most of them were arriving in Trinidad 'with only about ten shillings'.[129]

On 20 January 1939, the *Trinidad Guardian* reported that the Barbados Chamber of Commerce had written to the secretary of state for the colonies to ask for a ban on further Jewish refugees to be introduced in Barbados too. One of its members claimed that many of the refugees in Trinidad were 'walking the streets of that colony seeking jobs, and he certainly would not like to see that state of affairs existing in this island'. According to its president, 'every one of these people who secured a job in this island was automatically putting or keeping a local person out of employment'.[130] The Chamber of Commerce in Barbados may have been motivated in part by concern about the tourism industry, which was quickly gaining importance in the colony. The governor of the Bahamas, Sir Charles Dundas, had argued against Jewish immigration on similar lines in 1934, alerting the Colonial Office to the fact that the bulk of tourists coming to the colony during the winter were 'Americans of the better class, whose antipathy to all Jews is a bye word [sic] in their own country'.[131]

While the *Trinidad Guardian* clearly voiced its support for restrictions on further immigration, it also gave room to expressions of compassion for the plight of the Jewish refugees. On 12 January, the *Trinidad Guardian* published a letter from Albert Gomes, written two days earlier, on the day on which the imminent ban on further immigration was announced. Debates regarding immigration were paying insufficient attention to the 'human aspect' of the problem, Gomes complained. 'Laws, after all, and particularly this law', he insisted, 'vitally concern human relationships, and having regard to this it were well if we made provision in cases where our eagerness to preserve ourselves meant cruelty to someone else'.[132] On 15 January, the day on which the ban came into effect, an editorial followed, which claimed that 'the restrictions which have been imposed are not intended to be cruel or oppressive, but are dictated by economic reasons which can readily be appreciated'.[133]

It is noteworthy that the *Trinidad Guardian*'s presentation of the refugees who had arrived in the colony regularly stressed the social class of the recent arrivals from Austria and Germany. In an article published on Christmas Day 1938 with the title, 'The Strangers Within Our Gates', for instance, the correspondent of the *Sunday Guardian* wrote:

> At the outset I must say I have been struck by their general appearance, [and] the evident high standard of education and knowledge shown on all matters on which we conversed. I think it will interest those who have not had the opportunity of meeting the newcomers to know that these recent arrivals comprise professional men, such as, doctors, dentists, engineers, lawyers, dairy men, farmers and so on.[134]

A fortnight earlier, the *Sunday Guardian* had announced the arrival of a Viennese dress designer, Helen (originally Helene) Hammermann, in the colony, and accompanied the article with a sketch of one of her designs. As the paper reported, Hammermann 'soon hopes to be able to tell the Trinidad girl what the best-dressed women should wear in the tropics'. Indeed, she hoped that, with her input, 'Port-of-Spain may one day become the Paris of the tropical world – that is so far as fashion is concerned', the *Guardian* hastened to add.[135] 'Helen Hammermann reviews the dress-designer's impressions of our Christmas Race Meeting Fashions', the *Trinidad Guardian* titled an article and sketches by her covering a quarter of a page in its 29 December issue.[136] On 15 January 1939, the *Sunday Guardian* informed its readers that 'Helen Hammermann, in answer to numerous requests, has designed four dresses suitable for daytime in the tropics'. Alongside the sketches, Hammermann explained her rationale: 'I have decided', she wrote, 'that the main need is for everyday dresses that combine original smartness with a minimum of expense'. Her four designs, she suggested, 'would grace any local lady's wardrobe'. That she hardly had the majority of Trinidadian women in mind is clear, for example, from her guidance that the first design was 'suitable for morning shopping, the office or as an afternoon frock for the younger girl'.[137] The focus of Hammermann's contributions thus reinforced the notion of a link between the professional refugees and the upper classes in the colony. Yet Helen Hammermann and her family in fact gained little from her fifteen minutes of fame. Before being interned, she later recalled, 'my sister made hats for the British gentry, I decorated the shop windows in the only General Store and sold ads for the *Trinidad Guardian*, Mutti shopped at the local market and produced our meals on a camp stove, and Dad brooded'.[138]

Indeed, in her recollections, Helen Breger (as she now was), reported that they 'met much snobbery among the gentry, and we made fun of them, inventing conversations in our bad imitation of upper-class English; a gallows humour that was necessary in our unstable lives'. She reproduced one such conversation:

'Vienna is so terribly gay, we saw "The Great Waltz", utterly charming, did you ever met Johann Strauss?'
'Rawtha!, he is my second cousin; we often danced in the streets while my uncle played the violin.'
'Smashing. I say old girl, how long shall you be on holiday here?'
'Oh, it depends on the Polo. The season might not be all one is expecting, Still, one shall see.'
'Can't let the side down, can one? Shall you be dining at Government House tonight?'
'Rawtha.'
'I suggest you don't take your Bentley; the black urchin who parks it is rather smelly.'
'Oh, never fear, we always ride our bicycles there. It is so jolly!'
'So, you are visiting here. I've been to your country and saw the kangaroos in the outback!'
'Don't you mean Australia?'
'Good heavens, it is not, is it?'[139]

While the Hammermann sisters were able to engage in activities at least related to their professional training, many of the refugees were unable to practise their professions. It was a cause of considerable anxiety amongst West Indians that the refugees might compete for, and ultimately take away, local employment opportunities. This fear was expressed from a number of perspectives, and economic and racial considerations often comingled. The following communication from Edgar Pereira to the Joint is a particularly striking case in point. His plea that Jewish refugees from Germany and Austria should be prevented from peddling was predicated on the notion that in so doing they would stoop to the level of black West Indians – something that does not seem to have concerned him in connection with the Jewish immigrants from Eastern Europe who had previously arrived in the colony:

I desire you to get the position very clearly. The great majority of the inhabitants of this Colony are of the coloured race almost to the extent of 85%, and it is extremely necessary that the prestigue [sic] of the white race should be maintained, and Government carefully sees to it that nothing is done that would lower this prestigue. Therefore, it is necessary that we should stop Europeans accustomed to a high standard of living, such as the immigrants we have here, going on the roads of the Colony as pedlars and doing work that hitherto has been done by the coloured people. I must emphasize the importance of this not only for political aspects but also for the benefit of our race. It is for reasons such as these and the heartbreaking sight of seeing men of culture suffering indignities at the hands of coloured people that spurs on my efforts to get something started quickly which would assist the situation materially and morally.[140]

The Jewish immigrants from Eastern Europe presumably counted neither as 'Europeans accustomed to a high standard of living' nor as 'men of culture' and were consequently free to debase themselves as pedlars.

The fear that Jews were successfully competing for local employment opportunities was also expressed by members of other minority groups. Early in January 1939, for instance, the *Trinidad Guardian* reported on a court case under the heading, 'Syrian Pedlar Blames Jew Rival for his Failure'. A Lebanese pedlar who had been taken to court over non-payment of a debt claimed that his livelihood had been ruined because of competition from Jews who had 'spoiled his business'.[141]

Yet whilst some of the earlier Lebanese immigrants may have felt that Jewish competition was to blame for the hardship they faced, as a general rule West Indians were more inclined to lump Syrian and Jewish immigrants together, and to view the involvement of both in small business and trading as a threat to their own livelihoods. This is demonstrated in a striking fashion by a calypso of 1939 by Growler (Errol Duke), with the title, 'I Don't Want Any Syrians Again'. Even though its narrator conceded that he found Jewish immigrants preferable to their Chinese or Lebanese counterparts because the Jews extended credit to their customers, he nevertheless suggested that they 'should be in Jerusalem or Palestine, instead of in this Country of mine'.[142]

Calypsos

Calypsos are an important source when trying to assess the public mood in the British West Indies, and in Trinidad in particular. They were frequently used as a medium for the expression of political and social dissatisfaction and unrest, and were deeply 'implicated in the articulation of ... national belonging, politics of representation, and power relations'.[143] They have been described as 'a kind of auditory newspaper, spreading information about current issues'.[144] They originated in 'African musical practices on colonial plantations', and 'drew from and creatively combined an array of musical traditions, blending a variety of influences from Africa, Europe, and the Americas', rendering them a 'highly hybrid' means of expression.[145] By the 1930s, Calypsonians played to local audiences in villages, rum shops and cinemas, and the bamboo 'tents' in which they had performed in the 1920s became more permanent and commercial enterprises. As their popularity increased, calypso artists became commercially successful as Decca, Cook Records and other companies began to produce and sell calypso recordings in the United States and elsewhere in the Caribbean.[146] This commercialization notwithstanding, many calypsos continued to articulate biting social satire, often falling foul of censorship as the colonial authorities deemed their content too inflammatory to be recorded or broadcast.[147]

Gordon Rohlehr identified no fewer than six calypsos focusing specifically on the (potential) influx of Jewish refugees that were submitted to Trinidad's commissioner of police between late 1938 and early 1940 with the request that he 'would kindly have same censored'.[148] They are: the already mentioned 'I Don't Want Any Syrians Again' by Growler; 'Jews Astray' by Ryan; 'The Jews Immigration' by King Radio (Norman Span); 'Jews in the West Indies' by Gorilla (Charlie Grant); 'The Persecuted Jews' by Atilla the Hun (Raymond Quevedo); and 'Song of the Jews' by Lord Executor (Philip Garcia). The sentiments expressed in these calypsos ranged from outright hostility to a more welcoming position, with a variety of ambivalent notes struck in most of them. Except for the last two, they were all banned by the censors.[149]

Ryan's 'Jews Astray' articulated outright and unmitigated animosity:

Jews in the land better we give them the laws command.
And post them back to Jerusalem.

I want to know why they must flock down here
Leaving Hitler they high Master
Them and Mussoline [sic] is family so get them out of the Colony.

Why Hitler band [sic] such good-looking breath
They must be commit some surel dees [sic],
They come like dark sons off zebadie
To bring the country in slavery.

They trying the screw like the Chinese
And very soon the making poulit on eve
Coming to open they glass factory
Because they hear Trinidad have the money tree, [sic]

The Jews look wicked and Barbarous
They really ain't no nation to trust
Jews cannot deal with Samaritans
So get them out of the native land.[150]

'The whole of this calypso', the censor noted, 'is in bad taste in view of the British policy of extending hospitality to Jews everywhere, and should not be allowed'. The effrontery of this claim is quite breathtaking, given the consistent attempts of the colonial authorities and the Colonial Office to keep Jewish refugees out of the British West Indies, but they obviously could not condone such a clear-cut incitement to anti-Jewish hatred.

In King Radio's 'The Jews Immigration', the balance tended more towards the critical than the welcoming or compassionate. 'We form no objection', it began,

> With the Jew immigration
> But we want representation
> But we all had agreed and received a few
> But to come in by the thousand that wouldn't do
> In the ages of humanity.
>
> Trinidad is a cosmopolitan little Island in the West
> And it is considered to be the best
> The Foreigners leaving all their homes and here they look to run
> Like Trinidad is the dumping ground,
> The place is so congested friends I must say
> Yet the Foreigners are pouring in every day
> So I disagree that shouldn't be in a small little Colony.[151]

Having elaborated on this thought, the calypso then continued:

> Now they [disadvantaged Trinidadians] got trouble with the Jews
> The fact I must put to you
> Needn't my friends doubt it they know it's true
> They are going to form an opposition
> With every single merchant
> As to run them competition
> Any part of town you see a Jew Store,
> Bet your life he is selling cheap to the rich and the poor
> It's plain to see.[152]

The verse then stated, somewhat surprisingly, 'and we all must agree / They will be some help to the Colony'. Yet the rest of the calypso then returned to the previous negative tone.

> A Jew can live in a hole, when he means to control
> And Business throughout the world,
> We know that the Jews they are prosperous
> But now they bring Hitler's old junks to throw on us …
>
> San Fernando first explain we don't want no Jews here again
> Cause we have no place to remain,
> They are giving twice as much as the people used to pay
> And taking their rooms away

And the bad minded agents always agree
And given their tenants notice immediately
That shouldn't be I am appealing to the Authority
For more protection in this Colony.[153]

'Jews in the West Indies' by Gorilla took a generally positive approach:

Tell me what you think of a dictator
Trampling the Jews like Adolph Hitler,
Tumbling them out of Germany
Some running for refuge in the West Indies.

Some land in Demerara and Granada,
They land in Trinidad very regular
The way they are coming all of them,
Will make Trinidad a New Jerusalem.

When a Steamer comes to La Trinity
Run down to the jetty what you think you'll see,
Male and Female Jews in a band,
Begging the Authorities to let them land.[154]

Yet the following verses seem to introduce a more ambivalent tone:

Since Jews coming to this Colony
They are marrying and raising a family,
In a couple years believe it's true
Trinidad children will be only Jews.

Imagine how a bunch of them congregate
Sleeping in a garret by the six and eight,
See them in the morning down at their store,
You wouldn't believe they are sleeping ona [sic] garret floor.[155]

Rather disturbingly, the following verse then begins by stating that 'Anywhere you go you can tell a Jew / The nose in their face not like me or you'. Yet it then turns out that the calypso's message overall is in fact an optimistic one:

But the women all look rosy
Like a Christmas apple in a Grocery.

Very very soon we are going to see
Jews quite up to date in this Colony
For they are industrious and will progress,
For in all professions they are of the best.[156]

Of the two calypsos that did make it past the censors, 'The Persecuted Jews' took a clearly positive approach. It began by drawing a parallel between the current plight of the Jews and the earlier suffering inflicted by the Atlantic slave trade.

> Let's give serious contemplation
> To the question of Jewish immigration
> Just like our forefathers in slavery
> From the brutality of tyrant they have to flee,
> So it's nothing but Christian charity
> To give these oppressed people sanctuary.
>
> Negroes our slave fathers long ago
> Suffered all kinds of tribulation and woe
> With yokes round their necks beaten day and night
> Their only salvation remained in flight,
> So in remembrance of their agony
> And gratitude to those who showed them sympathy
> We shall extend to the Jews hospitality,
> As a monument to our ancestors' memory.[157]

The focus of the calypso then shifted to contemporary affairs:

> When Abyssinia was raped so horrible
> By that despite [sic] dictator Mussolini
> Our brother Ethopian [sic] had to flee,
> For succor and aid to many a country,
> In the fullness of our heart imagine that you'd say
> If England Spain France or Turkey had turned them away
> This barbaric cruelty you would abuse,
> So think of them before criticizing Jews.
>
> The last Negro King Haille Selassie
> From the Tenor of Fascism had to flee
> And many a sad story these Jews can tell,
> Of what is it to live in a fascist hell.
> But Negroes and Jews as you plainly see
> Have suffered from these arch tyrants equally
> So from attacking Jews we must refrain
> As we'd be upholding the Hitler Mussolini reign.[158]

This calypso gave the colonial censors something of a headache. While they welcomed its call for solidarity with the Jewish refugees, the flipside of this call – the equation of their fate at the hands of the National Socialists with that of earlier West Indians at the hands of their (British) slaveholders – was rather more problematic. This was, in the words of Gordon Rohlehr, 'hardly the sort of link that the colonial administrators, some perhaps themselves the direct descendants of slave owners, wanted to see made, at a time when they were trying to impress on the world their difference from the Nazis'.[159] Even so, given its positive sentiment towards those Jewish refugees who did make it to Trinidad, it was approved.

'Song of the Jews' is ultimately the most intriguing of these calypsos, not least because the censors approved it. Hence it arguably tells us as much about the mindset of the censors as it does about the intentions of its creator, who combined traditional Christian anti-Judaism with what might be interpreted as a positive response to the refugees. The calypso starts on a promising note:

> The song of the Jews
> To shelter them we could not refuse,
> Italy Germany and Mexico
> Have sent them away they have nowhere to go
> Now they rejoice they feel so glad,
> For they have a haven in Trinidad.[160]

Yet then the calypso pursues a rather different line of thought, drawing on the traditional Christian notion that the Jews had been punished and abandoned by God for not accepting Christianity. From there it moves on to the trope of the eternal wandering Jew, but in a way that implies that it is in fact the Jews' decision to 'roam' the countries of others rather than return to their own.

> If the pages of sacred history we trace,
> You'll see where the Jews are a sacred race
> That remained so long after the time,
> Of the miraculous turning of water into wine.
> But as the prophet's message they would not believe,
> Chastisement and punishment they will receive,
> From the hands of every nation,
> Except America and Great Britain.

> The tragedy of the Jewish nation
> Their sorrows and lamentations
> Depicted from the days of old,
> By the Prophets and Sages as we are told,
> There is a mystery about their birth,
> Why should they thus suffer upon this earth,
> Ah the Jewish generation
> They forsake Jerusalem.

> You remember when the Victorious Romans,
> Fought in the remarkable siege of Jerusalem

> Bringing destruction and havoc within the City wall,
> By Pompeii the Great that history recall
> From that moment every Jew decided to roam
> And will not go back to their beautiful home,
> Now they rejoice and feel so glad,
> To arrive in the Island of Trinidad.[161]

The calypso then turned explicitly to the November Pogrom of 1938, and criticized Herschel Grynszpan for provoking the Nazis, as though the assassination of Ernst vom Rath had been the cause of, rather than just a pretext for, the pogrom.

> The murder of the German Ambassador
> Has caused every Jew to suffer
> The Assassination took place in Paris,
> An ignorant Jew was the cause of this,
> That was like adding fire to fury,
> For Hitler had sworn against them bitterly
> He opened the door
> And said to them depart forevermore.

> The synagogues were taken and made hotels
> Their mansions confiscated for Germans to dwell,
> England received them to her bosom dear,
> At America they knelt and offered a prayer,
> Some had to live like rats in a hole
> By the tyrant Hitler without heart or soul
> Now they rejoice and they feel so glad,
> For they have found a haven in Trinidad.[162]

While some of the German Jewish communities indeed maintained impressive synagogues, the suggestion that they were (or could have been) turned into hotels betrays fairly dramatic misunderstandings both in terms of the measure of destruction wrought on most synagogues in Greater Germany during the pogrom, and regarding their suitability as potential hotels. Note also the implication that Jews (invariably?) owned mansions expropriated to provide housing for Germans (who apparently are, by definition, non-Jewish, while Jews, in turn, cannot be Germans).

Presumably what the censors read when examining this calypso was an affirmation of the fact that Trinidad was morally compelled to take in the refugees, praise of the fact that the refugees had been given cause to 'rejoice and ... feel so glad' now that they were in the colony, and an acknowledgement of the contention that Britain and the United States had a singular and proud track record of accommodating Jews – hence, they approved it. Yet the calypso obviously lends itself to a rather more subversive reading. If all the other countries, in refusing to tolerate Jews, had effectively been implementing their divine punishment, then the preparedness of Britain and the United States to accept them was actually quite problematic. Moreover, the Jews had in no small measure brought their current plight upon themselves, in general terms by refusing to 'go home', and more specifically by provoking the already enraged Nazis. As a consequence of the problematic behaviour of the Jews, on the one hand, and of Britain and the United States, on the other – the role of the Nazis features as more of a background phenomenon in the account offered by this calypso – Trinidadians were now forced to accept the refugees, undesirable as this was. That none of the references to God's punishment of the Jews or to the wandering Jews' obstinate refusal to go home raised any suspicion among the censors is telling in its own right. It helps to explain the extraordinary hard-heartedness the colonial authorities continued to display towards the increasingly desperate attempts of Jewish refugees to save themselves by fleeing Nazi-dominated Europe.

Notes

1. Prinz, 'Role of the Gestapo', 214–18.
2. Strauss, 'Jewish Emigration (II)', 367; Marrus, *The Unwanted*, 177.
3. London, *Whitehall and the Jews*, 114.
4. John G. Hibbert to Sir John Shuckburgh, 6 February 1939, TNA CO 323/1602/17. The pretext for the November Pogrom had been the assassination of a German diplomat in Paris by Herschel Grynszpan, a German-born Polish Jewish refugee, whose family had been among the roughly fifteen thousand Jews of Polish extraction rendered stateless by the Nazis and forcibly deported to the Polish border in late October 1938, where the refusal of the Polish authorities to admit them initially left them stranded in no man's land for several days.
5. Razovsky, 'Bound for Nowhere'.
6. New York Office of the Joint, Memorandum, 29 December 1938, JDC, File 1047.
7. Edgar Pereira to Cecilia Razovsky, 19 December 1938, JDC, File 1047.
8. Cecilia Razovsky, Memorandum To All Cooperating Agencies, 29 December 1938, JDC, File 1047.
9. Ibid.
10. 'Immigration General Policy 1939', Colonial Office memorandum summarizing immigration regulations (undated and unsigned), TNA CO 318/440/5.
11. Edgar Pereira to Charles Liebman, Refugee Economic Corporation, New York, 12 December 1938, JDC, File 1047.
12. Dr B. Pulver, Secretary of the JAT, to Cecilia Razovsky of the National Coordinating Committee, 7 January 1939, JDC, File 1047.
13. Razovsky, 'Bound for Nowhere'.
14. Henry Pels, Secretary of the Chief Rabbi's Religious Emergency Council (CREEC), to [Mr] Taylor [identity unclear], 25 December 1938, AJA, MS175 139/1F.2; Werner Röder and Herbert A. Strauss (eds), *Biographisches Handbuch der deutschsprachigen*

Emigration nach 1933 vol. 1 (Munich: Saur, 1980), 477; 'Max Markreich', in Fred Grubel et al. (eds), Catalog of the Archival Collections of the Leo Baeck Institute New York (Tübingen: Mohr Siebeck, 1990), 94. It is unclear who purchased the ticket for Markreich and whether he received assistance from any of the refugee organizations.

15. Colonial Office memorandum (undated and unsigned), TNA CO 318/440/5; John G. Hibbert, Colonial Office memorandum on the *Königstein* and the *Caribia*, 3 February 1939, TNA CO 123/376/6.
16. Colonial Office memorandum on immigration regulations in West Indian colonies (unsigned and undated), 1939, TNA CO 318/440/5.
17. John G. Hibbert, Colonial Office memorandum, 3 February 1939, TNA CO 123/376/6.
18. William Dunlop of the Foreign Office to Hilton Poynton of the Colonial Office, 28 February 1939, TNA CO 318/440/5.
19. Hilton Poynton to William Dunlop, 3 April 1939, TNA CO 318/440/5.
20. Edgar Pereira to Cecilia Razovsky, 7 January 1939; Dr B. Pulver to the National Coordinating Committee, 7 January 1939; Edgar Pereira to Cecilia Razovsky, 12 January 1939, JDC, File 1047.
21. Edgar Pereira to Cecilia Razovsky, 16 January 1939, JDC, File 1047.
22. Siegel, 'Unintended Haven', 66, 70.
23. Dr B. Pulver, Secretary of the JAT, to Cecilia Razovsky of the National Coordinating Committee, 18 January 1939, JDC, File 1047.
24. Sir John Huggins, Acting Governor, to the JAT, 3 March 1939, JDC, File 1047.
25. Governor of British Honduras to the Secretary of State for the Colonies, 14 January 1939, TNA CO 123/376/6; Kenneth Robinson, Memorandum referring to telegrams from British Guiana and British Honduras, 17 January 1939, TNA CO 123/376/6; idem, Memorandum regarding Jamaica, Barbados and Leeward, 24 January 1939, TNA CO 318/440/5.
26. Circular from Malcolm MacDonald, 1 December 1938, TNA CO 323/1604/1.
27. Harold Beckett, Colonial Office memorandum, 5 January 1939, TNA CO 318/440/5.
28. William Johnston, Governor of British Honduras, draft Statutory Rules and Orders 1939, No. 51, Order 'Prohibiting the entry of certain kinds of aliens into the Colony', TNA CO 123/376/6.
29. Kenneth Robinson, Minute to the Secretary of State for the Colonies, 30 March 1939, TNA CO 123/376/6.
30. Secretary of State for the Colonies to the Governor of British Honduras, telegram no. 66, 7 April 1939, TNA CO 123/376/6.
31. British Guiana, Ordinance No. 9 of 1939, passed February 1939; Barbados, Law No. 23, passed May 1939; British Honduras, Ordinance No. 14 of 1939, passed June 1939; Trinidad, Ordinance No. 21 of 1939, passed September 1939. Source: IALS.
32. *Trinidad Guardian*, 20 January 1939 (copy, page number could not be verified).
33. Edgar Pereira to Cecilia Razovsky, 16 January 1939, JDC, File 1047.
34. Edgar Pereira, Western Union Cablegram to National Coordinating Committee, 20 January 1939, JDC, File 1047.
35. Dr Ulrich Schächter (JAT) to Cecilia Razovsky, 13 April 1939, JDC, File 1047.
36. Communication from the Governor of Jamaica to the Secretary of State for the Colonies, 7 November 1946, TNA CO 318/472/13.
37. Executive Council, Trinidad, 29 December 1938, TNA CO 298/177.
38. Minutes of the Executive Council, 22 February 1939, TNA CO 298/178.

39. The figure of 105 is based on the number of cases discussed at the meetings of the Executive Council on 15 February, 15 March, 3 May, 17 May, 28 June, 9 August and 7 September 1939. From minutes of the Meetings of the Executive Council, 1939, TNA CO 298/178.

40. Edgar Pereira to the Joint, 21 June 1939, JDC, File 1047.

41. The following account draws on Siegel, 'Unintended Haven', 135–45.

42. Ibid., 136.

43. John Shuckburgh to Sir Cosmo Parkinson, 18 December 1939, TNA CO 295/615/5, quoted in Siegel, 'Unintended Haven', 136.

44. TNA CO 295/615/5, quoted in Siegel, 'Unintended Haven', 138.

45. Siegel, 'Unintended Haven', 138–39.

46. John Hibbert to Harold Beckett and John E.M. Carvell, 4 April 1940, TNA CO 295/615/5, quoted in Siegel, 'Unintended Haven', 140.

47. Siegel, 'Unintended Haven', 143.

48. Sir John Shuckburgh to Sir Cosmo Parkinson, 28 May 1940, TNA CO 295/619/16, quoted in ibid., 142–43.

49. John Hibbert, 27 May 1940, TNA CO 295/619/16, quoted in ibid., 143.

50. Ibid.

51. Sherman, *Island Refuge*, 231.

52. Lord Winterton to Sir Herbert Emerson, IGCR meeting, 13 July 1939, cited in ibid., 253.

53. 'Confidential. West India Royal Commission. Views of Seven Members on Proposed Jewish Settlement in British Guiana', sent by Sir Thomas Lloyd (Secretary of the Royal Commission) to Malcolm MacDonald, 5 May 1939, TNA CO 950/248.

54. Quoted in Martin Gilbert, 'British Government Policy towards Jewish Refugees (November 1937–September 1939)', *Yad Vashem Studies* 13 (1979), 131–32.

55. House of Commons Debate, 12 May 1939 (vol. 347, cc. 862–64), http://hansard. millbanksystems.com/commons/1939/may/12/refugees-settlement-british-guiana (last accessed 9 May 2019).

56. House of Commons Debate, 15 May 1939 (vol. 347, cc. 981–83), http://hansard. millbanksystems.com/commons/1939/may/15/british-guiana-refugees (last accessed 9 May 2019).

57. Sherman, *Island Refuge*, 254.

58. 'Conference of the Inter Governmental Committee on Political Refugees, 18 October 1939', in Mendelsohn and Detwiler, *Selected Documents Vol. 6: Jewish Emigration 1938–1940: Rublee Negotiations and the Intergovernmental Committee*, Document 8, 93.

59. Walter Citrine to Malcolm MacDonald, 8 May 1939, TNA CO 950/248.

60. Roger Makins, Minute, 1 December 1938, cited in Sherman, *Island Refuge*, 189.

61. See Feingold, *Bearing Witness*, 124–27.

62. Meeting of the Subcommittee for Central and South America, 13 April 1939, JDC, File 112.

63. 'Report on the Activities of the Freeland League' (undated), AJA, MS 116/159 Part 2.

64. Leopold Kessler, Chairman of British Section of the Freeland League, to *The Times*, 2 January 1939, AJA, M SI 16/159, Part 2 (AJ398/2).

65. Edgar Pereira to Cecilia Razovsky, 16 January 1939, JDC, File 1047.

66. Quoted in Gilbert, 'British Government Policy', 131–32.

67. Ernst Otto Fischer, 'An Austrian Jew in Trinidad Writes About: Changing Europe', *Sunday Guardian*, 11 December 1938, 28. Fischer and his wife, Liesl Fischer, née

Neubauer, left Vienna in 1937, together with their daughters Inge and Lucy who initially stayed in Britain for two years and then joined their parents in Trinidad. See http://collections.ushmm.org/findingaids/2011.378.1_01_fnd_en.pdf (last accessed 9 May 2019).

68. Manfred Goldfish, 'A Danger to Security', typescript, 1, 3. Su Goldfish collection, copy in my possession.
69. *Sunday Guardian*, 19 February 1939, 5.
70. Classified Announcements, *Trinidad Guardian*, 17 January 1939, 10.
71. Friedrich Borchardt and David Glick, Report to the Joint on Trinidad, 22 March 1939, JDC, File 1047.
72. Edgar Pereira to Cecilia Razovsky, 16 January 1939, JDC, File 1047; JDC Report on Loan Fund, Meeting of the Subcommittee on Refugee Aid in Central and South America, 17 May 1940, JDC, File 113.
73. Friedrich Borchardt and David Glick, Report to the Joint on Trinidad, 22 March 1939, JDC, File 1047.
74. Ibid.
75. Herbert Philip, Secretary of the Jewish Refugee Society, to Cecilia Razovsky, 14 April 1939, JDC, File 1047.
76. Report on the JRS's aims at the meeting of the Joint Subcommittee on Refugee Aid in Central and South America, 19 May 1939, JDC, File 112.
77. Edgar Pereira to Cecilia Razovsky, 15 May 1939, JDC, File 1047.
78. Meeting of the Joint Subcommittee on Refugee Aid in Central and South America, 19 May 1939, report on Trinidad, JDC, File 112.
79. Edgar Pereira to Cecilia Razovsky, 10 May 1939, JDC, File 1047.
80. Claude H. Hall, Jr., to the Secretary of State, Washington DC, 5 January 1939, Dispatch no. 226; Subject: German refugees in Trinidad. This dispatch was also copied to the American Consulate General in Berlin. NARA, Record Group 59, Decimal File 1930–39, Box no. 6222, File no. 844G.5562/1.
81. Max Markreich to the Committee on Refugee Jewish Ministers, 19 May 1939, LBI NY, Max Markreich Collection (hereafter MMC).
82. Undated manuscript sheet, MMC.
83. Chairman of the JAT to the WUPJ, London, 19 April 1939, MMC.
84. Lily Montague of the WUPJ to Dr Ulrich Schächter of the JAT, 10 May 1939, MMC.
85. Religious Committee of the JAT to the WUPJ, 11 June 1939, MMC.
86. WUPJ to Max Markreich, 23 June 1939; JAT to the WUPJ, 24 July 1939; WUPJ to the JAT, 15 August 1939, MMC.
87. Religious Committee of the JAT to the WUPJ, 22 September 1939, MMC.
88. Lily Montagu to Max Markreich, 30 October 1939, MMC.
89. Rabbi Alexander Burnstein, Executive Secretary of the Committee on Refugee Jewish Ministers, to the President of the JAT, 28 April 1939, MMC.
90. Max Markreich to the Committee on Refugee Jewish Ministers, 19 May 1939, MMC.
91. Henry Pels, Secretary of the CRREC, to Max Markreich, 17 March 1939, MMC.
92. See Under-Secretary of State in the Home Office to Henry Pels, 19 November 1938, AJA, MS175 139/1F.2.
93. Trepp was able to move to the United States in January 1940, where he subsequently had a distinguished career, serving congregations in Massachusetts, Washington and California (including Berkeley). He held a number of honorary doctorates and prestigious visiting university appointments. He died in San Francisco in 2010 as one of the

last surviving members of the generation of rabbis who had served congregations in Nazi Germany.

94. Moses W. Beckelman, Report to the Joint in New York, 19 October 1941, JDC, File 1048.
95. Max Markreich to the JAT, 24 March 1939; Dr Ulrich Schächter, Dr Ferdinand Bronner and Dr B. Pulver of the JAT to Max Markreich, 27 March 1939, MMC.
96. Max Markreich, Exposé des religiösen Komitees an die Verwaltung der Jewish Association of Trinidad, 28 November 1939; JAT to the Religious Committee, 30 November 1939, MMC.
97. JAT to the *Trinidad Guardian*, undated, MMC.
98. *Trinidad Guardian*, 27 October 1939, 3.
99. Jewish Association of Trinidad to His Worship the Mayor, Port of Spain, 2 November 1939, MMC.
100. Town Clerk to Lew Girion, Secretary of the JAT, 27 October 1939, MMC.
101. *Trinidad Guardian*, 31 May 1940 (copy, page number could not be verified).
102. See Claude H. Hall, Jr., American Consul in Trinidad, to the Secretary of State, Washington, DC, 'Rejection of Government of Trinidad to Designating Jewish Chaplain as Marriage Officer', 25 May 1943, NARA, RG 59, Box No. PI-157, 740, 811.34544/2946.
103. Secretary of War to the State Department, 30 June 1943, NARA, RG 59, Box No. PI-157, 740, 811.34544/2978.
104. Joanna Newman, 'A Caribbean Jerusalem', Radio 4, 11 August 2001.
105. Helen Breger, *Lines: A Sketched Life* (Berkeley, CA: Helen Breger, 2009), 13.
106. Mann, *Drastic Turn of Destiny*, 24–25.
107. Question No. 52, Adrian C. Rienzi, Member for Victoria, 1 April 1938, 'Settlement of Jews in the Colony', Debates in the Legislative Council of Trinidad and Tobago 1938. Hansard. Trinidad 1938 (hereafter Hansard, Trinidad 1938).
108. Question No. 55, Timothy Roodal, Member for St. Patrick, 22 April 1938, 'Jews – Settlement in Colony', Hansard, Trinidad 1938.
109. Hansard, Trinidad 1938, 300.
110. Ibid., 301.
111. Ibid., 302.
112. See Report of the Immigration Restriction Committee, Executive Council Meeting, 28 September 1938, Executive Council Minutes, January to June 1938, TNA CO 298/177; Report on recommendations of the Committee, *Trinidad Guardian*, 10 December 1938, 6.
113. Report of the Immigration Restriction Committee, 28 September 1938, Executive Council Minutes, TNA CO 298/177.
114. *Sunday Guardian*, 30 October 1938, 17.
115. Kurt Kersten, 'Farbiger Antisemitismus', typescript, 9 pp., here p. 4, LBI NY, Kurt Kersten Collection, Series III, Box 1, Folder 14: Manuscripts: 2 (unpublished) A–Z.
116. Meeting of Executive Council Trinidad, 6 January 1939, TNA CO 298/178.
117. Joint Report: 'Recent developments regarding emigration to Trinidad', 19 January 1939, JDC, File 1049.
118. 'No Crowding in Jewish Homes', *Trinidad Guardian*, 23 June 1939, 5.
119. *Trinidad Guardian*, 10 January, 1, 11; *Sunday Guardian*, 15 January, 6; *Sunday Guardian*, 19 February 1939, 5.
120. *Sunday Guardian*, 20 November 1938, 1.
121. Quoted in *Trinidad Guardian*, 18 November 1938, 3.

122. Marshall, *The Caribbean at War*, 20.
123. Marcus Garvey, President, Universal Negro Improvement Association, to Malcolm MacDonald, 22 November 1938, TNA CO 323/1604/5.
124. *Trinidad Guardian*, 23 November 1938, 8.
125. *Sunday Guardian*, 19 February 1939, 5.
126. 'Action Suspended', *Trinidad Guardian*, 28 September 1939, 4.
127. *Sunday Guardian*, 8 January 1939, 2.
128. 'Jamaica Bars Aliens', *Port of Spain Gazette*, 8 January 1939, 19.
129. *Sunday Guardian*, 8 January 1939, 2.
130. *Trinidad Guardian*, 20 January 1939, 11.
131. Sir Charles Dundas, Governor of the Bahamas, to Sir John Maffey, Permanent Under-Secretary in the Colonial Office, 20 April 1934, TNA CO 323/1271/1.
132. *Trinidad Guardian*, 12 January 1939, 6.
133. 'A Sensible Precaution', *Sunday Guardian*, 15 January 1939, 6.
134. *Sunday Guardian*, 25 December 1938, 5.
135. *Sunday Guardian*, 11 December 1938, 12.
136. *Trinidad Guardian*, 29 December 1938, 17.
137. *Sunday Guardian*, 15 January 1939, 29. Hammermann was the younger sister of Juana Merino Kalfel, née Hammermann. She was able to change her identity with the help of the Chilean Consular General in Paris, Armando Marine, who facilitated the escape of significant numbers of Jews to Chile. She was able to emigrate to the USA in 1941.
138. Breger, *Lines*, 13.
139. Ibid., 17.
140. Edgar Pereira, Jewish Refugee Society, 15 May 1939, JDC, File 1047.
141. *Trinidad Guardian*, 6 January 1939, 3.
142. See Gordon Rohlehr, *Calypso and Society in Pre-Independence Trinidad* (Port of Spain: Gordon Rohlehr, 1990), 314.
143. Jocelyne Guilbault, *Governing Sound: The Cultural Politics of Trinidad's Carnival Musics* (Chicago: Chicago University Press, 2007), 1. C.L.R. James, commenting on the development of Trinidadian musical culture, suggested that 'in dance, in the innovation of musical instruments, in popular ballad singing unrivalled anywhere in the world, the mass of the people are not seeking an identity, they are expressing one' (James, *Black Jacobins*, 417).
144. Trevor G. Marshall, 'Bajans Come Back to Calypso', in Rachel Wilder (ed.), *Insight Guide: Barbados* (Singapore: APA, 1990), 235.
145. Guilbault, *Governing Sound*, 29, 30.
146. Rohlehr, *Calypso and Society*, 147.
147. Ibid., 202–5.
148. Ibid., Plate 24; see also Casteel, *Calypso Jews*, 180–82.
149. Unless indicated otherwise, the material presented in this section is from the National Archives of Trinidad and Tobago, C.S.O. No. 41126 Pt. II.
150. Courtesy of the National Archives of Trinidad and Tobago.
151. Courtesy of the National Archives of Trinidad and Tobago.
152. Courtesy of the National Archives of Trinidad and Tobago.
153. Courtesy of the National Archives of Trinidad and Tobago.
154. Courtesy of the National Archives of Trinidad and Tobago.
155. Courtesy of the National Archives of Trinidad and Tobago.
156. Courtesy of the National Archives of Trinidad and Tobago.
157. Courtesy of the National Archives of Trinidad and Tobago.

158. Courtesy of the National Archives of Trinidad and Tobago.
159. Rohlehr, *Calypso and Society*, 314.
160. Courtesy of the National Archives of Trinidad and Tobago.
161. Courtesy of the National Archives of Trinidad and Tobago.
162. Courtesy of the National Archives of Trinidad and Tobago.

Part III

CONFRONTING THE NEED FOR RESCUE

Chapter 4

BOAT PEOPLE

Saul Friedländer closes the first volume of his *Nazi Germany and the Jews* (1997), covering the pre-war period, with excerpts from a review of an evocative performance by the Jewish Kulturbund in Berlin of J.B. Priestley's *People at Sea* in April 1939. As the reviewer, the Associated Press bureau chief in Berlin, Louis P. Lochner, who won a Pulitzer prize for his reports from Berlin that year, explained, the performance had only been made possible by the fact that 'the British playwright has renounced all claims to royalties from German Jews'.[1] As many of the remaining Jews in Greater Germany 'awaited quota numbers to emigrate, and emigration dreams were realized only via ship passage to foreign ports', the resonances of Priestley's 1937 account of a disoriented group of passengers from Britain and the United States adrift in the Caribbean on a damaged ship 'that might not make it to its destination' and awaiting rescue,[2] must have been considerable. On Lochner's account, the audience 'wistfully nodded when Fritz Grünne as Carlo Velburg complained again and again that he had no passport'.[3] Fritz Grünne, for one, was not able to rescue himself. He and his wife committed suicide when faced with a deportation order in February 1943.[4]

Almost invariably, Jewish refugees to the Americas and the Caribbean arrived by boat. Some emigrated with a sense of adventure and found their journey and arrival in the Caribbean an exhilarating experience. Take the following previously unpublished account by Manfred Goldfish, written in 1989. Goldfish was born in 1911 in the illustrious German spa town of Bad Ems, where his parents, Lina and Eugen Goldfisch, owned the Hotel

Löwenstein. Due to the combined impact of the Great Depression and Nazi rule, the Goldfisches lost the hotel in 1936. They moved to Cologne and were later deported to Theresienstadt where Eugen Goldfisch died in 1942 and his wife two years later. Searching for employment, Manfred Goldfisch moved to Königsberg in Eastern Prussia and emigrated from there with his first wife, Malka (later Martha) Goldfisch, at the end of 1938.[5]

As he later recalled, he had been presented with two options. The first was 'a booking on a freighter bound for Shanghai, and the second a first-class cabin on the *Andes* bound for the West Indies'.[6] The second option seemed preferable but compelled them to travel 'first class, which we could ill afford, because those were the only berths left ... Perhaps our decision to migrate under these conditions was reckless even foolhardy, but there was no real alternative and in the end it proved to be the right one'.[7] They arrived in Port of Spain on 1 January 1939. This is the full account that Manfred Goldfish wrote years later, remembering his arrival in Trinidad:

The 1. January 1939 is a date that can truthfully be described [as] the watershed, the turning point, the terminator, or any other cliché you can think of, they'll all fit.

On that fateful day I stepped ashore in Port of Spain, Trinidad and into a new and exotic world. Here was I with a brand new wife, no money and not the faintest idea how we were going to earn a living in this unfamiliar environment.

It [had] all started 3 months earlier, when encouraged by friends and relatives I married a Lithuanian girl and decided to emigrate to an overseas country because living in Germany became more dangerous every day. This proved to be difficult. First there were problems in obtaining passports, and when we finally managed to get some sort of travelling paper, there were long waiting lists for visas everywhere.

In our desperation we contacted some shipping agents, who told us that it was possible to obtain entry and work permits by depositing a certain sum of money (mostly US dollars). The agent told us that he could arrange passages for us to Havana, Cuba ($500 each), Barbados ($250) and Trinidad ($250 each). There were also passages to Shanghai available, with free access to the international settlement. But as the city itself was occupied by the Japanese and there was a war on, there was no guarantee that after a five-week journey we would be able to land there. We thanked the agent and went home.

For the next few weeks, we carried on with our jobs and the need to make a final decision seemed still far in the future. We lived at that time in the city of Koenigsberg, far in the north-east on the Baltic coast, winter was approaching and it got colder and the days got shorter.

Early in November 1938 a letter [came] from my uncle in France with the welcome news that he had deposited US$ 500 with Barclay's bank in my name. This was indeed a break and we could now proceed more seriously with our plans. We contacted the agent to get more information about available sailings. We told him over the phone that a deposit had been arranged and we would like to leave before the end of the year if this was possible.

But fate suddenly intervened after the German ambassador to France had been assassinated,[8] allegedly by a Polish Jew. This was the cue for 'Krystalnacht' [*sic*] that brought terror and destruction as rampaging brownshirts bombed synagogues, burnt and looted Jewish-owned shops and arrested thousands. Action was desperately urgent now if we wanted to escape. When the turmoil had settled somewhat, we dared to pay a visit to the agent and told him we would like to book a passage on the 'Cordillera' which was to sail from Hamburg in mid December.

He phoned the line headquarters and after a few minutes he turned to us and said, 'You are in luck, the liner is almost fully booked but I can offer you the last two berths for Trinidad. The next trip leaves Hamburg on the 16. December but you must pay me a deposit now and the rest within seven days, the total cost DM 3600'.[9]

I paled, 'So much? we thought it would be about half that amount'. 'Look here', he said irritably, 'do you want the tickets or not. There are hundreds out there just waiting for such a chance'. Outside the first snow of the season had begun to fall and through the flurries I could just see the still smoldering ruins of the great temple. I said no more and wrote a cheque for the full amount, leaving only a small balance in our account.

The following days were spent settling our affairs, hurriedly packing such items which we thought might be useful in any situation, and dispatched them by rail to Hamburg as hold luggage.

There was nothing else left but to say goodbye to a few friends, and at the end of November we were ready to leave the now gray and wintry Baltic.

We boarded a train to Cologne to spend a last week with my parents, and then the sad moment of parting had to be faced. There were no tears, no sighs, only grim faces all round when the whistle blew and the Hamburg express started to pull out of the station. Exhilarated by the romance of a leisurely journey into the sun, the importance of this farewell did not fully register with me and I felt actually quite cheerful. Gradually the figures of my dear parents faded into the steamy mist of the big railway junction and I had a feeling, almost a premonition, that I would never see them again. The express gathered speed and within a few hours we arrived at the big North Sea port.

We phoned the line's offices and learned that we should board at 9 am the following day, and that they had booked a room for us at the hotel 'Excelsior' (with the compliments of the company.) The excitement of the imminent departure kept us awake and it was almost morning before our eyes closed. At 7 am the desk woke us as arranged, and an hour later a bus took us to the quay; the great adventure was about to begin. It was bitter cold, with the temperature almost −30°. The liner was to sail at noon, and icebreakers were busy keeping channels open so that departure would not be delayed.

In spite of the biting cold I could not resist to go on deck to watch tugboats getting into position to pull the giant hulk into the stream. Then a shudder went through the ship as the powerful diesels down below started their run that would not stop for 14 days and nights.

I watched as, to the sound of grinding and crushing ice, the liner slowly edged away from the ice-covered concrete wall of the quay. A strip of black water appeared, we had lost contact with German soil. With long angry blasts of their sirens, the tugs began to pull and we were on our way.

For the past two weeks the M/V Cordillera had been battling the long Atlantic rollers and was approaching its destination, the island chain of the lesser Antilles. Apart from a spot of rough seas in the Gulf of Biscay, which had most of us seasick for a day or two, it was a routine journey and very enjoyable.

We were getting ready for our last dinner on board and there would be a new year's party later that night which we decided not to attend. We were simply not in the mood for celebrating. Tomorrow we would disembark and the carefree life on board would only be a memory. After dinner we went to our cabin to pack our few belongings and went to bed.

Earlier that week about halfway across the Atlantic we had encountered a huge ocean swell generated by some distant northern storm. We had just met our sister ship the 'Caribia' on her way back to Europe. I was standing on the promenade deck scanning the blue emptiness of the ocean, when a veritable mountain of water rose before my eyes. The top of the wave was well above the point where I stood. I was terrified and started to run toward the comparative safety of the companionways, but fortunately the wave did not crest and simply lifted the large liner like a toy and then we were over the top and rushed down the lee, with a shudder and a vibration that sent glasses, bottles and crockery crashing to the decks.

I was dreaming about this event, but in my dream the watery mountain brought with it some monstrous sea creature trying to get into our cabin through the porthole. Finding the opening too small it began moaning loudly in a low vibrating note.

I was terrified by the nightmare and woke up screaming, something had grabbed my shoulder, but the moaning continued. 'You must have had some dream' said my wife, letting go of my shoulder. The moan was only the ship's siren welcoming the new year, and from the upper decks came shouts of 'Happy New Year' and sounds of music from the Captain's party.

Brilliant sunshine greeted us as the tender deposited us at the Customs wharf, a brown-skinned officer offered a hand to help Marion ashore. 'Welcome to Trinidad', he said; the temperature was +30º.[10]

Even allowing for the tricks the memory can play on the mind, there can be little doubt that the journey and Goldfish's arrival in Trinidad impressed themselves on his recollection as eminently positive experiences. Yet, as we will see, for many the passage to the Caribbean was altogether less pleasant.

Goldfish arrived exactly a fortnight before Trinidad, followed by many of the other colonies, put in place its ban on the further admission of refugees from Europe. That fortnight already brought clear signs of what was to come. As the *Washington Post* reported on its front page on 12 January 1939 under the heading, 'Forbidden to Land Anywhere', thirty-seven refugees with 'fraudulent' visas for Peru were trapped on board a Chilean boat, the *Imperial*. They had embarked on the passage despite 'warnings that they would be barred from landing at their destination ... hoping that a solution could be found' on arrival. Cecilia Razovsky had initially appealed to the US commissioner of immigration and naturalization, James L. Houghteling, for the refugees 'to be taken off the *Imperial* at Ellis Island at the expense of her organization, which was seeking entrance for the group in Trinidad'.

Rather remarkably, the report then went on to explain that Razovsky, having been informed of the impending ban on the entry of further refugees to Trinidad from 15 January onwards, 'requested Ellis Island officials not to accept the 37 refugees unless another country which would let down its immigration bars to them could be found overnight' (the *Imperial* was already on her way from Baltimore to New York).

> If none was found, she said, the refugees would be forced to continue to their original destination, Peru, where officials have been advised by the Peruvian consul in Antwerp not to permit them to land ... 'The refugees themselves are not certain just what their "improper papers" mean', Miss Razovsky said. 'We know that Peruvian government officials have been instructed not to allow them to land at Callao ...' Meanwhile, her organization is querying Trinidad in efforts to arrange papers which would permit the 37 to land there.[11]

This gives a clear indication of Razovsky's mounting sense of frustration as more and more Jews were forced to embark without papers, visas or landing permits on ships destined for ports in the Western hemisphere, and German steamship companies, in turn, furnished refugees with invalid or illegal visas from various consular officials.[12] While the refugee organizations had previously still had some limited leeway to direct the migration of refugees they were assisting, the new restrictions, combined with the acceleration of forced emigration from Greater Germany, reduced their role to one of negotiating for refugees who were already on the high seas, and spending most of their funds to facilitate the landing of refugees who had been 'dumped illegally'.[13]

At the time, the National Coordinating Committee was already trying to find a solution for a group of passengers who had arrived in New York on the *Gerolstein* on 2 January on the way to the Dominican Republic, which had introduced new regulations when the *Gerolstein* was already on its way, requiring all new immigrants with no realistic prospect of return to pay $500 on entry. 'Santo Domingo Law Maroons 9 Austrian Refugees in N.Y.', the *Baltimore Sun* reported on 12 January 1939 on its front page, not without clarifying that 'their bills at present are being paid by a refugee committee'. A reporter had visited the refugees, finding them 'in a disconsolate huddle in a little midtown hotel' where they 'drearily picked at the strangest immigration puzzle that has arisen here since the great exodus from Nazi Austria began'.[14]

In the event, the Peru-bound Jewish refugees on the *Imperial* were apparently able to proceed after all. As the Jewish Telegraphic Agency reported from New York on 13 January 1939, under the heading, 'Closing of Trinidad to Refugees Creates Serious Situation in Emigrant Aid':

> the difficulties of 37 refugees who arrived here on the Chilean liner Imperial yesterday en route to Peru were temporarily settled today. They had feared that their visas would permit to remain in Peru only 48 hours, but when their documents were examined this morning, it was discovered they had tourist visas.[15]

Yet to the detriment of refugees on board the *Königstein* and the *Caribia*, the Colonial Office took a hard line. Despite having emphatically warned its European affiliates against sending further refugees, the Joint in New York was informed by its Paris Office that both the *Caribia* and the *Königstein* had 'assisted cases' on board, who had been allocated places before knowledge of the ban had been circulated. Approximately two hundred of the passengers had been forced to leave in order to be released from concentration camps.[16]

Refugees aboard the steamship *Königstein* who, as indicated, had set sail after 15 January, were refused entry to Barbados, Trinidad and British Guiana, despite having booked their passage well in advance of that date. As *The Times* reported on 28 February:

> The German ship arrived off the Demerara beacon on Saturday and sent a wireless message to the authorities asking for permission to land 165 Austrian Jewish refugees, stating that they possessed $30,000. The permission was refused under the terms of the recent immigration ordinance. It is understood that similar attempts at Barbados and Trinidad were also unsuccessful.[17]

The *Observer* likewise emphasized that 'the Jews had £6,000 and other funds available for settlement, but the government refused permission to land on the ground that no accommodation was available'.[18]

More than a month later, the Venezuelan government relented, as Lawrence S. Haas (of the United Press agency) reported in the *Washington Post* on 2 April under the heading 'Refugee Band Find New Life and Hope in Venezuela. Group of 165, Barred at 3 Ports, Now Happy in Camp'. It said the *Königstein* had, 'as a last resort, … put in to the Venezuelan port of La Guaira, where it lay for five days until a Jewish refugee aid committee in Caracas obtained permission for them to land'.[19] From there they were eventually able to travel to Ecuador.

On the strength of the agreement between the Jewish Association of Trinidad and the colonial authorities that allowed relatives of refugees already residing in the colony to enter, a tiny number of passengers aboard the steamship *Caribia* were given permission to land in Trinidad.[20] The remaining passengers, however, were turned away. The governor of Trinidad, Sir Hubert Young, felt justified in taking this stance on the grounds that the *Caribia* had set sail five days after the new legislation had been made known to the German authorities. Having been turned away by the Trinidadian authorities, the *Caribia* set sail for British Honduras. Yet the governor there, Sir Alan Burns, informed the local agent of the Hamburg Amerika line that the refugees would not be allowed to land there either. Eventually, the refugees on the *Caribia* – thanks to international appeals and the coordinated efforts of Jewish refugee organizations – found refuge in Venezuela.

Shortly after turning the *Caribia* away, Burns was approached by the National Coordinating Committee who offered to deposit the sum of $20,000 to cover the costs involved in maintaining the immigrants until they could support themselves. On 3 February, Burns cabled the Colonial Office to inform them of this offer and advise them that, assuming they approved, he was inclined to admit the refugees, provided they undertook not to engage in any work other than agriculture.[21]

The Colonial Office, however, decided that the only way to prevent Germany from expelling evermore refugees would be to take a 'firm line' against tactics seen as blackmail, and to send those who had already been expelled back to Germany. John Hibbert noted:

> It is a rather difficult decision to make. It is more than probable that hardly any of the refugees on board will be agriculturalists by profession, but they will certainly all say that they are prepared to engage in agriculture simply in order to avoid the risk of being taken back to Germany … Moreover, if the Governor admits even a few of them, it will be seized upon as a precedent by the Germans to send another shipload to Belize. At the present time they are using peaceful persuasion to push out Jewish refugees on German, Italian and Japanese ships to any port where they can at present be admitted upon payment of £50 or so. They have sent thousands to Shanghai. My rather extensive knowledge of the Germans enables me to say at once that there is only one argument which will appeal to the German mentality, and that is to refuse to allow these refugees to land and to send them back to Germany. That may seem a cruel thing to do, but it may be a kindness to other refugees in the long run.[22]

Consequently, the draft response to Burns advised him to refuse the refugees entry to British Honduras. Should the current investigations of the Moyne Commission identify suitable settlement areas in the colony, the needs of the West Indian population should in any case take precedence.[23] In the event, the draft was never sent because the news reached the Colonial Office that the refugees had been allowed to enter Venezuela.

Against the backdrop of the difficulties encountered by the refugees on the *Caribia* and the *Königstein*, the Joint office in New York contacted its counterpart in Paris, suggesting that the Jewish relief organizations needed to agree a common policy. 'This is not a matter of immediate cash available', they wrote,

> but [a] question of large important policy, which important Jewish organisa-
> tions must consider together. We [are] in [a] great quandary although [the]
> judgement [of] many members [of] our committee and officers is that with
> continuous similar dumping of shiploads we have no alternative but to refuse
> financial help. [This is an] Important question in principle [to] be canvassed
> with other organisations to determine [a] decision re these passengers and
> [the] future.[24]

The Paris office welcomed the proposal, suggesting a conference of the steam-ship companies and agents with the participation of the Council for German Jewry, the Jewish Colonization Association, the Joint and HICEM, and proposed that a statement should be agreed on the 'future attitude of the private organizations towards the people who leave with no visas or with irregular ones'.[25] Although the Joint was fully aware that by refusing financial help passengers would be returned to their country of origin, they were also conscious that it was their continued assistance that allowed corrupt officials to go on issuing false visas and landing permits.[26] Their dilemma is encapsulated in the following telegram sent by the Joint in Paris to the New York office:

> Please consider fully [suggestion that] British Council, ICA, HICEM reach
> common approach [regarding] policy respecting entire problem of dumped
> panic migration [to] Central [and] South America [and the] Far East. [It is]
> Quite clear [that the] resources [of] private philanthropic Bodies [are] strained
> [to the] utmost [to] deal [with] even more normal orderly emigration under
> [the] supervision [of] responsible Bureaus. [The] Dumping [of] refugees [is]
> resulting [in] panic migration [and] exploitation by unscrupulous steam-
> ship agencies, lawyers [and] venal officials, [which] raises alarming problems
> involving long-continuing or indefinite maintenance, [and refugee organiza-
> tions] making huge guarantees quite beyond [the] financial possibilities [of]
> private Bodies. Moreover, this dumping [is] carried out [with the] assump-
> tion [that] Jewish organizations will pay this form [of] blackmail. How to

deal [with the] whole situation is [a] fundamental problem [of] international Intergovernmental scope.[27]

Yet in the event, these considerations notwithstanding, the Joint and its affiliates in fact continued to do their best to support 'dumped' refugees and find them places of refuge.

Floating 'No Man's Lands'

The term 'No Man's Lands' was increasingly used by the JDC to refer to ships that were, again in the words of a JDC report, 'bound for nowhere' – unable to find destinations willing to accept the refugees.[28] The most in/famous case involving a large number of Jewish refugees stranded on the high seas is that of the St Louis, which arrived in Havana on 27 May 1939 and, having cruised for several days between Havana and Florida,[29] was finally forced to begin its return journey to Europe on 5 June. On board were more than nine hundred passengers who had paid between 600 and 800 Reichsmark for the passage, as well as a supplementary contingency fee of 230 Reichsmark to cover a possible unexpected return passage.[30] 'No event is more emblematic of American apathy' towards the plight of the refugees, has been the accepted notion.[31] C. Paul Vincent has argued compellingly, though, that the widely known narrative regarding the St Louis 'includes as much myth as it does history', and has suggested a more even-handed interpretation of events surrounding the St Louis.[32]

One of Vincent's main contentions is that the negotiator the Joint sent to Havana, the president of the Cuban–American Chamber of Commerce, Lawrence Berenson, radically misjudged the situation, not least because he was 'handicapped by his own optimism'. The landing permits had been issued to the passengers on the St Louis by the director general of immigration, Manuel Benitez Gonzalez, who was a client of Batista, the president of Cuba. The issue thus became embroiled in the 'deepening power struggle' between Batista and President Laredo Brú. To make things worse, Brú seems to have been genuinely 'annoyed by Hapag's [the Hamburg Amerika line's] collusion in Benitez's corruption'.[33] In the event, neither Batista nor Benitez were at any point involved in the negotiations with Berenson, which should surely have given him cause for concern.[34]

Until the very end, however, Berenson maintained his optimism about the likely outcome and consequently kept virtually all his collaborators and allies (including Cecilia Razovsky, who had travelled to Havana with him) in the dark about the seriousness of the situation, even when he had been 'virtually cut out of the negotiations'.[35] Against this backdrop, there seemed to be no reason for the US State Department to exert greater pressure and thus 'risk accusations of official American meddling'.[36]

When it finally became clear to all parties involved how dire the situation was, namely, that the *St Louis* really was being forced to return to Europe, the deputy director of the Intergovernmental Committee on Refugees established at Evian, Robert Pell, acting on instructions from US Under-Secretary of State Sumner Welles, played a crucial role in helping the Jewish relief organizations to bring about – while the *St Louis* headed back 'as slowly and circuitously as possible'[37] – the solution that led to the returnees receiving temporary permits to enter Britain, France, Belgium and the Netherlands (254 of them subsequently died in the Holocaust). The critique of the US administration therefore needs to be tempered, Vincent argues, not least in light of the fact that the drama of the *St Louis* was being played out against the backdrop of the 'final closed-door deliberations on the Wagner–Rogers bill', which proposed the admission of twenty thousand German refugee children to the United States. Given how controversial an issue immigration was at the time, the administration had to pick its fights; and in the light of the optimistic noises coming from Berenson, it may well have been considered wise for the administration not to champion the cause of the refugees on the *St Louis* as well as that of the bill. Yet when (the administration knew that) it counted, Welles, through Pell, did all he could to ensure a positive outcome.

While Vincent's account is plausible enough, Rafael Medoff has complicated the picture yet further by pointing out that the US Treasury secretary, Henry Morgenthau, suggested to the secretary of state, Cordell Hull, on 6 June that the refugees on board the *St Louis* could go to the Virgin Islands[38] (the former Danish West Indies, which the US had bought during the First World War). The governor and Legislative Assembly of the Virgin Islands had declared their willingness to admit Jewish refugees from Germany following the November Pogrom. Yet Hull rejected this suggestion on the grounds that Germany had banned the refugees from ever returning. As Medoff has put it rather aptly: 'It was a cruel irony: they were not admitted because they could not return to Germany, so they were ordered to return to Germany'. Morgenthau's suggestion is of particular interest in so far as this solution would not have required an executive order – in other words, the administration could have facilitated this option without having to pick a fight in Washington.[39]

Zava Litvac Glaser, by contrast, places Cuban duplicitousness centre stage in her account of the affair. Even as the League of Nations Refugee Commission warned the German authorities and the Joint informed its European partners that the refugees on the *St Louis* were highly likely not to be admitted to Cuba,[40] Benitez continued to declare the opposite and actively discouraged refugees from acquiring the correct bonds that would have allowed them to enter.[41]

In Cuba, meanwhile, the public were already being mobilized against the refugees on the *St Louis* before it had even left Germany. 'One thousand foreigners will arrive on the San [*sic*] Louis', the headlines in *El Pueblo* exclaimed on 4 May, with 'immediate displacement of our workers. Government efforts to alleviate unemployment will be frustrated if the immigration continues. Great problem for the government and the nation'. The paper referred to the refugees as 'strangers whose desire is only to enrich themselves to make a fortune and then to take their money with them'.[42]

The Joint eventually undertook to fulfil all the financial conditions set by the Cuban president, and on 5 March the Cuban government announced that it would now allow the refugees from the *St Louis* to land in Cuba. The following morning, Berenson had an appointment with Brú. He was kept waiting for three hours, and then informed that he had missed the deadline by which he would have been required to accept the government's offer – a deadline nobody had previously mentioned.[43] Glaser suggests that the explanation for the government's ostensible change of heart is simple enough: the Joint had agreed to meet the sum demanded as a guarantee for the refugees, but had refused to pay a substantial bribe, above and beyond this sum. As the Joint's vice president, Joseph Hyman, noted privately:

> The minutes will not say, and cannot say, that while all of the discussions were going on, overtures were being made to our representatives for the payment of a very large sum of money, almost one-half million dollars, quite apart from and independent of any guarantees and money deposits that might run into one-half million dollars or more.
>
> It is quite conceivable that if we had yielded to this type of ransom or extortion some or all of the passengers might have been landed, but it would have meant opening ourselves, and many of the refugees in Cuba, to continuous harassing and demands. ... We are firmly convinced that there never was any intention of the Cuban authorities to admit those unfortunates, and I am personally quite as sincerely convinced that only by the payment of huge graft would there have been any real possibility of getting into Cuba.[44]

'The children of the *St. Louis* thank you with their whole heart', Liesl Joseph wrote to Morris C. Troper of the Joint on 17 June 1939, her eleventh birthday, from the *St Louis*, 'for rescuing us from deepest despair. We entreat G-d's blessing upon you. Unfortunately, no flowers grow here on shipboard; we would have liked to have sent you a bouquet'.[45] Liesl Joseph and her parents, Josef and Lilly Salmon Joseph, were initially brought to England, after which Josef Joseph was interned on the Isle of Man. In 1940, they were able to remigrate to the United States where they settled in Philadelphia. Josef Joseph chaired the passenger committee on the *St Louis*.[46]

The countries that had agreed to take the refugees continued to haggle over them until the last moment, and the distribution of the refugees took place on the boat in Antwerp. The British tried to pre-empt competing claims by presenting a list of 180 refugees for whom sponsorship had been arranged, and who just so happened to be the best placed refugees. For all their disagreement, all the governments involved were united in not wanting to accept Polish Jewish refugees, and having a strong preference for those with definite remigration prospects. In the end, the British got their preferred refugees provided they also took the remaining undesirables once the other countries had picked their contingents. The 181 refugees accepted by the Netherlands were placed in a camp with guards, guard dogs and barbed wire when they arrived in Rotterdam.[47]

For the Joint, the outcome, while a relief, also signalled massive problems. The negotiations had cemented a trend that had become increasingly prevalent since the winter of 1938/39, namely, that even with substantive political support the Joint could at best hope to attain temporary permits for stranded refugees (most of whom, in this case, actually had valid quota numbers for the US) on condition that it carried all costs involved in maintaining those refugees – costs that were being calculated at evermore outrageous per capita rates – as well as the ultimate responsibility for finding them a permanent home elsewhere. None too surprisingly, the Joint was anxious to emphasize that the case of the *St Louis* had been exceptional, and should not be seen as creating a precedent. In the words of one Joint official, 'we look upon Cuba as being near to home; most of the refugees ultimately come into this country, and I think we have to deal more liberally with the Cuban situation than we are generally in a position to do'.[48] On 21 June 1939, it issued the following policy statement:

> The emergency is over. It is essential, however, to take into account the bearing that this incident may have on the future … It must be obvious to all that, aside from the fundamental questions of policy which are involved, the financial and administrative burdens of such 'dumped', chaotic, forced, and disorganized emigration are entirely beyond the scope of private philanthropic resources or the facilities of existing organizations … Under these circumstances, the Joint Distribution Committee must place on record that it cannot regard its action on behalf of the St. Louis passengers, and the enormous sacrifices it has made in the financial commitment undertaken for this relatively small number of persons, as constituting a precedent for any similar action … Conscious of its responsibilities in all of the vital necessities of the Jewish populations overseas, the JDC, as a trustee for the funds turned over to it by contributors throughout the country, cannot undertake to expend huge sums

for a comparatively small number of refugees in any such type of enforced and disorderly emigration. In the circumstances, the St. Louis must be regarded, as in fact it was, as a special problem that required special treatment.[49]

Yet, in fact, the case of the *St Louis* was special at best in terms of the measure of publicity it received. Indeed, further refugees arrived in Havana on the *Flandre* – having previously been refused entry to Mexico – and the *Orduna* just after those on the *St Louis*; they ran into the same difficulties and were also included in the negotiations.[50] When the refugees from both ships were forced to return to Europe, ninety-seven Czech and German Jews from the *Flandre* were allowed into France, while those from the *Orduna* were returned to Liverpool on the *Orbita*.[51]

The sister ship of the *St Louis*, meanwhile, the *Orinoco*, left Hamburg for Cuba on 27 May 1939 with 200 passengers on board – 103 of them Jewish refugees. As it became clear that the *St Louis* had run into trouble in Havana, the *Orinoco* changed its route and spent several days outside Cherbourg, waiting for further news as negotiations ensued. Neither the British nor the French government were willing to offer permits to the refugees on board, and nor in the end were the US administration. The ship eventually returned to Cuxhaven (the port on the mouth of the Elbe river leading to Hamburg), where the 103 Jews were taken off the ship before the remaining passengers continued their journey to Cuba.[52]

What is more, the Hamburg Amerika line's *Iberia* had arrived in Havana with fifty-two Jewish refugees on board on 15 May, a fortnight prior to the *St Louis*. They were interned at the Tiscornia immigration station. On 24 June, the *New York Times* reported that they were to be returned to Germany on the *Orinoco*, which was scheduled to sail from Havana on 4 July.[53] Yet in this case President Laredo Brú did eventually relent, and the *New York Times* was able to report on 16 August 1939 that Brú had signed a decree the previous day, allowing the fifty-two refugees to enter Cuba because 'the legal formalities have now been fulfilled … through efforts of the local Jewish relief committee'.[54]

Throughout the first half of 1939, refugees found themselves temporarily stranded on a steady succession of ships, either because they had genuinely been sold invalid permits or because governments reneged on valid visas. After the Paraguayan government cancelled large numbers of visas issued in Europe, Montevideo became a particular flashpoint, since the Uruguayan authorities were not willing to admit the refugees who would not now be able to continue their journey to Paraguay. Between January and March 1939, Jewish refugees were prevented from leaving the *Conte Grande* (twice), the *General San Martin*, the *Lipari* and the *Cap Arcona*.[55] In June, Jewish refugees (two hundred, according to the *New York Times*) on board the *Caporte*, the

Monte Olivia and the *Mendoza* were unable to land in Montevideo and, after trying their luck in Buenos Aires, were forced to return to Europe.[56]

With the prospect of war looming, some refugees took matters into their own hands. A dramatic case in point is that of 'eleven refugee veterans of the Spanish civil war' who arrived in Trinidad on 19 August 1939, 'only half-dressed and hungry after a 50-day trip across the Atlantic in their schooner *Alexandrine Eudoxie*'.[57]

Jewish Relief Work under War Conditions

With the outbreak of war in September 1939, the Jewish relief organizations were forced to adapt their activities in a number of ways. Initially, they continued to focus principally on helping Jewish refugees flee the Nazis' advance. As this goal became increasingly unrealistic, assistance to those who had already managed to leave but had often found only temporary or precarious refuge took up more and more of the organizations' attention. Once it became clear that the Germans had embarked on the systematic extermination of European Jewry, campaigning for rescue plans took on an increasingly prominent role. Intense pragmatic cooperation between Jewish organizations notwithstanding, old controversies, especially regarding the relative merits of (ostensibly) non-political relief work and more partisan political campaigning, resurfaced in the course of the war.

Not least, the war brought with it a number of perhaps less obvious practical problems, foremost among them increasing restrictions on international money transfers. Consequently, the Central British Fund for the Relief of German Jewry (formerly Council for German Jewry) was no longer able to contribute financially to HICEM. Following the German victory over France, the assets of the Jewish Colonization Association (ICA) were frozen and so it too could no longer help to finance the refugee relief work. Consequently, HIAS shouldered much of the financial burden in 1940. In 1941, the Joint began to cover most of the transportation costs while HIAS continued to contribute to the administrative costs and helped with some transportation expenses. The share of the HICEM budget covered by the Joint rose from 52 per cent in 1940 to 86 per cent in 1941.[58] Similarly, the Joint was compelled to take on sole financial responsibility in 1941 for the transportation fund for German Jewish refugees that had been established by the ICA, the Joint and the Council for German Jewry in 1935. Likewise, HIAS was left shouldering the burden of an East European fund it had set up jointly with the ICA. Between September 1939 and June 1941, the Joint operated a clearance system, which avoided the need to send US currency to Axis countries. Jewish organizations there took deposits in local currency from prospective emigrants and used them for internal aid programmes. The Joint, in turn, paid non-German shipping lines for the transportation of the refugees. Yet in June 1941, the US government froze the assets of all Axis, Axis-occupied and Axis-dominated countries in the United States by executive order. Henceforth a licence from the US Treasury was required for any transfer of funds to any of these countries.[59]

The greater financial strength of the American Jewish organizations is explained easily enough. Jewish aid organizations depended principally on fundraising appeals, and the Jewish population was much larger in the United States than in any other Western country. Moreover, much of the money collected by Anglo-Jewish organizations was needed for the support of refugees in Britain. Following the November Pogrom of 1938, Britain took in a substantial number of refugees – an estimated eighty thousand by the spring of 1940 – of which a large percentage depended on some form of aid from the Jewish Refugee Council.[60] Consequently, the financial resources of the Jewish organizations in Britain were stretched to breaking point. In February 1940, the House of Commons was informed that refugee organizations had spent a total of £5 million on refugee assistance since 1933. They were currently providing £60,000 per month and about to run out of funds. The Cabinet Committee on Refugees had agreed in 1938 to match the Jewish organizations' contributions pound for pound, and from February 1940 onwards their resources were finally supplemented by government contributions.[61]

The resources available to American Jewry may have been great, but unlimited they were not. The Joint generated most of its income from the annual United Jewish Appeal, which was complemented by individual donations and legacies. Although British policy had slowed emigration to Palestine to a trickle, the United Palestine Appeal continued to receive 40 per cent of the sums raised by the Joint annual appeal. By the end of 1939 the Joint had accrued a deficit of $1.8 million, and its income decreased in 1940 and 1941 as many donors evidently continued to prioritize domestic issues. Since the Joint's income was derived mainly from public fundraising, Yehuda Bauer has suggested that it can be understood as an indicator of American Jewry's response to the genocide against European Jewry. 'American Jewry', Bauer wrote, 'gave JDC very little money until 1944 ($37,909,323 in 1939–43) and somewhat more in 1944 and 1945 ($35,551,365). The $194,332,033 it raised in 1945–48 showed how late the reaction to the disaster of the Holocaust was'.[62]

Between 1939 and 1945 the Joint spent most of its budget, approximately $78 million in total, on relief and rescue activities within occupied Europe. Of these funds, roughly 11 per cent was channelled to Poland through the Joint's Warsaw office, which continued to operate legally until the entry of the United States into the war in December 1941. The Joint's Warsaw staff, including its former directors, Yitzhak Giterman and Daniel Guzik (who would go on to serve as the Joint's first post-war director in Poland), then continued their work illegally, relying on loans from local Jews whose post-war repayment by the Joint they guaranteed. For those who could afford to make substantial contributions, this was potentially a worthwhile investment. The most likely alternative was that the Germans would expropriate them, and the surviving creditors were indeed repaid by the Joint after the war.[63] Giterman, who was closely associated with Emanuel Ringelblum and Oyneg Shabes, was murdered by the SS on 18 January 1943 while trying to warn his neighbours that the Germans had entered the ghetto.[64]

The constant need to raise funds led to fierce competition between refugee bodies, especially between the Joint and the World Jewish Congress. Their difficulties in providing funding notwithstanding, Anglo-Jewish groups continued to be involved in the coordination of relief and refugee work in neutral, occupied and safe territories. The chairman of the Joint, Paul Baerwald, began to discuss the best possible division of labour between the organizations with Norman Bentwich of the Council for German Jewry in April 1939, insisting that refugees to South America and the Caribbean should not be the sole responsibility of the American Jewish organizations. Their welfare needed to be a matter of 'joint consideration and joint action'.[65]

In September 1939, it was agreed that the Joint would take responsibility for the transport of refugees from Greater Germany and Poland. HIAS, subsidized in part by the Joint, would take care of all other European countries through its continued support of HICEM.[66] The Central Council for Jewish Refugees would act as the central body responsible for Jewish refugees in Great Britain and the Dominions and colonies.[67] In the event, refugees who were able to enter British colonies with the help of the Joint did then frequently contact Anglo-Jewish organizations. Yet its formal responsibility for the refugees in the Empire notwithstanding, the Central British Fund for German Jewry (CBF) simply lacked the requisite funds to offer sufficient support, and so it was, for the most part, limited to an advisory role. It passed on information to other organizations and sought to use what influence it had in government circles to press refugee cases.

The Joint and HIAS, whose headquarters were in New York, both maintained offices in Europe, which liaised with various affiliated organizations in countries of refugee departure and reception. In June 1940, the British section in London took on the role of WJC headquarters under the charge of Maurice Perlzweig. It also established a relief committee in Geneva and a relief department in New York under Arieh Tartakower. Following the German invasion of France, the Joint and HIAS moved their European headquarters from Paris to Lisbon. In addition, HICEM maintained additional offices in Marseilles and Casablanca. Once the United States entered the war,

Joint and HICEM representatives were withdrawn from the occupied countries, rendering the remaining offices in Lisbon, Marseilles and Casablanca all the more significant.

HICEM, which established an administrative committee in New York in 1940, continued to maintain the largest number of points of contact throughout Europe, South and Central America, Africa and Asia. The Joint transmitted some funding directly for relief work but most of its expenditure for emigration was in fact processed through HICEM. Only between July and December 1941 did the Joint maintain a special Transmigration Bureau of its own in Lisbon for refugees from Germany and German-occupied countries. It was closed when the United States entered the war.

Representative bodies such as the American Jewish Committee and the Board of Deputies of British Jews did not wish to be considered partisan because they feared this would jeopardize their refugee work and lead to accusations that they prioritized the rescue of foreign Jews over their allegiance to the Allied war effort. Yet in practice, supposedly non-political refugee relief work and political campaigning functioned in tandem, and impacted on each other. More politically oriented Jewish organizations like the World Jewish Congress depended on information provided by the relief agencies to campaign for specific rescue plans and, through their work, raised public awareness of the plight of European Jewry, which, in turn, helped to throw the need for further emergency work into sharper relief. Rescue proposals tended to include calls to remove the immigration restrictions for Palestine, to send food and medical supplies to Jews in occupied Europe, to encourage neutral countries to receive refugees, to issue visas to refugees in occupied Europe, and to create temporary havens for refugees able to reach neutral territories.

It was certainly one of the Joint's central tenets that the organization should be non-political, concerned only with the dispensing of aid and relief, and until 1941 the Joint felt bound by Roosevelt's declaration of neutrality. Policy decisions in the Joint were made by a number of committees, most importantly the Executive Committee and the Administration Committee, which was formed after the outbreak of war to take swift decisions in response to current events. When the Joint, its principal orientation towards the American Jewish Committee notwithstanding, co-opted representatives of the American Jewish Congress (along with delegates from the Zionist and Orthodox organizations) onto its Executive Committee in November 1939, it was hoped that this might lead to a stronger politicization of the Joint, yet in the event, as Bauer has pointed out, this only transformed the committee into 'an unwieldy body unsuited for rapid decision making'.[68] HICEM and a number of other aid organizations likewise argued that it would threaten their standing as humanitarian aid organizations if they aligned themselves with a particular political position. Consequently, in December 1943, the Joint rebutted the proposal of the American Jewish Congress to form a single Jewish agency for rescue activities. Baerwald informed the AJC that the Joint 'consistently refrained from participation in activities [that] have a dominant political objective'; that said, any 'project, plan or measure, however initiated or created, and by whomsoever sponsored' would be fully considered and, if practicable, acted upon by the Joint.[69]

Differences did not end there. Like so many Jewish relief organizations in the past, the Joint and its affiliated associations operated on the assumption that the sooner refugees integrated into their new host societies, the more likely it was that further refugees might be admitted. Moreover, if the integration of Jewish refugees could be shown to run smoothly elsewhere – and especially in the United States' own backyard – so the hope that the US administration might be more amenable to the admission of more refugees. Finally, it was considered of paramount importance that the presence of Jewish refugees should under no circumstances be seen to stoke antisemitism or pro-German sympathies in Central and Southern America. Jewish refugees should therefore behave in as 'non-conspicuous' a manner as possible.[70] Against this backdrop, refugees in the Caribbean drew a remarkable measure of attention from the Joint and its affiliated relief organizations, given the relatively small numbers of refugees in the region.

In contrast to the Joint and similar organizations, the WJC drove a Zionist agenda and sought to organize Jewish communities as independent political entities, rendering them not less but more conspicuous. The Coordinating Committee, established in October 1940 by the Joint, HICEM, the Refugee Economic Board and a number of similar organizations to promote the integration of Jewish refugees, recognized that the WJC was an attractive option for many refugees because it offered them the opportunity to become 'articulate as its representatives in their worldwide Jewish program ... instead of being recipients of philanthropy from Jewish organizations'.[71] Given the Joint's intense focus on the Caribbean, the region emerged as a battleground on which the divergent visions of the Joint and the WJC clashed.

Once it became clear that the Germans really had embarked on the systematic extermination of European Jewry, this conflict only intensified. Inevitably, the Jewish relief organizations were pervaded by an escalating sense of helplessness in the face of the unfolding genocide, and specific schemes relatively close to home on which they could still exert some measure of influence took on a heightened significance as beacons of hope in a landscape of unyielding darkness. Some measure of hope was necessary not only in order to uphold the morale in the relief organizations themselves but also to ensure they could go on persuading the public that they were engaged in worthwhile activity deserving of further funding. As Yehuda Bauer has pointed out, 'fearing that too gloomy a picture might cause American Jewry to give less', the Joint emphasized in the run up to the Bermuda Conference (which will be discussed in the following chapter) that Europe's Jews 'are not yet dead, not by far. Even in darkest Poland there is organized Jewish life – committees that still function and leadership that guides Jews through these difficult days. It is up to us to preserve as much of this as possible'.[72]

That the Joint focused an extraordinary measure of attention on the British West Indies, given the relatively small number of refugees who either made it there or had a realistic prospect of getting there, is also borne out by its expenditure. Between 1936 and 1943, the Joint spent $2,794,450 in total on activities in twenty-five Central and South American countries. Of this, 5.5 per cent ($153,700) went towards its engagement in the British West Indies.[73] In 1940, for example, the Joint subsidized refugee activities in Argentina with $1,350 but spent $1,680 on Trinidad alone.[74] While only a tiny fraction of the refugees in Argentina required assistance, the Joint had to provide aid to a substantial proportion of the refugees in the British West Indies, including virtually all the Jewish refugees in Gibraltar Camp.

The Phoney War

With the onset of war it became even more difficult for Jewish refugees from Europe to cross the Atlantic. As the belligerent powers sought to divert as much shipping capacity as possible to the military, civilian shipping was squeezed. Ships crossing the Atlantic had to travel through the waters of a variety of states that were now pitted against one another. Frequently, Jews from Greater Germany travelling on German ships as they desperately sought to flee Nazi persecution were nevertheless subject to controls and obstacles because they were considered enemy aliens by the powers pitted against Germany (and, as we will see in the following chapter, they were often interned as a consequence). Last but by no means least, there was the risk that ships transporting refugees might be attacked and sunk.

One of the ships with refugees on board that was overtaken by the war was the *Wangoni*. The *New York Times* suggested on 24 September that the

war has produced few situations with more tragic irony than the plight of forty German Jews who were en route to South Africa on the German liner Wangoni when the crisis developed, and who apparently have no option but to spend years waiting aboard ship here [in the Spanish port of Vigo] until the conflict ends.

The Wangoni, which sailed from Hamburg on Aug. 11, was past the Canary Islands when she received orders to turn back and put in at Vigo. ... [S]ince the refugees are of German nationality, even though they are fleeing Nazi rule, they have been told that their existing permits to enter South Africa are no longer valid.

The Spanish government had agreed to let the refugees proceed to Portugal, but 'the Portuguese government thus far has refused'. Among the refugees trapped on the *Wangoni* was one Max Levy, 'a middle-aged Berlin interior decorator, whose father was an American and who lived in New York from 1897 to 1900. He has a brother, Ernst Lewy, living in Los Angeles'. Apart from the forty Jewish refugees on the *Wangoni*, another four were on the *Orizaba*, which had been en route to Venezuela but was now also stuck in Vigo. They were 'Mr. and Mrs. Max Oppenheimer and Mr. and Mrs. Meyer Oppenheimer, all of Frankfort on the Main. … [B]oth couples have sons living in Chicago'.[75]

On 18 November 1939, the Dutch ship, *Simon Bolivar*, en route from Amsterdam to Paramabiro in Dutch Guiana,[76] was sunk by a German mine off Harwich. It was one of eight ships sunk by German mines off the English east coast over the weekend of 18/19 November, signalling a substantial escalation of German naval warfare.[77] 'Among the passengers', the *Daily Boston Globe* reported, 'were Netherland citizens traveling to the West Indies, British citizens bound for Barbados and Trinidad, and German refugees'.[78] According to initial estimates, it was assumed that more than one hundred passengers and crew had lost their lives, but the number was later corrected to 86.[79] Among the Britons killed were Victor H. Brooke, assistant superintendent in the Trinidadian police,[80] and the manager of the Barclay's Bank branch in Barbados, W.A. Martin.[81]

Among the severely injured were Flory Cohen and Felix Levi, refugees from Germany, who would later marry and take on the surname Van Beek. Following their recovery in England they were sent back to the Netherlands, where they survived in hiding, initially in the house of Piet (Petrus Franciscus) Brandsen – a strict Catholic who refused to hide them together unless they married first, and who has been honoured as one of the righteous among the nations[82] – and his family and, following his arrest in January 1944, in the home of the Hornsveld family. In 1948, they emigrated to the United States.[83]

The *Simon Bolivar* had previously taken Jewish refugees to Trinidad in November 1938, among them Erich Tauscher, his wife Bertha Tauscher, née Stecher, and their daughters, Trudie and Alice (see Figure 3.1). Erich Tauscher had been arrested during the November Pogrom but Bertha Tauscher was able to secure his release on the strength of their planned emigration to Trinidad where they joined her brother, Victor Stecher, who had arrived on the island on 13 October 1938 with his wife, Sophie Stecher, née Baltinester, and their son, Hans, as well as Victor Stecher's brother Wilhelm and Sophie Stecher's sister, Wilhelmine Baltinester. Baltinester was a widely published author of mostly light-hearted short pieces in a range of German and Austrian periodicals. We will meet the Tauscher and Stecher families again later on.

After the End of the Phoney War

As naval warfare intensified, Bermuda became one of the convoy points for Allied shipping across the Atlantic. While this did not in itself make Bermuda any less vulnerable to the impact of shipping shortages and interrupted supply lines due to shipping losses, it did benefit from being one of the convoy points. As the *Baltimore Sun* reported in February 1941 under the heading 'Shipping Boom Brought to Bermuda by War. Island Made Busiest Maritime Junction in World for its Size', the number of ships 'entering and clearing at Hamilton and St. George's ... was nearly double' that of the previous year. 'These figures', it noted, 'disclose what the establishment of a convoy base here last May has meant to the colony in the way of shipping dues'.[84]

Bermuda's status led to some tension between Britain and the United States over Britain's right to inspect and censor US goods and documents being sent either way. In late August 1940, the *Chicago Daily Tribune* published a report with the title, 'Bermuda Again is Bottleneck for Mail to U.S.'. It explained that '842 mail bags had been removed from American export-ships at Hamilton in the last 18 days'.[85] A few days earlier, the *New York Times* had reported the arrival of more than one hundred new censors in Bermuda 'to strengthen the local censorship staff engaged in examining mail – a work that has been vastly increased lately with the calls of American Export liners on weekly voyages from the United States to Lisbon'. It added that 'more than 1,000 bags of mail have been taken from two American Export liners calling here in the last fortnight'.[86]

One case that caused particular outrage was that of the *Exochorda*. Until the end of the Phoney War, the *Exochorda* had run between Haifa and the United States, stopping at a variety of Mediterranean ports. On her last journey on this line, she had been damaged by an Italian anti-aircraft shell while docking in Genoa. Following the German defeat of France, and Italy's entry into the war in June 1940, Roosevelt declared the Mediterranean a combat zone, and from the end of June to the end of October the *Exochorda* ran between Lisbon and the US as one of the four ships that provided the already mentioned weekly direct service on this line. At the end of October, she was requisitioned by the military.

On 31 August 1940, the *Baltimore Sun* reported that the authorities in Bermuda had taken three German passengers off the ship in what was 'believed to be the first British removal of passengers from an American vessel'. They had been identified by the ship's captain, Wenzel Habel, as 'Dr. H. Block, A. Sandous and H. Schiffmann'.[87] There was subsequently some confusion in the press about the identity of the three passengers. According to the *New York Times* they were 'Dr. Herbert Bloch, 37 years old, on his way here to teach at a medical school in Boston; Hans Schiffmann, 33, and Adolph Sandhaus, 41, an Austrian jeweller who had been working in Belgium'. A fourth passenger, 'Mr. Sandhaus's brother-in-law, Sigmund Engelhart, also a jeweller, being 59 and therefore above military age, was allowed to remain on the ship'.[88] The *Hartford Courant*, on the other hand, was convinced that the first passenger was in fact not called Bloch but Block, and reported that he had 'told passengers that he was en route to Boston to teach political economy in a college'. Schiffmann, moreover, 'had informed shipboard acquaintances that he was en route to Richmond, Va., to visit relatives whom he did not name'.[89] If the *New York Times* was correct in reporting that 99 of the 166 passengers on board the *Exochorda* were US citizens, 'and the others refugees from virtually every country in Europe', then one has to assume that the three Germans taken off the ship in Bermuda were also refugees.[90]

It is unlikely, though, that the removal of these three passengers would have drawn quite as much attention if the authorities in Bermuda had not also confiscated some film reels from an American photographer travelling on the *Exochorda*. The *Hartford Courant* continued its report:

> More exciting to the passengers than the removal of the three Germans was the seizure of film from Frank W. Van Lew, of Lawton, Okla.
>
> Van Lew said he had been given 16 rolls of German war films in Switzerland and that some of the films, made by Germans, showed action in the historic British retreat from Dunkerque, France.
>
> When the British censor demanded the films, the photographer said a general scuffle ensued on the ship's deck.
>
> Later, he said, the censor went ashore and 'came back with three big police officers who took them from me forcibly'.[91]

In early October, one of the other ships running on the weekly line between Lisbon and the United States, the *Exochorda*'s sister ship, the *Excalibur*, 'received a thorough going-over at the hands of the British officials' in Bermuda. On this occasion, 'one Gino Treves, a 23-year-old Italian Jew, was removed for internment despite the tearful pleas of his mother, Mrs. Inez Treves'.[92]

When the *Exochorda* returned from her final trip from Lisbon, arriving in Jersey City on 26 October 1940, she brought with her, inter alia, the general secretary of the Socialist and Labour International, Friedrich Adler, with his wife Katia and their son Felix; the former Heidelberg professor and joint recipient of the 1922 Nobel Prize for Physiology or Medicine, Otto Meyerhof; and the critical journalist, Konrad Heiden.[93] Anticipating her arrival in a few days' time, the *New York Times* had reported that 'the Exochorda is also bringing from Lisbon 2,343 sacks of mail, which', it added, 'will probably be reduced by half when the liner goes into Bermuda and it is taken ashore for examination by the British censors'.[94]

In the meantime, another ship found itself potentially facing a situation similar to that of the *St Louis* in the spring of 1939. The *Quanza* left Lisbon in the second week of August 1940, destined for Mexico. The refugees on board had acquired transit visas from the Mexican consul in Lisbon to allow them to travel to Guatemala. As Guatemala had since refused to let them enter, the Mexican authorities consequently no longer honoured the transit visas, and the *Quanza* was turned away when it arrived in Veracruz.[95]

She then tried her luck in New York and in Norfolk (Virginia), but to no avail. As the *Washington Post* noted on 13 September, the *Quanza* was 'tied up at Sewell's Point [in Norfolk] … to load coal for the return trip to Lisbon'.[96] The day before it had reported in more detail on the 'eighty-nine disconsolate European refugees' on the *Quanza*. While the coal was being taken on board, 'the women in the group of mixed nationality, some with children at their side, wept at the rail as they talked with friends and relatives gathered on the rainy and windswept pier. Immigration officers kept the two groups apart'. One of the passengers, Hilmar Wolff, had jumped off the ship and managed, 'after a hard battle with current and surf', to swim ashore, but he was then caught and returned to the *Quanza*.[97] According to the *Baltimore Sun*, he was 'one of two Germans aboard the ship' and he 'said his return to Germany would mean his death'.[98]

In order to delay the ship's return to Europe, lawyers sued the owners of the *Quanza* on behalf of four of the passengers in the hope that the ship would be able to remain in the United States until court proceedings had been completed. After a four-day stand-off, however, the situation was resolved positively. As the *New York Times* reported on 16 September 1940, the 'eighty-odd European refugees, held aboard the Portuguese steamer Quanza for nearly four days before being permitted to land, were visitors on American soil yesterday. Permission to leave the ship was granted [to] the refugees after days of questioning by immigration officials and under legal latitude given [by] the Immigration Service'.[99]

On 16 January 1941, all refugees and holders of Italian or German passports, among them twelve Jewish refugees, were taken from the steamship *Argentina*, which was passing through Trinidad en route from Buenos Aires to New York, and transferred to the internment camp in Trinidad. Drawing on Joint funds, the local refugee committee cared for the refugees whilst the

New York office of the Joint sorted out their papers. On 14 February, all of them, except for one Italian Jewish refugee, were able to proceed to New York.[100]

Total War

On 22 June 1941, Germany invaded the Soviet Union. Emboldened by the spectacular initial success of the Soviet campaign, Hitler decided that the Nazis no longer needed to put off a 'Final Solution of the Jewish Question' until the end of the war.[101] By the middle of October a rough plan for the systematic extermination of European Jewry had been decided upon, and on 23 October the regime banned further Jewish emigration. By early 1942 at the latest, Western governments knew about the genocide, though this knowledge was not made widely available to the public until December of that year.

When the Phoney War ended, Lisbon began to play a more prominent role. Now it was the only remaining exit route open to Jewish refugees trying to leave Europe. As shipping capacity continued to be squeezed and naval warfare continued to escalate, Lisbon became an ever-tighter bottleneck and ticket prices skyrocketed, making it yet more difficult for refugees to flee Europe. As the backlog ballooned, Portuguese officials became increasingly reluctant to grant entry to any further refugees, especially if they had no valid visas to travel on from Lisbon. Several thousand were left stranded in Spain where they were interned, many in the concentration camp in Miranda del Ebro.[102]

In order to expedite emigration from Lisbon, the Joint began to purchase in advance the entire passenger space available on vessels sailing from Lisbon to Western destinations under the flags of neutral countries. The Joint's representatives in Lisbon estimated the numbers of refugees with valid papers and then booked corresponding numbers of tickets, which were paid for by the New York office with the help of Treasury licences. The tickets were then distributed to affiliated organizations and emigration committees such as HICEM, who would choose the individual refugees for each passage. Between December 1941 and May 1942, approximately a dozen ships left Lisbon for transatlantic destinations, carrying about five thousand refugees aided by the Joint and HICEM, all of whom had bona fide visas for one country or another in the Americas. For once, the Jewish refugee organizations were largely in control of the process, and the transports ran relatively smoothly.

Yet many refugees continued to make their own arrangements and often fell into the hands of unscrupulous agents who would book them onto unseaworthy vessels – many of them freight ships with few if any cabins, and hastily improvised dormitories – and sold them invalid visas. Today, the best-known account of the misery the passage to the Americas entailed for many refugees is that by the (then still largely unknown) anthropologist Claude Lévi-Strauss, in *Tristes Tropique*, telling of his journey to Martinique on the *Capitaine Paul Lemerle*, which left Marseilles on 24 March 1941. Yet *Tristes Tropiques* was not published until 1955, nor does there seem to be any contemporaneous mention of the *Paul Lemerle* in the anglophone press. At the time, it was the case of the *Navemar* that alerted the public to the conditions many refugees were enduring on their passage across the Atlantic.

Under the heading, 'Refugee Ship Waits at Pier in Bermuda', the *New York Times* reported on 31 August 1941:

> Packed aboard the small Spanish freighter Navemar with normal accommodations for fifteen passengers, about 1,200 European refugees are vicariously sampling the New World freedom from the crowded deck of the vessel alongside the Hamilton docks.
>
> The Navemar arrived yesterday and at present it is uncertain whether she will continue to Cuba or the United States ... Most of the refugees ... are destined for the United States, with some bound for Cuba.
>
> It is believed that the ship is under private charter and her closely huddled passengers, bunking in tiers in the holds, are said to have paid from $400 to $1,500 for passage.

Of the 1,200 passengers, '212 ... are reported without country, and 593 are German Jews. The others include Belgians, Poles, French, Czechs and Russians'. Eleven passengers apparently landed in Bermuda and 330 subsequently in Havana, before the remaining '769 exiles' proceeded to Brooklyn.[103] Rather remarkably, the initial report went on to state that 'visitors aboard the ship describe the refugees as happily indifferent to their cramped quarters'.[104]

Yet a very different picture emerged once the *Navemar* had arrived in Havana. The *Christian Science Monitor* noted on 6 September that the boat had 'creaked and groaned at anchorage today', and was being 'described as the saddest vessel ever to reach this white-washed harbour city'.[105] When it arrived in Brooklyn on 12 September, the *New York Times* too headlined that the *Navemar* had been 'Packed Like a Cattle Boat' and mentioned 'soiled bunks and rickety steamer chairs', noting that, 'after seeing the ship, with its improvised outside kitchen, the two "decks" of tiered bunks below in the windowless holds ... officials expressed surprise that "casualties" had been so few'.[106] Six passengers had died en route, and 'thirty-five in various stages of illness were taken to Ellis Island' on arrival.[107]

Public attention was sustained by the fact that a constantly growing number of passengers took legal action against the owners of the *Navemar*, the Compania Espanola de Navegacion Maritime, S.A. On 19 September, the *New York Times* reported under the headline 'Navemar Owners Sued by Refugees. Spanish Vessel Held "Floating Concentration Camp"'.[108] By the end of January 1942, the number of passengers who had joined the action had risen to 593.[109] Of these, 575 persevered, roughly half of them represented by Saul Sperling, and in February 1943 they were awarded a settlement of $250,000.[110]

The Pulitzer prize-winning writer, Edna Ferber, who championed the cause of refugees fleeing the Nazis, wrote in the *Christian Science Monitor*:

> Everyone knows that the ship was a thing of stench and filth … I talked with many of them [the passengers] and I know that they slept on the decks or on the floor in the hold without sheets or blankets, and rats ran over them. … [T]he stewards slapped them, and if they complained, threatened them with the promise that the ship would turn around and go back.

Resorting to considerable hyperbole, Ferber suggested that 'since the days of the slave traders, it is doubtful if a more ghastly ship has sailed the Atlantic'.[111]

The reporting on the *Navemar* also reflected on the treatment the passengers had received while in Bermuda. On 18 September, the *Los Angeles Times* published excerpts from an account by one of the passengers, Raissa Gutman, under the heading 'Diary of "Hell Ship" Relates New Horrors'. Gutman noted that British officials were shocked by the bad sanitary conditions on board. Her account continued:

> Toys and parcels with chocolate are given to the children by the British. The passengers loudly cheer at the inhabitants who throw oranges for the children.
> …
> The inhabitants have sent new and old clothes aboard. Many passengers came from concentration camps and the clothes come in very handy to them.
> Children up to 6 years with their mothers, and others up to 16 unaccompanied, have been invited by local women for a walk.
> Brushing and washing of children. They are unrecognizable. All are taken to a small island where they spend several hours and are offered chocolate and sweets. They return happy and excited.[112]

The solidarity of the local population was also mentioned in other press reports. Already on 1 September, the *New York Times*, under the heading 'Refugees Like Bermuda. "First Real Humanity" Is Found There En Route from Europe', reported that 'the local Daughters of the British Empire collected clothing and other gifts for the refugees'.[113]

Relating his experiences on the *Paul Lemerle* earlier that year, Lévi-Strauss wrote in *Tristes Tropiques*:

I did not begin to understand the situation until the day we went on board between two rows of helmeted *gardes mobiles* with sten guns in their hands, who cordoned off the quayside, preventing all contact between the passengers and their relatives or friends who had come to say goodbye, and interrupting leave-takings with jostling and insults.[114]

'Far from being a solitary adventure', as he had fantasized the passage might be, 'it was more like the deportation of convicts. What amazed me even more than the way we were treated', he continued,

was the number of passengers. About 350 people were crammed onto a small steamer which – as I was immediately to discover – boasted only two cabins with, in all, seven bunks. ... The rest of my companions, men, women and children, were herded into the hold, with neither air nor light, and where the ship's carpenters had hastily run up bunk beds with straw mattresses.[115]

Lévi-Strauss suspected that the *Paul Lemerle* was also 'carrying some kind of clandestine cargo', since 'both in the Mediterranean and along the west coast of Africa, we spent a fantastic amount of time dodging into various ports, apparently to escape inspection by the English navy'.[116]

Once the *Paul Lemerle* advanced southwards and heat increasingly became a problem, it was impossible to remain below and the deck was gradually turned into dining-room, bedroom, day-nursery, wash-house and solarium. But the most disagreeable feature was what is referred to in the army as the sanitary arrangements. Against the rail on either side – port for the men, starboard side for the women – the crew had erected two pairs of wooden huts, with neither windows nor ventilation; ... the unventilated huts were made of planks of unseasoned, resinous pine which, after being impregnated with dirty water, urine and sea air, began to ferment in the sun and give off a warmish, sweet and nauseous odour.[117]

Consequently, on Lévi-Strauss's account,

When, after a month at sea, we sighted the Fort de France lighthouse in the middle of the night, it was not the prospect of an edible meal, a bed with sheets [or] a peaceful night's sleep [that] caused the passengers' hearts to swell with anticipation. ... Instead of the call 'Land! Land!' as in traditional sea stories, 'A bath, at last a bath, a bath tomorrow!' could be heard on every side.[118]

Yet, 'the passengers were soon to learn', said Lévi-Strauss, 'that their filthy, overcrowded boat was an idyllic refuge in comparison with the welcome they were to receive almost as soon as the ship docked'.[119]

While Lévi-Strauss was extremely fortunate in having secured a place in one of the two cabins, even his more prominent fellow passengers were evidently less fortunate. On board was also the German writer, Anna Seghers – who has left one of the most memorable accounts of the vagaries involved in assembling all the right papers and permissions to leave non-occupied France at this juncture in her novel, *Transit* – the French surrealist writer, André Breton, and the veteran Russian revolutionary, Victor Serge, who famously described the *Paul Lemerle* as an 'ersatz concentration camp'.[120]

The *Paul Lemerle* was one of at least six ships that took refugees from Marseilles to Martinique in the spring of 1941. Eric Jennings has described the scheme that opened up this short-lived escape route as 'the only … government-endorsed colonial emigration scheme ever pressed into service'.[121] The 'hybrid rescue-expulsion' scheme was initiated by the interior minister of the Vichy regime, Marcel Peyrouton, who was a colonial official by training and therefore well connected in the French colonial administration.[122] Even so, it was met with considerable resistance in Martinique and was born of 'a curious blend of humanitarianism and xenophobia'.[123] Jennings suggests that Peyrouton's initiative marked the 'crucial transition phase' between the propagation of Jewish emigration/expulsion by the Vichy regime and its subsequent complicity in the deportation of Jews to the death camps.[124]

The scheme was brought to a sudden end when, on 25 May 1941, the *Winnipeg*, with its 732 passengers on board, 419 of them refugees with transit visas, along with the *Arica*, was stopped in the Caribbean by a Dutch warship, the *Van Kingbergen*, acting on behalf of the British and US navies.[125] The Allies evaluated Peyrouton's scheme against the backdrop of the U-boat war raging in the Caribbean.[126] By the end of 1942, an estimated 36 per cent of all merchant shipping losses worldwide had occurred in the Caribbean. The estuary of the Mississippi in the Gulf of Mexico, the Windward passage and the area around Trinidad were the main flashpoints.[127] Thousands of lives were lost, foremost among them those of merchant seamen, many of whom were recruited from the Trinidad Royal Naval Volunteer Reserve, and for whom 'the sunny Caribbean became a place of horror. They died in their thousands from the effects of torpedo explosions, of heat stroke, of thirst, of despair, or simply by drowning and by the ever-present sharks'.[128]

The result was felt both in Britain, which was cut off from colonial supplies, and in the Caribbean, where most colonies depended on imported goods. The sinking of a ship would often leave one or more colonies without urgently needed supplies for weeks at a time.[129] The combined impact of shortages in civilian shipping, the heightened risk of passages to and through the Caribbean, and food shortages in the colonies lent further support to the argument against the option of directing further refugees towards the British West Indies.

That French ships should be making their way unharmed to Martinique under these circumstances sufficed to convince Britain and the United States that their tolerating this route ultimately favoured German interests. Moreover, they hoped that by cutting the connections between mainland France and the French West Indies, the latter might be cajoled into going over to De Gaulle. Finally, the British were grateful for every opportunity to appropriate shipping capacity from the enemy.

Among all three Allies with interests in the Caribbean – the Netherlands, Great Britain and the United States – there was also a considerable fear of 'fifth column' activities that might be initiated by Germans using the route to infiltrate the region. One of the Vichy-loyal passengers on the *Winnipeg*, a colonial officer called R.M. Sallé, reported that after the ship had been seized, while its fate was being determined, some of the younger passengers passed the time by singing Alfred Roland's *Halte-là, les Montagnards sont là*. Some British officers apparently confused 'Halte-là' for 'Heil Hitler'.[130] Reporting on the arrival of the *Winnipeg* in the colony, the *Trinidad Guardian* remarked that 'most of the faces seemed tired and worn from the ravages in Europe. Many of them had the refugee look'. Yet the paper then added that 'examinations will reveal how many of the refugee claims are spurious'.[131]

Manfred Goldfish later recalled the excitement that came to Camp Rested, the internment camp in Trinidad, when the passengers from the *Winnipeg* arrived.

Suddenly one morning we awoke to see a large fleet of buses arriving and discharging hundreds of people, while we were wondering how on earth this camp could accommodate this mass influx of people. [M]ore trucks arrived with soldiers who began immediately to set up tents. Our kitchen staff ... sent out frantic calls for helpers.[132]

Most of the refugees who were taken off the *Winnipeg* and brought to Trinidad had valid visas for the United States and were soon able to continue their journey. Yet in the meantime, on Goldfish's account, 'we got on well with our visitors, who included a theatrical group from Vienna who treated us with an absolutely wonderful performance of Offenbach's operetta "La Belle Helene", which was a huge success before a captivated, captive audience'.[133]

The *New York Times* reported on 14 June 1941 that 238 of the passengers taken from the *Winnipeg* had arrived in New York on the *Evangeline*. Among them were Rose Hilferding, the wife of the former Social Democratic German finance minister, Rudolf Hilferding; and Erika Biermann, the daughter of the former German chancellor, Hermann Müller, and secretary of the leading German Social Democrat, Rudolf Breitscheid. They had both been handed over to the Germans by the Vichy regime in February and did not survive. Also on board were the German photographer Yolla Niclas-Sachs and her husband, the lawyer Rudolf Sachs;[134] the granddaughter of the actress Sarah Bernhardt, Lysian Bernhardt; and, so the *New York Times* reported, 'Hermann Thorn, a former Viennese lawyer, accompanied by his wife, Finy, an opera singer'.[135] On 17 July, the *Los Angeles Times* reported the arrival there, by rail on the Union Pacific Challenger, of a Polish refugee who had been on the *Winnipeg* and was taken to Trinidad before reaching New York on the *Evangeline*, Edith Bienastocki, 'widowed refugee from France', with her five-month-old son, Peter.[136]

Among those able to continue on to the United States fairly soon were the Hockenheimer family from Karlsruhe, who settled in the Bay Area.[137] Julius Hockenheimer and his wife Milly Hockenheimer, née Loewenthal, had their children Rudolf ('Rudi') and Marianne with them. The family had owned a butcher supply business in Karlsruhe. Julius Hockenheimer had been interned in Gurs and was apparently released largely due to the fact that Rudolf Hockenheimer had volunteered with the American Friends Service Committee (AFSC) as a translator and was able to use his connections to the Quakers. Julius Hockenheimer never fully recovered, and died in San Francisco in 1952. Having assumed that they would proceed to the US via Martinique, the Hockenheimers had transferred their funds there and now found themselves temporarily unable to access them from Trinidad.[138] While in Camp Rested, one of the Hockenheimers' fellow refugees from the Netherlands, G.W. Mooy, created a watercolour portrait of Rudolf Hockenheimer.

At least seventeen passengers from the *Winnipeg*, all with German or Austrian passports, were unable to proceed, and remained interned in Trinidad whilst efforts were made to find other destinations for them. Their visas had all either expired or were invalid. Two passengers, for instance, had received their immigration visas to the United States in January in Marseilles, but the earliest direct passage they could have secured would have been in July. Hence their visas expired and they travelled on the *Winnipeg* on the assumption that they would be able to renew them in Martinique. Other passengers had visas for San Domingo and Cuba but lacked the transit visas for the United States that they needed to get there.[139] Notwithstanding efforts by the Joint in New York and the Jewish Refugee Society in Trinidad, some refugees from the *Winnipeg* were still interned in Trinidad in October 1941.[140]

The Vichy regime did not let the opportunity to accuse Britain and the United States of hypocrisy pass, as the *New York Times* reported under the heading 'Vichy Chides British For Seizing Emigres':

Charges of the British radio that the French ship Winnipeg, recently seized by the British Navy near Martinique, was carrying German nationals, called forth today the following retort from official circles here:

Figure 4.1 Portrait of a teenage Rudolf Hockenheimer by G.W. Mooy, courtesy of the U.S. Holocaust Memorial Museum.

It is impossible to satisfy everybody in this war. On one hand, in America, there is continued urging that France allow interned foreigners to leave the country. And, on the other, when she does so, the British Navy intercepts them as spies.

> The Winnipeg, it is said, was bound from Marseille to Martinique. All the foreigners aboard were political refugees from French internment camps, it is asserted, and they held visas not only from the countries to which they were bound but also for the countries of transit. For all those of German nationality, American relief or aid organizations had intervened, assuming responsibility for their departure from France.[141]

The demise of Peyrouton's scheme immediately affected another group of refugees who were trapped on the *Alsina*. The *New York Times* reported that they had left Marseille on 15 January 1941, scheduled to reach Rio de Janeiro, via a number of West African stops, on 7 February. Yet when they reached Dakar on 23 January, the Vichy-loyal authorities there refused to let the ship proceed further, 'apparently … motivated by fear that the British would seize the ship as they had [the *Alsina*'s sister ship] the Mendoza'. Confined to the docked ship in Dakar, the refugees were 'being ravaged by tropical fevers and undernourishment'.[142] Following the interception of the *Winnipeg* and the collapse of the Martinique route, it seemed clear that the refugees on board the *Alsina* had no realistic prospect of crossing the Atlantic, and they were taken from Dakar to Casablanca where they were interned, according to the *Christian Science Monitor*, together with 'passengers from two other refugee ships, the Wyoming and Monte Viso', both of which had 'arrived recently in Casablanca from Marseille'. As the *Christian Science Monitor* explained, 'the French Admiralty decided earlier this month to discontinue trans-Atlantic refugee sailings after a Royal Netherlands Navy warship intercepted the French liner Winnipeg and escorted her to Port-of-Spain, Trinidad'.[143] The *New York Times* likewise reported that the *Alsina* had been taken to Casablanca 'after the seizure by the British of the steamship Winnipeg'.[144] Against this backdrop, HICEM established an office in Casablanca in the hope that it might be able to assist the refugees from the *Alsina*.

In early October 1941, forty passengers from the *Alsina* were released and their expired visas were renewed by the Brazilian Consul in Casablanca. They were then transferred to a Spanish ship, the *Cabo de Buena Esperanza*, which was en route to Brazil. Yet when they reached Rio de Janeiro, the Brazilian authorities refused to accept the validity of their visas and they sailed on to Buenos Aires. When the Joint staged a concerted intervention, Argentina agreed to offer the refugees a ninety-day permit, provided they stayed in special accommodation in Buenos Aires.

Yet within days the Argentine government reversed its decision and ordered the refugees to board the *Cabo de Hornos*, which had since arrived in Argentina carrying yet more of the refugees who had been left stranded by the *Alsina*. The *Cabo de Hornos* began its passage back to Europe, 'her rails lined with eighty-six weeping Jewish refugees'. The ship's captain, Jose Lanz

Mayro, was quoted as saying he was sure he would not reach Cadiz with all of them, 'since the majority prefer suicide to the sombre future awaiting them'.[145] Yet the ship returned to Brazil after four days, in the hope that the intercessions on behalf of the refugees submitted not only by Jewish refugee organizations but also by Polish, Belgian, US and British officials might yet offer a solution.

The World Jewish Council, the Joint, HICEM and the Central Council for Refugees collaborated closely with affiliated Jewish aid organizations in Lisbon, Argentina, Brazil, Curaçao and Trinidad to try to find a solution. Throughout October and the first half of November 1941, cables went back and forth between Stephen Wise of the American Jewish Congress, Chief Rabbi Hertz in London, the Central Council for Refugees, and local refugee committees in Buenos Aires and Curaçao. In London, the Central Council for Refugees and Chief Rabbi Hertz negotiated with the deputy high commissioner for refugees and the Netherlands government in exile.[146] The refugees also requested entry to Mexico, where the Polish ambassador intervened on their behalf.

While 'tenacious negotiations' with the Mexican authorities were still ongoing,[147] the Dutch government in exile finally agreed, on 18 November 1941, to offer the refugees sanctuary in Curaçao for ninety days. This offer was made on the strength of an agreement worked out with the Joint, who had agreed to shoulder all costs of maintenance and find final destinations for the refugees.[148] On arrival, the eighty-three refugees were divided up by gender and interned in separate male and female internment camps. At the end of the war, nineteen refugees from the *Cabo de Hornos* were still in Curaçao and still being maintained by grants from the Joint.

That same month, November 1941, a group of Polish Jewish refugees arrived in Trinidad on board the *Lorenzo Marquez* and were granted entry on transit permits. Their visas for Costa Rica, issued in Lisbon in August 1940, had expired. They had come to Trinidad via France, Spain and Portugal, the East African Portuguese colony of Lorenzo Marquez, and Cape Town.[149] Most of them were able to move on to Cuba, but in 1942 eight of them were still in Trinidad. They were dependent on the aid and assistance of the Joint, the local refugee committee, and the Council for Refugee Settlement, an organization based in Johannesburg, which had funded their journey from Cape Town to Trinidad.[150]

The burden of supporting refugees who were temporarily stranded in Trinidad fell directly on the local Jewish refugee committees. Although they were reimbursed by the Joint in New York,[151] refugees regularly arrived without warning and the funds from the Joint were only adjusted retro-actively. Nor was money the only difficulty. On 26 November 1941, the president of the Jewish Association of Trinidad, Dr Oscar Pillersdorf, wrote to the Joint in New York about the refugees who had arrived on the *Lorenzo*

Marquez. They had been offered temporary accommodation in the internment camp but had turned it down because they were 'very religious people
and find it easier to eat koscher [*sic*]'. They were therefore housed with
local Jewish residents for the first few days, and the association paid for the
boarding costs. Pillersdorf used the opportunity to emphasize that, given the
ever-increasing number of refugees in transit, the association's resources were
becoming extremely stretched:

> As they live among us, we cannot see them starving. But, on the other hand,
> it is certainly unjust to put such a burden on the shoulders of a young and
> poor community. We need not tell you that there is hardly a day without new
> arrivals and passings of refugees through Trinidad. Many of them come to us
> for help. We are doing our utmost, and in many a time more than we can.[152]

Notes

1. Quoted in Saul Friedländer, *Nazi Germany and the Jews. Vol. 1: The Years of Persecution,
   1933–39* (London: Weidenfeld & Nicolson, 1997), 332.
2. Rebecca Rovit, 'Jewish Theatre: Repertory and Censorship in the Jüdischer Kulturbund,
   Berlin', in John London (ed.), *Theatre under the Nazis* (Manchester: Manchester
   University Press, 2000), 206; eadem, 'Cultural Ghettoization and Theater during the
   Holocaust: Performance as a Link to Community', *Holocaust and Genocide Studies*
   19(3) (2005), 460. See also eadem, *The Jewish Kulturbund Theatre Company in Nazi
   Berlin* (Iowa City: University of Iowa Press, 2012), 155–56.
3. Friedländer, *Nazi Germany and the Jews*, 333.
4. See Rebecca Rovit, *The Jewish Kulturbund Theatre Company in Nazi Berlin* (Iowa:
   University of Iowa Press, 2012), 213.
5. For Goldfish's biographical details see Su Goldfish (ed.), *Manfred Goldfish: The
   Schooldays of Freddy Karpf,* Bad Emser Hefte No. 310 (2010).
6. Goldfish, 'A Danger to Security', 2. Goldfish and his wife in fact travelled on the
   Cordillera.
7. Ibid., 2, 3.
8. The murdered diplomat, Ernst vom Rath, was a counsellor at the German Embassy in
   Paris, but not the ambassador.
9. The currency would obviously have been Reichsmark, not DM.
10. Unpublished typescript, courtesy of Su Goldfish. The sequence in this account of the
    ship voyage with the nightmare was included later by Goldfish and I have inserted it
    into the manuscript.
11. *Washington Post*, 12 January 1939, 1. Much of the following account is reconstructed
    on the basis of newspaper reports. Newspaper reports are likely to include errors and
    inaccuracies, but their use in this context is merited not least because a sense of the
    extent to which the newspaper-reading public could know about the events in question
    has an important role to play in judging relevant policy decisions.
12. Wischnitzer, *To Dwell in Safety*, 197.
13. Committee on Refugee Aid in South America, 1939, 4, JDC, File 112.

14. *Baltimore Sun*, 12 January 1939, 1. It named the refugees as: Heinrich Bank – 'a short, square-shouldered little dentist' – his wife, Pauline, and their daughter, Helga; Heinrich Bank's brother, Robert Bank, his wife, Margaret, and their son, Carl; Eric Pam and Isaac Gans and his wife, Helen (who also 'appeared to be vaguely related to the Banks'); and, finally, Dr. Alfred Wilder.
15. Jewish Telegraphic Agency (hereafter JTA), 13 January 1939, http://www.jta.org/1939/01/13/archive/closing-of-trinidad-to-refugees-creates-serious-situation-in-emigrant-aid (last accessed 1 May 2019).
16. Joint office Paris to Joint office New York, 21 February 1939, JDC, File 1059.
17. *The Times*, 28 February 1939, 13.
18. *Observer*, 26 February 1939, 18.
19. *Washington Post*, 2 April 1939, 7.
20. Razovsky, 'Bound for Nowhere', 4, JDC, File 1059.
21. Telegram no. 30, 2 February 1939 confidential. Governor of British Honduras (Burns) to the Secretary of State for the Colonies. TNA CO 123/376/6.
22. John G. Hibbert, 3 February 1939, TNA CO 123/376/6.
23. John G. Hibbert to H.E. Brooks, 4 February 1939, TNA CO 123/376/6.
24. Joint office New York to Joint office Paris, 28 February 1939, JDC, File 1059.
25. Morris Troper, European Executive Council of the Joint, to Joseph C. Hyman, Executive Director of the Joint, New York, 3 March 1939, JDC, File 1059.
26. Joint office New York to Joint office Paris, 21 February 1939, JDC, File 1059.
27. Jointfund Paris to Joint office New York, 10 March 1939, JDC, File 1059.
28. See Joint Running Publications, 4, JDC, File 151.
29. While anchoring off Miami, the JTA reported, 'the refugees got no sleep all night as floodlights lit up the ship to prevent passengers from jumping overboard. Most of the refugees lined the railings to greet friends and relatives who circled the ship in launches, but they saw hope vanish as the hours slipped by … More than a score of policy and marine boats accompanied the "floating refugee camp" out of Cuba's territorial waters as thousands of Cubans and Jews gathered on the shore to watch what many termed "a funeral of the living". Some groups of Cubans shouted: "Expel the Jews from the country!" Others replied: "Down with a Government which supports Fascism!"' Quoted in Zhava Litvac Glaser, 'Refugees and Relief: The American Jewish Joint Distribution Committee and European Jews in Cuba and Shanghai, 1938–1943', PhD thesis, CUNY Graduate School, 2015, http://academicworks.cuny.edu/gc_etds/561/ (last accessed 16 June 2019), 114.
30. Ibid., 101.
31. Sara L. Bloomfield, 'Museum Director's Foreword', in Sarah A. Ogilvie and Scott Miller, *Refuge Denied: The* St. Louis *Passengers and the Holocaust* (Madison: University of Wisconsin Press, 2006), ix–x, here ix.
32. C. Paul Vincent, 'The Voyage of the *St. Louis* Revisited', *Holocaust and Genocide Studies* 25(2) (2011), 252–89.
33. Ibid., 256.
34. Ibid., 264. In the event, Benitez first took a two-month leave of absence and then resigned on 1 June (Glaser, 'Refugees and Relief', 105, 108).
35. Vincent, 'Voyage of the *St. Louis*', 263.
36. Ibid., 265.
37. Ogilvie and Miller, *Refuge Denied*, 25. Following a second suicide attempt on board, the refugee passengers organized a suicide watch committee and enlisted 36 passengers to serve as suicide patrols (Glaser, 'Refugees and Relief', 116).

38. The Virgin Islands form part of the archipelago known as the Leeward Islands (southeast of Puerto Rico, west of Barbados and north of Trinidad). During the First World War the United States bought the western-most islands, formerly the Danish West Indies, which are now called the Virgin Islands of the United States. They are located to the west and south-west of the British Virgin Islands.

39. Rafael Medoff, 'American Responses to the Holocaust: New Research, New Controversies', *American Jewish History* 100(3) (2016), 390.

40. Glaser, 'Refugees and Relief', 98–100.

41. Ibid., 97.

42. Quoted in ibid.

43. Ibid., 120.

44. Joseph Hyman to Joseph P. Loeb, 19 July 1939, JDC, Cuba, 1933/44:507, quoted in ibid., 124.

45. Patricia Heberer (ed.), *Children during the Holocaust* (Lanham, MD: AltaMira Press, 2011), 79.

46. Liesl Joseph Loeb papers, United States Holocaust Memorial Museum Collection, Gift of Liesl Joseph Loeb, Accession Number: 1991.164.118, http://collections.ushmm.org/search/catalog/irn72801 (last accessed 2 May 2019).

47. Frank Caestecker and Bob Moore, 'From Kristallnacht to War, November 1938–August 1939', in eidem (eds), *Refugees from Nazi Germany and the Liberal European States* (New York: Berghahn Books, 2010), 300–301.

48. Lawrence Berenson and Cecilia Razovsky, 'Report on the JDC Efforts in the St. Louis Affairs' (Highly Confidential), 15 June 1939, JDC, Cuba, AR 1933/44:378, 119.

49. Vincent, 'Voyage of the *St. Louis*', 276.

50. *Washington Post*, 9 June 1939, 22.

51. Vincent, 'Voyage of the *St. Louis*', 281, note 43.

52. 'Seeking Refuge in Cuba', USHMM Holocaust Encyclopedia, https://www.ushmm.org/wlc/en/article.php?ModuleId=10007330 (last accessed 1 May 2019); *Globe and Mail* (Toronto), 2 June 1939, 1, cited in Amanda Grzyb, 'From Kristallnacht to the MS *St Louis* Tragedy: Canadian Press Coverage of Nazi Persecution of the Jews and the Jewish Refugee Crisis, September 1938 to August 1939', in L. Ruth Klein (ed.), *Nazi Germany, Canadian Responses: Confronting Antisemitism in the Shadow of War* (Montreal: McGill-Queen's University Press, 2012), 103.

53. *New York Times*, 24 June 1939, 5.

54. *New York Times*, 16 August 1939, 2.

55. *New York Times*, 15 January 1939, 30; JTA, 27 February 1939, http://www.jta.org/1939/02/27/archive/68-refugees-barred-from-uruguay (last accessed 16 June 2019); *New York Times*, 10 March 1939, 5.

56. *New York Times*, 3 June 1939, 4.

57. *New York Times*, 20 August 1939, 7.

58. Albert J. Phiebig et al., *HIAS Survey, 1940–1941* (New York: HIAS, 1942), 15. EmigDirect had stopped funding HICEM in 1934, and between 1933 and 1935 the Joint had already provided almost a third of the funds that HICEM disbursed to assist migrants. Yehuda Bauer, drawing on Joint sources, arrived at lower figures. On his account, the Joint contribution rose from 38 per cent of the HICEM budget in 1939 to 51 per cent in 1941 (Bauer, *American Jewry*, 30, note 17).

59. 'Aiding Jews Overseas: Report of the American Jewish Joint Distribution Committee, for 1941 and the first 5 months of 1942', 11, JDC, File 158.

60. Ronald Stent, 'Jewish Refugee Organisations', in Werner E. Mosse et al. (eds), *Second Chance: Two Centuries of German-Speaking Jews in the United Kingdom* (Tübingen: Mohr Siebeck, 1991), 583–84.
61. Ibid., 587.
62. Bauer, *American Jewry*, 458.
63. Samuel D. Kassow, *Who Will Write Our History? Rediscovering a Hidden Archive from the Warsaw Ghetto* (London: Penguin, 2009), 113–14.
64. Ibid., 356.
65. Paul Baerwald of the Joint to Norman Bentwich of the CGJ, 6 April 1939, JDC, File 1059.
66. Phiebig et al., *HIAS Survey*, 14.
67. Draft Report, Central Council for Jewish Refugees, 1939, 32, CBF Reel 2, F.5, AJA.
68. Bauer, *American Jewry*, 37.
69. David S. Wyman (ed.), *America and the Holocaust. Vol. 5: American Jewish Disunity* (New York: Garland, 1990), Document 282, Paul Baerwald of the Joint to the Rescue Commission of the American Jewish Congress, 7 December 1943.
70. Coordinating Committee, Brief Review of the Situation in Central and South America, 28 October 1940, JDC, File 115.
71. Minutes of the meeting of the Coordinating Committee on 22 October 1940, JDC, File 115.
72. Bauer, *American Jewry*, 192–93.
73. Committee on Refugee Aid in Central and South America, 'J.D.C. Work in Central and South America 1936–1943', 7 March 1943, JDC File 114.
74. Aiding Jews Overseas: Report of the AJJDC for 1940 and the first 5 months of 1941, 33–51, JDC, File 157.
75. *New York Times*, 24 September 1939, 39.
76. *New York Times*, 19 November 1939, 36.
77. *The Times*, 21 November 1939, 8.
78. *Daily Boston Globe*, 19 November 1939, 10.
79. *The Times*, 21 November 1939, 8.
80. *The Times*, 23 November 1939, 1.
81. *The Times*, 15 December 1939, 14.
82. Claudia Leonhard, *Das Unaussprechliche in Worte fassen: Eine vergleichende Analyse schriftlicher und mündlicher Selbstzeugnisse von weiblichen Überlebenden des Holocaust* (Kassel: Kassel University Press, 2013), 115–16; http://db.yadvashem.org/righteous/family.html?language=en&itemId=403895 (last accessed 1 May 2019).
83. See Felix and Flory Van Beek collection, United States Holocaust Memorial Museum Collection, Gift of Felix and Flory Van Beek and their Estate, Accession Number: 1990.23.241, http://collections.ushmm.org/search/catalog/irn109095 (last accessed 1 May 2019); for Flory Van Beek's own account see *Flory: Survival in the Valley of Death, Holocaust 1940–1945* (Santa Ana, CA: Seven Locks Press, 1998).
84. *Baltimore Sun*, 16 February 1941, 8. The story in fact came from the *New York Times*.
85. *Chicago Daily Tribune*, 27 August 1940, 4.
86. *New York Times*, 22 August 1940, 4.
87. *Baltimore Sun*, 31 August 1940, 4.
88. *New York Times*, 1 September 1940, 13.
89. *Hartford Courant*, 1 September 1940, C7.
90. *New York Times*, 1 September 1940, 13.
91. *Hartford Courant*, 1 September 1940, C7.

92. *Washington Post*, 6 October 1940, 16.
93. *New York Times*, 27 October 1940, 20.
94. *New York Times*, 24 October 1940, 51.
95. *Manchester Guardian*, 6 September 1940, 7.
96. *Washington Post*, 13 September 1940, 3.
97. *Washington Post*, 12 September 1940, 5.
98. *Baltimore Sun*, 12 September 1940, 13.
99. *New York Times*, 16 September 1940, 14.
100. Willi Grossmann, Secretary of the Jewish Refugee Society, Aliens Internment Camp, Trinidad to Robert Pilpel of the Joint, 16 January 1941, Joint, File 1048.
101. In the words of Christopher Browning: 'Nazi racial policy was radicalized at points in time that coincided with the peaks of German military success, as the euphoria of victory emboldened and tempted an elated Hitler to dare evermore drastic policies. With the "war of destruction" in the Soviet Union underway and the imminent prospect of all Europe at his disposal, the last inhibitions fell away. Hitler's final hesitations in August 1941 – to wait until "after the war" – were overcome in late September and early October, with the last great military encirclements that still promised an early victory' (Browning, *Origins of the Final Solution*, 427).
102. On Franco's concentration camp system, see Javier Rodrigo, 'Exploitation, Fascist Violence and Social Cleansing: A Study of Franco's Concentration Camps from a Comparative Perspective', *European Review of History* 19(4) (2012), 553–73.
103. *New York Times*, 13 September 1941, 19.
104. *New York Times*, 31 August 1941, 16.
105. *Christian Science Monitor*, 6 September 1941, 8.
106. *New York Times*, 13 September 1941, 19.
107. *New York Times*, 20 February 1943, 7.
108. *New York Times*, 19 September 1941, 25.
109. *New York Times*, 28 January 1942, 21.
110. *New York Times*, 20 February 1943, 7.
111. *Christian Science Monitor*, 25 September 1941, 24. For an extremely interesting and thoughtful discussion of Ferber's complex dealings with her own German Jewish relatives, see Laurel Leff, 'Ties that Bound, Ties that Broke: Edna Ferber's Sponsorship of Refugees from Nazi Germany' (video, 2010), https://repository.library.northeastern.edu/files/neu:cj82mf10m (at 28:10) (last accessed 16 June 2019).
112. *Los Angeles Times*, 18 September 1941, 7.
113. *New York Times*, 1 September 1941, 8.
114. Claude Lévi-Strauss, *Tristes Tropiques* (London: Penguin, 2011), 24.
115. Ibid.
116. Ibid., 25.
117. Ibid., 25–26.
118. Ibid., 26.
119. Ibid., 27.
120. Victor Serge, *Memoirs of a Revolutionary, 1901–1941* (London: Oxford University Press, 1963), 366.
121. Eric Jennings, 'Last Exit from Vichy France: The Martinique Escape Route and the Ambiguities of Emigration', *Journal of Modern History* 74(2) (2002), 291.
122. Eric Jennings, '"The Best Avenue of Escape": The French Caribbean Route as Expulsion, Rescue, Trial, and Encounter', *French Politics, Culture & Society* 30(2) (2012), 46; Jennings, 'Last Exit from Vichy', 293.

123. Jennings, 'Last Exit from Vichy', 295.

124. Ibid., 292.

125. Ibid., 300.

126. In the course of the Second World War, seventeen German submarines were sunk in the Caribbean, amounting to 2 per cent of all U-boat losses. Yet the number of merchant ships sunk by the Germans amounted to an average of 23.5 per sunk submarine. Nowhere was German submarine warfare more successful than in the Caribbean. Dwight R. Messimer, 'Foreword', in Kelshall, *U-Boat War*, xi–xii, here xi.

127. See Kelshall, *U-Boat War*, xiv–xvi.

128. Ibid., xvi.

129. Poole, *The Caribbean Commission*, 181. As J. Edgar Hoover reported to the Department of State in June 1942 about the state of affairs in Jamaica, 'there have been many complaints that storekeepers, who for the most part are Chinese, refuse sales to poor people and hold their goods for sale to wealthy customers from whom they are able to obtain higher prices. There has been a marked increase in the number of grocery store robberies, and the merchants have requested to arm themselves' (J. Edgar Hoover, FBI, to the Assistant Secretary of State, 5 June 1942, NARA, RG595062, Decimal File 1940–44, File no. 844D.1112/10-2644). The FBI was monitoring communist activity in Jamaica.

130. Jennings, 'Last Exit from Vichy', 311–12.

131. *Trinidad Guardian*, 31 May 1941, 1, 5, here 5.

132. Goldfish, untitled typescript, 9.

133. Ibid., 9–10.

134. http://digital.cjh.org/R/73TS5DPF6HJAEKFSMM7TU9VRVXC3Q1BLPTG56AM MADUR9ATJ8F-00299?func=dbin-jump-full&object%5Fid=503733&local%5Fbas e=GEN01&pds_handle=GUEST (last accessed 2 May 2019). See also Jennings, *Escape from Vichy*, 92–93, who lists the other photographers on board the *Winnipeg* on her last voyage to Martinique in May 1941 including Fred Stein, Josef Breitenbach, Ilse Bing, Chaim Lipnitzki, Charles Leirens and Ylla (Camilla Koffler).

135. *New York Times*, 14 June 1941, 8.

136. *Los Angeles Times*, 17 July 1941, 10.

137. For the following, see Ralph M. Hockley, *Freedom Is Not Free* (Houston, TX: Brockton, 2000).

138. Ibid., 72.

139. Jewish Refugee Society, Trinidad, to the Joint's Subcommittee on Refugee Aid in Central and South America, 4 August 1941, JDC, File 1048.

140. Moses W. Beckelman, Report to the Joint in New York, 19 October 1941, JDC, File 1048.

141. *New York Times*, 5 June 1941, 5.

142. *New York Times*, 3 March 1931, 4.

143. *Christian Science Monitor*, 20 June 1941, 6.

144. *New York Times*, 26 June 1941, 6.

145. *New York Times*, 9 November 1941, 6.

146. See WJC Buenos Aires, cable to Stephen Wise, 5 November 1941; Sumner Welles, cable to the American Jewish Congress, 7 November 1941; American Jewish Congress, cable to the Jewish Community in Curaçao, 11 November 1941 (American Jewish Archives, Cincinnati, WJC Series H, H213/Curaçao). See also Central Council for Jewish Refugees to Chief Rabbi Hertz, 14 November 1941; Deputy High Commissioner for Refugees to Chief Rabbi Hertz, 17 November 1941 (AJA, MS175 Hertz 1/3).

147. Daniel Gleizer, *Unwelcome Exiles: Mexico and the Jewish Refugees from Nazism, 1933–1945* (Leiden: Brill, 2014), 215.
148. JDC, File 158.
149. Edgar Gruen, Secretary of the Jewish Refugee Society, to Frederick Borchardt, Secretary of the Subcommittee on Refugee Aid in Central and South America, 24 November 1941, JDC, File 1048.
150. Dr Oscar Pillersdorf, President of the Jewish Association of Trinidad to the Joint, 26 November 1941; Otto Malameth, President of the JAT to Robert Pilpel, Secretary of the Subcommittee on Refugee Aid in Central and South America, 19 December 1941; Council for Refugee Settlement to the Joint, 24 July 1942; Robert Pilpel to the Jewish Refugee Society, 21 August 1942, JDC, File 1048.
151. See, 'Aiding Jews Overseas: Report of the American Jewish Joint Distribution Committee for 1941 and the first 5 months of 1942', 22, JDC, File 158; see also JDC, File 151. The support given to refugees who were (technically speaking) in transit in Trinidad in the course of 1941 and the first five months of 1942 amounted to $4,400.
152. Oscar Pillersdorf, President of the JAT, to the Joint, 26 November 1941, JDC, File 1048.

Chapter 5

INTERNMENT, CAMPS AND MISSED OPPORTUNITIES

For most of the Jewish refugees from Germany and Austria, the often arduous flight to the British West Indies by no means marked the end of their travails. Many of them arrived 'just in time to be interned' there following the out-break of the Second World War.[1] To make matters worse, the internment of 'enemy aliens' seems to have been implemented more strictly and tenaciously in the British West Indies than it was in Britain.

The presence of substantial German communities that had settled in neighbouring South and Latin American countries prior to 1933 heightened the fear of fifth-column activity in the West Indies. Jewish refugees repeat-edly sought to clarify that they were surely beyond suspicion. The Jewish Association of Trinidad felt this acutely. Already in late August 1939, days before the German invasion of Poland, they sent a telegram to the German-Jewish Aid Committee in London, asking it to 'convey to the Government the fact that the Jews of Trinidad, including refugees, are completely loyal to Britain'. The cable said the refugees were all 'mindful of the hospitality, and gratefully pledge their support'.[2] The telegram was presumably passed on to the government, but it was also reported by the JTA, ensuring cover-age across the Jewish Commonwealth. To reinforce the message locally, the Jewish Association of Trinidad followed this by submitting a rather forceful statement to the *Trinidad Guardian*:

> To the public of Trinidad: Remarks have been publicly made that many of the Jews here in Trinidad are German spies ... this is an absurd charge, for the Jews

of the world have no greater enemy than present-day Germany ... We ask the people of Trinidad that all remarks against us as German spies cease. Such matters are logically subjects for the police, who know best how to handle them. To make wanton attacks without proof against us Jews smacks too much of the German spirit: for that is the true German method. True British spirit is what we ask for, and expect, from everyone in Trinidad.[3]

Yet these efforts seem to have been largely futile. When comprehensive internment was rolled out following the end of the Phoney War, the *Trinidad Guardian* published an editorial under the heading, 'The Fifth Column'. It welcomed the recent internment of enemy aliens. 'Some of the Jewish enemy aliens who found refuge here from the horrors of Nazism', it noted,

> have written suggesting that our campaign was based on anti-Semitism and appealing against internment on the ground[s] that it is impossible to be a Jew and also a Nazi. No fair-minded person will deny that there is merit in the statement that it is extremely unlikely for any Jew to be a Nazi. It must also be remembered, however, [that] it is still very possible to be a Jew and [to] remain a German.

Britain, after all, was at war not just with Nazism but with 'the whole German people whose warlike spirit and lust created the fertile foundation on which Hitler and his gang of murderers were able to build a regime of lust such as Nazidom'.[4]

The authors of most of the letters to the editor published by the *Trinidad Guardian* agreed with these sentiments. 'A Britisher' called for all enemy aliens to be interned without exception.[5] Another letter-writer claimed that he had seen an alien switch a radio to a German station and say 'Heil Hitler', so all refugees, whatever their sympathies, should be interned.[6] 'Loyalist' argued that even though Jews in Trinidad had been expelled from Germany now, they and their families had lived there all their lives, perhaps for generations. Consequently, some might well still feel a sense of loyalty towards Germany. To be sure, internment would be hard on Jews who had started to build up businesses and rebuild their lives in the colony. Even so, 'we must realise that we are at war with Germany and with all Germans regardless of whether they be Jewish-Germans, English-Germans, French-Germans, or any other kind of Germans; and that those Germans in our Country should be made to take the same punishment as other Germans who have been captured in other Allied countries'. Indeed, the refugees should not only be interned but also made to 'work for us, make them build roads, or some such useful work'.[7]

Some letter-writers expressed undisguised anti-Jewish resentment. The German Jews 'tell us these fantastic stories' about their struggles, one Shah

Soodeen complained, yet in fact they were extremely wealthy. Not unlike earlier Lebanese immigrants, they complained of poverty whilst accumulating wealth. He was 'inclined to believe', he continued, 'that there is a well-organized Nazi spy ring operating here which perhaps would destroy our oilfields and sugar factories, thus putting thousands out of employment'.[8]

That said, the powers given to the governors under Defence Regulations were also repeatedly used to quell indigenous political activism, including the internment of labour leaders such as Alexander Bustamante. In January 1941, the US consul in Jamaica, Hugh H. Watson, informed the State Department in Washington that the interned labour leaders in Jamaica were opposed not to Britain or her war effort but to the policies of the colonial government. Consequently, they in fact posed no threat to the security of the colony, and so the governor, Sir Arthur Richards, was misusing his powers.[9] Richards himself, writing to the Colonial Office, conceded that he was on 'shaky ground' with these measures.[10]

Yet the use of internment to repress political opposition was not unique to Jamaica. In Trinidad, Butler was interned on Nelson Island for the entire duration of the war. As Manfred Goldfish later recalled:

> One section of the island was cordoned off with barbed wire and was out of bounds to us. It contained a little hut and we noticed a carefully tended kitchen garden, fenced in to protect the plants from a large white goat and a number of chickens. This area was inhabited by a quiet man and his wife. He was a trade union leader who had tried to organise the islanders into a workers', peasants' and ratepayers' union. As the population in general was very much underpaid at this time, his activities met with some success. He was a very religious man and all his public meetings, we were told, always started and ended with a hymn. However, he had strongly anti-colonial convictions and aimed for the independence of the British possessions in the Caribbean. His aims were achieved after the war, but for the moment he was deprived of his liberty for the duration.[11]

In principle, internment in the Colonial Empire followed the practices implemented by the British government in the United Kingdom. There, only small numbers of supposedly particularly dangerous 'enemy aliens' were interned at the outbreak of war. Only when the Phoney War ended, in the summer of 1940, did the government move to the mass internment of residents who had come to Britain from enemy countries. Given how many of the interned Germans and Austrians were in fact refugees whose hatred of the Nazis could not have been more wholehearted, public opinion soon turned against internment, especially in the face of the mass deportations of internees to Canada and Australia. As is well known, the sinking of the *Arandora Star* lent particular force to the opposition to internment. En route to Canada, it was sunk by a German U-boat, costing the lives of somewhere between 446 and 486 Italian and 243 German and Austrian internees. Within little more than a year of the original nine internment camps in Britain, only two on the Isle of Man were left.

The implementation of internment policy in the British West Indies was uneven and the historical record is patchy. Given their geographic and strategic positions, some of the Caribbean islands continued to play a significant role as refugee (and, consequently, internment) centres during the war, foremost among them Trinidad and Jamaica (on which this chapter will principally focus), as well as Dominica, which was the main collection point for refugees who fled the Vichy-controlled West Indian colonies hoping to join the Free French Forces,[12] and Curaçao, which was controlled, with Allied support, by the Dutch government in exile.

British Guiana and Barbados, it would seem, sent their residents who qualified as enemy aliens to Trinidad or Jamaica. In February 1940, for example, one non-Jewish German and two German Jews were transferred from British Guiana to Jamaica; and in November of that year, three refugees were transferred from Barbados to the internment camp in Trinidad.[13] In 1943, 'a group of Jewish refugees from Axis countries who reached British Honduras' was 'sent from there to the United States for internment as enemy aliens' in Seagoville, Texas, where the National Refugee Service was then able to secure their release.[14]

Alongside the internment of enemy aliens and suspected enemy sympathizers from the West Indies, internment camps in the Caribbean had several additional functions. Suspicious passengers and transit passengers from passing ships were held in the camps, as were wounded Allied and captured enemy merchant seamen. Moreover, when the Phoney War ended the British transferred several hundred internees from Western Africa to Jamaica.

The different parties involved obviously had strong reasons for portraying life in the internment camps in varying ways, and accounts of the camps doubtless need to be taken with a pinch of salt (and in some cases a considerable one, at that). Even so, it does seem clear that conditions in the camps varied widely. The facilities included a military prison – a hastily adapted building whose unsuitability for the purpose was soon aggravated by overcrowding – and a purpose-built camp with its own leisure facilities. In Bermuda, internees resided in the stately Huntley Towers. As the *Washington Post* reported in December 1940 under the title 'Concentration Camp Luxury':

> Bermuda has the most lavish concentration camp in the world. It is an old Victorian mansion which was formerly used for extension courses by the Wildcliff Junior College, of Swarthmore, Pa. It is elaborately furnished, and

a fine collection of oil paintings hang on the walls of three drawing rooms. There are palm trees around it, [along with] hibiscus flowers and bougainvillea vines and a general air of subtropics luxury. It is surrounded by barbed wire. Its name is Huntley Towers.

Interned in the concentration camp are 18 enemy aliens, Germans and Italians. They lead such a life of luxury that persons arrested in Bermuda ask to be sent to the concentration camp instead of the jail. Although they have army rations, a number of the inmates are quite wealthy and send out for additional delicacies. One of the best watch repair men in Bermuda is an inmate of the camp. Now, if you want your watch repaired, you send it into the concentration camp, where he repairs it and has it sent back. He is carrying on his business behind barbed wire.[15]

Even allowing for the possibility that the author of this report was wearing somewhat rose-tinted glasses when visiting Huntley Towers, the apparent comfort of the camp in Bermuda definitely stood in marked contrast to conditions in the other internment facilities.

Trinidad

Although only twenty-two refugees were initially interned, virtually all Jews in Trinidad (including those who had come from Poland and Romania) were required to comply with the Aliens Restriction Order of September 1939, which stipulated that they report daily to the police, observe a curfew and remain in Port of Spain. Initially, internees were taken to the Five Islands, located in the Gulf of Paria, some two miles to the west of Port of Spain. The men were brought to Nelson Island, which had served as the reception centre for indentured labourers – Trinidad's Ellis Island, as it were – between 1866 and 1917, and the women and children to Caledonia Island.

As Manfred Goldfish later recalled in an undated typescript called 'Nelson Island':

> There was no electricity on the island, and gasoline pressure lamps provided lighting. Water was another problem, as the island was too small to support natural springs. Rainwater had to be stored in large sheet-metal tanks and had to be used sparingly. Toilet facilities were somewhat unique and consisted of wooden huts built on platforms overhanging the 100-feet high cliff. They had wooden benches with appropriate holes cut, and you sat there suspended in mid-air, so to speak. It was a simple and hygienic arrangement, but somewhat uncomfortable when there was a high wind.

Hans Stecher, whom we met in the previous chapter, has described the mood of the internees as they found themselves separated by sex, yet

Figure 5.1 View of internment camp on Nelson Island, 2001. Photograph by the author.

within sight and shouting distance of each other; not far away is Carrera, the official prison island, and the waters around the area are said to be shark-infested. … I was young enough to see mostly the beauty of our surroundings, and played down the unpleasant parts of the situation. … They [the older internees] could not help but feel bitterness and resentment at being thus mistreated, of being deprived of their newly found freedom and, having just sent out new roots, [of] being so abruptly and rudely uprooted once more. The stigma of being branded 'enemy alien' was almost intolerable to us.[16]

By 1941, four camps had been established in Trinidad. Nelson Island now served as the location for a POW camp, while an internment camp ('Camp Rented'), a rest camp and a detention centre, had been set up in St James, a suburb of Port of Spain. Refugees of 'enemy alien' nationality were placed in Camp Rented.

Survivors from Allied ships that had been attacked by the Germans, most of them merchant seamen, were housed in the detention centre, as were the interned labour leaders. It also served as a transit facility for passengers taken from intercepted ships who were neither prisoners of war nor enemy aliens, and as a clearing centre for refugees taken from ships such as the *Winnipeg*. Once their papers had been checked, they were either allowed to proceed on their journey or, if they did not possess appropriate papers, moved to either the internment camp (if they were enemy aliens) or the rest camp (if they were not).[17] Refugees trapped in transit were often interned for considerable periods of time. Given that they had no legal status in Trinidad, internees in transit had no recourse to the Advisory Board and were thus unable to appeal against their internment.

Potential internees fell into three categories: nationals of enemy countries; those who had resided in enemy countries as aliens; and anyone else suspected of sympathizing with, or aiding, the enemy. Those in the first category were interned without exception under a general order; those in the second category were routinely detained unless the Aliens Investigation Committee specifically stipulated otherwise; and those in the third category were judged on a case-by-case basis, and interned only if the committee recommended their detention.[18] Refugees found themselves in all three categories. On 1 March 1940, the security forces in Trinidad informed the Colonial Office that of the 585 registered refugees in the colony, 366 fell under the Aliens Registration Order – 304 as enemy aliens and 62 because they had resided in enemy (or enemy-occupied) territory.[19]

By August 1940, 279 Jewish refugees had been interned in Trinidad. Upon appeal to the Advisory Committee, thirty-four Polish and stateless refugees were released. This almost certainly means that none of them came from Germany or Austria, because after the outbreak of war Britain did not acknowledge the decision of the Nazi regime to rob Jewish refugees of their citizenship. It was, in fact, the case of two Austrian brothers who had been detained in Trinidad as enemy aliens and were then transported to Britain, where they were interned until 1944 – *The King v Home Secretary, ex parte L* – that established this legal principle. The judgement mentioned neither the brothers' Jewishness nor the fact that, as was now clear, they had been forced to flee for their lives. It stipulated:

The Courts of this country will not in time of war recognize any change of nationality brought about by a decree of an enemy State, which purports to turn any of its subjects into a stateless person or a subject of a neutral state. Therefore, an alien enemy, who in consequence of such decree has become a stateless person, still retains, in law, his enemy status, and if interned in this country cannot move for a writ of *habeas corpus*.[20]

Those with German or Austrian passports were detained until August 1941 unless they were able to leave the colony altogether.[21] As we have seen, refugees only began to opt in significant numbers for the British West Indies once they found it impossible to emigrate to more obvious destinations; consequently, the stipulation that they could only be freed from internment once they had secured their short-term remigration elsewhere must have seemed particularly daunting.

Camp Rented consisted of eleven barracks and was divided into two sections, facilitating the separation of Jewish and non-Jewish internees. Each of the barracks comprised several rooms, and families were allowed to live together. As their speaker the internees elected Paul Richter, a refugee from Frankfurt (Main) whose wife, Toni Richter, née Weihermann, had been a German tennis champion before 1933. Classes in English and Hebrew were organized within the camp as well as a series of lectures on scientific topics by Dr Paul Laband, a refugee dentist who had come to Trinidad following his release from Buchenwald and would go on to marry Helen Hammermann's sister, Jean.[22] The authorities tried to alleviate the situation by giving much of the day-to-day administration of the camp over to the internees, who then divided the required tasks up amongst themselves. Manfred Goldfish, as he later recalled, 'was honoured to be elected chief translator' for the BBC broadcasts that reached the camp. 'The loudspeaker was fairly high up, so to be able to hear every word I had to stand at a table and take notes, while the audience sat quietly until the newscast ended and the translation would begin.'[23]

Even so, as a recent online publication of the National Archives of Trinidad and Tobago on the Second World War emphasizes, 'many suffered from depression and intense boredom' while in internment.[24] Hans Stecher recalls:

> We spent more than three and a half years in detention and … many … felt defeated and hopeless. The close proximity of living also caused people to get on each other's nerves. … Dr Karell, a doctor of philosophy, became deranged; [he] started to sit on the floor and to proclaim that he was a reincarnation of Abraham.[25] An old man, Mr Blei,[26] unfortunately hung himself.[27]

As Helen Breger later recalled, her father, Baruch Hammermann, 'was hurt by being interned as an "enemy alien"' and 'resented the forced proximity and the humiliations of camp life'.[28] He 'refused to cooperate in all communal activities, including joining us at meals in the mess hall, and I had to bring him his food to his solitary spot behind the barracks. He spent most of his time there reading early science-fiction novels and brooding'.[29]

Forty-five internees were able to leave for the United States between August and November 1940.[30] Among them was the Tauscher family from Vienna whom we met in the previous chapter. Erich Tauscher, who was married to the sister of Hans Stecher's father, Victor, had initially established a watch store in Port of Spain, proudly advertising himself as a 'Viennese watch maker and repairer' (see Figure 3.7).

Like the Stechers, the Tauschers were interned, initially on Nelson Island and Caledonia Island, and then in Camp Rented. They were able to remigrate

Figure 5.2 'Trinidad', sketch by Helen Breger in *Lines, A Sketched Life*, USA 2009, p. 14. Published with permission.

to New York on the *Medea* in November 1940. The following year, the Markreichs, who had also been interned, moved to New York, where they were reunited with their son. In 1947, having become the Markrichs, they moved to San Francisco where Max Markrich died in 1962.[31]

Given the constant arrival of new refugees in transit, some of whom were able to leave at relatively short notice while others were forced to stay for longer periods, and the ongoing, if modest, remigration of refugees already in the colony, the number of internees in Trinidad fluctuated, reaching up to one thousand at times. When the internment regime was softened in Britain, the colonial authorities in Trinidad only gradually followed suit. Jewish organizations in Britain, together with the high commissioner for refugees, asked the British authorities to urge their colonial counterparts into compliance with the regulations applied in Britain,[32] and in March 1941, Chaim Weizmann interrupted a trip to New York to go to Trinidad to visit the internment camp and discuss the requisites for a release of the internees with the governor.[33]

In August 1941, the Trinidadian government finally modified its internment policy and lowered the requirements for release. As a result, the majority of interned refugees were freed by February 1942. It is hard to say whether this decision was influenced by the Jewish organizations' efforts. Highbrow travel writers Lawrence and Sylvia Martin suggested that the crucial motive behind the far-reaching internment regime in Trinidad had been primarily economic all along. They wrote in an article published in *Harper's Magazine* in March 1941:

> Trinidad's open scandal is her internment of refugees in concentration camps. 'We must guard against fifth-column activities', intoned the press owned by Sir George Huggins.[34] But it is hard to keep anything a secret [on] a small island. Soon everyone knew about the conferences of the governor with Sir George and the big merchants of Frederick Street, of the governor's protest and finally his dutiful submission. The refugees had been opening new shops on Frederick Street and building small factories in the fields. The large traders wanted no such competition.

In October 1941, Young's successor as governor, Sir Bede Clifford, informed the Colonial Office that 165 refugees had been released on the advice of the Advisory Committee. The committee had recommended the freeing of a further eight of the remaining twenty-eight internees, provided they could secure entry visas allowing them to leave Trinidad.[35] While most of the refugees were greatly relieved to be freed, as the war dragged on, there were also some refugees who were reluctant to leave the camp, given that it provided them with basic board and accommodation. As time wore on, financial assistance from relatives elsewhere on the globe also tended to dry up.[36]

Take the case of Siegfried Beer. As the Jewish Refugee Society reported to the Joint in New York in late August 1941, he had been voluntarily interned alongside his son and daughter-in-law. Upon their release, he was asked to leave the camp, but was unwilling to do so. His relatives, who had lost the photographic studio they had established before the war due to their internment, were unable to support him as they were currently unemployed. There were two further couples in their seventies who had no relatives in Trinidad and no means of support. All of them wanted to emigrate to the United States.[37] In October 1941, the possibility of establishing a home for those elderly internees who were unemployable and had no means of support was discussed, but this plan never materialized, presumably for financial reasons.[38]

When the Joint sent Moses Beckelman to Trinidad to inspect the internment camp in October 1941, he found that eighty refugees were still being detained: forty-four men, twenty-nine women and seven children. At this point, fourteen refugees from the *Winnipeg* were still interned in the colony, having been unable to secure an alternative destination. They were eventually released in January 1942 and allowed to stay.[39] In January 1944, nine of the remaining sixteen internees were released. It is unclear whether in the end they had challenged their internment or had been forced to leave the camp.[40] Since all nine were destitute, the Joint increased its monthly grant to the Jewish Refugee Society to cover their maintenance.[41]

In December 1941, the Joint sent the former executive director of the National Committee for Resettlement of Foreign Physicians, Harry D. Biele, to Trinidad. He found that of the four remaining internees, three, all in their fifties, entertained 'unrealistic hopes' regarding their prospects, and refused to apply for release unless the Joint offered written guarantees that it would fund their maintenance for as long as they would need it. Their families had left the internment camp and were barely eking out an existence in Port of Spain. 'The longer they remain in the camp', Biele noted, 'the more peculiar their behaviour becomes'.[42] They too were released by July 1945 and became reliant on aid sent from the Joint to the Jewish Refugee Society for their upkeep.[43]

Jamaica

Given the Martins' suggestion that the internment regime in Trinidad may have been economically motivated, it is perhaps noteworthy that the first report on internment in Jamaica in the *New York Times* read as follows: 'The government today ordered all enemy aliens in Jamaica interned, and their business turned over to an official receiver. The government sought to prevent profiteering as food prices began to increase'.[44] Initially, twenty-two 'enemy aliens' were rounded up, taken to the Criminal Investigation Department headquarters on East Street,[45] and from there to the Stockade (i.e. the military prison) at Up Park Camp, where a unit of the Shropshire Guard was stationed at the time. It henceforth served as the internment camp for male detainees in the colony.[46] Half of the twenty-two internees were, by one definition or another, Jews, and their non-Jewish counterparts consistently shunned them. The 'Jewish group' elected the Hamburg-born dentist, Ernst Lobbenberg, as their spokesman. The other detainees were Arnold von der Porten and his brother Gerhard, Ludwig Klein[47] – an accountant from Vienna who, after the *Anschluss*, had initially fled to Italy and earned his living accompanying silent movies on the piano[48] – Richard Kaiser, Richard Kahn,[49] Fritz Lackenbach, and three refugees who had been released from concentration camps on condition that they emigrate instantly: Max Ebersohn from Vienna (whose brother-in-law, Fred Löffler, was also interned), Robert Hirsch, and Ernst Lobbenberg's brother, Fritz.[50] They were subsequently joined by Ernst Schönbeck, the chief chemical engineer at the WISCO Frome Sugar Estate, who had one Jewish parent but had been brought up as a Lutheran (we met him towards the end of Chapter 2),[51] and Willy Gertig, who originally came from Pomerania in north-eastern Germany and had been teaching at Friend's College in Highgate (located between Kingston and Port Maria).[52] On their arrival at the camp, the detainees were given numbers in lieu of their names. Initially, the cells were locked at night but this practice was abandoned when the internees protested against it. Visitors were permitted to bring goods for the detainees, but only to the gate as they were prohibited from speaking to them.[53] With the exception of Richard Kahn, Richard Kaiser, Ludwig Klein and Willy Gertig, the detainees from the 'Jewish group' were released again on 15 November 1939.[54]

When the Phoney War ended, they were rounded up again and returned to Up Park Camp (with the exception of Robert Hirsch who had since moved on to Brazil with his family).[55] This time, Richard Kahn's seventeen-year-old son, Wolfgang, was also interned. Soon after, naturalized citizens of 'enemy alien' origin and the wives and children of the detainees were also interned – the men in a separate section of Up Park Camp, the women and children at 93 Hanover Street.

Among the naturalized detainees now interned were Hans Stamm and Gerhard von der Porten, who had been granted citizenship while interned for the first time in the autumn of 1939. Arnold von der Porten, his brother Gerhard and Gerhard's wife Dorrie (Dorothea) thus found themselves in three different internment camps, unable to communicate with one another.[56] After some weeks they were given permission to write to one another, but their letters were subject to strict censorship. Eventually, Arnold von der Porten was given permission to visit his brother Gerhard for an hour once a week.[57] Conditions for the naturalized internees were more comfortable and they each had a room of their own.[58]

When the British transported some seven hundred internees from Western Africa to the Up Park Camp, the 'Jewish group' acquired four new members. One of them, on von der Porten's account, was an 'Italian Jew from Kano in northern Nigeria by the name of Levi', who was 'a real loner'. Another was Rudolf Aub. Born in Augsburg in 1901, Aub had trained as a doctor. When Nazi legislation led to his being sacked from his hospital position, he built up a private practice.[59] Since Jewish doctors were no longer allowed to practise after 1 September 1938, Aub began to intensify his efforts to emigrate, not least by taking courses in English and medical English. He was able to secure an affidavit for himself, though not his family, to enter the United States in 1939. Yet his planning was overtaken by the November Pogrom of 1938. Aub had agreed with his wife that should he be arrested she would contact her brother in Sierra Leone who, in turn, would apply for a permit for Aub to come there. Aub was imprisoned in Augsburg for a fortnight and forced, with his peers, to salvage coal from the synagogue and other buildings of the Jewish community. After two weeks, he was transferred to Dachau. His brother-in-law was able to secure his entry to Sierra Leone, provided he could demonstrate that he would be able to remigrate from there. Given the affidavit he had already obtained for the US, he was able to fulfil this requirement. He was released from Dachau on 14 January 1939, and exactly one month later he left Germany on the *Usaramo* for Freetown. His wife, Jula Aub, née Axenfeld, was the daughter of a pastor (with no Jewish ancestors) and thus protected, and there was an option for their three children – Martin, Gertrud and Konrad – to find refuge in Switzerland if necessary. On the *Usaramo*, Aub was seated separately from the other passengers in the dining room, though the ship's captain did join him demonstratively on one occasion. His brother-in-law, a wholesaler and shopkeeper, lived in Makeni, roughly 100 miles from the coast, where Aub joined him and worked as his assistant.

When war broke out six months later, Aub was interned, together with his brother-in-law, in a school in Freetown. In December 1939, all but three of the German internees in Freetown were transferred to Britain. Aub was released and was then able to work in a number of auxiliary medical positions until he was interned again in June 1940. A few days later, he received a message from the US consulate in Lagos, Nigeria, asking him urgently to attend the consulate in connection with his US visa. When Nigeria refused him entry, the consulate in Lagos transferred his case to the consulate in Monrovia, Liberia. Liberia was willing to let Aub enter, but Sierra Leone now refused him an exit visa. On Aub's own account, he was eventually the only Jew among eight hundred internees in Freetown. In November 1940, all the internees were put on a ship, which eventually returned to Freetown two days later. A few days after that, they were transferred to another ship, and eventually arrived in Kingston on 3 December 1940.

At Up Park, Aub worked informally as the secretary of the military doctor in the camp. He received regular correspondence from his family via the International Committee of the Red Cross (ICRC). It turned out that in the meantime, two elderly sisters who would later commit suicide to evade their deportation had persuaded relatives in the United States to provide an affidavit for Aub's wife; however, the family in fact stayed in Germany until after the war. Eventually, Ernst Lobbenberg was able to persuade the authorities to release Aub, given the serious lack of doctors in the colony, and Aub left Up Park on 26 March 1943.

All in all, the 'Jewish group' now comprised twenty-two detainees.[60] They were joined by a small number of non-Jewish anti-Fascists who also wanted and, indeed, needed to be isolated from the other German internees, making up a group of thirty in total.[61] Given the limited expertise of the official military dentist, Ernst Lobbenberg performed more complicated procedures 'on soldiers and prisoners alike … while Fritz pedalled to keep the drill going'.[62] Max Ebersohn took over as the Jewish group's representative.[63]

On the whole, the members of the Jewish group seem to have been on relatively good terms with their guards, especially those from the Canadian Winnipeg Grenadiers who 'proved to be very congenial and informal human beings'.[64] Von der Porten was particularly impressed with a sanitary inspector,

> a tall, powerful-looking young Jew. Unfortunately, I forgot this admirable man's name. When he saw our group, he was outraged. Jews interned in a British internment camp! And then with 1,200 Nazis and Racists! That was too much.
>
> He contacted his superior officers, his chaplain, and Rabbi Silverman. When he got nowhere, he petitioned to be released as a conscientious objector, as he could not guard Jews in good conscience. He was discharged and sent home.[65]

While the non-Jewish German detainees, as mentioned, generally shunned their Jewish counterparts, either from conviction or because of the massive (and occasionally violent) peer group pressure among them, there were exceptions. Von der Porten recalls the case of one Dr Marschall, a 'German specialist for tropical diseases who had come with the contingent from Africa'. Porten describes him as 'a very sensitive man who obeyed his conscience rather than any political authority, and who was already ostracized by the Nazis, as he kept having friendly conversations with Dr. Lobbenberg'. He became 'very depressed' and committed suicide.[66]

In 1941, Ernest Schönbeck/Edward Schonbeck became something of a cause célèbre in the colony when Ronald Kirkwood, the director of WISCO and a local politician, started a campaign for the release of his employee. The *Daily Gleaner* took a keen interest in the campaign, yet Kirkwood criticized it, arguing that the paper was stirring up opposition to Schönbeck's release by calling attention to his German nationality. Kirkwood was particularly incensed, given the leading role that Jews played in the management of the paper. Since there were 'a number of gentlemen of Jewish extraction con-nected with the "Gleaner"', he wrote, 'I think that your editorial staff might at least have taken the trouble to stress the fact that Schonbeck is a Jew – and not a German'.[67] The *Daily Gleaner* responded robustly:

> Mr. Kirkwood says in the first paragraph of his letter that Mr. Schonbeck is 'a Jew who happens to be German'. In his second paragraph, he says that we should have taken the trouble to stress the fact that 'Schonbeck is a Jew and not a German'. We cannot reconcile this contradiction. We have always understood that a man's nationality does not necessarily indicate his race, and vice versa, and this in spite of anything Mr. Hitler may say.[68]

The campaign was successful, though. Schönbeck was freed in June 1941, and following his release, 'one after the other of our hut and of the British compound was released several days apart'. Von der Porten was released on 28 October 1941, though Gerhard and Dorothea (his brother and sister-in-law) were not released until six months later.[69] On von der Porten's account, as a result of their camp experience, 'both Dorrie and Gerhard remained very bitter and suspicious of everybody with whom they came into contact for the rest of their lives'.[70]

The Hanover Street Camp for the interned women developed into a considerable bone of contention. The *Daily Gleaner* reported on 15 June 1940 that 'the internment camp for enemy alien women is now open and it has ten occupants. It is situated at 93 Hanover Street, where the Deaconess Home was formerly established. The premises have been enclosed by a strong and high barbed-wire fence, and an armed guard keeps constant patrol around it'. The paper named the ten women as: Kathe Norman, Julia Kahn, Rosa Lackenbach, Dorothy Von der Porten, Hugette Heise, Matilda Kroneker,[71] Emelie Sara Stamm, Nimi Erna Stamm, Johanna Ann Schone and Karoline Ebersohn.[72] Karoline Ebersohn had her ten-year-old daughter, Susan, with her; and Julia Kahn had her fourteen-year-old son with her.[73] Susan Ebersohn was subsequently released and fostered by 'Jewish refugees from Czechoslovakia who knew German'.[74]

According to von der Porten, Hanover Street was 'the main street for prostitutes' in Kingston, suggesting that the location of the internment camp there was a 'disgusting insult'. On the one hand, it is certainly true that the Hanover Street Camp was located on a condemned block earmarked for the new Council Chamber.[75] On the other hand, the Kingston Central Group of the Left Book Club met regularly at 83 Hanover Street,[76] so the insult cannot have been all that great.

On von der Porten's account, conditions in the Hanover Street Camp were a major concern for the men at Up Park Camp. Here is von der Porten's account:

> Rumors started that the women in the Hanover Street Interment House were being ill-treated. The internees from Africa had swelled the population … to 60 women and about 100 babies under three years old. The husbands and fathers of the women internees kept petitioning the Colonial Secretary to be allowed to see their wives and daughters. As a result, the husbands were bussed down to Hanover Street. They came back with shocking stories. …
>
> Eventually, six women committed suicide … Hitler himself threatened in a radio broadcast that he would take revenge on British prisoners if the German women imprisoned in Jamaica were not treated more humanely. …
>
> The Jamaican Government reacted. A deaconess from the Methodist Church, a well-respected lady of English descent, was put in charge. The house

next door was added, thus doubling the space for the internees. No armed guards, nor any other males, were allowed inside the compound. ...

The *Daily Gleaner* ... published stories that Black people were [to be] replaced by Whites on Hitler's orders. This was welcome propaganda for the anti-British independence movement. ... The *Daily Gleaner* proved to be a disgrace not only to its country, but to the entire newspaper profession as a whole. As for the discharged matron, there are no words mean enough to describe her.[77]

While the specifics are not entirely clear, a German protest against the fact that German internees were being guarded by black personnel was indeed lodged in March 1941.[78]

The removal of the matron of the Hanover Street Camp certainly led to major controversy in the Legislative Council in March 1941. On 27 March, the *Daily Gleaner* reported on 'a lively discussion as Government was charged with colour discrimination for removing a coloured matron from the Female Internees Camp to meet the wishes of the internees'. The Jamaican colonial secretary, Sir Alexander Grantham, insisted that the removal of the matron had occurred for purely pragmatic reasons, had been undertaken prior to the arrival of the second wave of female internees, and certainly not in order to appease the internees. Yet Oswald Anderson, who led the charge, would have none of it: 'If they were going to say that a German alien was too good to be taken care of by a Jamaican, a loyal Britisher, because of colour, then the time had come when they must call a halt'. Legislative Council member Little supported Anderson: 'It was very strange that the people they were making provision for were not Britishers, and not in sympathy with us, yet a woman of this country was discriminated against in favour of our enemies'.[79] Arthur B. Lowe was cited as stating:

It must not be forgotten how Germans think of dark people – he believed they shot a great many of the coloured soldiers they captured in France and treated others like dogs; and when they had the Germans here the best thing was to teach them a lesson, and say: 'You are now in a country where we regard everybody's rights'. It would have been a very good thing to let them know that they were not in their own country, and we would not cater to their fancies.[80]

There is also some indication that a greater effort was made in the spring of 1941 to make the conditions for the interned women more bearable. In February, the *Daily Gleaner* reported about 'a programme of music, song and recitation, also motion pictures' organized by the Salvation Army 'at the Hanover Street camp, where there are about 80 women and half as many children ... After the singing of "Now thank we all our God" and prayer, Mrs Lt. Colonel Simpson read in German a portion from St. Luke's Gospel, then followed item after item'. Among the highlights that 'delighted the audience' was 'the singing of the Colonel's little daughters, Misses Margaret and Marylla'.[81] Perhaps more importantly, the *Daily Gleaner* explained in June 1941 that 'in order to give German women interned here the benefit of an occasional outing from the internment camp in Hanover Street, the Rockfort mineral bath is to be closed to the public on Wednesday mornings between 6 o'clock and 8 o'clock'.[82]

Later in the same meeting of the Legislative Council at which the removal of the matron was discussed, J.A.G. Smith raised the question of why the colonial government was paying £1,150 for the maintenance of male internees but £5,428 for female detainees. In response, Grantham explained that the lower sum covered only the Jamaican male internees (of whom there were 37 at the time) while the much larger amount covered not only the Jamaican female internees (of whom there were 13) but also those sent to Jamaica from elsewhere (another 121). The colonial government would be reimbursed for the costs covering the latter group.[83]

Gibraltar Camp

Alongside the two internment camps at Up Park and Hanover Street, a fourth, much larger camp, Gibraltar Camp, was being hastily established in the summer of 1940 on the former Mona plantation, which was owned by the Jamaican Water Commission,[84] to house (as the name indicates) evacuees from Gibraltar. Given the high strategic importance given to Gibraltar by the British and the assumed likelihood that the colony would become the object of intense and sustained fighting, it was agreed in April 1940 that the civilian population would be evacuated to French Morocco.[85] In the course of May and June, some thirteen thousand Gibraltarians were evacuated, but following the German victory over France, they needed to be relocated yet again. The British authorities were desperately keen to transfer them to any location but Britain, and a number of localities in South Africa, the West Indies and other parts of the Empire were considered.[86] As this search dragged on into July, the Vichy-loyal French authorities in Morocco deported the Gibraltarian evacuees, forcing them to return to Gibraltar. This left the British authorities with no other choice but to bring the Gibraltarians to Britain in the first instance and then to try to disperse them from there. Between June and August 1940, some eleven thousand Gibraltarians were brought to London where they were maintained in hotels, hostels and tenement blocks. This left a further three thousand evacuees in Gibraltar, and in August it was decided to move some of them directly to Jamaica, where Gibraltar Camp was hastily being constructed.[87]

On 19 July 1940, the governor of Jamaica, Sir Arthur Richards, received instructions to build a camp that could house four thousand evacuees. As the director of the Jamaican Public Works Office, P. Martin Cooper, later reported,

> the time factor was considered one of very great urgency. It was necessary to build a camp for 2,000 evacuees in one month. Six days were used in making the preliminary arrangements, leaving only 25 days for actual construction. At end of one month it would have been possible to accommodate the 2,000 evacuees, but the kitchen arrangements were not quite complete, and were completed a week later. At the end of three months, accommodation was ready for 4,000 evacuees.[88]

In the meantime, on 15 September 1940, further instructions followed, stipulating that additional accommodation for another five thousand evacuees should be constructed, taking the total capacity to nine thousand. 'Mona Springs to Life as Home of 9,000', was the headline of one of the *Daily Gleaner*'s reports on this development.[89]

Yet in the event, the British authorities never did move on any of the Gibraltarians who had been evacuated to Britain. On 10 October, Lord (George) Lloyd, the colonial secretary, wrote to Richards about the resistance of the Gibraltarians to their further evacuation. 'Indeed', he explained, 'we may have to use force to get them to go at all'.[90] On 9 November, Richards received a telegram from Lloyd, informing him that 'circumstances have arisen [that] now make it unlikely that any Gibraltar evacuees will be sent to Jamaica from this country in the near future', and instructing the governor that he 'should not enter into any further avoidable commitments'.[91] The building work that was already too advanced to halt was completed, and by the time construction was suspended on 13 November 1940, the camp had a capacity of slightly under seven thousand. The material that had been acquired to complete the remaining two thousand places was kept in storage to ensure the originally planned capacity could yet be reached at short notice, should the need to do so arise.[92] Cooper-Clark suggests that, following the arrival of the evacuees who were brought over directly from Gibraltar, 'approximately 50' of the 112 barracks in the camp were still unoccupied.[93] If this is true, the implication would be that each occupied barrack accommodated only twenty-five evacuees, although the barracks had been constructed to accommodate sixty evacuees each. Had the 1,486 evacuees inhabited the barracks in groups of sixty, they would have used only 25 barracks, leaving 87 barracks (or room for more than five thousand additional evacuees or refugees) unoccupied. Even if Cooper-Clark is right, the evacuees could have been asked to occupy the barracks at capacity, had there been a serious political will to use the camp's remaining capacity to accommodate further refugees. In the event, some of the vacant barracks were used to establish a school, a hospital, a reading room, and a camp police station.[94]

Given the consistent resistance of the Colonial Office and the colonial governments to attempts to settle refugees in the British West Indies that we have seen throughout this study so far, one can only marvel at the prompt and unproblematic execution of the measures required to put Gibraltar Camp in place. Since (a) all the costs of the camp were to be carried by the British government, (b) both the erection and maintenance of the camp created jobs for Jamaicans, and (c) the evacuees were strictly precluded from undertaking any kind of paid work in the colony and would return home once the war ended, the scheme brought some advantages and did no immediate damage, and it was therefore generally welcomed.[95] Moreover, though mostly Spanish-speaking, the evacuees were, of course, British subjects. While the evacuees were mainly restricted to Gibraltar Camp, local Jamaicans who worked there reported back. In Louise Bennett's memorable twelve-stanza poem 'Jamaica Patois', their influence on the local population is described as 'Miss Liza's' … 'sister husban get /One job up a Mona!', and in the process, assimilated some of the speech habits of the foreigners: 'You want to hear her cut Spanish, like / She jus come out from Sea! / So till dem bwoy start fe call her / De dry-lan-refugee!'[96]

'So, This is Jamaica!' the *Daily Gleaner* headlined its front page on 26 October 1940, reporting in great detail on the arrival of the first group of detainees: 'Of the 1,104 arrivals', the paper explained, '185 are males, 673 are females, and 246 children under 12 years of age. … The youngest arrival is a two-day old baby, who was born in Caribbean waters'. The report went on to suggest that 'history was made in the island as the ship steamed in with its human cargo, for it was the first close-up this island has yet received of the devastating European war'.[97]

The camp commandant, John L. Worlledge, returned to Britain in March 1941, at which point Ernest A. Rae, who had resigned as deputy mayor of Kingston to take on the role of camp manager – and who is otherwise better known as one of Jamaica's outstanding test cricket players – became acting commandant. In the event, much of the employment created by the camp was in fact taken up by its inhabitants. In 1940, only 194 Jamaicans were employed by the camp, compared to 453 of the camp's inhabitants.[98]

Jamaicans were strictly precluded from entering the camp, and this ban was actively enforced.[99] On 28 November 1940, the *Daily Gleaner* reported that five defendants – Julius Wood, Eulist Robinson, Beatrice Williams, Gertrude Darby and Edward Hill – had been fined for 'gate crashing' Gibraltar Camp. The charge against Hill was that 'he unlawfully did within a distance of 100 yards, to wit four feet, from the boundary of the said precincts of the Gibraltar Camp sell fruits to persons within the said camp'.

The resident magistrate, John E.D. Carberry, 'warned that while these cases, as the first brought before him, were leniently dealt with, that there would be an increase of penalty in the event of breach of the regulation continuing'.[100] In February 1941, one W. Buie was fined, although his solicitor maintained 'that his client committed a technical breach under a misunderstanding'.[101] The exclusion of Jamaicans from the camp must have made it unnecessarily difficult for the evacuees to establish relations outside the camp, given that they could never reciprocate invitations.

The costs involved in setting up the camp were high. Writing to the Treasury, Andrew B. Acheson of the Colonial Office estimated the total cost at £330,000.[102] Running costs for the camp in 1941 amounted to more than £420,000.[103] Justifying the costs to the Treasury, Acheson explained:

> We have no material here on which to form any opinion as to whether these figures are open to criticism. The camp was constructed at very great speed under strong pressure from this end to use the utmost expedition, and that may well have increased the cost. In the circumstances, it is little short of lamentable that we should only have been able, so far, to arrange for some 1,500 evacuees to occupy the camp. It may be that the proposal to send some of the evacuees from this country to the West Indies will be revived. We can only hope that by these or other means the vacant accommodation will, sooner or later, be turned to practical advantage.[104]

One such practical advantage was eventually found, when the British government agreed to allow small numbers of refugees to come to Gibraltar Camp.

Refugees in Gibraltar Camp

Early in 1941, the Polish government in exile approached the high commissioner for refugees and the British government on behalf of approximately two hundred Polish Jewish refugees stranded in Lisbon. The ensuing negotiations were evidently tricky. Yet in December, the Polish ambassador in the United States, Jan Ciechanowski, contacted the Joint in New York, informing them that the British government would allow the refugees admission to Gibraltar Camp in Jamaica for the duration of the war, provided the Polish government in exile guaranteed the cost of their maintenance. However, the government did not have sufficient funds at its disposal, Ciechanowski explained. Would it be possible, he enquired, for the Joint or some other American Jewish organization to shoulder the financial burden 'in order to save these Jewish refugees of Polish citizenship'?[105]

The Joint agreed to carry the costs for the Polish refugees for one year. After that, it would 'continue to extend all possible help to this group of refugees in the same manner as we extend assistance to refugees in other parts of the world'.[106] The British authorities evidently accepted this guarantee as sufficient, because they were keen to keep the exit route via Lisbon open. As the refugee department in the Foreign Office clarified,

> the Jamaica scheme was set on foot with [the] main object of clearing away [the] 'hard core' of Polish Jews who had been in Portugal for a long time, and whose continued presence in Portugal was the pretext for Portuguese authorities wanting no further transit visas for Poles [or] Czechs whom we wished to get out of unoccupied France and elsewhere. We should not wish the impression to get about (which would be in any case erroneous) that it is our intention to make a permanent dumping ground in Jamaica for all aliens.[107]

The Joint thereupon informed the press that it had arranged for the emigration of 180 Polish Jews from Lisbon to Jamaica. It emphasized that 'this rescue operation ... [was] an instance of the interest of the Allied democratic powers in the maintenance of programs of overseas aid during the war as a part of the struggle for democracy on the "human front"'.[108]

The enthusiasm with which the Joint publicized its involvement in this scheme – and continued to exploit it for public relations purposes – is a clear reflection of the observation made in the previous chapter regarding the importance of 'success stories' in upholding morale within the organizations themselves, and in persuading the public of the continued worthiness of their work. In May 1942, the *J.D.C. Digest* contained a report by Joseph Schwartz on the voyage of the *Serpo Pinto* bringing the first group of Polish Jewish refugees to Jamaica. In March 1944, an article under the heading 'Happy Ending: Love Story' followed. It related the story of a couple who had met and fallen in love on the voyage to Gibraltar Camp, and then married in the camp. The Joint also issued a series of Loose Leaf Memos circulated to the organization's supporters. The work for the Polish Jewish refugees in Gibraltar Camp features prominently in these memos.

The Joint was by no means alone in this respect, and various organizations competed in trying to claim credit for this scheme or effective refugee relief work more generally. Even the WJC, having in fact had no involvement at all with the arrangements made for the Polish Jewish refugees to come to Gibraltar Camp, claimed that 'with the aid of our representatives in London, we succeeded in bringing a considerable number of Polish Jewish refugees from Portugal to the British colony, Jamaica'.[109] Its relief committee received reports on this group of refugees at every meeting throughout 1943 and 1944.

For all the enthusiasm about the transfer of the Polish refugees to Gibraltar Camp displayed in public, the officials of the Joint were fully aware of the fact that the Joint had been forced yet again to accept financial responsibility for measures on which it had not been consulted and over which it had no genuine influence. 'The Joint Distribution Committee did not initiate this step', one of them wrote to Lionel J. Simmonds, the widely respected departing superintendent of the Hebrew Orphan Asylum in New York, and continued:

> It was after the arrangements had been consummated among the governmental groups in question that the Polish Government turned to the J.D.C. and stated that it had solved the problem of these unfortunate people for the duration. ... We considered the matter very carefully. This, like many other situations, came to pass without our planning. We were called on, however, to make good arrangements already effected by other groups. We came to the conclusion that at the present time with the possibility of ingress to Latin and South American countries virtually blocked, and with no opportunity at this time [for] admission to [the] United States, because these people had no affidavits or sponsors for admission there, we had no alternative but to accept a measure of responsibility.[110]

The first steamship to take the Polish Jewish refugees to Jamaica sailed from Lisbon on 24 January 1942.

As well as passengers bound for Cuba and the United States, the *Serpa Pinto* carried 152 Polish Jewish refugees. They were accompanied by Bertram Jacobson of the Joint and his wife, formerly of the Budapest office of the Joint. In addition to the Joint's guarantee to cover their maintenance, the Jamaican Legislature also insisted that the refugees refrained from seeking employment or citizenship in the colony.[111] In February 1942, the Joint extended its original guarantee to allow an additional 200 refugees to be brought from Lisbon to Gibraltar Camp. In the course of 1942 a further 107 refugees from a number of Allied countries, including Luxembourgians and Czechs, were transferred from Lisbon to Gibraltar Camp.[112]

During 1942 and 1943, significant numbers of Dutch refugees, including Jews, were moved from Vigo and Lisbon to the Dutch West Indies and to Gibraltar Camp. In May 1942, 200 Dutch refugees were sent to Dutch Guiana. The Netherlands government in exile paid for their transportation while the Joint guaranteed their maintenance for one year.[113] In December 1942, a further group of 400 Dutch refugees were evacuated from Vigo and taken to Jamaica. Approximately 250 of them remained in Gibraltar Camp while the others travelled on to Paramaribo in Dutch Guiana.[114] Of the 250 refugees who stayed in Gibraltar Camp for the time being, approximately 175 were Dutch Jews who relied on aid from the Joint.[115]

In the course of 1943, three further groups of Dutch refugees arrived. In April 1943, 305 Dutch refugees were transferred to Gibraltar Camp where

Figure 5.3 A group of Jewish refugees pose on the pier in the port of Lisbon before boarding the SS *Serpa Pinto*. Photograph 59617, courtesy of the U.S. Holocaust Memorial Museum.

they remained until 31 March 1944. It is unclear how many of these refugees may have been Jewish, though it is possible to make an estimate of sorts based on the surnames of the refugees. Of the refugees on the list, 63 had surnames making it highly likely that they were Jewish (Baruch, Bialystok, Cats, Cohen, Cohn, Feiner, Finkelstein, Goudsmit, Goldschmidt, Kan, Katz, Samson, Speyer, Taytelbaum, Wertheim). Another 56 refugees had surnames that are listed in Lars Menk's *Dictionary of German-Jewish Surnames*,[116] and a further 13 bore likely Sephardi surnames (Casoetto, Coelho, Miranda, Penha and Vieyra). In short, some 130 of these 305 Dutch refugees may well have been Jewish.[117] On 3 October 1943, approximately 60 Dutch refugees arrived – 50 men and 10 women. The men were drafted into the

Figure 5.4 Jewish refugees look out from the deck of the SS *Serpa Pinto* before its departure from the port of Lisbon. Photograph 59619, courtesy of the U.S. Holocaust Memorial Museum.

military in short order. HICEM had expected 79 refugees, 66 of whom were Jewish.[118] In December, finally, a further 300 Dutch refugees were evacuated to Gibraltar Camp from Vigo. Their maintenance was covered entirely by the Netherlands government in exile, suggesting that none of them were Jews.[119]

With Diana Cooper-Clark's publication, *Dreams of Re-Creation in Jamaica*, we now have a detailed compilation of accounts of life in Gibraltar Camp. Ultimately, there were as many refugee experiences as there were refugees, and this holds true of the ways in which life in Gibraltar Camp was encountered too. There would be little point to my duplicating Cooper-Clark's detailed reconstruction of life in the camp here. As elsewhere, the younger refugees tended to find it easier to adapt. This is reflected in Fred

Figure 5.5 Postcard from England posted in March 1942 to Lisbon, Portugal, and redirected to Gibraltar Camp, Kingston, Jamaica, where it arrived on 4 November 1942. It was censored by the British and had chemical wash lines to see if there was any secret writing. Courtesy of William Kaczynski's Collection.

Mann's *A Drastic Turn in Destiny*, a particularly wide-ranging and lively, though arguably in many respects not particularly representative, account of life in the camp.

Emanuel and Zelda Mann from Leipzig and their son Fred (Manfred) were among the refugees on the *Serpa Pinto*. While Zelda Mann was originally from Poland, her husband, who was an Austrian, had, on the advice of a friend with close connections to the Polish consul in Leipzig, applied for, and received, a Polish passport in 1937.[120] The family was able to seek refuge in the Polish consulate both during the mass deportation of Polish Jews at the end of October 1938 and during the November Pogrom.[121] They eventually left Germany at the end of June 1939 for Belgium. Given the family's relative wealth, they were able to leave with all their possessions, though Emanuel Mann had to bribe the relevant official to let their property leave, given that they did not in fact have an entry visa for Belgium. The family then crossed the green border to Belgium illegally, aided by what would now be called 'people smugglers'.[122] Following the end of the Phoney War, they then fled via France and Spain to Portugal, where they eventually boarded the *Serpa Pinto* in January 1942.

Like other teenage refugees in Gibraltar Camp – he names Henry and Maurice Feigenbaum, Maurice Tempelsman, Adolf Lipmanowitz, Trudy

Figure 5.6 Fred Mann and his parents at Gibraltar Camp, Jamaica. Left to right: his father, Emanuel; Fred; and his mother, Zelda. Courtesy of the Azrieli Foundation.

Gross and Lizzi Eckstein – Fred Mann went to school outside the camp. They attended Jamaica College, Kingston College and Kingston Technical School, and were driven there and picked up from there by the camp's station wagon.[123] Mann also draws attention to his and his peers' lively sex lives both in and outside the camp.[124] Mann maintained relationships of various kinds outside the camp, and in September 1943 he started teaching French at the newly established Priory School where he met Jon Laidlaw, with whom he published a maths textbook for pre-teens.[125]

While Mann speaks generously of individual members of the established Jewish community in Jamaica, he is critical of the attitudes displayed by the community as a whole and, not least, by Rabbi Henry Silverman. 'About a month after our arrival in Jamaica', Mann wrote,

> we had a visit from another priest [other than Father Feeney, on whom more in a moment] who, to our amazement, spoke Hebrew. He wore a typical clerical collar that we identified with Catholic priests. He asked us how we were doing and whether we were happy in the camp. Needless to say, he got an earful. He listened politely and left about an hour later without any comment. Father Feeney happened to come by on a walk the following day, and we asked him who the priest was who had visited us the day before. Father Feeney laughed out loud and informed us that he was Rabbi Henry P. Silverman, the spiritual leader of Kingston's United Congregation of Israelites. ...

Figure 5.7 Fred Mann (centre) with friends in Jamaica. Courtesy of the Azrieli Foundation.

> Rabbi Silverman never visited again … The Jewish community of Jamaica, with very few exceptions, did nothing to assist us and, at worst, ignored our existence.[126]

Mann's account tallies with that of Arnold von der Porten. On his account, Silverman came to Up Park one day and 'told the Jews that he had done all he could for them and that any further effort to free them would be useless. There would be no hope to get out until the war was ended. He would do no more. He never came back'.[127] As Cooper-Clark reports, Fred Mann apart, 'none of the other refugees that I interviewed referred to Rabbi Silverman', which is surely telling.[128]

The Catholic priest in the camp, Father Feeney, by contrast, received warm praise from Mann as well as the other refugees whom Cooper-Clark interviewed.[129] On Mann's account, 'he was more compassionate than the rabbi and visited us on a regular basis. The only thing Father Feeney did not condone was our fraternizing with the Gibraltarian girls. When Father Feeney caught us trying to date a girl from Gibraltar, he would instruct her mother to forbid her daughter to go out with us'. On the whole, then, notwithstanding 'the infamous dengue fever epidemic' in the camp in 1943,[130] Mann's experiences were largely positive: 'My days were filled with teaching and my nights with cavorting'.[131] Yet as we will see in a moment, many of the Polish Jewish refugees in Gibraltar Camp felt altogether differently about life in the camp.

When the Polish Legation in London approached the Colonial Office in November 1942 on behalf of 120 Polish Jews who had arrived in Lisbon since the departure of the *Serpa Pinto*, the request was rejected. Given the continued influx of Dutch refugees this may seem surprising but there were four reasons why the Dutch refugees were admitted while the request to accept further Polish refugees was turned down. Firstly, the Dutch refugees had the realistic prospect of remigrating in relatively short order to Dutch Guiana. Consequently, the male refugees of military age would be able to serve the government in exile. Thirdly, the Netherlands government in exile helped to cover the costs for the maintenance of the Dutch refugees during their stay at Gibraltar Camp. Finally, the Polish refugees did themselves few favours by complaining in rather dramatic terms about conditions in the camp and apparently putting it about that they were interned in a concentration camp.

Unlike their Dutch counterparts, the Polish Jewish refugees had great difficulties in securing opportunities for remigration, and consequently had no prospect of actively supporting the war effort. Of 184 Polish refugees who arrived on the *Serpa Pinto* and *San Thomé* in December 1941 and April 1942, only thirty were able to move on in the course of 1942. Nineteen managed to enter the United States, nine emigrated to Cuba, one to Venezuela and one to Curaçao.[132] The Polish government in exile had insisted from the outset that it was in no position to contribute to the maintenance of the Polish refugees at Gibraltar Camp. As David Engel has shown, the policy of the Polish government in exile, when it came to Jews, was predicated on the assumption of a powerful world Jewry.[133] They may therefore have taken it for granted that the Joint could easily continue to carry the costs for the Polish refugees indefinitely; yet the Joint would only agree to fund them for one year. In the end, the Joint did in fact continue to carry the costs beyond the first twelve months, but the British government evidently did not want to risk being left with the bill.

If the Joint had reservations about the transfer of the Polish refugees to Gibraltar Camp, so too did the refugees themselves, and their dissatisfaction soon led to increasing alienation between the refugees and both the Joint and the British (colonial) authorities, which, in turn, partly explains the British government's refusal to allow further Polish refugees to enter the colony.

Some of the Polish refugees were also unhappy with the resident HICEM representative, Bernhard Glasscheib. He and his wife had accompanied the refugees on the *Serpa Pinto*, having previously worked for the HICEM office in Lisbon. Glasscheib continued to represent HICEM in Gibraltar Camp but he was also employed by the camp. Given that the refugees were instructed to report all their grievances to him, Glasscheib, in the eyes of many, seemed to be both an ineffective representative of their interests (he had been forced upon them – they had sought their own representation on a short-lived committee) and a representative of the camp regime itself. Rae dissolved their committee in June 1942 because of what he considered their unduly critical stance towards the Joint, HICEM and the Polish government in exile, arguing that the committee did not enjoy the support of the majority of the Polish refugees.[134]

Many of the Polish refugees evidently felt that compared to their Dutch counterparts in the camp they had received a raw deal. The refusal of the Polish government in exile to contribute to their maintenance suggested that it had effectively abandoned them. As the Joint's director for the Caribbean, Charles Jordan, reported, the Polish refugees 'do not feel … that it is the Joint's responsibility to look after them but the responsibility of the Polish government in exile, and they have, unsuccessfully, tried to contact their government. They feel that because of the interest of the Joint in their situation, it makes it harder for them to keep up their own relationship with their government'.[135]

The Polish 'prisoners' systematically rejected any attempt to portray their transfer to Gibraltar Camp as a positive step. Efforts to persuade the refugees to be photographed for Joint publicity purposes, for example, were rebuffed by the newly arrived refugees. Rae informed the Joint that 'the majority expressed dissatisfaction towards "the Joint", and were hostile to the whole idea of using them in pictures for propaganda purposes'.[136] They also responded negatively to positive reports in the American press about the Joint's efforts to bring them to Gibraltar Camp and the Polish refugees' supposed gratitude. In May 1942, their short-lived committee wrote to the Joint that it was 'with much surprise that we noticed in the American newspapers, articles on our behalf, the contents of which do not all correspond to reality. These publicity articles are not at all of a nature to satisfy our elementary needs, and we shall not declare ourselves satisfied'.[137] As one of the Polish refugees, Rosenbaum, explained to the Polish government in exile:

> I beg you to understand that we are not complaining about the camp organisation or camp life. It is simply marvellous, [and everything] is done to give us the most possible comfort. Nevertheless, we were not aware of the conditions under which we were to live here. When we left Lisbon, we were told that we were going to a free country as free men, with the possibility of building up our lives again. We have been told now that this is absolutely out of [the] question. We object to the feeling of having to live for the remaining duration of the war on charge of public charity, and therefore beg you to find a way that a visa could be granted us to such country where we could really immigrate and make ourselves useful.[138]

Rosenbaum also contacted Ignacy Schwarzbart, one of the two Jewish members of the Polish National Council and a prominent WJC activist. 'What is weighing most on us', he wrote, is the forced idleness. We therefore must consider our residence here only as a halting place and endeavour to reach countries where we can build up a new existence. I insist on what I said in my previous letter, and I know that your position will be difficult in getting a collective visa for all of us, but I hope that you will see your way to do me the favour I asked you to procure the necessary visas to Canada for my friends and myself.[139]

Pinning their hopes more and more on entry to Canada, a group of Polish refugees also wrote to Winston Churchill in August 1942, requesting that he intervene with the Canadian authorities to allow them entry, so that they could enlist in active service and war work there. They wrote:

While a world war rages and hecatombs of victims fall, we young people, wanting to fight and to work, and able to be useful through our technical and branch knowledges, are here in complete spirit and health-killing inactivity, in Gibraltar Camp. After three years, fleeing from the terrors of the flaming Europe, trying to save ourselves and ours from Nazis and Fascist concentration camps, we are now on the English territory, where we wish to give all our possible efforts of our technical and branch knowledges for our common cause. We would have considered ourselves as parasitical individuals if we were not conscious that we are leading these camp-lives absolutely against our own will. But our consciences do not leave us in peace; others fight and die, others work and help – and we live in uselessness. We feel very, very depressed, particularly now as the war seems to reach crisis point and when useful strength is more and more necessary. In our despair and helplessness, we decided to address ourselves to you and through your excellency to the Canadian Government, to deliver us and our families Canadian visas.[140]

This letter was forwarded by the Colonial Office to the Polish government in London and to the Canadian prime minister in Ottawa. The Colonial Office also asked the governor of Jamaica to inform the petitioners that the decision was one for the Polish and Canadian authorities, and not in the hands of the British government.[141]

The Polish refugees' bitterness only increased over time. In August 1943, two of them, Boruch Eksztajn and Samuel Schipper, wrote to the Joint, noting that

it is exactly one and a half years since by your action we arrived here. You will not be surprised to hear that our group remembers this jubilee with rather mixed feelings. ...

If the Joint took it upon them to 'rescue' us they ought to complete their 'rescue work' and not leave us halfway to our sad fate. What we desire is to be 'rehabilitated' just as so many others have been, and as this is impossible in this country under the hospitality conditions accepted by you for us, we must insist that we should be sent to another country where we will be allowed to be free, law-abiding, useful citizens, earning our living, and where we will not be obliged to live in barracks and spend our life in idleness.[142]

One key obstacle faced by the Polish refugees in seeking to remigrate was their legal status. Although they were governed by the same Defence Regulations as the Gibraltarian evacuees, the State Department in Washington considered them detainees, which automatically made them ineligible for entry into the United States.[143] Consequently, HIAS asked Glasscheib to approach the Jamaican authorities and ask them to help to clear up the confusion; and the organization, along with HICEM, the Joint and the World Jewish Congress became embroiled in a protracted struggle to obtain visas for the Polish refugees.[144]

Further confusion and friction arose when the Joint and the WJC approached the US administration independently of one another in order to try to resolve the issue. Repeated references to interned or detained refugees in HIAS annual reports and WJC committee meeting minutes reflect the ongoing muddying of the waters,[145] and this despite the fact that HIAS had secured confirmation of the fact that the State Department had considered Gibraltar Camp to be not an internment camp but an evacuee and refugee camp as early as July 1942.[146]

Arguably the most consequential initiative undertaken by (former) members of the short-lived committee of the Polish refugees was the public propagation of the claim that they were internees in a concentration camp. While this claim caused quite a stir in the short term, it ultimately precipitated a strong backlash and massively complicated relations between all parties involved – including the WJC, which was drawn into the negotiations at this point. In May 1942, Ernest Rae wrote to the Joint in New York, asking them not to represent Gibraltar Camp as a 'concentration camp' to Washington.[147] Yet subsequently *The Day* and a number of American Jewish publications printed a letter from the 'interned refugees in Gibraltar Camp'.[148]

The hyperbole of the Polish prisoners' committee impacted on relations between the US administration and the Joint, and between the Joint and the WJC; it made the Polish government in exile suspicious and, most importantly of all, helped to dissuade the governor and the British authorities from allowing further Polish refugees to come to Gibraltar Camp. This was certainly the impression of the Polish government in exile.

In February 1943, the minister plenipotentiary for the Polish Embassy in Washington, Michael Kwapiszewski, wrote to the Joint 'in connection with complaints [that] have been reaching this Embassy regarding the alleged mistreatment of Polish refugees in Jamaica'. He assured the Joint that the governor had given definite assurances to the Polish Embassy that none of the refugees had been interned, and he warned that 'all these unsubstantiated complaints, which found an echo in the United States, do not encourage the Governor to give his consent for the admission of a new contingent of refugees'. Moreover, he advised the Joint to send an 'expression of appreciation of the treatment of the refugees directed to the Governor of Jamaica'.[149]

Writing to Philip Rogers of the Colonial Office in December 1942, Alec Randall of the Foreign Office made explicit reference to the Polish refugees' unfounded claims. 'The High Commissioner for Refugees, Sir Herbert Emerson, is now faced with the problem of finding asylum for refugees escaped and escaping from France into Spain and Portugal', he wrote.

> The President of HICEM, Max Gottschalk, has asked whether room can be found for them in British colonies. Emerson has enquired whether we can let him know the position, particularly in regard to Jamaica where a statement has been made to him that there is room in existing barracks for about 4,000 persons ... In view of the unfavourable insinuations about Jamaica which certain Jewish ex-internees have been spreading on reaching the United States, it may seem odd that the Jewish organisations should appear to want more accommodation in the Colony; but if we can truthfully tell Sir Herbert Emerson that the island's accommodation is entirely used up, so much the better.[150]

In October 1942, the Jamaican governor, Sir Arthur Richards, explained to the colonial secretary, Lord Cranborne, that

> among various other misrepresentations of Jamaica now being given currency in the United States [were] references to Gibraltar Camp as a sort of 'Concentration Camp', not widely different from similar institutions in Germany. There is no doubt that this campaign has been instigated by Polish Jews who have left the Camp for the United States, and who hope by telling harrowing and untruthful stories to persuade the US Authorities to grant entry permits to a large number of Polish Jews now in Gibraltar Camp.[151]

On 17 December, the very day on which the governments of Britain and the United States finally came out in force to publicize and protest the systematic extermination of European Jewry being perpetrated by the Germans in Eastern Europe, John H. Emmens of the Colonial Office, commenting on Richards' communication, wrote in a memorandum: 'I am getting tired of these Jewish refugees. In Jamaica we have a letter from some of them expressing gratitude for good treatment in Jamaica: now we have complaints such as those described [by Richards]. If these people really think that conditions in Jamaica are no better than in concentration camps in Germany, it is a pity they didn't remain there'.[152] Two days later, John B. Sidebotham of the Colonial Office wrote to Randall at the Foreign Office to approve the reassignment of twelve units – equivalent to accommodation for up to one thousand refugees – at Gibraltar Camp for military purposes.[153]

In mid January 1943, the colonial secretary, Oliver Stanley, wrote to Richards, asking the governor to confirm that no further accommodation for Jewish refugees from Europe was available at Gibraltar Camp.[154] Richards informed Stanley that there was in fact still room for an additional five hundred refugees, but it was 'being reserved for emergencies such as a sudden influx by refugee ships'. It would be 'inconvenient', Richards argued, if the remaining space 'were given up permanently'.[155]

For many, the Allied Declaration of 17 December 1942 regarding the genocide against European Jewry was anything but news. Michael Fleming has recently reassessed the question of 'who knew what when', though he focuses most of his attention specifically on knowledge about Auschwitz rather than the systematic mass shootings following the invasion of the Soviet Union and the subsequently established Reinhard camps of Belzec, Sobibor and Treblinka II.

As Fleming makes abundantly clear, there was no immediate correlation between the information available to the British government and the information circulated to the public. Censorship played a key role in holding back information on the evolving genocide against European Jewry. 'Both the US and British governments', Fleming explains, 'were concerned that stories about Jews could provoke anti-Semitism on the one hand, and stimulate demands from civil-society activists for rescue and refuge on the other'.[156] The dearth of relevant documentation in the government papers held at the National Archives in Kew that has drawn much comment, Fleming suggests, contrary to 'the commonly accepted view that such documents do not or did not exist', actually results from the fact 'that they were weeded from' the regular files 'and redirected to selected officials with a view to post-war war crime trials'.[157]

A policy document circulated in the BBC in 1940, 'Presentation of News: Giving flesh to the bones – Description, interpretation, and comment', indicated very clearly that the availability of 'information' as such was not the problem. 'Truth being often stranger than fiction', BBC personnel were advised by this document, 'plenty of true reports have to be rejected on the grounds of incredibility'.[158] On 25 July 1941, just as the Einsatzgruppen in the Soviet Union were readying themselves to massacre every Jew they could lay their hands on, the Ministry of Information in London published a planning document with the title, 'Combatting the apathetic outlook of "What have I got to lose even if Germany wins"'. It explained that material intended for publication should not be too extreme. Sheer 'horror' stuff such as the concentration camp torture stories ... repel the normal mind. In self-defence, people prefer to think that the victims were specially marked men – and probably a pretty bad lot anyway. A certain amount of horror is needed, but it must be used very sparingly and must deal always with treatment of indisputably innocent people. Not with violent political opponents. And not with Jews.[159]

On the other hand, as early as 27 August 1941, Nigel de Grey, who at the time was head of research at Hut 3 in Bletchley Park, reported the following to Churchill: 'The fact that the police are killing all Jews [who] fall into their hands should now be sufficiently well appreciated. It is therefore not proposed to continue reporting these butcheries specially, unless so requested'.[160] Churchill saw this report on 12 September 1941.

Nor does Chief Rabbi Hertz seem to have been in any doubt as to what was occurring. As the *Manchester Guardian* reported on 8 September 1941, Hertz was 'issuing a call to all Jewish communities throughout the British Empire to join in a "week of re-dedication" in the period culminating in the Day of Atonement'. Hertz would 'open the week by a broadcast address in the Home Service on September 21, and in the North American service [the] next day'.[161] 'It is now many centuries since Judaism and Jewry anywhere stood so near [to] the brink of annihilation', Hertz explained in his message for Rosh Hashanah. 'Only the triumphant victory of Britain and her Allies will finally exorcise the demoniac terror which overhangs Continental populations. On that victory depends the future of Israel in Europe and beyond, as well as the survival of civilisation.'[162]

'Information', then, was not the problem. Yet with the exception of 'two choreographed reporting peaks' in June/July and December 1942, information about the ongoing genocide was systematically downplayed – that is, if it was brought to the public's attention at all, the persistent efforts of the Chief Rabbi and Board of Deputies notwithstanding.[163] On 2 June 1942, the BBC informed its listeners about a report by the Bund on the mass killings, followed on 9 July by a press conference in London chaired by the minister of information, Brendan Bracken, that highlighted the Bund report and put the number of murdered Jews to date at seven hundred thousand. That same evening, the archbishop of Westminster referred to this information in a BBC Home Service broadcast.[164]

On 13 December 1942, Hertz preached at Bevis Marks synagogue in the City of London to mark a 'day of fasting, mourning, and prayer for the victims of mass massacres in Nazi land'. The *Manchester Guardian* quoted Hertz as stating that

'I am dumbfounded by the indifference in some quarters, both high and low, in this country to the tragedy of millions of defenceless people' ...

Describing the Nazi slaughter of the Jews in Europe today as unsurpassed in the annals of barbarism by the vastness of its extent and its diabolic methods, Dr. Hertz said that many people in England appeared to be unshaken by the pronouncements of the leaders of the churches, and that in some sections of the press and some Government quarters 'a studied silence' had been adopted, which could not but be taken by the criminals in Berlin as an encouragement to perfect their technique.

'It is a sin to stand by with folded hands', said Dr. Hertz. 'What are the United Nations prepared to do? Will they at least be ready to open their gates to receive the survivors who have escaped, and the children. Public opinion must be roused in this beloved England ...

Shuddering seizeth us at the murderous decree to destroy, to slay, and to cause to perish all Jews, both young and old, women and little children. Their blood is flowing like water in Poland, Rumania, and in all other lands under the heel of arrogant iniquity.'

The *Manchester Guardian* noted that 'crowds were unable to get into this service ... and stood outside its doors throughout the service. ... As the most moving memories of Armistice Day have often been two minutes' silence in streets usually busy and noisy', the report concluded,

> so the intercession in Petticoat Lane yesterday will be remembered by Londoners who were in the East End for the Day of Mourning.
>
> Just before eleven o'clock, Christmas shopping was at its noisiest. Stallholders were shouting their offers of dolls, statuettes, stockings, and women's hair grips when walking down the crowded streets came a Jewish crier appealing for silence. Dolls and stockings were put down, many of the stallholders bowed their heads, and though not all the buyers [and] sellers were Jewish, the jostling crowd ceased to push and the only conversations were in undertones.
>
> At the end of five minutes, pandemonium started again, but though the streets were crowded, the East End was only half itself. Jewish bakers and butchers had their shutters up and many restaurants were closed.[165]

By now, sufficient pressure had mounted to convince the British government and the US administration that a contained and carefully stage-managed information campaign was their best option. On 17 December, the following statement was read to both Houses of Parliament on behalf of the nascent United Nations:

> The attention of the Governments of Belgium, Czechoslovakia, Greece, Luxemburg, the Netherlands, Norway, Poland, the United States of America,

the United Kingdom of Great Britain and Northern Ireland, the Union of Soviet Socialist Republics and Yugoslavia, and of the French National Committee, has been drawn to numerous reports from Europe that the German authorities, not content with denying to persons of Jewish race in all the territories over which their barbarous rule has been extended, the most elementary human rights, are now carrying into effect Hitler's oft-repeated intention to exterminate the Jewish people in Europe. From all the occupied countries Jews are being transported, in conditions of appalling horror and brutality, to Eastern Europe. In Poland, which has been made the principal Nazi slaughter-house, the ghettos established by the German invaders are being systematically emptied of all Jews except a few highly skilled workers required for war industries. None of those taken away are ever heard of again. The able-bodied are slowly worked to death in labour camps. The infirm are left to die of exposure and starvation, or are deliberately massacred in mass executions. The number of victims of these bloody cruelties is reckoned in many hundreds of thousands of entirely innocent men, women and children.

The above-mentioned Governments and the French National Committee condemn in the strongest possible terms this bestial policy of cold-blooded extermination. They declare that such events can only strengthen the resolve of all freedom-loving peoples to overthrow the barbarous Hitlerite tyranny. They reaffirm their solemn resolution to ensure that those responsible for these crimes shall not escape retribution, and to press on with the necessary practical measures to this end.

On the suggestion of the Labour MP for Islington South, William Cluse, the members of the House of Commons stood in silence 'in support of this protest against disgusting barbarism'.[166] In the House of Lords, Labour's Lord (Christopher) Addison remarked that, 'a more awful exposure to horrors, I imagine, has never been issued by any Government in the history of the world … if ever, in the history of the world, there was a crime for which the obliteration of those responsible was merited, surely it is to be found in this series of crimes'. His colleague, Viscount (Herbert) Samuel suggested that 'the only events even remotely parallel to this were the Armenian massacres of fifty years ago'.[167] Yet words were one thing, actions quite another, and it is telling that the Colonial Office resolved to intensify its stonewalling against the admission of further refugees on the very day on which the United Nations called the free world to action against the extermination of European Jewry by the Nazis.

Clearly, then, for all the pragmatic reasons the British and Jamaican authorities felt they had for refusing to accept further Polish Jewish refugees while continuing to admit their Dutch counterparts, this particular decision also reflected their continuing determination to keep the immigration of Jewish refugees to an absolute minimum, even once it became general knowledge that the Germans were systematically exterminating all the Jews they could bring under their control.

To be sure, it would be foolhardy to deny that the availability and security of the requisite shipping was a key issue when it came to considering the possibility of transferring larger numbers of refugees, Jewish or otherwise, to Gibraltar Camp, given that it had been built for seven thousand inhabitants yet was, to the best of our knowledge, never more than half full. Yet it is also difficult to deny that the arguments about shipping were as much political as they were technical in nature. An obvious case in point is the decision to end the evacuation of further Gibraltarians to Jamaica. Labour's Albert V. Alexander, as First Lord of the Admiralty, did call for a halt of the scheme in the War Cabinet on 25 October 1940, given 'the present position in the North Western Approaches'. Yet he also stated that 'the Navy could provide a sufficient escort' for those Gibraltarians who were actually willing to be transferred from London to Gibraltar Camp (some 500 out of a total of 10,600). Moreover, he did not argue that the scheme should be stopped altogether, but that further transfers should be postponed 'until the Admiralty had tested the results of the new convoy arrangements'. It seems evident from the minutes that the real problem consisted in the unwillingness of the Gibraltarians to leave Britain. Churchill argued that 'the Gibraltarians ought to go overseas and that they should be made to understand that we were determined that they should go. Their attitude could be altered by propaganda'. Consequently, the colonial secretary and the minister of health (who was responsible for maintaining the evacuees in London) were 'invited … to make suitable arrangements to induce the other Gibraltarian evacuees, by effective propaganda, to proceed to the West Indies as and when suitable shipping arrangements could be made'. Clearly, then, the War Cabinet was operating on the assumption that there was a realistic prospect of transferring the remaining ten thousand Gibraltarians to Jamaica in the foreseeable future.[168] A report submitted to the War Cabinet on 16 November 1940 again reiterated that 'difficulties have arisen over the re-evacuation of Gibraltarians from this country to the West Indies (Jamaica and Trinidad). All arrangements for their reception have been made, but there is a strong disinclination on the part of the great majority to go overseas'.[169]

Presumably in order to persuade the reluctant Gibraltarians of the merits of going to Jamaica, a propaganda film, 'The Gate at Gibraltar', was planned (I have been unable to ascertain whether it was actually produced). The first part of the script covered at some length the arrival of the first Gibraltarians; the second part focused on camp life once they had settled in. In both parts, the camp was praised with great pathos. 'The gates are opened', the script began; 'like giant arms outstretched they welcome to Jamaica and to safety those who were forced to seek refuge from the mad fury of a hell let loose in

Europe by Hitler and his Axis-partner-in-crime Mussolini'. Gibraltar Camp was 'a haven of safety for hundreds who have had to leave their homes and loved ones to traverse seas fraught with danger for a destination unknown'.[170] The second part of the script emphasized the degree to which:

> Life goes on: Life without fear of Enemy attacking from [the] Air. Life that knows only the assurance of Victory, and the salvation of the world through Democracy. ...
> Life goes on ... with that feeling of security, which is the right of every citizen in Britain's far-flung Empire.
> Families know that when each pleasant day comes to an end that they may retire to bed – peacefully and without fear.[171]

Presumably the crucial term in this ode is 'citizen', given how much less outstretched the camp's giant arms were when it came to accepting refugees in (arguably more) desperate need of help who were not British citizens.

In May 1941, the possibility of transferring a further four thousand evacuees directly from Gibraltar to Jamaica was again considered by the War Cabinet, indicating that shipping really was not the principal concern in letting the evacuations to Gibraltar Camp peter out.[172] Nor, evidently, did the order of November 1940 to stop further construction at Gibraltar Camp indicate that the British government had given up on the possibility of still sending substantial numbers of evacuees there. Yet if this was so, and smaller transfers to Gibraltar Camp continued until December 1943, then it clearly would not have been an insurmountable challenge to offer more Jewish refugees a temporary abode there.

The Bermuda Conference

If any further proof were needed that neither the British government nor the US administration ever seriously considered undertaking direct practical measures to help to rescue Jews from the German machinery of extermination, it was delivered by the Anglo-American Bermuda Conference that met in the colony's capital, Hamilton, in the second half of April 1943. None too surprisingly, the hope that this conference might turn out to be rather more useful than the Evian Conference of 1938 was articulated by numerous observers, yet in vain. However, the widespread public critique of the Bermuda Conference was predicated on a fundamental misunderstanding regarding the goal of the conference. As we will see, significant sections of the public both in Britain and the United States assumed that the conference had been convened to follow up on the Allies' concerted public protest against the systematic extermination of German Jewry of 17 December 1942 with commensurate action. The governments, meanwhile, never saw the conference in this light, though they presumably did hope that the conference might create the impression that they were doing something about the genocide.

The governments' priorities lay elsewhere altogether. For them, the conviction reigned supreme that victory over Germany was the best guarantee that the systematic extermination of European Jewry would end, and that any temptation to divert funds, goods or personnel from the war effort towards rescue efforts had to be avoided. Consequently, for the British government and the US administration, the Bermuda Conference was only ever meant to address an issue with which we are already familiar: their principal aim was to keep open the exit route via Spain and Portugal for potential Allied military personnel by extracting those stranded on the Iberian peninsula who were clogging up the pipeline. Estimates prepared for the conference focused on three categories: firstly, there were assumed to be some fourteen thousand French refugees in Spain and Portugal, mainly men of military age who were hoping to be posted to North Africa; secondly, it was estimated that some eight hundred Allied nationals, mainly Poles, were affected, who had been accepted into the armed forces of their countries and whom the Allies wished to take to Britain; this left, thirdly, some six to eight thousand Jewish refugees, mostly from Central Europe.[173] Of the latter, some two thousand had reached Spain prior to 1942 but were then left stranded because they lacked the requisite visas to travel elsewhere. The others were mainly young men who had fled France after the occupation of the former so-called Free Zone (i.e. Vichy France) by the Germans in November 1942.[174]

As had been the case when the British government agreed to the transfer of Polish Jewish refugees from Lisbon to Jamaica in the winter of 1941/42, Britain and the United States were motivated primarily by the desire to ensure that refugees who would go on to enlist in the Allied armed forces could continue to flee France via Spain and Portugal. The Jewish refugees, for the most part, were of concern only in so far as they threatened to block the exit route for potential Allied military personnel. The situation of the Jewish refugees in Spain and Portugal was dire, to be sure, yet, as things stood, they no longer needed to fear for their lives. It is therefore not without irony that the public largely looked on the Bermuda Conference as an opportunity to discuss means of rescuing Jews from the genocide.

However, anything undertaken to keep the exit route via the Iberian peninsula open did also benefit Jews still trapped in the former Free Zone and facing deportation from there to Drancy and on to the death camps, including those who had temporarily found protection in the Italian Zone but would come under German control again following Italy's surrender in September 1943. As an editorial in the *Manchester Guardian* put it rather wisely: 'The question is simple. Many Jews and other victims are still escaping, and will escape, from their tormentors. What can be done to save these, to increase the number, to encourage all who can lend a hand? It is a practical question, and no answer is to be found in defeatism and procrastination backed by platitudes'.[175] The expectations of various individuals and organizations, both Jewish and non-Jewish – including, inter alia, the archbishops of Canterbury, York and Westminster – certainly differed quite considerably from those of the two governments. This was reflected not least by the sustained demand for formal independent Jewish representation at the conference.

Early in April, the president of the Board of Deputies of British Jews, Selig Brodetsky, who was a leading British Zionist, called for accredited independent Jewish representation at the conference. He expressed his hope that it 'will not be a repetition of the Evian conference', but also his concern about statements by Lord Cranborne and the State Department that the conference would not focus on refugees of 'any particular race or faith'. After all, 'on no other people has a declaration of death been pronounced'.[176] Later that month, the Swiss section of Agudas Israel initiated the delivery of an appeal to Pope Pius XII, 'asking him to intervene at the Bermuda Conference'.[177]

Not only Jewish officials sought to exert pressure on the forthcoming conference. A broad coalition of religious and political organizations engaged in a sustained campaign for a more proactive approach of the Allies towards the possible rescue of Jews. On 15 April, to name just one example, a meeting at the Chicago Stadium mobilized 'more than 20,000 Jews and non-Jews' who 'adopted a resolution asking that the European Jews be rescued, which will be forwarded to President Roosevelt with the request that it be submitted to the Bermuda Conference'. The speakers 'included Judge Joseph Proskauer, president of the American Jewish Committee; Dr. Stephen Wise, president of the American Jewish Congress; Henry Monsky, president of the B'nai B'rith; Adolf Held, president of the Jewish Labor Committee; Governor Dwight H. Green of Illinois; Senator Brooks of Illinois; and Senator Truman of Missouri. Federal Judge William J. Campbell presided'. Illinois Senator Scott Lucas, one of the designated members of the US delegation at the conference, addressed the gathering 'over the telephone from Washington'. Reverend Harold Rop of the Chicago Church Federation warned that 'the Statue of Liberty will be veiled in gloom if no urgent measures are taken to save Jews from the Nazis'.[178]

On 20 April, as the conference was just getting under way, the JTA published an appeal for independent Jewish representation at the conference from the Joint Emergency Committee for European Jewish Affairs – 'comprising the American Jewish Committee; the American Jewish Congress; the B'nai B'rith; the Jewish Labor Committee; the American Emergency Committee for

Zionist Affairs of the Zionist Organization of America; Hadassah; Mizrachi; and the Poale Zion; the Synagogue Council of America; the Agudath Israel of America, Inc.; and the Union of Orthodox Rabbis in America'. 'We would be less than frank', the committee explained,

> if we did not convey to you the anguish of the Jewish community of this country over the failure of the United Nations to act until now to rescue the Jews of Europe. For many months it has been authenticated that the Nazis have marked the Jewish population of Europe for total extermination, and that it is estimated that almost three million Jews have been done to death, while a similar fate awaits those who remain. World civilization has been stirred to its depths by these horrors. Every section of public opinion throughout the world, and more particularly in England and in the United States, has spoken out in demand that the United Nations act before it is too late to save those who can still be saved. Six months have elapsed, however, and no action has as yet been taken. In the meantime, it is reported that thousands of Jews continue to be murdered daily.
>
> When first the conference, which is now to open in Bermuda, was announced, it was our hope that at last effective action would be immediately forthcoming on the part of the United Nations.

Yet in the meantime their hopes had been 'seriously disturbed'. There were three reasons for this. Firstly, both the British government and the US administration had 'announced that the Bermuda Conference is to be primarily exploratory'. Secondly, neither government had so far 'seen fit to call into consultation the representative organizations of the Jewish communities of their respective countries' or 'to invite delegations representing the organized Jewish communities of these two countries to participate in the deliberations'. Finally, 'the isolation of the Conference in a place completely inaccessible to the influences of public opinion or public personalities, except by Government permission', did not seem to bode well. 'When millions of human beings have already been done to death', the appeal continued,

> and the fact of their murder has been authenticated by the United Nations, the time for exploration has long since passed, and the time for action is long past due. Unless action is undertaken immediately, there may soon be no Jews left alive in Europe. In communicating these views to you, it is our purpose at this time also formally to place before you the request that a delegation representing the Joint Emergency Committee for European Jewish Affairs be invited to the Bermuda Conference to present our views on the program of rescue to be undertaken for the Jews of Europe. It is our sincere hope that you [i.e. US Under-Secretary of State Sumner Welles], who have long had an intimate and, we believe, sympathetic knowledge of this problem, will lend your influence to ensure that the Bermuda Conference may serve as the instrument

of humanity in rescuing a defenseless people who are otherwise doomed to complete annihilation.[179]

While the committee was correct as far as independent Jewish representation at the conference was concerned, it is worth noting that the US delegation was in fact accompanied by a small group of experts, one of whom was the vice president of the Joint, George Backer.

Protests concerning the lack of formal Jewish participation at the conference and its increasingly apparent lack of ambition continued throughout the conference. On 20 April, thirty-seven members of the Massachusetts Senate 'signed resolutions presented by Senator Maurice M. Goldman of Boston asking Secretary Hull to request the refugee conference now in session at Hamilton, Bermuda, to allow the Joint Emergency Committee for European Jewish Affairs to appear before it to present its program for the rescue of Jews in Europe'.[180]

On 23 April, the JTA, under the title, 'Disappointment in Britain at Spirit of Bermuda Parley', reported, inter alia, on an editorial in the *Manchester Guardian*.[181] 'Why', the author of the editorial asked, 'does the Foreign Office and why do the opening speeches at the conference ignore (so far as the published versions show) the Jewish side of the persecution?' After all, 'the Bermuda conference has sprung from the horrors of the extermination of the Jews'.

Just as the conference was drawing to a close, the JTA noted that the president of the Congress of Industrial Organizations, Philip Murray, a Scottish-born former miner – acting on 'a cable from the Histadruth, Federation of Jewish Labor in Palestine, asking American labor to exert its influence on the conference' – had lodged

a formal protest with the State Department ... emphasizing that the membership of the CIO 'is profoundly shocked at the outrageous mass murder of the Jewish people in Axis-dominated Europe', and criticizing the action of the State Department in closing the doors of the Bermuda Conference to representatives of American war relief groups. ...

'The closed-door policy gives us deep concern that this conference might be a mere diplomatic nicety. We would regret a repetition of the futile Evian conference'.[182]

The pathos and sense of urgency expressed by various individuals and organizations could not have been further removed from the pace at which the preparations for the conference and the conference itself commenced. The US delegation was headed by the president of Princeton, Dr Harold W. Dodds, a political scientist. He was joined by Senator Scott Lucas of Illinois, and congressman Sol Bloom who represented New York's Upper East Side.

They were accompanied by a handful of experts. Initially, the JTA suggested that, alongside George Backer, these would be the executive secretary of the President's Advisory Committee on Refugees, George Warren, and Robert Clark Alexander, the assistant chief of the State Department's Visa Division. It later reported that the delegation had consulted throughout the conference with the former consul in Copenhagen, Robert Borden Reams, and Julian Foster, a shipping expert in the State Department.[183] Maybe all of them were present.

The British delegation was headed by the Parliamentary Under-Secretary of State for the Foreign Office, Richard Law, the son of the former prime minister, Andrew Bonar Law. He was joined by the Parliamentary Under-Secretary of State for the Home Office, Osbert Peake, and George Hall, the Parliamentary Under-Secretary of State at the Admiralty. They had with them a team of five experts. They were Sir Bernard Reilly of the Colonial Office (the former governor of Aden), Sir Frank Newsam of the Home Office, Alec Randall of the Foreign Office, Bernard F. Picknett of the Ministry of War Transport, and William G. Hayter, the first secretary of the British Embassy in Washington.

The Jewish organizations were doing their best to read the tea leaves. As the JTA informed its readers on 14 April,

> the most significant indication of the possibilities of the Bermuda Conference, Jewish leaders feel, is the fact that one of the three British delegates is the Under-Secretary of the Admiralty, George Hall. This is taken here to mean that the question of providing transportation facilities for refugees will probably be one of the central points of discussion at the parley. Transportation difficulties have, hitherto, been the crux of the entire refugee problem.[184]

Yet the following day, the JTA delivered chastening news: 'It was learned here today [that the conference] will not deal with the problem of rescuing Nazi victims in occupied countries, but will restrict its discussion to the problem of the refugees who have succeeded in leaving Nazi-countries and who are at present in Spain, Portugal and Switzerland'.[185]

On the eve of the conference, the *Washington Post* related that Law and Dodds 'were expected to "get acquainted" with one another at a small informal dinner at the Governor's villa tonight'.[186] On the first day of the conference, proceedings lasted 'for one hour … Delegates adjourned to spend the rest of the day in informal talks, marking time until the arrival of Senator Scott Lucas of Illinois, whose departure from the United States had been delayed by illness'. Dodds was quoted as explaining in his opening address that 'the problem is too great for a solution by the two governments here represented'. Peake used the opportunity to inform journalists that the British

West Indies 'are overcrowded and face an acute feeding problem'. Reilly added 'that British Guiana needed two years of preparatory construction to provide havens for refugees', and that 'Jamaica has not only 400 refugees, but also 1,500 English evacuees from Gibraltar, and provides no further possibilities'. At least in terms of the existing free capacity at Gibraltar Camp this was not in fact true.

The next day, the conference made considerable progress: the delegates present (Lucas was still missing) were able to agree 'that Dr. Harold W. Dodds and Under-Secretary Law will alternate as chairman at future sessions of the conference'. Moreover, Dodds informed the press 'that he has been conferring with Mr. Law on the agenda, and that the two have reached an agreement regarding the subjects of discussion'. Giving a clear indication of his priorities, Law explained that 'we must take great care to see that we are not betrayed by our feelings of humanity and compassion into courses of action which at best would postpone the day of liberation, and at worst might make liberation forever impossible'. He added:

> We are hopeful that two things at least we shall be able to achieve. Where joint action may be possible, we may hope to lay the foundations for such action. Where other countries may be involved – and since this is not a national problem but an international problem, other countries are inevitably involved – we may be able to work out tentatively some basis for wider international discussion with a view to wider international organization and action.[187]

Even allowing for diplomatic conventions, this was hardly an ambitious programme. Two days later, the JTA noted that 'Senator Scott Lucas of Illinois ... is still in the United States, unable to leave the country because of illness'. It had been 'stated here today' (i.e. on 22 April) that this was 'preventing the conference from getting into full swing since the American delegation is not complete'.[188] On 23 April, the *New York Times* reported that the 'movement of refugees on a large scale during the war seems to the delegates to be out of the question'.[189]

The statement issued at the end of the conference – such as it was, given that the ostensible results were declared too sensitive to publicize – matched the aspirations of this beginning:

> The United States and the United Kingdom delegations examined the refugee problem in all its aspects, including the position of those potential refugees who are still in the grip of the Axis powers without any immediate prospect of escape. Nothing was excluded from their analysis, and everything that held out any possibility, however remote, of a solution [to] the problem was carefully investigated and thoroughly discussed.

From the outset it was realized that any recommendation that the delegates could make to their governments must pass two tests: Would any recommendation submitted interfere with or delay the war effort of the United Nations? And was the recommendation capable of accomplishment under war conditions? The delegates at Bermuda felt bound to reject certain proposals which were not capable of meeting these tests.

The delegates were able to agree on a number of concrete recommendations which they are jointly submitting to their governments and which, it is felt, will pass the tests set forth above, and which will lead to the relief of a substantial number of refugees of all races and nationalities. Since the recommendations necessarily concern governments other than those represented at the Bermuda conference and involve military considerations, they must remain confidential. It may be said, however, that in the course of discussion the refugee problem was broken down into its main elements.

Questions of shipping, food and supply were fully investigated. The delegates also agreed on recommendations regarding the form of intergovernmental organization which was best fitted in their opinion to handle the problem in the future. This organization would have to be flexible enough to permit it to consider without prejudice any new factors that might come to its attention.

In each of these fields the delegates were able to submit agreed proposals for the consideration of their respective governments.[190]

This lacklustre communiqué precipitated harsh criticism from a number of quarters. 'Press in England Disappointed with the Bermuda Conference', the JTA headed its report on the conference on 29 April 1943. Several London papers had argued 'that the British people would welcome a more generous approach to the refugee problem than that shown by the Anglo-American delegations at Bermuda'.[191] On 4 May, the JTA related, under the heading 'American Press Urges Admission of More Jews from Nazi Europe', a number of public activities on, and responses to, the 'Day of Compassion' for European Jewry organized the day before by the Federal Council of Churches. It quoted from the *New York Herald Tribune*, which had written:

Compassion which does not show to each man his own faults and falseness illumines little … Compassion which does not bring forth some act to ease the lot of those suffering and wronged or, if that is not possible, to avert any likely suffering, any likely wrong against other men and women is empty sentiment, worthless alike to giver and to receiver.

In Boston, a 'protest demonstration against the Nazi extermination of Jews' had taken place, 'in which more than 20,000 persons participated'. The JTA quoted the commentary of the *Boston Globe*:

The mass meeting, one of a series being held throughout the country, coincides with the closing days of the joint British-American Conference on Refugees held in Bermuda. It was hoped that this conference would result in a program of action for those refugees from Hitlerism who so far have escaped the Nazi hangman. But the news from Bermuda is not encouraging, and one can well imagine the disappointment of those who looked to it with great hope.[192]

The president of the Synagogue Council of America, Rabbi Israel Goldstein, described the conference as 'not only a failure but a mockery ... The job of the Bermuda conference apparently was not to rescue victims of the Nazi terror, but to rescue our State Department and the British Foreign Office from possible embarrassment'.[193] He added that it was 'a sad commentary upon the disparity between our professed war aims, which speak in terms of humanitarianism, and our actions, which are motivated by timidity and by catering to the forces of reaction in our midst'.[194] Adolph Held, the president of the Jewish Labor Committee, called the conference 'a failure and a great disappointment',[195] the Committee for a Jewish Army spoke of a 'cruel mockery',[196] and Stephen Wise of 'a tragic disappointment'.[197] The JTA reported that 'the London Economist ... wonders whether the Bermuda Conference "will become a by-word of indecision, compromise and deferred hope"'.[198] The *Los Angeles Times* noted that the conference was being 'Seen As Second Munich'.[199] The JTA Daily News Bulletin reported:

> Several hundred rabbis in New York today [24 May] adopted a resolution expressing disappointment at the outcome of the Bermuda Conference ... 'We cannot believe that Bermuda is the answer to the agonizing cry of the millions of innocent victims', said the resolution. 'Evasion and helplessness must not be the way of the United Nations now, any more than concession and appeasement should have been the pre-war policy of the democracies'.[200]

The actual report of the Bermuda Conference, which was never published, was circulated confidentially to the War Cabinet by the Foreign Office on 4 May 1943. It recommended that the French refugees should be sent to camps in North Africa and that Allied nationals would be accepted into service in the armed forces. As far as the six to eight thousand Jewish refugees were concerned, the possibility was suggested of allowing small groups to emigrate to the United States and Palestine, and offering temporary refuge to others either in Gibraltar Camp or in camps in North Africa. Generally, though, the British West Indies had been ruled out as a possible destination because 'there would be the gravest difficulties in receiving refugees owing to the acute supply position, especially in regard to food, fuel and accommodation'. Not least, Europeans could hardly be expected to exist without some of the food stuffs to which they were accustomed but which were 'unobtainable' in tropical locations. British Honduras and British Guiana had already been examined as possible refugee destinations, the report pointed out, but the requisite construction projects were not feasible during wartime.[201]

In the event, no more Polish Jewish refugees were transferred to Gibraltar Camp, but two further groups of Dutch refugees were temporarily housed in the camp, arriving in October and December 1943. The first of these groups comprised mostly Jewish refugees, with a substantial number in the second group also. The arrival of these two groups clearly demonstrates that it was still possible to transfer refugees safely to the Caribbean. Evidently, the crucial distinction between the Polish and Dutch refugees was that the Dutch government in exile was willing to make a substantial financial contribution to the maintenance of its refugees, while its Polish counterpart was not. In this light alone, British refugee policy at this juncture can indeed be aptly characterized as 'self-interested', and the Bermuda Conference as a 'low-cost' attempt 'to assuage domestic Jewish opinion'.[202]

The conference was scheduled for discussion in the House of Commons on 19 May. 'The coming debate on the Bermuda Conference', the *Manchester Guardian* commented, 'will show whether we still claim, or deserve, the old reputation' of being a country willing to provide asylum to refugees.

> Ministers who have been pressed in Parliament to do something substantial now have fallen back on the supposed achievement of the past as though, even were it true, it justified our failure either to do anything ourselves or to get others to do anything that would abate the horrors of Hitler's extermination policy. …
> Our humanitarian feelings having so far failed to issue in practical results, the Bermuda Conference becomes the test of both our sincerity and our capacity of action.

The British delegates at the conference, the *Manchester Guardian*'s editorial continued, had been

> representative of the departments which have been either flatly negative or tearfully despondent. But they can now wipe that cut. They can show that we have at last decided a creditable, because a determined and energetic, course. If not, it will be disappointing, but it will be more disappointing still if Parliament does not in that case plainly express the dissatisfaction which the public cannot but feel.

Twice the editorial referred to the fact that it had now been five months since 'we learned fully what was going on and … condemned it with impressive rhetoric' – that is to say, since the Allied Declaration of 17 December 1942, criticizing 'our five months' lack of policy'.[203]

The government was certainly taken to task by a number of impassioned speakers in the House of Commons – Eleanor Rathbone noting that 'it is maddening that the Government shows so little sense of urgency'[204] – yet to no discernible effect. The government's speakers mainly resorted to reticence and regret, and emphasized the confidentiality of the conference's results. Osbert Peake reiterated the government's central argument:

> We must, I think, recognise that the United Nations can do little or nothing in the immediate present for the vast numbers now under Hitler's control. He is determined not to let those people go.[205] The rate of extermination is such that no measures of rescue or relief on however large a scale could be commensurate with the problem ... Any slackening of our war effort or any delay to shipping in the attempted rescue of refugees could only delay the day of victory and result in the infliction of greater suffering on the subjugated peoples of Europe.[206]

Other speakers were rather more forthright, repeating worn arguments about the risk that further Jewish immigration would intensify domestic antisemitism, and claiming that there were no fewer than 120 million potential refugees in Europe, only waiting for Britain to give an inch. 'What a hollow farce, what a pitiful exhibition of political cynicism, was the solemn declaration subscribed to by the House five months ago',[207] the London *News Chronicle* protested in response to the parliamentary debate.

On 28 July, the conference was finally discussed in the House of Lords (on initiative not of the government but of David Davies, a former Welsh MP for the Liberals, philanthropist and staunch supporter of the League of Nations). As the *Manchester Guardian* commented, 'unfortunately Lord Cranborne could report little progress. ... But with what energy has the Government thrown itself into this task?' the editorial asked, adding:

> The great protest in the House of Commons was made on December 17, the Bermuda Conference ended in the last week of April. Britain and the United States decided at Bermuda to set up an Inter-Governmental Committee to watch over the execution of the Conference decisions. Now, three months later ... Lord Cranborne announces that international negotiations are proceeding with regard to the first meeting of this Committee, and I am glad to say that those negotiations are progressing favourably.
>
> If the two Governments had had their hearts in the job, and if the refugees had been British or American and not aliens, there could not have been this dreary, discreditable delay. Three months and the Committee has not met! But let us be grateful – and let the refugees be grateful too – since the negotiations are 'progressing favourably'.[208]

The reorganized Intergovernmental Committee for Refugees did not hold its first plenary session until August 1944.[209]

Dr Pulver, whom we previously met as secretary of the Jewish Association of Trinidad, also referred to the Bermuda Conference in his New Year Address on behalf of the World Jewish Congress, which was broadcast on Trinidad's Rediffusion Programme on the evening of 29 September 1943. 'We called the attention of the civilized world' to the extermination of European Jewry 'by December 1942', he explained.

> Hitler has not as yet exterminated all the Jews but he has done a long step towards that.
>
> From the reports transmitted through the State Department to Dr. Stephen Wise, the President of the World Jewish Congress, it appears that four million Jews have been murdered by the Nazis since the summer of 1942. According to this report the entire Jewish population of Poland (formerly 3,300,000) has been annihilated ...
>
> The terror against the Jews in Nazi-occupied Europe has reached a peak never known in the history of religious persecutions.

Pulver referred to goings on in Eastern Europe in some detail, illustrating the measure of information already available in the West at the time, even if not all of it was entirely precise. He also mentioned explicitly the Warsaw Ghetto uprising, in which 'the Jews have offered armed resistance for ten days'. 'Not only a Jew will understand my sorrow for my mother and father, brothers and sisters', Pulver continued,

> but any one of you listening to me now will feel the same repulsion, and will be of the opinion that something must be done before the remainder of the victims have been exterminated.
>
> So far, very little has been done: a conference has been called for this purpose in Bermuda in April 1943 but up to now we have seen no action. The Intergovernmental Committee which had to be formed for a rescue program has taken six months to be set up and has not started work as yet. ...
>
> The only hope for the Jews is the invasion of Europe and the total victory of the Allies. We are waiting and preparing for this. But something must be done to stop the killing of Jews in the meantime.[210]

Pulver felt that his address was a great success. 'The radio broadcast was listened to by thousands of local friends (non-Jewish)', he wrote to Baruch Zuckerman of the World Jewish Congress in October 1943, 'and by the majority of the Jews. From all the reactions shown so far it appears that it had a good reception from the listeners'.[211]

That the Jewish refugees and the wider public in the British West Indies knew about events in Europe, including the Ghetto uprising in Warsaw, is also demonstrated by an article in the *Daily Gleaner* of 4 August 1943 on one of the more active and vocal Polish refugees, Arthur Steigler, who evidently had at least some success in overcoming the isolation at Gibraltar Camp. As the *Daily Gleaner* reported,

> The May–June issue of the 'Polish Jew' organ of the American Federation for Polish Jews in the United States, published an article concerning Dr. Arthur Steigler, who is residing at present at Gibraltar Camp.
>
> The article is headed 'Jewish Composer at Gibraltar Camp Writes Anti-Hitler Song'. [It] states: 'Dr. Arthur Steigler, who has been in constant communication with the American Federation for Polish Jews since he arrived in Gibraltar Camp from Cracow, has composed an Anti-Hitler song entitled "Quo Vadis, Domine!" Dr. Steigler, a Jew, composed this song when news arrived that the Burgomaster of the Jewish ghetto in Warsaw, Adam Czerniakow, had committed suicide. Dr. Steigler is responsible not only for the pathetic verse referring to the Jews and Poles, but also for the music. The author has put into the mouth of Czerniakow, speaking from his grave, a challenge for the United Nations to upset the infernal plans of Hitler to exterminate the entire Jewish population in Poland, where it is well known they are being herded and slaughtered by the thousands'.[212]

Increasingly aware of what was happening to European Jewry, yet unable to contribute to the war effort or even to obtain more specific information on friends and relatives they had been forced to leave behind, many of the refugees, as Miriam Stanton recalled, 'felt a terrible sense of loss; we felt that we did not belong anywhere anymore'.[213]

Ultimately, most of the criticism of the Bermuda Conference hinged on the fundamental misunderstanding outlined at the beginning of this discussion. Significant sections of the public assumed that the task of the conference was to come up with substantive action to match the Allied Declaration of 17 December 1942. For the two governments, by contrast, the conference, like all else, had only one purpose, namely, to strengthen the war effort, in this case by guaranteeing the continued influx of expertise and manpower via Spain and Portugal. If the Bermuda Conference was, consequently, as much of a disappointment to all those concerned with the plight of the refugees as the Evian Conference had been, there was, of course, one fundamental difference. In the meantime, the Germans had moved from the expulsion to the systematic extermination of the Jews. Yet even now, British officials feared that easing the entry requirements for Jewish refugees might encourage the Germans to unleash an insurmountable flood of refugees on the Allies. Extraordinarily, it was pointed out in the document from the British Embassy in Washington to the Department of State, in which the British first proposed what would become the Bermuda Conference, that, 'there is a possibility that the Germans or their satellites may change over from the policy of extermination to one of extrusion, and aim as they did before the war at embarrassing other countries by flooding them with alien immigrants'.[214]

The Jewish Relief Organizations after the Bermuda Conference

The limitations of the Bermuda Conference doubtless marked a turning point for Jewish refugee and relief organizations. Writing to the US Under-Secretary of State, Sumner Welles, on behalf of the Joint Emergency Committee for European Jewish Affairs shortly after the conference, the American Jewish Congress expressed its 'desire to convey the sense of despair of the American Jewish community over the failure of our Government to take any effective steps to save the Jews in Nazi-occupied Europe from the certain death that awaits them'.[215] For Jewish organizations the outcome of the conference was clearly an unmitigated disaster, given how clearly it demonstrated the reluctance of the Allies to pursue even limited rescue schemes, the viability of which was not really in question. Given the apparent failure of attempts to commit the Allies to rescue initiatives, important Jewish organizations began to redirect their focus firmly towards demands for the post-war period.

From August 1943 onwards, the American Jewish Conference placed the demand for the creation of a Jewish state in Palestine centre stage, subscribing to the programme first formulated in May 1942 at the Biltmore Conference: 'The Conference demands that the gates of Palestine be opened; that the Jewish Agency be vested with the necessary authority for up-building the country, including the development of its unoccupied and uncultivated lands; and that Palestine be established as a Jewish commonwealth integrated in the structure of the new democratic world'.[216]

Even so, some persisted, most importantly perhaps the Bergson group, whose significance in the ongoing struggle for rescue measures has only recently been widely acknowledged.[217] It consisted of Zionist Revisionists from the Yishuv who owed no loyalty to either the United States or the American Jewish leadership. They campaigned vociferously for rescue measures, including a possible agreement with the Romanian government, and organized an Emergency Conference in New York in July 1943. Late in 1943, Treasury Secretary Henry Morgenthau, Jr., submitted a report to Roosevelt that he had commissioned 'on the Acquiescence of this Government in the Murder of Jews'. It detailed ways in which information about the systematic extermination of European Jewry had been suppressed, and rescue schemes obstructed, by the administration. The main recommendation of the report was that a government agency should be created to tackle the rescue and relief issue.

Given the widespread criticism of the Bermuda Conference, which had been mobilized in no small measure by the Bergson Group, and with elections looming, Roosevelt decided to follow the recommendation. On 22 January 1944, he established the War Refugee Board and tasked it with the provision of administrative support for rescue operations (including relevant negotiations with foreign governments) and the evacuation of, and care for, refugees. This did indicate an important change in refugee policy on the part of the United States administration, and thus, on Tony Kushner's reading, amounted to a split between the US administration and the British government on this issue.[218] It is important to note that it was not the purpose of the War Refugee Board to engage in rescue work itself, but rather to offer administrative support to organizations undertaking rescue activities for which the funding was already in place.[219] To this end, it received $1 million from Roosevelt's Presidential Emergency Fund, as well as a number of major donations, including $100,000 from HIAS, most of which never went through the books. These donations included funds from the Joint. In her recent study of the War Refugee Board, Rebecca Erbelding refers to at least one instance in which War Refugee Board funding was returned because the Joint had already stepped into the breach, and acknowledges that 'it is unfortunate that the War Refugee Board did not repay the Joint for their important donations'.[220] Even so, on Erbelding's account, the widely accepted notion that the War Refugee Board was underfunded and effectively financed by the Jewish organizations is untenable. Its finances may have been complicated and procedures often cumbersome, but it was adequately funded for the role it had been assigned. As Erbelding points out, one also has to consider the alternatives. The chances of getting Congress to play ball were minimal, and any fundraising drive would have taken too long and would in any case have competed with other crowd-sourcing projects, including the United Jewish Appeal.

After the war, blame was apportioned to the Joint, especially by the World Jewish Congress, for failing to facilitate the rescue of more European Jews, not least by turning down the proposal of the American Jewish Congress to form a single refugee organization. As a result, the Joint continued to be the only American Jewish organization licensed by the US Treasury to carry out rescue initiatives in occupied countries until the formation of the War Refugee Board in 1944. The Joint did in fact collaborate with the WJC in neutral countries, but this cooperation transpired unofficially, and looking back, the WJC evidently had no intention of acknowledging it.[221] The strength of feeling articulated by WJC officials may have sprung not least from their desire for self-exculpation, given that in reality the WJC too, as Zohar Zegev has recently shown, 'cooperated with other Jewish elites and with the US administration with a view to moderating the American Jewish reaction to the Holocaust'.[222] 'For two years', Nahum Goldmann, president of the World Jewish Congress, complained at a WJC conference in London in 1945, the WJC had 'futilely appealed to Jewish relief organizations' like the Joint 'to help obtain permission to send relief; but their "ideology" did not permit them to mix relief with politics, and the result was that thousands of Jews [who] could have been saved were exterminated'.[223] Yet it is, in fact, much more likely that any attempt to bring all the relief work and political campaigning under one institutional umbrella would have led to paralysis, given how disparate the ideological orientations of some of the organizations were that would have needed to fine-tune their activities. Hence the pragmatic collaboration that did transpire almost certainly achieved more than any single, unified rescue and relief organization would have done.[224]

The Closure of Gibraltar Camp

'With the possibility of the evacuees at Gibraltar Camp going by the end of next week or the beginning of the following week', the *Daily Gleaner* reported on 30 September 1944, 'the authorities have given the majority of the local employees notice'.[225] Two days later, two advertisements followed, inviting offers to purchase 'A Herd of 350 to 400 Pigs, Consisting of Boar, Sows, Shoats, Barrows and Piglets' and 'The Entire Stock in the Dry Goods Canteen, Consisting of Piece Goods, Haberdashery, Boots & Shows, Underwear, Shirts, etc., etc.' at Gibraltar Camp.[226] This signalled the departure of the Gibraltarian evacuees who returned home later that month.

Unfortunately, the clarification that they were refugees and not internees had done little to improve the Polish Jewish refugees' remigration prospects, but most of them too were able to find refuge elsewhere by the end of 1944, a hundred of them in Cuba.[227] In November 1944, eighteen of them were still in Gibraltar Camp,[228] of whom fourteen remained there until the autumn of 1947.

'While stores, equipment, furniture etc. are successively being sold at the moment', the *Daily Gleaner* reported in April 1945, 'Gibraltar Camp is gradually being closed in order to make place for the Military who will be taking over the camp shortly.' There were, though, 'some 30 refugees' overall still on the site who would remain there 'until provisions are made by the local or the Imperial Government for their resettlement here or elsewhere'.[229] In late May, they were allowed to move into the convent buildings that had previously been inhabited by nuns looking after the Gibraltarian evacuees, which considerably improved their living conditions.[230] Even so, as Miriam Stanton recalled, it was 'really frightening to live in the empty city'.[231]

In the autumn of 1947, it was decided to accommodate the remaining fourteen refugees privately. 'It appears that the prospect [*sic*] of getting rid of these refugees from Jamaica, at any rate in the immediate future, are slight', the authorities noted on 15 October. 'Few, if any of them, are ever likely to be in a position to support themselves. On the other hand, it appears out of all proportion to have to maintain a camp at a total annual expenditure of $4,397 for the maintenance of 14 persons only'.[232]

Those who remained either had no relatives in any relevant country, or no money to procure visas let alone cover travelling expenses, or suffered from poor health (or were affected by some combination of these factors). One of the female refugees had to be committed to a psychiatric hospital in Kingston in 1946. Her husband left the camp, together with their son, for the United States and instigated divorce proceedings against her.[233] Another Polish Jewish refugee, Samuel Rubenfeld, died in Kingston Public Hospital on 4 March 1946 and was buried the following day by Rabbi Silverman in the presence of 'Mr. Fabian P. Lopez, Commandant of the Camp ... and L. Brauner, representing the Polish group from the Camp. A beautiful wreath was laid on the grave from the administration of the Camp'.[234]

The Manns had, in the meantime, established a flourishing business, which set them apart from most of their peers. Emanuel Mann was an avid reader of the *Aufbau*, which arrived in the camp regularly, if with some delay. While studying the adverts in the paper, he had noticed that there was evidently a shortage in the United States of certain goods 'that were plentiful in Jamaica', such as coffee, sugar, jams and marmalades, and dried fruits. He set up E. Mann & Sons and, with the help of a Chinese wholesaler, began to send food parcels to the United States. Once the business had taken off, they rented a room in Kingston and employed two workers to process the parcels when they had been packed. Eventually they were sending up to 250 parcels a week, and they continued this business until they left for the United States in 1948.[235]

On 27 January 1946, the first anniversary of the liberation of Auschwitz by the Red Army, the *Sunday Gleaner* printed the English translation of Steigler's song with the following foreword by Leslie Ashenheim, a scion of one of Jamaica's most prominent Jewish families.[236] 'Sometime early in the year 1942', Ashenheim wrote,

> a Polish War Refugee first came into my Office and I made the acquaintance of Dr. Arthur Steigler, Doctor of Philosophy and Law of the Universities of Vienna and Cracow.

Figure 5.8 Business card for the export business that Fred and his father, Emanuel, operated in Jamaica from 1944 to 1948. Courtesy of the Azrieli Foundation.

He has perforce spent all his sojourn in Jamaica at the Gibraltar Camp and desired fervently to place his talents at the disposal of the War effort, particularly along the lines of Anti-Hitler Propaganda. For reasons best known to the Defence Regulation Authorities his offers were refused, and in spite of vigorous representations on his behalf, he was not even permitted to publish his patriotic Anti-Hitler Song – 'Quo Vadis In Poloniam'.

The music has been privately performed in Jamaica, and found good by those qualified to judge. The words, which were written in Polish by the Author, have been rendered into the English version by Mr. C.A. Escoffery, with a sympathy and vigour which all who read it may appreciate.

Today, Dr. Steigler knows what he did not know whilst writing the words and music of his song, that in Birkenau Concentration Camp … his only daughter, 16 years old, was confined, and, no doubt, murdered, after having been separated from her Mother, of whom no word has been heard, but who, no doubt, met a similar fate in some other Nazi Slaughter House.

The text of the song itself then followed, as per my shortened version below:

'Quo Vadis In Poloniam'

Ye Nations United, oh listen
'Tis Poland calls to be free –
Her People – her Jews and her Gentiles
Are scattered over land and sea –
The brown wolf hath entered her children's fold

And savaged their freeman's birth!
But her hope is in you, oh valliant Knights,
To rescue our tortured Earth:

Once more the good God of all pity
Appears amidst dying cries:
'Quo Vadis, Domine' we ask –
'In Poloniam', he replies:
From the ghetto's hell to save the Jews
Now victims of their blood
And man endow for evermore
With Peace and Brotherhood.

CHORUS

Orphaned children calling
Ravished mothers calling
To the herded, murdered band –
And now the love of C[z]er[ni]akow
Bids brother's hand clasp hand
And malices hate and mean distrust
Abolish from the land.
Oh listen! Voices whisper.
Whisper in our ear: –
'O Lord, wither dost Thou go?'
To Poland. Do not fear!
To bless with Peace her rooftrees
Jews' heritage to save –
It cannot die, for 'tis for aye
Till time shall disappear.

Evidently, for some at least among Jamaica's indigenous Jewish population, the truth about the genocide against European Jewry was now gradually beginning to sink in.

Notes

1. Arnold von der Porten, *The Nine Lives of Arnold: The Story of My Life from Hamburg, Germany 1917, to leaving Jamaica, B.W.I. 1953* (Bloomington, IN: 1stBooks Library, 2007), 225.
2. JTA, 27 August 1939, http://www.jta.org/1939/08/27/archive/40000-refugees-in-britain-face-internment (last accessed 1 May 2019).
3. *Trinidad Guardian*, undated cutting, MMC.
4. *Trinidad Guardian*, 28 May 1940, 6.
5. *Trinidad Guardian*, undated cutting, MMC.

6. Ibid.
7. Ibid.
8. Ibid.
9. Hugh H. Watson, US Consul, Jamaica, to the State Department, Washington, DC, 'Political Developments in Jamaica', NARA, RG59, 5062.
10. Sir Arthur Richards, Governor of Jamaica, to the Colonial Office, TNA CO 323/1797/14.
11. Manfred Goldfish, untitled typescript (11 pages), 3. Sue Goldfish collection, copy in my possession.
12. See Baptiste, *War, Cooperation, and Conflict*, 208; Lennox Honychurch, *The Dominica Story: A History of the Island* (Dominica: Macmillan Education, 1975), 134–36.
13. Telegram from the Governor of Trinidad, Sir Hubert Young, to the Secretary of State for the Colonies, 3 February 1940, TNA CO 323/1799/2; Jewish Refugee Society to Robert Pilpel, Subcommittee on Refugee Aid in Central and South America, 30 November 1940, JDC, File 1047.
14. JTA, 15 April 1943, http://www.jta.org/1943/04/15/archive/national-refugee-service-secures-release-of-jewish-internees-in-texas-camp (last accessed 1 May 2019).
15. *Washington Post*, 19 December 1940, 9. According to the *New York Times*, 'seven persons "of enemy alien birth" had been "rounded up by the police" in Bermuda on 14 June 1940. Five Italians were rounded up Monday [i.e. 10 June] soon after Italy declared war' (*New York Times*, 15 June 1940, 4).
16. *Memoirs*, unpublished draft manuscript by Hans (John) Stecher, in my possession.
17. See Governor of Trinidad to the Secretary of State for the Colonies, 4 March 1943, TNA CO 980/26; 15 April 1943, TNA CO 980/26; 21 September 1944, TNA CO 323/1879/12.
18. See telegrams no. 329 (17 May 1940) and no. 22 (8 July 1940) from the Governor of Trinidad to the Secretary of State for the Colonies, TNA CO 323/1799/2.
19. Supt. W.E. Rumbelow, Security Office Report: 'Refugees in Trinidad and Tobago', 1 March 1940, TNA CO 323/1799/2.
20. Quoted in Paul Weis, *Nationality and Statelessness in International Law* (Dordrecht: Kluwer, 1979), 122; see also Didi Herman, *An Unfortunate Coincidence: Jews, Jewishness, and English Law* (New York: Oxford University Press, 2011), 108–9.
21. Jewish Refugee Society to Robert Pilpel of the Joint, 2 September 1940 and 30 November 1940, JDC, File 1047.
22. Stecher, *Memoirs*; Peter Laband collection, United States Holocaust Memorial Museum, Accession Number: 1997.A.0154, https://collections.ushmm.org/search/catalog/irn501644 (accessed 17 June 2019); Breger, *Lines*, 19–20.
23. Goldfish, untitled typescript, 8.
24. See 'World War II: The Trinidad and Tobago Experience', National Archives of Trinidad and Tobago, http://natt.gov.tt/sites/default/files/images/World%20War%20boards%20final%2011March2015%209.pdf (last accessed 9 May 2019).
25. Fritz Karell (born in Vienna in 1911) who died on 13 April 1942; see https://www.findagrave.com/memorial/130137370/fritz-karell (last accessed 9 May 2019).
26. Presumably Paul Bley (born in Vienna in 1869), who died on 1 June 1942; see http://www.findagrave.com/cgi-bin/fg.cgi?page=gr&GScid=2209945&GRid=130136669& (last accessed 9 May 2019).
27. Stecher, *Memoirs*.
28. Breger, *Lines*, 19.
29. Ibid., 18.

30. Jewish Refugee Society to Robert Pilpel of the Joint, 30 November 1940, JDC, File 1047.

31. *Biographisches Handbuch der deutschsprachigen Emigration*, 477. A history of Bremen Jewry that Markreich circulated in 1956 in manuscript form (the LBI NY holds a copy) has recently been published as *Geschichte der Juden in Bremen und Umgegend* (Bremen: Edition Temmen, 2009).

32. See Reports of the Central Council for Jewish Refugees for 1940 and 1941, LBI NY Microfilm collection, reels SI 10 and 11; Report of Activities of the CRREC for period ending 31 October 1941, AJA, MS183/576/1, part 1.

33. Julius Sass, President of the JRS, to Robert Pilpel of the Joint, 28 March 1941, JDC, File 1048.

34. Huggins was the chairman of the Trinidad Publishing Company, which owned the *Trinidad Guardian*. He died in June 1941.

35. Jewish Refugee Society to Robert Pilpel of the Joint, 4 August 1941, JDC, File 1048; Sir Bede Clifford to the Secretary of State for the Colonies, telegram no. 1153 (secret), 12 October 1942, TNA CO 980/26.

36. Edgar Gruen, President of the JRS, to Robert Pilpel of the Joint, 18 February 1942, JDC, File 1048.

37. Jewish Refugee Society to Robert Pilpel of the Joint, 30 August 1941, JDC, File 1048.

38. Moses W. Beckelman, Report to the Joint in New York, 19 October 1941, JDC, File 1048.

39. Ibid.; Jewish Refugee Society to the Joint, 16 January 1942, JDC, File 1048.

40. Professor Robert Moll, delegate of the International Red Cross Committee, reporting to the Joint on his recent visit to Port of Spain, 9 August 1944; Ferdinand Bronner, Jewish Refugee Society, to Robert Moll, 27 October 1944, JDC, File 1048.

41. Committee on Refugee Aid in South America, Memorandum to the Joint Administration, 31 January 1944, JDC, File 114; Jewish Refugee Society to Robert Pilpel, 11 January 1944, JDC, File 1048.

42. Harry D. Biele, Internal Joint memorandum, 5 December 1944, JDC, File 1048.

43. Edgar Gruen, President of the Jewish Refugee Society, to Robert Pilpel of the Joint, 9 November 1945, JDC, File 1215.

44. *New York Times*, 6 September 1939, 11.

45. Von der Porten, *Nine Lives*, 194.

46. Ibid., 195.

47. Ludwig Klein was naturalized in Jamaica in 1951. See TNA HO 334/268/6471.

48. Von der Porten, *Nine Lives*, 199.

49. Richard Kahn was also naturalized in Jamaica in 1951. See TNA HO 334/268/6312.

50. Von der Porten, *Nine Lives*, 205.

51. Ibid., 200.

52. Ibid., 199, 201.

53. Ibid., 200.

54. Ibid., 210.

55. Ibid., 222.

56. Ibid., 235.

57. Ibid.

58. Ibid., 236.

59. The following account is based on Rudolf Aub, 'From My Life', August 1988, typescript (16 pages), 1–9, American Jewish Archives, Cincinnati, SC-575. A German translation of this account has been published as 'Handlanger in Sierra Leone – Amtsarzt in

Jamaika', in Wolfgang Benz (ed.), *Das Exil der kleinen Leute: Alltagserfahrung deutscher Juden in der Emigration* (Munich: C.H. Beck, 1991), 80–91.
60. Von der Porten, *Nine Lives*, 238.
61. Aub, 'From My Life', 8 ('Amtsarzt in Jamaika', 89).
62. Von der Porten, *Nine Lives*, 225–26.
63. Ibid., 230.
64. Ibid., 245.
65. Ibid., 246.
66. Ibid., 264–65.
67. Ronald L.M. Kirkwood, Letter to the Editor, *Daily Gleaner*, 9 June 1941.
68. Ibid.
69. Von der Porten, *Nine Lives*, 287.
70. Ibid.
71. Matilda Kronecker's husband, Louis, was also interned at Up Park Camp (236).
72. *Daily Gleaner*, 15 June 1940, 1. See also Karoline [Ebersohn] (surname deleted in the original), to the Chief Rabbi, 29 September 1941, AJA, CBF Reel 14, 70/19.
73. Von der Porten, *Nine Lives*, 234–35.
74. Ibid., 237.
75. *Daily Gleaner*, 13 April 1943, 1.
76. *Daily Gleaner*, 14 March 1940, 2; 9 May 1940, 23; 12 October 1943, 2.
77. Von der Porten, *Nine Lives*, 250–51.
78. Wolfgang Weber, 'Gibraltar liegt in Amerika: Zur Geschichte des Internierungslagers Gibraltar in Kingston 1940–1948', in *Historisches Jahrbuch der Stadt Linz* (2003/2004), 870.
79. On Oswald Anderson, see Henrice Altink, 'A True Maverick: The Political Career of Dr. Oswald E. Anderson, 1919–1944', in *New West Indian Guide, Vol. 87* (2013), 3–29.
80. *Daily Gleaner*, 27 March 1941, 10.
81. *Daily Gleaner*, 19 February 1941, 8.
82. *Daily Gleaner*, 3 June 1941, 1.
83. *Daily Gleaner*, 27 March 1941, 11.
84. Weber, 'Gibraltar liegt in Amerika', 865.
85. The governor of Gibraltar was given compulsory powers to evacuate the civil population on 30 April 1940. See TNA CO 91/518/14.
86. Undated note prepared by the Colonial Office for the War Office, TNA CO 91/518/14.
87. Undated Colonial Office report to the War Cabinet, TNA CO 91/518/14.
88. Director of Public Works Office, Interim Report on the Construction works carried out at Camp Gibraltar, Mona, for the Colonial Secretary, 13 February 1941, TNA CO 91/515/12.
89. See facsimile in Suzanne Francis Brown, *Mona Past and Present: The History and Heritage of the Mona Campus, University of the West Indies* (Kingston: University of the West Indies Press, 2004), 27.
90. Colonial Secretary Lord Lloyd to Sir Arthur Richards, 10 October 1940, TNA CO 323/1846/8, quoted in Diana Cooper-Clark, *Dreams of Re-Creation in Jamaica: The Holocaust, Internment, Jewish Refuges in Gibraltar Camp, Jamaican Jews and Sephardim* (Victoria, BC: FriesenPress, 2017).
91. Telegram from the Colonial Secretary to the Governor of Jamaica, 9 November 1940, National Archives of Jamaica (hereafter NAJ), IB/5/38/2, quoted in Claus and Katja Füllberg-Stolberg, 'Jüdisches Exil im Britischen Kolonialreich – Gibraltar Camp

Jamaica 1942–1947', in Marlis Buchholz, Claus Füllberg-Stolberg and Hans-Dieter Schmid (eds), *Nationalsozialismus und Region: Festschrift für Herbert Obenaus zum 65. Geburtstag* (Bielefeld: Verlag für Regionalgeschichte, 1996), 90.

92. Ibid., 90, note 13; Suzanne Francis Brown, *Mona Past and Present: The History and Heritage of the Mona Campus* (Kingston: University of the West Indies Press, 2004), 25.

93. Cooper-Clark, *Dreams of Re-Creation*, 13.

94. Ibid.

95. Director of Public Works Office, Interim Report on the Construction works carried out at Camp Gibraltar, Mona, for the Colonial Secretary, 13 February 1941, TNA CO 91/515/12.

96. Louise Bennett, *Jamaica Labrish: Jamaica Dialect Poems* (Kingston: Sangster's Book Stores, 1966), 87–88.

97. *Daily Gleaner*, 26 October 1940, 1.

98. Weber, 'Gibraltar liegt in Amerika', 869.

99. Ibid., 866.

100. *Daily Gleaner*, 28 November 1940, 1.

101. *Daily Gleaner*, 9 February 1941, 16.

102. Andrew B. Acheson of the Colonial Office to Cecil Syers of the Treasury, 1 April 1941, TNA CO 91/515/12.

103. Weber, 'Gibraltar liegt in Amerika', 869.

104. Andrew B. Acheson to Cecil Syers, 1 April 1941, TNA CO 91/515/12.

105. Jan Ciechanowski, Polish Ambassador in Washington, DC, to Joseph Hyman, Executive Vice Chairman of the Joint, 3 January 1942, JDC, File 884.

106. Joseph Schwartz of the Joint in Lisbon, cable to the Joint office in New York, 31 December 1941, JDC, File 884.

107. Foreign Office refugee department to the British Embassy in Lisbon, 23 March 1942, TNA FO 371/32655/205, quoted in Füllberg-Stolberg and Füllberg-Stolberg, 'Jüdisches Exil', 94. See also London, *Whitehall and the Jews*, 180.

108. Joint Press Release, 9 January 1942, JDC, File 884.

109. Special Committee on Relief Questions, Report by Dr. Tartakower, 17 April 1942, American Jewish Archives, Cincinnati, WJC Series D, D2/6.

110. Unsigned, Joint Official, General and Emergency Committee, to Lionel J. Simmonds, 3 February 1942, JDC, File 884.

111. Charles Jordan, Report on Gibraltar Camp for the Joint, New York, 17 December 1943, YIVO, XIII-8 Jamaica.

112. British Embassy, Washington, DC, to Joseph Hyman of the Joint, 23 April 1946, enclosing copies of Joint guarantees originally sent to the British Embassy in Lisbon on 5 January and 11 February 1942, JDC, File 893. On 6 March 1942, the Joint guaranteed the maintenance costs for 58 Luxembourgian citizens in Gibraltar Camp (see Moses A. Leavitt to Leon Schaus, Gouvernement du Grand-Duché de Luxembourg, Montreal, Canada, JDC, File 885). On 3 April 1942, 33 Czech and Luxembourgian nationals were brought to Jamaica by the Joint (see Loose Leaf Memos, JDC, File 153). On 27 April 1942, HICEM received lists of 16 Czech and Luxembourgian immigrants sent to Gibraltar Camp from Lisbon on the *San Thomé* (see Ilya Dijour to Isaac Asofsky, HICEM, New York, 27 April 1942, YIVO, XIII-3 Jamaica). In total, 35 refugees came on the *San Thomé*: the already mentioned 16 Czech and Luxembourgian refugees, 13 Polish Jews and 4 Dutch refugees. Two additional passengers left the ship in Jamaica for security and health reasons respectively (Cooper-Clark, *Dreams of Re-Creation*, 32).

113. Joint Loose Leaf Memos, 15 May 1942, JDC, File 153; HIAS Annual Report for 1943, 'Rescue Now!', 30, YIVO, I-43.
114. Charles Jordan, Report on Gibraltar Camp for the Joint, 17 December 1943, YIVO, XIII-8 Jamaica; Minutes of the meeting of the Committee on Refugee Aid in Central and South America, 1 June 1943, 4, JDC, File 114.
115. Ilja Dijour to Bernhard Glasscheib, 30 December 1942, YIVO, XIII-5 Jamaica; Bernhard Glasscheib to HICEM, New York, 14 January 1943, YIVO, XIII-10 Jamaica.
116. Lars Menk, *Dictionary of German-Jewish Surnames* (Bergenfield: Avotaynu, 2005).
117. Dutch Refugees: Ex s/s 'Marques De Comillas', (undated printed) list of refugees. NAJ 1B/5/77. I am grateful to Professor Claus Füllberg-Stolberg of the Leibniz University in Hannover for providing me with this list. Among the Jewish refugees on the *Marques De Comillas* was Bernard Katz, a prominent art dealer from Dieren. Apparently, the rumour spread in Gibraltar Camp that he had secured his own rescue and that of two dozen of his relatives by handing over several valuable paintings to Goering free of charge, which were in fact forgeries (Mann, *Drastic Turn*, 208–9). Katz may well have put this version of events into circulation himself, given that in fact his business had continued to sell art to high-ranking Nazis during the Phoney War. Katz returned to the Netherlands after the war and took over the business again, which had been taken care of by non-Jewish associates in the meantime (https://rkd.nl/nl/explore/artists/360298, last accessed 1 May 2019).
118. Bernhard Glasscheib to Ilya Dijour, HICEM, New York, 3 October 1943, YIVO, XIII-11 Jamaica.
119. See Charles Jordan, Report on Gibraltar Camp for the Joint, 17 December 1943, YIVO, XIII-8 Jamaica. Also among the Dutch refugees were Hendrika Engelander and Boo [Abraham Albert] van Praag, both from Amsterdam, who were married by Rabbi Silverman in April 1943 in the presence of Boon van Praag's parents, Engelander's sister, Sipora (who was married to Harry Leon Cats), and the sisters' uncle, Mr. de Miranda. The ceremony was attended by Ernst Rae and his wife, and Charles M. Dozy, the Dutch consul general in Washington, who was posted to Kingston for a year while substantial numbers of Dutch refugees were in Gibraltar Camp. The *Daily Gleaner* related that Hendrika Engelander had 'travelled under pressure through war-torn Europe, before she finally came on to Jamaica to join her fiancé at Gibraltar Camp, from whom she had been separated in Holland at the commencement of the war' (*Daily Gleaner*, 12 April 1943, 4).
120. Mann, *Drastic Turn*, 30.
121. Ibid., 39–41, 43.
122. Ibid., 54–56.
123. Ibid., 195.
124. See, for example, ibid., 202–3, 211, 231.
125. Ibid., 218–21.
126. Ibid., 196.
127. Von der Porten, *Nine Lives*, 205.
128. Cooper-Clark, *Dreams of Re-Creation*, 43.
129. Ibid., 44.
130. Mann, *Drastic Turn*, 210.
131. Ibid., 236.
132. Data prepared by Bernhard Glasscheib for Ilya Dijour, Executive Secretary of HICEM, New York, 17 January 1943, YIVO XIII-10.
133. David Engel, *In the Shadow of Auschwitz: The Polish Government-in-Exile and the Jews, 1939–1942* (Chapel Hill: University of North Carolina Press, 1987), 113–83.

134. Report by Ernest Rae, 16 June 1942, YIVO, XIII-3 Jamaica.
135. Charles Jordan, Report to the Joint, 17 December 1943, YIVO, XIII-8 Jamaica. That said, they were certainly keen to ensure that the Joint did continue to pay for their maintenance. They rejected direct assistance from the local Jewish community because, as Owen K. Henriques – the chairman of the German Refugee Fund (set up in 1940 by the local Jewish population to assist the refugees) and a scion of one of Jamaica's most prominent established Jewish families – reported to the Joint in May 1942, 'it is the general belief in the camp that by accepting assistance from us on a small scale they are lessening their chances of receiving from you the help to which they believe themselves entitled' (Owen K. Henriques to Moses A. Leavitt of the Joint, 28 May 1942, JDC, File 884).
136. Ernest Rae to the Joint, 17 October 1942, JDC, File 884; see also letter from the Joint to the Committee of the Polish Group, 13 May 1942 (YIVO, XIII-7 Jamaica), and the committee's response, 25 May 1942 (YIVO, XIII-4 Jamaica).
137. Committee of the Polish Group to the Joint, 11 May 1942, YIVO, XIII-7 Jamaica.
138. S. Rosenbaum, Gibraltar Camp, to the Polish government in exile in London, 28 February 1942, YIVO, XIII-3-Jamaica, 000013.
139. S. Rosenbaum, Gibraltar Camp, to Dr. Ignacy Schwarzbart in London, 26 February 1942, YIVO, XIII-3 Jamaica, 000014.
140. Group of Polish Refugees at Gibraltar Camp to Prime Minster Winston Churchill, 24 August 1942, TNA CO 323/1846/6.
141. John B. Sidebotham of the Colonial Office to Alec W.G. Randall, Head of the Refugee Section at the Foreign Office, 29 October 1942, TNA CO 323/846/6, Reg. no. 29/14381/1/42.
142. Boruch Eksztajn and Samuel Schipper to the Joint, 11 August 1943, YIVO, XIII-7 Jamaica.
143. HIAS, New York, to Bernhard Glasscheib, 27 April 1942, YIVO, XIII-3 Jamaica.
144. Bernhard Glasscheib to HICEM, New York, 15 May 1942, YIVO, XIII-1 Jamaica.
145. See, for example, HIAS Annual Report for 1942/43, p. 27, and HIAS Annual Report for 1944, p. 27, YIVO I-43; minutes of the meetings of the WJC Relief Committee, 29 July 1943, p. 3, and 26 August 1943, p. 1, American Jewish Archives Cincinnati, WJC, D1/8.
146. Isaac Asofsky of HIAS to Ilya Dijour of HICEM, 24 July 1942, YIVO, XIII-5 Jamaica.
147. Ernest Rae to the Joint, 18 May 1942, YIVO, XIII-4 Jamaica.
148. Ilya Dijour to *The Day*, 24 July 1942, YIVO, XIII-5 Jamaica.
149. M. Kwapiszewski, Minister Plenipotentiary and Counsellor of the Polish Embassy in Washington, DC, to Moses A. Leavitt of the Joint, 9 February 1943, JDC, File 885.
150. Alec W.G. Randall of the Foreign Office to Philip Rogers of the Colonial Office, 4 December 1942, TNA CO 323/1846/7.
151. Sir Arthur Richards, Governor of Jamaica, to the Colonial Secretary, Lord Cranborne, 13 October 1942, TNA CO 323/1846/6.
152. John H. Emmens, Colonial Office memorandum, 17 December 1942, TNA CO 323/1846/7.
153. John B. Sidebotham of the Colonial Office to Alec W.G. Randall of the Foreign Office, 19 December 1942, TNA CO 323/1846/7.
154. Colonial Secretary Oliver Stanley to Governor Sir Arthur Richards, 15 January 1943, TNA CO 323/1846/6.
155. Governor Richards to Colonial Secretary Stanley, 18 January 1943, TNA CO 323/1846/6.

156. Michael Fleming, *Auschwitz, the Allies and Censorship of the Holocaust* (Cambridge: Cambridge University Press, 2014), 6.

157. Ibid., 11.

158. Quoted in ibid., 59.

159. Quoted in ibid.

160. TNA HW16/45, 27.8.41, item 1; HW1/62, item 9, quoted in ibid., 67.

161. *Manchester Guardian*, 8 September 1941, 6.

162. Quoted in *Manchester Guardian*, 19 September 1941, 7.

163. Fleming, *Auschwitz*, 67.

164. Ibid., 63.

165. *Manchester Guardian*, 14 December 1942, 3.

166. House of Commons Debate, 17 December 1942 (vol. 385, cc. 2082–2087), http://hansard.millbanksystems.com/commons/1942/dec/17/united-nations-declaration (last accessed 1 May 2019).

167. House of Lords Debate, 17 December 1942 (vol. 125, cc. 607-612), http://hansard.millbanksystems.com/lords/1942/dec/17/persecution-of-the-jews-allies (last accessed 1 May 2019).

168. Minutes of the War Cabinet, 25 October 1940, 245, TNA CAB 65/9/39.

169. Reports for the Month of October 1940 for India, Burma and the Colonies, Protectorates and Mandated Territories, 16 November 1940, 8, TNA CAB 68/7/24.

170. 'The Gate at Gibraltar'. Film Script, p. 1. I am grateful to Claus Füllberg-Stolberg for letting me have a copy of this script, which he received from Father Feeney.

171. Ibid., 6, 8.

172. Conclusions of a meeting of the War Cabinet, 5 May 1941, 11, TNA CAB 65/18.

173. Marrus, *The Unwanted*, 264.

174. Report to the Governments of the United States and the United Kingdom from their Delegates to the Conference on the Refugee Problem held at Bermuda, 19–29 April 1943, printed for the War Cabinet, May 1943, TNA CO 733/449.

175. *Manchester Guardian*, 22 April 1943, 4.

176. JTA, 5 April 1943, http://www.jta.org/1943/04/05/archive/jewish-representation-at-bermuda-refugee-conference-demanded-by-british-jews (last accessed 1 May 2019); the JTA sent the wife of its founder and managing editor, Ida Landau (née Bienstock), to Bermuda to cover the conference (JTA, 6 May 1986, http://www.jta.org/1986/05/06/archive/ida-landau-dead-at-86, last accessed 1 May 2019). When they married in 1921, Ida Landau, a solicitor, was forced to relinquish her US citizenship and the right to practise law because Jacob Landau had not been naturalized. Their predicament considerably raised public awareness, and was instrumental in bringing about a change in the relevant legislation.

177. JTA, 14 April 1943, http://www.jta.org/1943/04/14/archive/jews-send-plea-to-pope-to-intervene-for-action-by-bermuda-parley (last accessed 1 May 2019).

178. JTA, 16 April 1943, http://www.jta.org/1943/04/16/archive/chicago-meeting-attended-by-20000-urges-united-nations-to-save-european-jews (last accessed 1 May 2019).

179. JTA, 20 April 1943, http://www.jta.org/1943/04/20/archive/american-jewish-organizations-make-public-their-appeals-to-the-bermuda-parley (last accessed 1 May 2019).

180. *New York Times*, 21 April 1943, 27.

181. JTA, 23 April 1943, http://www.jta.org/1943/04/23/archive/disappointment-in-britain-at-spirit-of-bermuda-parley (last accessed 1 May 2019).

182. JTA, 28 April 1943, http://www.jta.org/1943/04/28/archive/sumner-welles-says-bermuda-conference-is-not-secret-rejects-labor-protest (last accessed 1 May 2019).

183. JTA, 29 April 1943, http://www.jta.org/1943/04/29/archive/bermuda-parley-closing-today-more-neutrals-to-join-intergovernmental-committee (last accessed 1 May 2019).
184. JTA, 14 April 1943, http://www.jta.org/1943/04/14/archive/jewish-organizations-in-england-drafting-joint-memorandum-to-bermuda-conference (last accessed 1 May 2019).
185. JTA, 14 April 1943, http://www.jta.org/1943/04/15/archive/bermuda-conference-will-deal-with-refugee-problem-not-with-rescuing-jews-in-nazi-lands (last accessed 1 May 2019).
186. *Washington Post*, 19 April 1943, 4.
187. JTA, 21 April 1943, http://www.jta.org/1943/04/21/archive/rescue-of-jewish-children-from-bulgaria-may-come-as-result-of-bermuda-parley (last accessed 1 May 2019).
188. JTA, 23 April 1943, http://www.jta.org/1943/04/23/archive/bermuda-conferees-rule-out-large-scale-rescue-of-nazi-victims (last accessed 1 May 2019).
189. *New York Times*, 23 April 1943, 9.
190. JTA, 30 April 1943, http://www.jta.org/1943/04/30/archive/bermuda-conference-closes-decisions-remain-confidential-general-statement-issued (last accessed 1 May 2019).
191. JTA, 29 April 1943, http://www.jta.org/1943/04/29/archive/press-in-england-disappointed-with-the-bermuda-conference (last accessed 1 May 2019).
192. JTA, 4 May 1943, http://www.jta.org/1943/05/04/archive/american-press-urges-admission-of-more-jews-from-nazi-europe (last accessed 1 May 2019).
193. *Hartford Courant*, 29 April 1943, 17.
194. *Christian Science Monitor*, 29 April 1943, 6.
195. JTA, 5 May 1943, http://www.jta.org/1943/05/05/archive/conference-was-a-failure-and-a-disappointment-labor-convention-is-told (last accessed 1 May 2019).
196. JTA, 7 May 1943, http://www.jta.org/1943/05/07/archive/lucas-defends-bermuda-parley-on-senate-floor-attacks-jewish-army-committee-statement (last accessed 1 May 2019).
197. JTA, 10 May 1943, http://www.jta.org/1943/05/10/archive/bermuda-conference-was-tragic-disappointment-rabbi-wise-says (last accessed 1 May 2019).
198. JTA, 6 May 1943, http://www.jta.org/1943/05/06/archive/london-press-silent-on-bermuda-results-british-empire-can-absorb-million-jews (last accessed 1 May 2019).
199. *Los Angeles Times*, 5 May 1943, A12.
200. JTA, 25 May 1943, http://www.jta.org/1943/05/25/archive/rabbis-ask-roosevelt-churchill-to-secure-release-of-jews-in-europe (last accessed 1 May 2019). Scott Lucas, incidentally, was extremely outraged by the criticism of the conference. Attempting to convince the Senate of his profound commitment to the cause of European Jewry, he told his fellow senators 'that some of his best friends in this country are of the Jewish faith' (JTA, 7 May 1943, http://www.jta.org/1943/05/07/archive/lucas-defends-bermuda-parley-on-senate-floor-attacks-jewish-army-committee-statement, last accessed 1 May 2019).
201. Report to the Governments of the United States and the United Kingdom from their Delegates to the Conference on the Refugee Problem held at Bermuda, 19–29 April 1943, printed for the War Cabinet, May 1943, TNA CO 733/449.
202. Phil Orchard, *Refugees, States, and the Construction of International Cooperation* (Cambridge: Cambridge University Press, 2014), 143, 145.
203. *Manchester Guardian*, 19 May 1943, 4. 'Five months have passed and still there is no organized international action', it remonstrated again the following day (20 May 1943, 2).

204. JTA, 20 May 1943, http://www.jta.org/1943/05/20/archive/bermuda-recommenda tions-leave-little-hope-for-refugees-eden-tells-commons (last accessed 1 May 2019).
205. This was an obvious allusion to Victor Gollancz's 'Let My People Go: Some Practical Proposals for Dealing with Hitler's Massacre of the Jews and an Appeal to the British Public', which Peake also went on to cite directly. Published in late December 1942, Gollancz's 32-page pamphlet sold more than 100,000 copies in the first month after its appearance, indicating considerable public interest in possible rescue measures and, by implication, widespread knowledge of the need for rescue measures; see Tom Lawson, *The Church of England and the Holocaust: Christianity, Memory and Nazism* (Woodbridge, UK: Boydell, 2006), 85.
206. House of Commons Debate, 19 May 1943 (vol. 389, cc. 1117–1204), https://api.par liament.uk/historic-hansard/commons/1943/may/19/refugee-problem (last accessed 17 June 2019).
207. Quoted by the JTA, 23 May 1943, https://www.jta.org/1943/05/23/archive/con flicting-reaction-in-british-press-to-parliamentary-debate-on-bermuda-conference (last accessed on 17 June 2019).
208. *Manchester Guardian*, 31 July 1943, 4.
209. JTA, 17 August 1944, http://www.jta.org/1944/08/17/archive/refugees-will-not-be-forced-to-return-to-native-lands-italy-grants-them-citizenship (last accessed 1 May 2019).
210. American Jewish Archives, Cincinnati, Series HWJC, Box H361, Folder Trinidad BWI.
211. Ibid.
212. *Daily Gleaner*, 4 August 1943, 8.
213. Miriam Stanton, *Escape from the Inferno of Europe* (London: Imprint unknown, 1996), 203.
214. British Embassy to the Department of State, 'Aide Memoire: Refugees from Nazi-Occupied Territory', 20 January 1943, in *Foreign Relations of the United States, 1943. General*, Vol. 1, 134, http://digicoll.library.wisc.edu/cgi-bin/FRUS/FRUS-idx?type=article&did=FRUS.FRUS1943v01.i0010&id=FRUS.FRUS1943v01&isize=M (last accessed 1 May 2019). Quoted in Orchard, *Refugees*, 144.
215. David S. Wyman (ed.), *America and the Holocaust. Vol. 3: The Mock Rescue Conference: Bermuda* (New York: Garland, 1990), Document 28: American Jewish Congress to Under-Secretary of State Sumner Welles, 13 May 1943.
216. Quoted in Allon Gal, 'David Ben-Gurion's Zionist Foreign Policy, 1938–48: The Democratic Factor', *Israel Affairs* 10(1–2) (2004), 22.
217. See Medoff, 'American Responses', 399–401.
218. See Tony Kushner, *The Holocaust and the Liberal Imagination: A Social and Cultural History* (Oxford: Blackwell, 1994), 173–201.
219. The following account of the War Refugee Board's finances follows Rebecca L. Erbelding, 'Appendix B: The Funding of the War Refugee Board', in eadem, 'About Time: The History of the War Refugee Board', PhD thesis (Fairfax, VA: George Mason University, 2015), 716–25.
220. Ibid., 724.
221. See Bauer, *American Jewry*, 197–216.
222. Segev, *World Jewish Congress*, 8.
223. 'Information Bulletin: Activities of the World Jewish Congress. Reports on the World Jewish Situation', draft, New York, 1 October 1945, Jewish Theological Seminary Library Special Collections, New York, Arch. 96–12.

224. After the war, intensified recruitment by the WJC resonated well with the refugee committees in Barbados and Trinidad, but not with the established Jewish community in Jamaica. As the chairman of the WJC's organizational division, Isaac Schwartzbart, wrote to his US-based colleague in the fundraising department, Isaac M. Gotlib, on the occasion of a pending trip to the region, the 'leadership there [in Jamaica] is apparently utterly in bondage to the Anglo-Jewish Association, this being the main reason for our futile efforts' (American Jewish Archives, Cincinnati, WJC Series H, H82/2).
225. *Daily Gleaner*, 30 September 1944, 14.
226. *Daily Gleaner*, 2 October 1944, 12.
227. Unsigned, undated list, YIVO, XIII-19 Jamaica.
228. HIAS Annual Report for 1944, 26, YIVO, 1-43; Ilya Dijour of HICEM to Owen K. Henriques of the German Refugee Fund in Jamaica, 15 August 1944; Ilya Dijour to his HICEM colleague Arnaud, 10 November 1944, YIVO, XIII-16 Jamaica; Arnaud to Dijour, 29 September 1944, YIVO, XIII-15 Jamaica.
229. *Daily Gleaner*, 11 April 1945, 13.
230. Mann, *Drastic Turn*, 238.
231. Stanton, *Escape*, 217.
232. Gibraltar Camp Estimates 1947/48. Minutes, 15 October 1947, NAJ IB/5/77/200, quoted in Füllberg-Stolberg and Füllberg-Stolberg, 'Jüdisches Exil', 101.
233. Fabian P. Lopez, Camp Commandant, Data on refugees, 30 April 1947, JDC, File 893.
234. *Daily Gleaner*, 20 March 1946, 6.
235. Mann, *Drastic Turn*, 230–32.
236. Lesie Ashenheim's great-great-great-grandfather was one of the first Ashkenazi Jews legally to settle in Edinburgh in the late eighteenth century, and a prominent member of the first Jewish community established there in 1816, the year in which his son Lewis was born. Lewis Ashenheim became a medical doctor – he is assumed to have been the 'first Scottish-born Jew to hold qualifications from a Scottish university' (see http://news.bbc.co.uk/local/edinburghandeastscotland/hi/people_and_places/religion_and_ethics/newsid_8318000/8318312.stm, last accessed 1 May 2019) – and emigrated to Jamaica, where he married into the DeCordova family who belonged to the high nobility of Sephardi Jewry in the colony. His wife was one of the granddaughters of Haham Joshua Hezekiah DeCordova, head of the Jamaican Jewish community from 1755 until 1797, and author of 'the first American volume of Jewish apologetics', *Reason and Faith*, published in 1788 – see Bertram W. Korn, 'The Haham DeCordova of Jamaica', *American Jewish Archives* 18(2) (1966), 141; Stanley Mirvis, 'Joshua Hezekiah Decordova and a Rabbinic Counter-Enlightenment from Colonial Jamaica', in Brian Smollett and Christian Wiese (eds), *Reappraisals and New Studies of the Modern Jewish Experience. Essays in Honor of Robert M. Seltzer* (Leiden: Brill, 2015), 104–233. In fact, the two families continued until quite recently to intermarry as a matter of course – see Thomas G. August, 'Family Structure and Jewish Continuity in Jamaica since 1655', *American Jewish Archives* 41(1) (1989), 35. In 1834, the DeCordova family founded the *Daily Gleaner*. Members of the Ashenheim family stood at the helm of the paper for much of the twentieth century. When Jamaica gained independence in 1962, Leslie Ashenheim's brother, Sir Neville Ashenheim, was Jamaica's first ambassador to the United States.

EPILOGUE

In Paul Gilroy's seminal work, *Black Atlantic*, he suggests that the concept of 'diaspora' is an underutilized device with which to explore the fragmentary relationship between blacks and Jews, and the difficult political questions to which it plays host: the status of ethnic identity, the power of cultural nationalism, and the manner in which carefully preserved social histories of ethnocidal suffering can function to supply ethical and political legitimacy.[1]

In the twenty-first century, there is little trace of the Jewish refugees who came to the Caribbean in the 1930s and 1940s, or indeed of earlier periods of Jewish immigration and emigration. However, as Caribbean post-war fiction and poetry demonstrates, the theme of Jews and the Caribbean, and the memory of the various encounters, forms part of the tapestry of West Indian identity.[2] The Sephardic community in Jamaica is still functioning, but in most West Indian countries, consciousness of Jews is limited to some street names, shop stores, and family names. With so few Jewish communities across the Caribbean, the history of Jewish immigration to the West Indies is explored and retold as part of the rich cultural diversity of West Indian heritage. In Jamaica, the site of Gibraltar Camp is now part of the University of the West Indies. The complex history of the Caribbean is encapsulated in this description of Gibraltar Camp's history by Suzanne Brown:

> The Mona campus of the UWI encapsulates a rich store of recorded past experience, events and artefacts spanning hundreds of years. These include the inferred legacies of the Tainos and the Spanish; the documentary records and

Figures 6.1 and 6.2 Two photographs of still standing parts of the original Gibraltar Camp, taken in 2001 by the author.

architectural remains left by the English plantation owners; the labour input of the African slaves and East Indian indentured workers; the river flow captured in the aqueduct and coveted by water authorities; the barracks occupied by the Gibraltarian evacuees, the Jewish refugees and the interned Germans and Italians; the army camp; and the regional university.[3]

In Barbados in the 1950s, the Jewish community bought back from the government and restored the land and building of the ancient Sephardic synagogue (built in 1651, one of the first synagogues in the Western hemisphere). It is now a point of pride for the remaining community, and a tourist attraction mentioned in most guide books and Jewish travel guides. As a point of tourism, Jewish heritage in the West Indies is repeatedly drawn on. The story of Jewish immigration has been integrated into a history of the West Indies that emphasizes tolerance and acceptance, and the role of the West Indies as a haven.[4] In these accounts, little is made of the restrictions and hostility that Jews faced in the seventeenth to nineteenth centuries, or the reluctant welcome that they faced in the 1930s and 1940s. West Indian responses to Jews were complex and drawn from elements of antipathy, ambivalence and sympathy, but they have been flattened in order to fulfil the celebratory needs of heritage nostalgia.

There is no doubt that the physical space that Jewish refugees entered in the 1930s was fraught with historical parallels and a difficult historical legacy. In Cooper-Clark's history of Gibraltar Camp, she points out that: 'Jamaica's history includes racism, exclusion, and slavery. Today, visitors can see the ruins of the old slave plantation and the remnants of Gibraltar Camp II on the grounds of the university'. She also reminds us that the refugees themselves would have been conscious of the use that the site they occupied had been put to: 'When the refugees were in the camp, they could still see the overseer's house, an icon of slavery that survived intact until just after World War II'.[5]

As has been shown in this book, there was much local sympathy for the plight of the Jews, and an empathy based on a shared experience of racism and persecution, as well as fears about the economic impact of new immigrants. Sarah Casteel writes about a generation of Caribbean/diaspora writers who grew up during the Second World War, and 'whose adolescences were shaped by an awareness of the war, [and who] invoke calamitous moments of Jewish history as part of a larger effort to confront slavery and its legacies. In so doing, they probe what Paul Gilroy describes as "the knotted intersection of histories", deepening their investigation of Caribbean creolization in all its many iterations'.[6]

The attitudes of West Indians, from Marcus Garvey in his letter of protest about the British Guiana scheme, to school children debating Jewish immigration, are understandable within the context of small island dependencies, nascent small island states. But it is harder to understand the responses of the Colonial Office and the British government to the refugee crisis.

In the 1930s, the international community had no legal obligation towards refugees. The majority who did find refuge did so under existing immigration requirements. Indeed, the immigration of Jewish refugees to the West Indies was viewed with ambivalence by most parties involved. The Colonial Office was rightly diligent in protecting West Indian interests. Yet there were many instances where, because of a failure of imagination on the part of a Colonial Office administrator, at times blatant antisemitism, or a reluctance to go beyond what was expected of the job, many opportunities were missed. The British government was happy to use its slim figures of refugee admittance to its colonial Empire as an example of a generous refugee policy; but once pressure built from the West Indies to prevent further numbers, such as in Trinidad in 1938 and 1939, action was taken to stem Jewish immigration. Was the West Indies, as with many so-called 'exotic' locations of refuge, in a better position than Britain or the United States to accommodate refugees or mass refuge plans? The situation brings to mind one of many historical parallels: the uncomfortable fact that the majority of refugees and displaced people today live in poor and developing countries, often adjacent to conflict zones, and are unable to gain access to countries with more resources to accommodate them.

In the 1930s, Britain and the United States both dealt with the refugee crisis by a process of selectivity before war broke out and after September 1939, at all times focusing on an Allied victory as the main way in which refugees could be helped.[7] In this vein, mass refuge in British Guiana was offered by the British government as an option when preventing further refugee migration to Palestine. But few government ministers or officials concerned in the Home, Colonial or Foreign Offices, felt the offer was, in seriousness, a viable scheme that would come to fruition. For British West Indians, schemes to develop land in British Guiana would have been of benefit to those in the colony and possibly a solution to overpopulation in other colonies, such as Barbados and Jamaica. Yet the suggestion of a Jewish refugee settlement, funded privately by American Jewish organizations, took the project away from West Indian concerns and was viewed by many in the West Indies and the Colonial Office as an attempt to 'dump' a European problem on West Indian land. For the vast majority of refugees fleeing Nazi Europe, settlement schemes, such as the Sosua Scheme that came up at Evian, or in British Guiana a year later, were not viable solutions. These schemes ignored who the majority of refugees were: on the whole, not the young and fit, but those displaced from metropolitan lives. It is possible that some refugees would have contributed and found employment and refuge, but this would not have applied to the potential 250,000 refugees that the plan first discussed. In the Dominican Republic a generous offer was made to Jewish refugees, and a farming colony was attempted with far fewer numbers, but the results were mixed. The majority of refugees found it impossible to make a living in agriculture, and soon became reliant on overseas aid, or moved from the settlement and became involved in Dominican life in other productive ways.[8]

Jewish organizations also became involved in investigations with schemes like British Guiana unwillingly. Objections included the economic reality that the JDC was running at a deficit and would not be able to fund such a large endeavour. Practical objections were based on their long experience in the settlement of refugees. Both the Evian Conference and the British Guiana Commission reveal how little influence Jewish refugee organizations possessed at governmental level, despite their established record in helping to resettle emigrants and refugees from the mid nineteenth century. At the same time as the British Guiana plan, President Roosevelt's Political Advisory Committee compelled Jewish refugee organizations to take part (and fund) numerous fruitless explorations of locations, from the Philippines to the US Virgin Islands.

With the outbreak of war, refugee settlement was no longer a government concern or priority. In the example of Gibraltar Camp, any Colonial Office objections were overruled by the Foreign Office's perceived political exigency of moving Gibraltarians to Jamaica. Gibraltar Camp, with an initial capacity to house 9,000 evacuees, was never used to its full potential, and only 1,700 of the proposed 7,000 Gibraltarians were evacuated to Jamaica during the summer of 1940. Between then and the arrival of the SS *Serpa Pinto* in January 1942, the camp was woefully underused. Whilst it could be argued that the British government could have allowed the camp to be used (it had space for seven thousand) for refugees who had escaped Nazi Germany to neutral territory, this ignores the situation from a British perspective. During 1940 and 1941, the British government felt no particular obligation to rescue Jewish refugees during a period when fear of invasion was high, and domestic policy involved the mass internment of German and Austrian Jews. Yet when it was in the British interest to do so, the camp was used. As we have seen, in 1942 and 1943 refugees were moved from Spain and Portugal to Jamaica.

Taken from an uncertain future in Portugal, refugees were at first enthusiastic and grateful for their removal to Jamaica. But once the restrictions of life in the camp became clear, they became increasingly restless. The slow rate of emigration only added to a sense of betrayal by the refugee organizations, who they blamed for bringing them to the camp. For Jewish organizations, the camp served as a reminder of their powerlessness. Whilst responsible for refugees in the camp, they were unable to initiate further movements there, with requests to do so being declined at various points, before and after the Bermuda Conference in April 1943. Whilst in private the JDC may have felt worried about the project, in public they used it as a success story in publicity to bolster fundraising and morale among staff and supporters.

By examining the position of refugee organizations, important parallels can be drawn to their situation today. The dilemma encapsulated in the JDC's report 'Bound for Nowhere: Disorganized Panic Migration' has not gone away.[9] Since 1945, the number of non-governmental organizations working for refugees has proliferated, as has the number of refugees. There are, today, 68.5 million people who have been forcibly displaced from their homes around the world, which is unprecedented.[10] Despite the post-war legal recognition of refugee status, it would seem that little has changed to empower organizations to make more of a difference. The theme of refugees and the sea, and refugee policy, is as alive today as it was for those refugees who took perilous journeys by sea on steamships such as the *Cordillera, Köenigstein, Caribia, St Louis, Orinoco, Alsina, Navemar, Paul Lemerle, Winnipeg, Serpa Pinto* and others.

It has been evident throughout this book that the British West Indies only really came into view as a possible destination for Jewish refugees from Greater Germany from the winter of 1938/39 onwards, because for many there were virtually no alternatives. In the words of Hans Stecher, by late 1938 'one would have gone to Timbuktu just to get out'.[11] It is therefore hardly surprising that most of the refugees who did make it to the Caribbean never seriously considered staying. For Henry Altman, however, Barbados did become his home. In an interview in 1989, he described the process by which he became a Barbadian:

> When we first came to Barbados it happened that most of us had blue eyes and the original Jews had black eyes, the ones who came from the Mediterranean, the Spanish and Portuguese, and they were suspicious; they [the West Indians] thought that we were Germans. It is a fact, and people called us Germans until war broke out. Then slowly they realized that we were not. We are Polish Jews. Most of us are Polish Jews. We always thought that we would leave the Island and go somewhere else, like to New York, America, Canada. But somehow, we loved it here and we are Barbadians.[12]

Henry Altman's experience was probably influenced by the fact that he was never interned and had left Poland as an emigrant rather than as a forced migrant. For many, the Caribbean was simply not 'European' enough. To quote Harry Schachter, who arrived in Trinidad with his parents, Ulrich and Miriam Schächter, on board the *Cordillera* – 'our ship was the "3rd to last" that [was] allowed entry into Trinidad' – in January 1939:[13]

> We were Europeans ... and so ... even though [Trinidad] was a wonderful home and a wonderful refuge, it was always a temporary home, and my parents, even though they loved the place, ... they missed the European things, they missed the European music, the larger Jewish community connections, so I don't think there was any question that the family would move on when the opportunity arose.[14]

The experience of internment hardly made the refugees feel particularly welcome and did little to endear a place of refuge to them that they had only chosen as a last resort in the first place. It also irrevocably damaged the businesses that many of those who were considering the possibility of remaining were beginning to establish and obstructed their attempts to put down roots. Even after their release from the internment camps, many of them faced considerable difficulties. Though no longer detained, they were still subject to restrictions as enemy aliens. In Trinidad, for instance, they had to live in Port of Spain, report daily to the police and maintain a curfew.[15] Some 150 East European Jews who had settled in San Fernando had been compelled to move back to Port of Spain when these regulations came into force at the beginning of the war, and consequently lost their livelihoods. Jewish pedlars were no longer able to sell their wares outside Port of Spain, nor were they able to collect what they were owed by their customers. The Jewish Refugee Society estimated that pedlars who had sold goods on credit were owed some $15,000 in May 1940. By June, the amount had risen to $25,000.[16] Not least, the affordable credit provided by Jewish businesses may well help to explain the fact that despite all the scaremongering of the winter of 1938/39 and some remaining ambivalence, the internees drew relatively little attention and no longer seem to have been considered a major problem following their release.

The fact that they were not allowed to leave Port of Spain also ruled out numerous employment opportunities, for instance on the construction sites of the American bases that were being erected on the island. Not least, it also drove up rents in Port of Spain.[17] Moreover, in November 1942, Edgar Gruen reported to Friedrich Borchardt of the Joint that 'all American firms attached in Trinidad, and also some British companies, refused from the beginning to employ Jewish people released from the detention'. Even so, Gruen added, 'we have still some confidence for the future' since 'in contempt of all those obstacles a certain number of us have settled [our]selves again'.[18] Many of the released internees had considerable difficulties making a living for the remainder of the war, and it must have been a matter of some frustration to the Joint that, instead of focusing their efforts on the provision of loans to facilitate the establishment of small businesses, as they had done before internment curtailed the refugees' activities, the organization was now called upon to maintain numerous destitute refugees who had to begin afresh after their release. By the summer of 1944, the Joint found itself again having to make monthly payments to assist refugees in Trinidad that were equivalent to those it had made at the height of the panic migration of 1938–39.[19]

While the subsequent biographies of the refugees were shaped by many individual factors, one can roughly divide the refugees into four groups: firstly, those who left the British West Indies as soon as they could; secondly, those who probably would have liked to leave but did not succeed; thirdly, those who initially stayed but later left, for instance, in response to the rise of Black Power and the ensuing upheaval in the 1970s; and, finally, those who stayed for good.[20]

Jamaica

This section focuses on three of the refugees we have met earlier, either in Up Park or Gibraltar Camp: Arthur Steigler, Arnold von der Porten and Rudolf Aub. Although Steigler was one of those refugees still languishing in Gibraltar Camp long after most of his peers had secured their remigration elsewhere, he clearly falls into the first category in the sense that he had no intention of staying and sought to move on as soon as possible. Von der Porten and Aub fall into the third category, as despite initially deciding to stay, they both eventually left: von der Porten in the early 1950s, partly for personal, partly for political and economic reasons; Aub not until the 1980s, for political reasons.

Initially it looked as though Steigler too would move on to Cuba like many of his fellow refugees. On 6 October 1944, he received a Cuban visa dated 5 August.[21] Yet on the eve of Steigler's departure, planned for 28 December 1944, he was informed that his visa had been revoked. Within days of the arrival of his visa, the new Cuban president, Ramón Grau San Martín, had taken office. Grau had garnered considerable public support in the 1930s by tapping into widespread anti-immigrant resentment. Famously, his speaker, Primitivo Rodriguez, urged a mass demonstration against the influx of Jewish refugees in Havana in 1939 to 'fight the Jews until the last one is driven out'.[22]

On 28 January 1945, Steigler wrote to Ramón Grau San Martín to request that he be allowed to come to Cuba after all. 'I have prepared my departure, liquidated my things, [and] purchased an airplane ticket for Havana', he explained, 'only to be informed by the Pan American [on] the 27th December, on the eve of the presumptive departure, that the immigration department "does not accept me for travel". No reason for the annulling of my valid visa has been given'. Steigler took it for granted that he had been refused entry because of critical comments about the Cuban treatment of the *St Louis* he had published in the French daily, *L'Aube*, back in 1939. In the light of Grau's anti-corruption drive, Steigler suggested, he should let bygones be bygones.[23]

Rau's office politely thanked Steigler for his letter and passed it on to the immigration authorities who informed Steigler, just as politely, on 26 February 1945, that immigration was subject to legal regulations and that he did not meet the requirements of the Cuban decree no. 1072 of 1942, which had barred enemy aliens (including refugees from countries under enemy occupation) from entering.[24] Given that scores of his peers had only just remigrated to Cuba without any mention of this exclusion clause being made, Steigler can be forgiven for taking the matter personally. Even so, it is obviously much more likely that his visa was annulled due to the tougher immigration regime under the new government rather than his critical comments about Cuba during the *St Louis* crisis, and he was not the only refugee stuck in Gibraltar Camp because of the change in Cuban policy. A detailed HIAS-ICA list names several Polish Jewish refugees (including several entire families) who had been 'expecting visa[s] from Cuba when government changed'.[25] Either way, Steigler was not best pleased when the director of the American Federation for Polish Jews, Isaac Kornfeld, subsequently suggested to the American Friends Service Committee (AFSC) that 'Dr. Steigler did not use the visa that had been granted him until it was too late'.[26] In some ways this was an unfair criticism; on the other hand, had he acted promptly when the visa arrived, he might well have made it to Cuba before the immigration regime was tightened up.

Steigler now enlisted the Quakers in an attempt to move to the United States. He was able to secure an affidavit but various complications arose before he could finally remigrate. The more he pursued every contact he could think of to garner support for his immigration, the more exasperated his contacts became. When aid organizations consulted with some of the contacts he had named, they effectively disavowed him.[27] The AFSC last heard directly from Steigler in December 1945: 'I am living very hard days', he wrote.

> My sister-in-law communicated to me from Geneva in Switzerland that my only daughter, my sole child, wrote the last time in October 1943 from the concentration Camp Birkenau in Germany. She wrote the last time only few words. My sister-in-law does not mentioned [*sic*] the name of my wife at all. It is the first news about my family since 1941 … It is evident that the Nazis did separate child from mother and send them in different camps. I have no more wife and child. From my mother, my seven brothers, my three married sisters, all in Poland, there are no news at all. I have nobody more.

'My visa gives me much worries', Steigler continued. He suspected that his most recent affidavit was invalid. 'I don't know what to do', he went on,

> I lost my equilibrium, I am not able to continue my optical studies. To it comes a revival of rheumatism in my hands, this time very strong and painful. Two years ago, I was in the Island's mineral bath and got a big improvement. This time I cannot go there. I have no money. I need money also for other

very urgent purposes. I need about 25–30 pounds. I don't know where to get it from. Your attention and goodwill encourage me to ask you if you would be able to procure me a loan. I would return it later in the U.S.A. I am not able to address my different personal friends in the States for material help. During the four years of my residence here, nobody of them did ask me, nobody offered me any help. I never addressed them with such a request and I do not like to do it now.[28]

Over the following six months, the AFSC made several unsuccessful attempts to contact and locate Steigler. In the spring of 1946, they asked Marion Ballysingh of the Jamaican Quakers to look into Steigler's situation.[29] In May, Ballysingh informed the AFSC that 'it did not seem suitable for me to make a visit to the men's internment camp'. Consequently, she had asked the secretary of the local YMCA to locate Steigler, yet 'he says that he can find no trace of him, and the camp authorities do not seem to know about him'. Apparently, 'the internees have been placed all over the island in various places and they do not seem to know where he is. Isn't that amazing?'[30]

On 11 June 1946, Steigler's guarantor, Elias Laub, who ran a print shop in New York, informed the AFSC by telephone that Steigler had suddenly cabled to say he would be arriving in New York the following day. The last entries in Steigler's AFSC file are from 6 December 1946.[31] There was some suggestion that Steigler might spend time in the AFSC's Sky Island Hostel, which was in the process of changing from a home for the recuperation of refugees to a reception centre for DPs arriving in the United States.[32] Contacting Olive Whitson of the Friends Center in New York City in order to secure a place for Steigler at Sky Island, his case worker, Agnes Gallagher, wrote that 'it is our impression that Dr. Steigler['s] experiences in recent years have had a rather unstabilizing effect on him and he may have some difficulty adjusting in this country. We feel, however, that he has made such a valiant effort to help himself and to keep occupied that he deserves whatever help can be given him'.[33] At this point, as far as the archive is concerned, we lose all trace of Arthur Steigler.

Arnold von der Porten recalls something of a mixed reception in Kingston following his release from Up Park. He experienced a high measure of solidarity from some, yet 'others made it quite clear that they would not have anything to do with a "damned German". Some', he wrote,

went so far that, when we were approaching each other in the street, they rather crossed the street, so that they would not have to say hello to me. Every now and then I was invited to a party but invariably had to leave early, as there were always a few boys who, after a few drinks, wanted to pick a fight with me to show their patriotism.[34]

Figure 6.3 Portrait of Edna Manley by Arnold von der Porten. Photograph courtesy of Professor Jeffrey Giles.

Once he was able to go out in the evenings again, he began to attend an art class at the Institute of Jamaica with Edna Manley, the wife of Norman Manley, the founder and leader of the People's National Party. Von der Porten painted a portrait of her, and apparently engaged in vehement political controversy with her throughout the three sittings, which, he suggests, helps to explain her fierce appearance in the portrait.[35]

When the Allies finally defeated Germany, von der Porten joined the Quakers. He suggests that he had been reluctant to do so sooner lest it appear as though he were doing so to attain personal advantage. He helped to found the Kingston Monthly Meeting of Friends, which met on Caledonia Avenue. It was the first regular unprogrammed meeting in Jamaica since the group visited by George Fox in 1672 had stopped gathering.[36]

He had begun to establish a neon sign business before his internment, which was now 'as good as dead',[37] though he was able to re-establish it later. Von der Porten spent much of his time working at the Jamaica Macaroni Factory run by his brother and sister-in-law. Gerhard von der Porten went on to genuine commercial success when, with the help of Chinese bottlers on the island, he headed up the Zimba Cola operation in Jamaica.[38] Both brothers also played an important role in establishing and consolidating the Jamaican Manufacturers' Association.

Von der Porten married Amy Barry, the daughter of Herbert F. Barry, the Jamaican administrator general. They rented their first shared home from his former fellow internee, Fritz Lackenbach.[39] Initially, he had taken it for granted that he would stay in Jamaica and applied for naturalization, yet his application was rejected for reasons he was never able to ascertain.[40] Their first child was born with substantial health problems and died within a year. When Amy von der Porten became pregnant again, she was weary of relying on the Jamaican health system should problems arise with their second child. Von der Porten in any case felt increasingly uneasy about Jamaican nationalism, and they left Jamaica in January 1953 for the United States,[41] where he worked as 'a glassblower, industrial foreman, production manager, and a mechanical designer'. In 1965, he graduated from Rutgers University College with a BSc in Business Administration. He retired in 1980, and in 1994 Arnold and Amy von der Porten moved to Gainesville, Florida, where, up until recently, they occasionally attended the local Quakers meeting.[42] Amy von der Porten died in 2017.[43] Gerhard and Dorrie von der Porten eventually moved to Greenville, North Carolina, to join their daughter.[44] Dorrie von der Porten died in 1983, aged 82, her husband the following year at the age of 95.[45] Arnold von der Porten still has the blanket that he made in the internment camp in Jamaica, described by him as the 'Jew Camp'. In his memoir, Nine Lives, Arnold tells the story of how inmates constructed a loom from discarded fence posts and barbed wire (left lying around when the camp expanded from 22 inmates to over 1,000):

> We made the heddles and the comb from the straightened barbed wire, six
> pedals and hinges for them. Out of the bullet wool I made a six-toothed

ratchet wheel and pawl and mounted the ratchet on the warp beam to keep the warp tightly. We made several heddles to be able to make a great variety of patterns. The loom could make a blanket 2'-6" wide. By sewing two together we could make a good sized blanket. Now, that the loom was complete, we needed wool, a card (a kind of comb to prepare wool for spinning) and a spinning wheel. The Quakers managed to find us a card cover, i.e. two sheets of rubber with hundreds of stainless steel wires sticking out. We had to make a roll, bearings and a handle to mount one sheet on, so that it could have a combing action against the other sheet. We also received a broken spinning wheel which we repaired to work like new. The wool was 'butchers' wool', i.e. from sheep which had recently been slaughtered. We had to wash it and dry it. We combed it on the card and … I learned how to spin wool yarn. We made a shuttle for the loom and made several blankets.[46]

Rudolf Aub was released from Up Park in March 1943 due to the serious shortage of medical staff in Jamaica.[47] He immediately began to work as an assistant medical officer. Given that he lacked a British medical licence, he was subject to a special decree that allowed him to practise in public hospitals, but only under the supervision of a consultant.

As an internee, Aub had been able to stay in touch with his family back in Germany on a regular basis. Now that he had been released, he would be an ordinary resident trying to send mail to enemy territory, which was illegal. In order to stay in touch with his family, Aub therefore had to maintain the pretence that he was still interned; the camp authorities played along with this, channelling the mail through the camp. Given that the mail was censored, this meant that he also had to leave his family under the impression that he was still interned, and so they did not find out that he had actually been released until the end of the war.

Aub began working in a very busy general emergency department, which familiarized him with the diversity of Jamaica's population. On Aub's own account, he was accepted unquestioningly by his new Jamaican colleagues. Socially, former fellow internees supported him. When the war finally ended, Aub decided, without being able to discuss this with his family, to stay in Jamaica, and he became a regular medical officer. Alongside his work in the emergency department he now ran a ward with seventy beds and was asked to reorganize the way in which the hospital raised its statistics. As it turned out, his wife had anticipated his decision, and on 12 November 1947, Julia Aub arrived in Kingston with their three children, Martin, Gertrud and Konrad.[48] Rudolf Aub and the children were naturalized in 1948.[49]

By 1951, he was no longer able to continue his hospital work because of his lack of formal qualifications and, with the help of his wife, who died in 1967, he opened a private practice, from which he retired in 1976, aged 75. He then ran a clinic for hospital personnel until he was 80, when, against

Figure 6.4 Arnold von der Porten, with Professor Jeffrey Giles, at his home in Gainesville, Florida, holding a blanket made in the internment camp with a loom made from barbed wire and fence posts, 12 April 2019. The blanket is still in remarkably good condition after eighty years. Photograph courtesy of Professor Jeffrey Giles.

the backdrop of a mounting economic and political crisis in Jamaica, Aub decided to return to Germany, and settled in Lindau on the Bodensee. He visited Jamaica in 1982 and 1984. On the latter occasion he again considered his options, yet ultimately returned to Lindau, where he died in

1989. Although he was able to brace his apprehension – he had previously visited Germany in 1958 and 1965 – he was never entirely at ease again in Germany. 'The trauma of exile', he explained shortly before his death, 'is inextinguishable.'[50]

Martin Aub read maths and physics at the University of London. He then taught at the University of the West Indies and worked for the Farquharson Institute of Public Affairs. He married a Jamaican woman and they adopted three Jamaican children. Gertrud Aub Buscher read modern languages at universities in Edinburgh, Paris and Strasbourg. She married a German and initially returned to Jamaica where she taught French at the University of the West Indies. She went on to become director of the Language Centre at the University of Hull. Konrad Aub Robinson read geography at Cambridge and went on to teach at Aarhus University.

Of Max Ebersohn we know only that he embarked on the production of women's undergarments following his release.[51] Willy Gertig eventually left Jamaica for New York on 9 April 1946 on a visa for educational purposes.[52] On 10 June 1946, Lili Koehler of the AFSC informed Helen Abrikian of the Jamaican Quakers that everything was now in place to allow Willy Gertig 'to go to Alfred University, which he wants so much, and we are very happy that everything has been arranged'.[53] Alfred University, located in Alfred, 60 miles south of Rochester in Upstate New York, was one of the earliest co-educational and racially integrated institutions in the United States.

Trinidad

Jewish life in Trinidad offered few attractions to entice refugees to stay. Writing to Chief Rabbi Hertz in London in November 1941, Oscar Pillersdorf of the Jewish Association of Trinidad described the situation as follows:

> There are among us about 60 bachelors in the age between 20–35 years, but on the other hand unmarried Jewish women are practically non-existent in the Colony. Being far away from England and America, the situation would deteriorate. There are a few children among us, but those who are, do not receive a Jewish education. We have no synagogue, no Jewish home, no Jewish books. We are too poor to see about it ourselves. In our Colony are stationed at present many Jewish boys from the English and American armed forces. But there is nothing we can offer them in the way of Jewish atmosphere. We turn to you for advice. There are many among us willing to build up a Jewish life in this Colony, but they need inspiration and help.[54]

In February 1944, the Jewish Refugee Society counted approximately 400 Jewish refugees in Trinidad. Of these, 189 were Polish and Romanian

Jews, and 140 were Germans, Austrians and Czechs. Some 330 of them were registered with the Committee, though it only assisted eight of them.[55] Harry Biele estimated that approximately 150 Jewish refugees had managed to emigrate to the United States between 1939 and 1944.[56] In June 1945, an estimated 320 Jewish refugees were still in Trinidad, of which 250 were able to sustain themselves. The group comprised 187 refugees from Poland and Rumania, 128 from Germany, Austria and Czechoslovakia, and a handful of Italian and stateless refugees.[57] Throughout 1945 and 1946, the JRS continued to receive $300 from the Joint each month to cover the assistance required by ten refugees.[58]

Relations between the Jews who had come to Trinidad from Eastern Europe, organized mainly in the Jewish Association of Trinidad, and the refugees from Greater Germany, organized predominantly in the Jewish Refugee Society, had been tense from the outset. Internment, which disproportionately affected those represented by the JRS, hardly helped. The Joint consistently tried to engineer a rapprochement between the two groups, but to no avail.

Following the release of its leading members from internment, the JRS proposed to the Joint in January 1942 that it should be recognized in its own right, and requested funding to rent an office. The Joint was not convinced. 'Time has passed and conditions have changed', Robert Pilpel responded, 'so that perhaps the old sources of irritation may be forgotten … There is no point in blanking the fact that the points of view of Jews from Eastern and Western Europe have been opposed to a degree. At the same time, this opposition has in many places and in many instances been overcome'.[59] Yet this was wishful thinking on Pilpel's part, and the cultural and religious distinctions between East European and Central European refugees largely persisted and certainly dwarfed the notional juxtaposition of the JAT as a permanent organization and the JRS as a temporary aid society.

Not until 1945 was an agreement of sorts secured between the two committees. As Edgar Gruen, now in his capacity as chair of the newly formed Council of Jewish Organizations, informed the Joint in December 1945, 'after years of efforts to have general Jewish interests represented in Trinidad and abroad by only ONE Committee', this goal had now been attained.[60] The council comprised representatives of the JAT and the JRS as well as WIZO, the Jewish Dramatic Circle, United Zionists, the Committee of the World Jewish Congress and also the newly formed Jewish Religious Society.

Given the long-standing preponderance of the Jewish Association of Trinidad throughout the refugee crisis and the war, and the resentment of the Jewish Refugee Society at not being treated by the Joint on an equal footing with the JAT, it is not without irony that in the long run Hans Stecher emerged as the stalwart of Trinidadian Jewry right up until his death in May 2014 at the age of 90. His father, Victor Stecher, lost the business he had begun to set up on arriving in Trinidad as a result of the family's internment, which lasted for three and a half years. Following their release, Victor Stecher began producing hats and handbags, and after the war, Victor and Hans Stecher built up the successful chain of Stechers duty-free shops, selling luxury goods that still has ten branches in Trinidad today. Stecher's father died in 1953 at the age of 69, while his mother, Sophie Stecher, died in 1980 aged 82.[61] Her sister, Wilhelmine Baltinester, who was three years younger, died the same year. She was never able to resume her career as a writer, and was forced to reinvent herself by running a hat shop. In Hans Stecher's words, just 'like a plant transplanted from its accustomed soil cannot bud again', his aunt, who had been 'like a second mother' to him, had never written again after her departure from Vienna.[62]

'"Giant of a man" laid to rest', the *Trinidad Guardian* reported when Stecher was buried in Mucurapo cemetery in May 2014.[63] It quoted the honorary Israeli consul in Port of Spain, Barbara Malins-Smith:

'Hans has served his adopted country with distinction, in tourism as chair of the Tourist Board, as Chamber of Commerce president and as longest-serving Rotarian … He was also honorary consul for Austria.' She described him as a 'walking encyclopaedia', knowledgeable on everything from architecture to

Figure 6.5 Hans Stecher, at the Jewish graveyard in Port of Spain, Trinidad. Photograph by the author, 2001.

Figure 6.6 Gravestone of Hans Stecher's father, Dr Victor Stecher, in the Jewish cemetery, Port of Spain, Trinidad. Photograph by the author.

Figure 6.7 Jewish section of the graveyard in Port of Spain, Trinidad. Photograph by the author.

languages and geology. 'He was the most gracious man I ever knew, and we have lost a treasure. It is the end of an era', she added.

Lifelong friend Jean-Paul Simonet described Stecher as 'a man who was passionate about life and travel, had a wealth of knowledge and loved to share. He was wise, kind, a great leader and loyal friend. A true renaissance man'.[64]

He had, in his own words, become a 'Trinidadian by adoption', but one who also insisted that 'one can be more than one thing'.[65]

Hans Stecher, then, was one of those who stayed, and stayed for good. Many of his fellow refugees did not. Among those to leave as soon as possible was Julius Sass, the former president of the Jewish Refugee Society, who moved to Cincinnati after the war, together with his wife, Gertrude Sass, née Alexander, and her mother, Bertha Alexander. Julius and Gertrude Sass were naturalized in September 1946, not without being 'admonished … to avoid the pitfalls of subversive activities and organizations, and to give their undivided loyalty to the land of their adoption'.[66] They had come to Trinidad in 1939, while Gertrude Sass's sister, Elsa Levinsohn, née Alexander, emigrated to New Zealand. Their younger brother, Curt Alexander, fled to Denmark in 1937.[67] After the war, Curt Alexander joined his mother and sister in Cincinnati.[68] When Elsa Levinsohn came to visit her mother and siblings in Cincinnati in 1958 and they were all reunited for the first time in twenty-one years, the *Cincinnati Enquirer* deemed the occasion worthy of a substantial report on the front page, including a photo of the three siblings and their mother at the airport.[69] Gertrude Sass died in November 1976, and Julius Sass early in 1979.[70]

The family of Ernst Otto Fischer, the Viennese journalist we met in Chapter 3 explaining in the *Trinidad Guardian* how little was known about the British West Indies as a possible refugee destination, also remigrated to the United States at the first opportunity. Fischer himself died in 1944, aged 62, following surgery.[71] The Fischers were all interned for some twelve months during the war. In 1945, Fischer's widow, Liesl Fischer, and her two daughters were able to move on to the United States, where Inge Fischer married Walter Engel, a former theatre and cabaret actor and director, who had emigrated to the States from Vienna in 1938, fought in the US army during the war and then went on to a distinguished career in broadcasting, eventually heading up the broadcasting department at the American Embassy in the West German capital, Bonn, and two radio stations, RIAS and Voice of America.[72] In 2011, a musical by Andrew Geha of the Friends Academy in New York was performed at the Edinburgh Fringe Festival in Fischer Waldstein's presence.[73] It was based on Inge Engel's diaries from the 1930s and on interviews with her and her younger sister, Lucy Fischer Waldstein, portraying their emigration from Vienna via England and Trinidad to the United States.

Helen Hammermann, whom we met in Chapter 3 writing fashion columns for the *Trinidad Guardian*, was interned, as were her parents, Esther and Baruch Hammermann. Released in 1943, the family moved to the United States in 1945. Esther Hammermann, née Wachsmann, went on to become a well-known folk art painter in the USA. Helen Breger, née Hammermann, worked as the fashion artist of *The Jewish Chronicle* from 1954 to 1960 before becoming an independent artist (specializing in etchings) and teaching at the California College of Arts and Crafts.[74] Baruch Hammermann died in 1950, Esther Hammermann in 1977 and Helen Breger in 2013.[75] Helen Breger's daughter, Michelle Shelfer, has produced a documentary, 'Vienna in the Heavenlies' (2012), in which Breger tells her story in the context of a trip to Vienna with her two adult daughters.[76] For many years an influential fashion illustrator for the *New York Times*, Breger's elder sister, Juana Nadja Merino Kalfel, née Hammermann, arguably became the most famous member of the family. Her story has been told in the documentary film, 'Dancing on the Volcano', by Gary Merz (2012, Federal Street Productions), which won the Audience Choice Best Documentary Award at the New Hope Film Festival.[77]

Josefine Koffler Bley and Adolf Klinger were also among those who sought a speedy exit. Koffler Bley's daughter, Hertha, was married to Klinger's son, Walter. The four of them had fled Austria after the *Anschluss*, and eventually arrived in Trinidad. Walter Klinger, who had worked for Warner Bros and Metro-Goldwyn-Mayer in Vienna and Berlin, initially continued to work for Warner Bros and set up a company for screen advertising in Trinidad, but after the German victory over France, all four of them were interned. Walter and Hertha Klinger moved to the United States in 1941, and the parents eventually followed in 1947.[78]

Miriam Schächter, née Freund, who had worked as the secretary of the editor of the Viennese Jüdische Presse, initially opened a restaurant called Allies Café in Trinidad following her release from internment, which was frequented especially by sailors from the US naval base. Ulrich Schächter was eventually able to open a dental practice in Port of Spain. Their son, Harry Schachter, meanwhile, attended St Mary's College where 'no attempt was made to convert the Jewish kids … The priests knew our history and respected our Jewish religion'.[79] Yet in 1950, Ulrich and Miriam Schächter emigrated to Toronto, and their son rejoined them the following year, having completed his education at St Mary's College and received the prestigious Island Scholarship to study at the University of Toronto,[80] where he is a professor emeritus. He was awarded the Rosalind Kornfeld Award for Lifetime Achievement in Glycobiology in 2010 and the Austrian Cross of Honour for Science and Art (First Class) the following year.

The Hockenheimers too moved on to the United States as soon as they could, and there became the Hockleys. Marianne Pennekamp, née

Hockenheim/Hockley, went on to study at Berkeley and the Sorbonne, and became a distinguished scholar of school social work. In 2013, she was awarded the Randy A. Fisher Lifetime Achievement Award of the School Social Work Association of America.[81] Ralph Hockley, as he became, joined the US army and served as an intelligence officer in Bremen during the initial phase of denazification after the war.

A number of refugees are buried in Mucurapo cemetery who died within a few years of the end of the war, some of them at a fairly young age, some of them quite old, suggesting that they belonged to the second group – those who would have liked to move on but were not well placed to do so. Irene Huth, for instance, died just days ahead of VE Day, on 2 May 1945, aged 69; Oscar Huth died early in 1951 at the age of 72.[82] Egon Huth, presumably their son, died in June 1959, aged 55.[83] The German-born Erna Marx, née Bloch, who had lived in Utrecht before leaving Europe for Trinidad, died in July 1949, aged 51.[84] Karl Falkenstein, the youngest son of the cigar manufacturer Salomon Falkenstein from Hochneukirch (located near the Dutch border in what is now North Rhine Westphalia), who fled to Trinidad in 1938 and was followed by his wife, Lucie, and their four children, Margot, Ronald, Rene and Lisa, in 1939, died the same year, aged only 59.[85] Following his death, his family moved to the United States. Berta Marx, née Cahn, who had come to Trinidad from the south of what is now North Rhine Westphalia with her husband, Isidor Marx, died in 1946, aged 61. Isidor Marx died in 1959, at the age of 76. Theirs is an imposing double grave in Mucurapo cemetery, joined by a large shield of David.[86]

Among those who stayed for good were Willi (Wilhelm) and Herma (Hermine) Schwarz from Vienna. Willi Schwarz was arrested during the November Pogrom of 1938 but released when he provided evidence that he was already in the process of emigrating to Trinidad. His wife and son, Heinz Herbert, followed in July 1939. They were interned from March 1940 until November 1941. While Heinz Herbert Schwarz secured a scholarship to study at Northwestern University, Illinois, and then trained as a psychiatrist at the University of Michigan Medical School, his parents spent the rest of their lives in Trinidad.[87] Willi Schwarz apparently ran the Cozy Nook restaurant;[88] he died in 1963 at the age of 76.[89]

Paul Richter and his wife, the former tennis star Toni Richter, also stayed in Trinidad. She died there in 1961, aged 66, followed by Paul Richter in 1972 at the age of 68.[90] Otto Gumprich from Borghorst, a small town near the Dutch border in what is now North Rhine Westphalia, was naturalized in February 1948,[91] and continued to live in Trinidad until he died in October 1958, aged 63,[92] as did Walter Julius Hahn from Cologne, who died in March 1958, aged 55, and Wihelmina Hahn, who died in 1978 in her mid-70s.[93] There are the graves in Mucurapo cemetery of three further refugees who had spent the rest of their lives in Trinidad: Johann Schwarz from Vienna, who died in 1983 at the age of 92;[94] Ernestine Köhler, who died in 1960, aged 75;[95] and Georges T. Königsberg, who died the same year, aged 52.[96]

A list of Trinidadian contributors to the Joint's 1950/51 annual appeal indicates that at the time Edgar Gruen and Paul Laband were still in the colony. It also includes a few more distinctly German-sounding names, though I have not been able to secure any independent evidence for the suggestion that they too were refugees. They are: Bernhard Mahler, Moritz Schnapp, Robert Altholz, Edgar Wolfram and David Wagschal.[97]

David Wagschal was the second husband of Manfred Goldfish's first wife, Malka, now Martha. He adopted the Goldfishes' children, Harry (born 1939) and Marion (born 1943). In 1951, the Wagschals emigrated to Montreal with the two children. Harry Wagschal trained as a violinist at the Juilliard, in Vienna and in Nice, and played in the Kingston Symphony, the Quebec Symphony and the CBC Orchestra. He later shifted his focus to teaching and educational theory. He died in Pointe-Claire, Greater Montreal, in 2011.[98] Marion Wagschal taught history of art at Concordia University in Montreal and is a highly respected painter. The Montreal Museum of Fine Arts held a major retrospective of her work in 2015, and a selection of her portrayals of the female figure was shown at Canada House in London in the Spring of 2016.

In August 1951, Manfred Goldfish married Phyllis McEwen who had come to Trinidad from London after the war.[99] Their daughter, Su Goldfish, was born in 1958. Goldfisch had initially secured a probationary position as an assistant in a radio repair department, yet it turned out that he lacked both the technical and linguistic skills for this position. His employer, who was of Chinese descent, did, however, encourage him to return, once his English had improved.[100] Goldfisch then worked on the docks for a while before being re-employed by his former firm on the strength of his knowledge of the European music scene. He was asked to select European records for sale in the shop.[101] His remit grew when he was also commissioned to select (and deliver) suitable records for the local programmes that ran on the island's radio relay service.[102]

After the war, Goldfish worked for Emory Cook's Cook Records and became deeply immersed in the local music scene. Cook's mobile recording devices allowed the label to produce recordings of local steel bands and calypso music in the locations in which they were generally played rather than a conventional studio setting. Over time, Goldfish became studio manager and eventually the manager of Cook Caribbean.

Following the rise of the Black Power movement and the military mutiny against the state of emergency in April 1970, Manfred and Phyllis Goldfish no longer felt safe in Trinidad, gave up their electrical store in Port of Spain and, with their daughter Su, emigrated to Sydney. Even though he had stayed, Goldfish too insisted that Trinidad had chosen him, he had not chosen it.

The Goldfishes were by no means the only Jews to leave the West Indies at this juncture. Among their numerous peers who left the islands against this backdrop were also Leo Siegel and his wife, Adela Siegel, née Dornbusch. Their son Markus had left to study at Northwestern in 1945, followed by their younger son, Arthur, who went up to Berkeley in 1946.[103] Yet Leo and Adela Siegel remained in Trinidad, and for three decades Leo Siegel played a prominent role in the Jewish Religious Society.[104] Only then did they leave to join Arthur Siegel in Montreal. Arthur Siegel was a widely respected journalist who, in 1976, took up a position in Communication Studies at York University. He died in April 2010. Alisa Siegel is his daughter.

Arriving in Australia, Manfred Goldfish, now in his early sixties, found work as a salesman in a department store, while his wife worked as a housekeeper, and their financial situation was difficult. Although Goldfish visited Germany in 1962 with his family, and continued to receive letters from one surviving aunt living in Strasbourg, he was generally tight lipped in the extreme about his past – indeed, Su Goldfish grew up knowing neither that she was Jewish nor that her father had been married before. Her documentary, 'The Last Goldfish', offers a moving account of her efforts gradually to reconstruct and connect with her father's past, her half siblings and the fate of the family and relatives whom Goldfisch and his first wife left behind when they quit Germany for Trinidad following his arrest during the November Pogrom of 1938. Only very late in life did Goldfish come to feel more at ease about his earlier life in and before Trinidad, though he was also plagued by intense survivor's guilt as he confronted the truth, no longer as an abstraction but as definitive information, about the murder of virtually all his German relatives.

When Su Goldfish met her half-brother and sister for the first time in Montreal, she received a gift from Marion Wagschal: a fish knife and fork from Hotel Löwenstein, the hotel that Manfred Goldfish's parents, Lina and Eugen Goldfisch, had run in Bad Ems before the Nazi ascendancy. Lina and Eugen Goldfisch had given the cutlery to their son; Manfred and Malka Goldfish had taken them along to Trinidad; Malka, now Martha Wagschal, took them with her to Canada in 1951; and from there Su Goldfish took them back to Manfred Goldfish in Sydney, only for him to claim that he did not remember the hotel or understand its significance. When Su Goldfish travelled to Bad Ems she found that the hotel had been transformed into an apartment block, now inhabited by Turkish and Iraqi immigrants, including one Lebanese-born Turkish Kurd who at the time had been living in Germany for twenty-two years, and who told her that he felt a strong resonance between his own experience and that of her family.

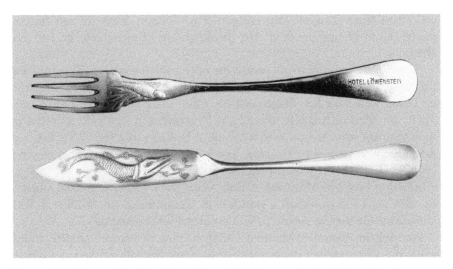

Figure 6.8 Photograph of the fish knife and fork given to Su Goldfish by her sister Marion Wagschal, from Hotel Löwenstein. Photograph given to author with kind permission by Su Goldfish.

The story of the knife and fork that Su Goldfish brought to Australia is a story of tragedy and resilience, of overcoming great odds, and of memory and identity. As such, it is strongly emblematic of so many stories of forced migration, that refugees have told over the ages. In its own way, it encapsulates the scale of the havoc wreaked by the National Socialist determination to annihilate European Jewry, even upon the lives of those Jews who were fortunate enough to get away. As this study has demonstrated, in the context of the British West Indies too, even allowing for all the various pragmatic concerns and caveats, the efforts of the British government and the US administration to help Jewish refugees from Nazi-dominated Europe never even came close to confronting this enormity seriously.

Notes

1. Paul Gilroy, *The Black Atlantic: Modernity and Double Consciousness* (London: Verso, 1993), 207.
2. See, for example, Sarah Casteel's critique of novelists including Jamaica Kincaid, John Hearne, M. NourbeSe Philip, Michèle Maillet, Michelle Cliff and Caryl Philips in *Calypso Jews*, 175–270; see also novels by Andrea Levy, *Small Island* (London: Tinder Press, 2004); V.S. Naipaul, *A House for Mr Biswas*, reprint (Picador, 2011); idem, *Miguel Street*, reprint (Picador, 2011); Lawrence Scott, *Night Calypso* (London: Allison & Busby, 2006).
3. Brown, *Mona Past and Present*, 46.

4. See, for example, Paul Bartrop, 'From Lisbon to Jamaica: A Study of British Refugee Rescue During the Second World War', *Immigrants and Minorities* 13(1) (March 1994), 62, where he argues that the rescue 'goes some small way towards rehabilitating British honour'.

5. Cooper-Clark, *Dreams of Re-Creation*, 126. In 2016, she organized a reunion in Gibraltar Camp; see, for example, this report from St Andrews School, Jamaica – https://sahs.edu.jm/fond-memories-of-sahs-from-a-gibraltar-camp-refugee/ – for a description of how Inez Baker, née Schpektor, the only refugee to come back to Jamaica for the reunion, visited the school that, as an 11 year old, she attended in Jamaica (last accessed on 6 January 2018).

6. Casteel, *Calypso Jews*, 2–3.

7. See, for example, Kushner, *The Holocaust*, and London, *Whitehall and the Jews*. See also Tony Kushner, 'The Big Kindertransport Myth', *The Jewish Chronicle*, 15 November 2018, https://www.thejc.com/news/news-features/the-big-kindertransport-myth-kind ertransport80th-anniversary-1.472542 (last accessed 6 January 2019). Over two-thirds of the 10,000 unaccompanied children admitted to Britain had parents they had to leave behind.

8. See Marion A. Kaplan, *Dominican Haven: The Jewish Refugee Settlement in Sosúa, 1940–1945* (New York: Museum of Jewish Heritage – A Living Memorial to the Holocaust, 2008).

9. National Coordinating Committee for Aid to Refugees and Emigrants Coming From Germany, 1939, *Bound for Nowhere: Disorganized Panic Migration,* unpublished typescript report, JDC 1059.

10. Among them are nearly 25.4 million refugees, over half of whom are under the age of 18. Cited from: https://www.unhcr.org/figures-at-a-glance.html (last accessed 6 January 2019).

11. Joanna Newman, 'A Caribbean Jerusalem', Radio 4, 11 August 2001.

12. From transcript of interview with author, August 1989, Barbados, in author's possession.

13. Harry Schachter, email communication, 1 August 2016.

14. Joanna Newman, 'A Caribbean Jerusalem', Radio 4, 11 August 2001.

15. Julius Sass, President of the Jewish Refugee Society to Robert Pilpel of the Joint, 1 February 1941; Jewish Refugee Society to Robert Pilpel, 18 February 1942, JDC, File 1048; Memorandum, National Refugee Service, New York, 22 August 1940, JDC, File 1047.

16. D.J. Goldenberg, President of the Jewish Refugee Society to Robert Pilpel of the Joint, 30 May 1940; Paul Richter of the Jewish Refugee Society to Robert Pilpel, 22 June 1940, JDC, File 1047; Meeting of the Joint Subcommittee on Refugee Aid in Central and South America, 9 July 1940, JDC, File 113.

17. Moses W. Beckelman, Report to the Joint in New York, 19 October 1941, JDC, File 1048.

18. Edgar Gruen of the JRS to Friedrich Borchardt of the Joint, 17 November 1942; see also JRS to Friedrich Borchardt, Joint Subcommittee on Refugee Aid in Central and South America, 12 November 1941, JDC, File 1048.

19. For the relevant figures, see the minutes of the meetings of the Joint's Committee on Refugee Aid in South America between 1942 and 1944, JDC, File 114.

20. There were also those, of course, who died before the end of the war. We have already noted the death of Fritz Karell and the suicide of Paul Bley, both at Up Park in 1942. Richard Bronne from Wörrstadt near Worms, one of the oldest centres of Jewish

settlement in the German-speaking lands, succumbed to illness on 20 April 1943, aged only 28. His death was announced by his family in *Aufbau* on 3 September 1943. At the time, his father, Julius Bronne, was in Amsterdam from where he was later deported to Auschwitz. He was murdered on 11 December 1942. His mother, Hedwig Bronne, née Metzger, had managed to emigrate to Brazil, where she lived in Sao Paolo with her daughter, Lucie Salomon, née Bronne, and her son-in-law, Otto Salomon (https://jewishphotolibrary.smugmug.com/CARIBBEAN/TRINIDAD/TT PortofSpainWoodbrookCemetery/i-GWPPqPf; *Aufbau*, 3 September 1943, 20. Last accessed 9 May 2019). One Martin Tanz from Berlin, presumably also a refugee, given that he too was buried in the Jewish section of Mucurapo cemetery, died in 1942 at the age of 29 (http://www.findagrave.com/cgi-bin/fg.cgi?page=gr&GSsr=41&GScid=22 09945&GRid=130137322&, last accessed 9 May 2019). Both the gravestones for Bronne and Tanz give the precise date of their death but only the year of their birth, suggesting that both must have been very seriously ill by the time they attracted any serious attention. Ernst Otto Fischer died following surgery in 1944.

21. Arthur Steigler to Abe Kan of the *Forward*, New York, 9 April 1945, AFSC Case 7827, 43, USHMM.

22. See https://www.ushmm.org/wlc/en/article.php?ModuleId=10005267 (last accessed 9 May 2019).

23. Copy of the letter in AFSC Case 7827, 36–38, here 36, USHMM.

24. Copy of the responses, AFSC Case 7827, 34, USHMM.

25. HIAS-ICA Emigration Assn., 'Data on Refugees in Gibraltar Camp', JDC, File 893.

26. Isaac Kornfeld of the American Federation for Polish Jews, New York, to the AFSC, Philadelphia, 20 March 1945, AFSC Case 7827, 25, USHMM.

27. See, for example, Friedl Reifer of Oswego, New York, to Alexis O. Hay of the Unitarian Service Committee, 24 February 1945, AFSC Case 7827, p. 20, USHMM. Inter alia, Steigler wrote to Hannah Arendt who, he claimed, 'knows me well personally … but … did not answer' (Arthur Steigler to the AFSC, Philadelphia, 11 April 1945, AFSC Case 7827, p. 44, USHMM). There is no trace of Steigler in Arendt's correspondence at the Library of Congress.

28. Arthur Steigler to the AFSC, Philadelphia, 10 December 1945, AFSC Case 7827, 76, USHMM.

29. Agnes Gallagher of the AFSC, Philadelphia, to Marion Ballysingh, 20 March 1946, AFSC Case 7827, 80, USHMM.

30. Marion Ballysingh to Agnes Gallagher of the AFSC, Philadelphia, 17 May 1946, AFSC Case 7827, 81, USHMM.

31. Agnes Gallagher, summary of Steigler's case, undated, AFSC Case 7827, 89, USHMM.

32. Kathleen Hambly Hanstein, *Refugee Services of the American Friends Service Committee: An Historical Summary*, April 1967, https://www.afsc.org/sites/default/files/documen ts/1967%20Refugee%20Services%20of%20the%20AFSC%20-%20History%20 of%20AFSC%20WWII%20Work%20by%20K%20Hanstein.pdf (last accessed 1 January 2019), 14.

33. Agnes Gallaher of the AFSC, Philadelphia, to Olive Whitson of the Friends Center, New York, 6 December 1946, AFSC Case 7827, 86, USHMM.

34. Von der Porten, *Nine Lives*, 294.

35. Ibid., 375–79.

36. Ibid., 412.

37. Ibid., 323.

38. Ibid., 453–54.
39. Ibid., 480.
40. Ibid., 536.
41. Ibid., 539.
42. Ibid., 540; email from Bonnie Zimmer of the Gainesville Quakers, 30 July 2016.
43. See her obituary: https://www.legacy.com/obituaries/gainesville/obituary.aspx?n=amy-von-der-porten&pid=187667007&fhid=6683 (last accessed 1 May 2019).
44. Arnold von der Porten, *50 Years in America* (Bloomington, IN: AuthorHouse, 2004), 341.
45. Ibid., 397.
46. Von der Porten, *Nine Lives*, 239–40.
47. The following account again follows Aub, 'From My Life' ('Amtsarzt in Jamaika').
48. See also Hansjörg Ebell and Ursula Ebell, 'Fegt alle hinweg: Entzug der Approbation jüdischer Ärztinnen und Ärzte 1938'. Begleitheft zur Ausstellung [Guide to the exhibition] (Berlin: Bundesärztekammer, 2012), 16.
49. TNA HO 334/258/4509.
50. Ebell and Ebell, 'Fegt alle hinweg', 16.
51. Von der Porten, *Nine Lives*, 335.
52. AFSC Case 8192, 37, USHMM.
53. AFSC Case 8192, 53, USHMM.
54. Oscar Pillersdorf of the Jewish Association of Trinidad to Chief Rabbi Hertz, 27 November 1941, JDC, File 1048.
55. Jewish Refugee Society, statistical data provided to the Joint, February 1944, JDC, File 1048.
56. Harry D. Biele, Internal Joint memorandum, 5 December 1944, JDC, File 1048.
57. Jewish Refugee Society, statistical data provided to the Joint, June 1945, JDC, File 1215.
58. Robert Pilpel, memorandum to Isaac Levy and Louis Sobel, 5 January 1946, JDC, File 1215.
59. Robert Pilpel of the Joint to the Jewish Refugee Society, 6 January 1942, JDC, File 1048.
60. Edgar Gruen, Chairman of the Council of Jewish Organizations to the Joint, 21 December 1945, JDC, File 1215.
61. https://jewishphotolibrary.smugmug.com/CARIBBEAN/TRINIDAD/TTPortofSpain WoodbrookCemetery/i-Xsmc8fg; and https://jewishphotolibrary.smugmug.com/CAR IBBEAN/TRINIDAD/TTPortofSpainWoodbrookCemetery/i-VVvfCj5 (both last accessed 9 May 2019).
62. Joanna Newman, 'A Caribbean Jerusalem', Radio 4, 11 August 2001.
63. *Trinidad Guardian*, 16 May 2014, http://www.guardian.co.tt/article-6.2.382720.78 8d708b7f (last accessed 2 May 2019).
64. *Trinidad Guardian*, 15 May 2014, http://www.guardian.co.tt/news/2014-05-15/stech er-nazi-escapee-dies (last accessed 9 May 2019).
65. Preparatory interview with Hans Stecher for Joanna Newman, 'A Caribbean Jerusalem', Radio 4, 11 August 2001 (transcript in my possession).
66. *Cincinnati Enquirer*, 5 September 1946, 16.
67. *Cincinnati Enquirer*, 1 July 1958, 1.
68. He died there in June 1990 (*Cincinnati Enquirer*, 28 June 1990, B8).
69. *Cincinnati Enquirer*, 1 July 1958, 1.
70. *Cincinnati Enquirer*, 8 November 1976, B7, and 4 January 1979, C14.

71. https://jewishphotolibrary.smugmug.com/CARIBBEAN/TRINIDAD/TTPortof
SpainWoodbrookCemetery/i-bRvNZBD (last accessed 9 May 2019); Emil Welwart,
presumably Fischer's former colleague at the *Kronen-Zeitung*, died in 1946, aged 66
(https://jewishphotolibrary.smugmug.com/CARIBBEAN/TRINIDAD/TTPortofSpa
inWoodbrookCemetery/i-SW5qSLv, last accessed 9 May 2019).
72. See http://collections.ushmm.org/findingaids/2011.378.1_01_fnd_en.pdf (last accessed
17 June 2019); Susanne Blumesberger, Michael Doppelhofer and Gabriele Mauthe
(eds), *Handbuch österreichischer Autorinnen und Autoren jüdischer Herkunft 18. bis 20.
Jahrhundert* (Munich: Saur, 2002), Vol. 1, 278.
73. See 'Nazi refugee story to star at Fringe', in *Jewish Chronicle*, 10 June 2012, http://www.
thejc.com/news/uk-news/50080/nazi-refugee-story-star-fringe; http://www.andrewge
ha.com/we-didnt-have-time-to-be-scared (both last accessed 9 May 2019).
74. http://www.sfgate.com/bayarea/article/Bay-Area-artist-teacher-Helen-Breger-dies-49
29120.php (last accessed 9 May 2019).
75. https://www.annexgalleries.com/artists/biography/3659/Hamerman/Esther; http://
www.al.csus.edu/sota/ulg/pastexhibits/eyes-have-it/e_hamer.html; and http://www.jwe
ekly.com/article/full/67852/two-generations-render-holocaust-memories-through-art/
(all last accessed 9 May 2019).
76. http://baitstand.biz/Vienna.html (last accessed 9 May 2019).
77. http://thephilanews.com/dancing-on-a-volcano-wins-at-new-hope-film-festival-333
95.htm (last accessed 9 May 2019).
78. http://montrealgazette.remembering.ca/obituary/harry-wagschal-1066548959 (last
accessed 17 June 2019).
79. Harry Schachter, email communication, 1 August 2016.
80. Ibid.; Siegel, 'Unintended Haven', 319.
81. http://www.sswaa.org/?page=549 (last accessed 9 May 2019).
82. https://jewishphotolibrary.smugmug.com/CARIBBEAN/TRINIDAD/TTPortof
SpainWoodbrookCemetery/i-fV5b6Z8; and https://jewishphotolibrary.smugmug.com
/CARIBBEAN/TRINIDAD/TTPortofSpainWoodbrookCemetery/i-R9Nc22Z (both
last accessed 9 May 2019).
83. https://jewishphotolibrary.smugmug.com/CARIBBEAN/TRINIDAD/TTPortof
SpainWoodbrookCemetery/i-2bjVxSr (last accessed 9 May 2019).
84. https://www.ushmm.org/online/hsv/person_view.php?PersonId=5633422; and https:
//jewishphotolibrary.smugmug.com/CARIBBEAN/TRINIDAD/TTPortofSpainWoo
dbrookCemetery/i-pfFDDSz (both last accessed 9 May 2019).
85. http://www.steinheim-institut.de/cgi-bin/epidat?id=e19-10&lang=de; and http://ccb
funeral.com/?p=4169 (both last accessed 9 May 2019).
86. https://jewishphotolibrary.smugmug.com/CARIBBEAN/TRINIDAD/TTPortof
SpainWoodbrookCemetery/i-xdBWbzF (last accessed 9 May 2019).
87. http://www.holocaustcenter.org/research/testimonies/Schwarz.Heinz.
88. List of Contributors to JDC Campaign 1950/1, JDC, NY AR194554/4/80/1/989,
http://search.archives.jdc.org/multimedia/Documents/NY_AR_45-54/NY_AR45-54_
Count/NY_AR45-54_00104/NY_AR45-54_00104_00600.pdf (last accessed 9 May
2019).
89. https://jewishphotolibrary.smugmug.com/CARIBBEAN/TRINIDAD/TTPortof
SpainWoodbrookCemetery/i-443Sdj3 (last accessed 9 May 2019).
90. https://jewishphotolibrary.smugmug.com/CARIBBEAN/TRINIDAD/TTPortof
SpainWoodbrookCemetery/i-cLNswXw; and https://jewishphotolibrary.smugmug.

com/CARIBBEAN/TRINIDAD/TTPortofSpainWoodbrookCemetery/i-X9qzgxG (both last accessed 9 May 2019).

91. TNA HO 334/257/4235.
92. https://jewishphotolibrary.smugmug.com/CARIBBEAN/TRINIDAD/TTPortofSpa inWoodbrookCemetery/i-SqGXZcG (last accessed 9 May 2019).
93. https://jewishphotolibrary.smugmug.com/CARIBBEAN/TRINIDAD/TTPortofSpai nWoodbrookCemetery/i-R2cLHzs; and https://jewishphotolibrary.smugmug.com/CA RIBBEAN/TRINIDAD/TTPortofSpainWoodbrookCemetery/i-TLCJ2pq (both last accessed 9 May 2019).
94. https://jewishphotolibrary.smugmug.com/CARIBBEAN/TRINIDAD/TTPortofSpa inWoodbrookCemetery/i-mtL5Vmg (last accessed 9 May 2019).
95. https://jewishphotolibrary.smugmug.com/CARIBBEAN/TRINIDAD/TTPortofSpa inWoodbrookCemetery/i-jghjkxB (last accessed 9 May 2019).
96. https://jewishphotolibrary.smugmug.com/CARIBBEAN/TRINIDAD/TTPortofSpa inWoodbrookCemetery/i-HSZpgkR (last accessed 9 May 2019).
97. List of Contributors to JDC Campaign 1950/1, JDC, NY AR194554/4/80/1/989, http://search.archives.jdc.org/multimedia/Documents/NY_AR_45-54/NY_AR45-54_ Count/NY_AR45-54_00104/NY_AR45-54_00104_00600.pdf (last accessed 9 May 2019).
98. http://www.legacy.com/obituaries/montrealgazette/obituary.aspx?pid=148298895.
99. The following account follows Su Goldfish, *The Last Goldfish* (documentary film), Umbrella Entertainment, 2017.
100. Manfred Goldfish, 'A Danger to Security', 8.
101. Ibid., 12.
102. Ibid., 15.
103. Siegel, 'Unintended Haven', 313.
104. Ibid., 302.

SELECT BIBLIOGRAPHY

Archival Primary Sources

The National Archives, Kew Garden, London
CAB 65/9/39; CAB 65/18; CAB 68/7/24.
CO 91/515/12; CO 91/518/14; CO 123/370/2; CO 123/376/6; CO 295/615/5; CO 295/619/16; CO 298/177; CO 298/178; CO 318/412/4; CO 318/440/5; CO 318/472/13; CO 323/412/4; CO 323/846/6; CO 323/1271/1–2; CO 323/1296/13; CO 323/1345/6; CO 323/1347/8; CO 323/1602/17; CO 323/1603/1; CO 323/1604/1–3; CO 323/1604/5; CO 323/1605/2; CO 323/1797/14; CO 323/1799/2; CO 323/1846/6–7; CO 323/1879/12; CO 351; CO 733/449; CO 950/248; CO 980/26.
FO 372/3284.
HO 334/258/4509; HO 334/268/6312; HO 334/268/6471.

The American Jewish Joint Distribution Committee Archive, New York
Files 112–15, 151, 153, 157–58, 884–85, 893, 1047–49, 1059, 1215.

YIVO Archive, New York
Files I-43, XIII Jamaica.

American Jewish Archives, Cincinnati
WJC Series D: D1/8, D2/6.
WJC Series H: H82/2, H213, H361.
SC-575.

Leo Baeck Institute, New York
Kurt Kersten Collection, Max Markreich Collection, Microfilm collection, reels SI 10 and 11.

United States Holocaust Memorial Museum
AFSC Cases 7827 and 8192.

Jewish Theological Seminary Library Special Collections, New York
Archive 96-12.

Anglo Jewish Archives, University of Southampton
MS 116/159; MS175 Hertz 1/3, 139/1F.2; MS 177, 114/3; MS183/576/; CBF Reels 2 and 14.

National Archives and Records Administration, Washington, DC
RG 59, 1930–1939, 6222; RG59, 1940–1944, 5062.

National Archives of Trinidad and Tobago, Port of Spain
C.S.O. No. 41126 Pt. II.

Wiener Library, London
Book Section, Microfilm collection S49–S146, reel S123.

Printed Primary Sources and Memoirs

'Aid to Jews Overseas. Report of the AJJDC for the Year 1937'. New York: JDC, 1938.
American Jewish Year Book 40 (5699/1938–39).
Arbeitsbericht der Reichsvertretung der Juden in Deutschland für das Jahr 1938. Berlin, 1939.
Aub, Rudolf. 'Handlanger in Sierra Leone – Amtsarzt in Jamaika', in Wolfgang Benz (ed.), *Das Exil der kleinen Leute: Alltagserfahrung deutscher Juden in der Emigration* (Munich: C.H. Beck, 1991), 80–99.
Beek, Flory van. *Flory: Survival in the Valley of Death, Holocaust 1940–1945*. Santa Ana, CA: Seven Locks Press, 1998.
Breger, Helen. *Lines: A Sketched Life*. Berkeley, CA: Helen Breger, 2009.
Burns, Alan. *Colonial Civil Servant*. London: George Allen & Unwin, 1949.
Evian Conference Concerning Political Refugees: Memorandum of Certain Jewish Organisations Concerned with the Refugees from Germany and Austria. London: n.p. [1938].
Goldmann, Nahum. *The Autobiography of Nahum Goldmann*. London: Weidenfeld & Nicolson, 1970.
Hilfsverein der Juden in Deutschland [Jewish Aid in Germany] (ed.). *Jüdische Auswanderung: Korrespondenzblatt über Auswanderungs- und Siedlungswesen*. Berlin: Schmoller & Gordon, [September] 1936, 1939.
Hockley, Ralph M. *Freedom Is Not Free*. Houston, TX: Brockton, 2000.
Laws of Barbados, Vol. III, Part IV, Session 1932–1933. Barbados, 1933.
Lenk, Karl. *The Mauritius Affair: The Boat People of 1940/41*. GB: R. Lenk, 1993.
Letter of Resignation of James G. McDonald, High Commissioner for Refugees (Jewish and Other) from Germany. Addressed to the Secretary General of the League of Nations. London: Headley, 1935.
Lévi-Strauss, Claude. *Tristes Tropiques*. London: Penguin, 2011.

Mann, Fred. *A Drastic Turn of Destiny*. Toronto, ON: Azrieli Foundation, 2009.

Marshall, Oliver (ed.). *The Caribbean at War: 'British West Indians' in World War II*. London: The North Kensington Archive at Notting Dale Urban Studies Centre, 1992.

Ordinances of British Honduras Passed in the Year 1932. Belize, 1933.

Ordinances Passed by the Legislative Council of Trinidad and Tobago during the Year 1936. Trinidad, 1937.

Parkinson, Cosmo. *The Colonial Office Within*. London: Faber & Faber, 1947.

Phiebig, Albert J., et al. *HIAS Survey, 1940–1941*. New York: HIAS, 1942.

Porten, Arnold, von der. *50 Years in America*. Bloomington, IN: AuthorHouse, 2004.

——. *The Nine Lives of Arnold: The Story of My Life from Hamburg, Germany 1917, to Leaving Jamaica, B.W.I. 1953*. Bloomington, IN: 1stBooks Library, 2007.

Serge, Victor. *Memoirs of a Revolutionary, 1901–1941*. London: Oxford University Press, 1963.

Shuckburgh, John. 'Colonial Civil History of the War', Vol. 1. Unpublished typescript. London: Institute of Commonwealth Studies Library.

Stanton, Miriam. *Escape from the Inferno of Europe*. London: Imprint unknown, 1996.

Statistisches Jahrbuch für das Deutsche Reich, Vol. 49 (1930).

Strasberg, Zeno, and Lorna Yufe. *Our Calypso Shtetl*. Toronto: Immediate Impact, 1998.

Urban-Fahr, Susanne (ed.). *PHILO-Atlas: Handbuch für die jüdische Auswanderung*, Reprint der Ausgabe von 1938 [reprint of the 1938 edition]. Frankfurt: Philo Fine Arts, 1998.

West Indies. Report by the Honourable E.F.L. Wood, MP, on his visit to the West Indies and British Guiana, December 1921 – February 1922. London: HMSO, 1922.

West India Royal Commission Report. London: HMSO, 1940.

Secondary Literature

Adler-Rudel, Salomon. 'The Evian Conference on the Refugee Question', in *Leo Baeck Institute Year Book, Vol. 13* (1968), 235–73.

Afoumado, Diane. *Indésirables 1938: la conférence d'Évian et les réfugiés juifs*. France: Calmann-Lévy, 2018.

Alderman, Geoffrey. *Modern British Jewry*. Oxford: Clarendon, 1992.

Altink, Henrice. 'A True Maverick: The Political Career of Dr. Oswald E. Anderson, 1919–1944', in *New West Indian Guide, Vol. 87* (2013), 3–29.

Arbell, Mordechai. *The Jewish Nation of the Caribbean: The Spanish–Portuguese Jewish Settlement in the Caribbean and the Guianas*. Jerusalem: Geffen, 2002.

August, Thomas G. 'Family Structure and Jewish Continuity in Jamaica since 1655'. *American Jewish Archives* 41(1) (1989), 27–42.

Avni, Haim. 'Patterns of Jewish Leadership in Latin America during the Holocaust', in Randolph Braham (ed.), *Jewish Leadership during the Nazi Era: Patterns of Behavior in the Free World* (New York: Social Science Monographs, 1985), 87–130.

Ayearst, Morley. *The British West Indies: The Search for Self Government*. London: George Allen & Unwin, 1960.

Baptiste, Fitz. *War, Cooperation and Conflict: The European Possessions in the Caribbean 1939–1945*. New York: Greenwood, 1988.

Barkai, Avraham and Paul Mendes-Flohr. 'Renewal and Destruction 1918–1945', Vol. 4, in Michael A. Meyer (ed.), *German-Jewish History in Modern Times* (New York: Columbia University Press, 1998).

Bartrop, Paul. *The Evian Conference of 1938 and the Jewish Refugee Crisis*. London: Palgrave Macmillan, 2017.

———. 'From Lisbon to Jamaica: A Study of British Refugee Rescue during the Second World War'. *Immigrants and Minorities* 13(1) (March 1994), 48–64.

——— (ed.). *False Havens: The British Empire and the Holocaust*. Lanham, MD: University Press of America, 1995.

Bauer, Yehuda. *American Jewry and the Holocaust: The American Jewish Joint Distribution Committee, 1939–1945*. Jerusalem: Institute of Contemporary Jewry / Detroit: Wayne State University Press, 1981.

Bazarov, Valery. 'HIAS and HICEM in the System of Jewish Relief Organisations in Europe, 1933–31'. *East European Jewish Affairs* 39(1) (2009), 69–78.

Becker, Avi. 'Diplomacy without Sovereignty: The World Jewish Congress Rescue Activities', in Selwyn Ilan Troen and Benjamin Pinkus (eds), *Organizing Rescue: National Jewish Solidarity in the Modern Period* (London: Frank Cass, 1992), 343–460.

Bennett, Louise. *Jamaica Labrish: Jamaica Dialect Poems*. Kingston: Sangster's Book Stores, 1966.

Blumesberger, Susanne, Michael Doppelhofer and Gabriele Mauthe (eds). *Handbuch österreichischer Autorinnen und Autoren jüdischer Herkunft 18. bis 20. Jahrhundert*. Munich: Saur, 2002.

Bousquet, Ben, and Colin Douglas. *West Indian Women at War: British Racism in World War II*. London: Lawrence & Wishart, 1991.

Brinkmann, Tobias. 'The Road from Damascus: Transnational Jewish Philanthropic Organizations and the Jewish Mass Migration from Eastern Europe, 1840–1914', in Davide Rodrigo, Bernhard Struck and Jakob Vogel (eds), *Shaping the Transnational Sphere: Experts, Networks and Issues from the 1840s to the 1930s* (New York: Berghahn Books, 2015), 152–72.

———. 'Strangers in the City: Transmigration from Eastern Europe and its Impact on Berlin and Hamburg 1880–1914'. *Journal of Migration History* 2 (2016), 223–46.

Brown, Suzanne Francis. *Mona Past and Present: The History and Heritage of the Mona Campus, University of the West Indies*. Kingston: University of the West Indies Press, 2004.

Browning, Christopher R. *The Origins of the Final Solution: The Evolution of Nazi Jewish Policy, September 1939 – March 1942*. With contributions by Jürgen Matthäus. London: Heinemann, 2004.

Caestecker, Frank, and Bob Moore. 'From Kristallnacht to War, November 1938 – August 1939', in Caestecker and Moore (eds), *Refugees from Nazi Germany and the Liberal European States* (New York: Berghahn Books, 2010), 276–311.

Casteel, Sarah Phillips. *Calypso Jews: Jewishness in the Caribbean Literary Imagination*. New York: Columbia University Press, 2016.

Cohen, Robin. *Global Diasporas: An Introduction*. London: UCL Press, 1997.

Cooper-Clark, Diana. *Dreams of Re-Creation in Jamaica: The Holocaust, Internment, Jewish Refuges in Gibraltar Camp, Jamaican Jews and Sephardim*. Victoria, BC: FriesenPress, 2017.

Craig, Hewan. *The Legislative Council of Trinidad and Tobago*. London: Faber & Faber, 1952.

Crigler, Robin K. 'On Calypso's Island: The Rise and Rise of Carnival in Trinidad', 29 April 2017, https://www.academia.edu/33081388/On_Calypsos_Island_The_Rise_and_Rise_of_Carnival_on_Trinidad. Accessed on 29 April 2019.

Cwik, Christian, and Verena Muth. 'European Refugees in the Wider Caribbean in the Context of World War II', in Karen Eccles and Debbie McCollin (eds), *World War II and the Caribbean* (Jamaica: University of the West Indies Press, 2017), 247–72.

Daniels, Roger. 'American Refugee Policy in Historical Perspective', in Jarrell C. Jackman and Carla M. Borden (eds), *The Muses Flee Hitler: Cultural Transfer and Adaptation 1930–1945* (Washington, DC: Smithsonian, 1983), 61–77.

Ebell, Hansjörg, and Ursula Ebell. 'Fegt alle hinweg: Entzug der Approbation jüdischer Ärztinnen und Ärzte 1938'. Begleitheft zur Ausstellung [Guide to the exhibition]. Berlin: Bundesärztekammer, 2012.

Engel, David. *In the Shadow of Auschwitz: The Polish Government-in-Exile and the Jews, 1939–1942*. Chapel Hill: University of North Carolina Press, 1987.

Erbelding, Rebecca L. 'About Time: The History of the War Refugee Board'. PhD thesis. Fairfax, VA: George Mason University, 2015.

Farah, Donna. 'The Jewish Community in Trinidad, 1930s–70s'. Unpublished Caribbean Studies Project. Kingston, Jamaica: University of the West Indies, 1991.

Feingold, Henry. *Bearing Witness: How America and Its Jews Responded to the Holocaust*. Syracuse, NY: Syracuse University Press, 1995.

Feldman, David. *Englishmen and Jews: Social Relations and Political Culture, 1840–1914*. New Haven, CT: Yale University Press, 1994.

Fleming, Michael. *Auschwitz, the Allies and Censorship of the Holocaust*. Cambridge: Cambridge University Press, 2014.

Fortune, Stephen. *Merchants and Jews: The Struggle for British West Indian Commerce 1650–1750*. Gainesville: University of Florida, 1984.

Frankel, Jonathan. *The Damascus Affair: 'Ritual Murder', Politics, and the Jews in 1840*. New York: Cambridge University Press, 1997.

Friedländer, Saul. *Nazi Germany and the Jews, Vol. 1: The Years of Persecution, 1933–39*. London: Weidenfeld & Nicolson, 1997.

Fry, Helen. *Spymaster: The Secret Life of Kendrick*. London: Marranos, 2014.

Füllberg-Stolberg, Claus. 'The Caribbean in the Second World War', in Bridget Brereton (ed.), *UNESCO General History of the Caribbean, Vol. 5: The Caribbean in the Twentieth Century* (Paris: UNESCO, 2004), 82–140.

Füllberg-Stolberg, Claus, and Katja Füllberg-Stolberg. 'Jüdisches Exil im Britischen Kolonialreich – Gibraltar Camp Jamaica 1942–1947', in Marlis Buchholz, Claus Füllberg-Stolberg and Hans-Dieter Schmid (eds), *Nationalsozialismus und Region: Festschrift für Herbert Obenaus zum 65. Geburtstag* (Bielefeld: Verlag für Regionalgeschichte, 1996), 85–102.

Gal, Allon. 'David Ben-Gurion's Zionist Foreign Policy, 1938–48: The Democratic Factor'. *Israel Affairs* 10(1–2) (2004), 13–28.

Gazely, Ian. 'Manual Work and Pay, 1900–70', in Nicholas Crafts, Ian Gazely and Andrew Newell (eds), *Work and Pay in Twentieth-Century Britain* (New York: Oxford University Press, 2007), 55–79.

Gilbert, Martin. 'British Government Policy towards Jewish Refugees (November 1937 – September 1939)'. *Yad Vashem Studies* 13 (1979), 127–67.

Gilroy, Paul. *The Black Atlantic: Modernity and Double Consciousness*. London: Verso, 1993.

Glaser, Zhava Litvac. 'Refugees and Relief: The American Jewish Joint Distribution Committee and European Jews in Cuba and Shanghai, 1938–1943'. PhD thesis, CUNY Graduate School, 2015 (http://academicworks.cuny.edu/gc_etds/561/) (last accessed 17 June 2019).

Gleizer, Daniel. *Unwelcome Exiles: Mexico and the Jewish Refugees from Nazism, 1933–1945*. Leiden: Brill, 2014.

Goldfish, Manfred: 'Nelson Island', undated typescript in author's possession.

Goldfish, Su (ed.). *Manfred Goldfish: The Schooldays of Freddy Karpf*. Bad Emser Hefte, No. 310 (2010).

Goldfish, Su. Director/Writer/Producer, Carolyn Johnson Films, *The Last Goldfish* (2017). https://www.thelastgoldfish.com/ (last accessed on 2 January 2019).

Goldfish, Su, Joanna Newman, and Julie Ewington. 'The Last Goldfish'. *Alphaville: Journal of Film and Screen Media* 18 (2019). Forthcoming.

Grossmann, Atina. 'Remapping Relief and Rescue: Flight, Displacement, and International Aid for Jewish Refugees during World War II'. *New German Critique* 117, Vol. 39, No. 3 (2012), 61–79.

Gruner, Wolf. 'Local Initiatives, Central Coordination: German Municipal Administration and the Holocaust', in Gerald D. Feldman and Wolfgang Seibel (eds), *Networks of Nazi Persecution: Bureaucracy, Business, and the Organization of the Holocaust* (New York: Berghahn Books, 2005), 269–94.

Grzyb, Amanda. 'From Kristallnacht to the MS *St Louis* Tragedy: Canadian Press Coverage of Nazi Persecution of the Jews and the Jewish Refugee Crisis, September 1938 to August 1939', in L. Ruth Klein (ed.), *Nazi Germany, Canadian Responses: Confronting Antisemitism in the Shadow of War* (Montreal: McGill-Queen's University Press, 2012), 78–113.

Guilbault, Jocelyne. *Governing Sound: The Cultural Politics of Trinidad's Carnival Musics*. Chicago: Chicago University Press, 2007.

Hambly Hanstein, K. *Refugee Services of the American Friends Service Committee: An Historical Summary*. Online, 1967. Available at: https://www.afsc.org/sites/default/files/documents/1967%20Refugee%20Services%20of%20the%20AFSC%20-%20History%20of%20AFSC%20WWII%20Work%20by%20K%20Hanstein.pdf (last accessed 1 January 2019).

Hawkins, Richard A. 'Samuel Untermyer and the Boycott of Nazi Germany, 1933–1938'. *American Jewish History* 93(1) (2007), 21–50.

Heberer, Patricia (ed.). *Children during the Holocaust*. Lanham, MD: AltaMira Press, 2011.

Hellig, Jocelyn. 'German Jewish Immigration to South Africa during the 1930s: Revisiting the Charter of the SS Stuttgart', in James Jordan, Tony Kushner and Sarah Pearce (eds), *Jewish Journeys from Philo to Hip Hop*. London: Valentine Mitchell, 2010.

Herman, Didi. *An Unfortunate Coincidence: Jews, Jewishness, and English Law*. New York: Oxford University Press, 2011.

Holzberg, Carol S. *Minorities and Power in a Black Society: The Jewish Community of Jamaica*. Lanham, MD: NorthSouth Books, 1987.

Honeychurch, Lennox. *The Dominica Story: A History of the Island*. Oxford: Macmillan Education, 1995.

Israel, Jonathan. *Diasporas within a Diaspora: Jews, Crypto-Jews and the World Maritime Empires (1540–1740)*. Leiden: Brill, 2002.

James, C.L.R. *The Black Jacobins: Toussaint L'Ouverture and the San Domingo Revolution*, 2nd edition. New York: Vintage, 1989.

Jennings, Eric. '"The Best Avenue of Escape": The French Caribbean Route as Expulsion, Rescue, Trial, and Encounter'. *French Politics, Culture & Society* 30(2) (2012), 33–52.

———. *Escape from Vichy: The Refugee Exodus to the French Caribbean*. Cambridge, MA: Harvard University Press, 2018.

———. 'Last Exit from Vichy France: The Martinique Escape Route and the Ambiguities of Emigration'. *Journal of Modern History* 74(2) (2002), 289–324.

Johnson, Howard. 'The British Caribbean from Demobilization to Constitutional Decolonization', in Judith Brown and Wm Roger Louis (eds), *The Oxford History of the British Empire. Vol. 4: The Twentieth Century* (New York: Oxford University Press, 1999), 597–622.

———. 'Oil, Imperial Policy and the Trinidad Disturbances, 1937'. *Journal of Imperial and Commonwealth History* 4(1) (1975), 29–54.

———. 'The Political Uses of Commissions of Enquiry (1): The Imperial–Colonial West Indies Context, The Forster and Moyne Commissions'. *Social and Economic Studies* 27(3) (1978), 256–83.

Kaplan, Marion. *Between Dignity and Despair: Jewish Life in Nazi Germany*. New York: Oxford University Press, 1998.

———. *Dominican Haven: The Jewish Refugee Settlement in Sosúa, 1940–1945*. New York: Museum of Jewish Heritage – A Living Memorial to the Holocaust, 2008.

Kassow, Samuel D. *Who Will Write Our History? Rediscovering a Hidden Archive from the Warsaw Ghetto*. London: Penguin, 2009.

Kelshall, Gaylord T.M. *The U-Boat War in the Caribbean*. Annapolis, MD: Naval Institute Press, 1994.

Korn, Bertram W. 'The Haham DeCordova of Jamaica', *American Jewish Archives* 18(2) (1966).

Kushner, Tony. *The Holocaust and the Liberal Imagination: A Social and Cultural History*. Oxford: Blackwell, 1994.

Lansen, Oscar E. 'Victims of Circumstance: Jewish Enemy Nationals in the Dutch West Indies 1938–1947'. *Holocaust and Genocide Studies* 13(3) (1991), 441–42.

Lawson, Tom. *The Church of England and the Holocaust: Christianity, Memory and Nazism*. Woodbridge, UK: Boydell, 2006.

Lee, John M., and Martin Petter. *The Colonial Office, War, and Development Policy: Organisation and the Planning of a Metropolitan Initiative, 1939–1945*. London: Maurice Temple Smith, 1982.

Leff, Laurel. 'Ties That Bound, Ties That Broke: Edna Ferber's Sponsorship of Refugees from Nazi Germany' (Video, 2010). https://repository.library.northeastern.edu/files/neu:cj82mf10m (last accessed 1 January 2019).

Leonhard, Claudia. *Das Unaussprechliche in Worte fassen: Eine vergleichende Analyse schriftlicher und mündlicher Selbstzeugnisse von weiblichen Überlebenden des Holocaust*. Kassel: Kassel University Press, 2013.

Lesser, Jeffrey. *Welcoming the Undesirables: Brazil and the Jewish Question*. Berkeley: University of California Press, 1995.

Levine, Robert M. *Tropical Diaspora: The Jewish Experience in Cuba*. Gainesville: University Press of Florida, 1993.

Lewis, Gordon. *The Growth of the Modern West Indies*. London: MacGibbon & Kee, 1968.

London, Louise. *Whitehall and the Jews: British Immigration Policy, Jewish Refugees and the Holocaust*. Cambridge: Cambridge University Press, 2000.

Look Lai, Walton. *Indentured Labor, Caribbean Sugar: Chinese and Indian Migrants to the British West Indies, 1838–1918*. Baltimore, MD: Johns Hopkins Press, 1993.

Maingot, Anthony P. *The United States and the Caribbean*. London: Macmillan Caribbean, 1994.

Malmsten, Neal R. 'The British Labour Party and the West Indies, 1918–1939'. *Journal of Imperial and Commonwealth History* 5(2) (1977), 173–205.

Margaliot, Abraham. 'The Problem of the Rescue of German Jewry during the Years 1933–1939: The Reasons for the Delay in their Emigration from the Third Reich', in Yisrael Gutman and Efraim Zuroff (eds), *Rescue Attempts during the Holocaust: Proceedings of the Second Yad Vashem International Historical Conference, Jerusalem, 8–11 April 1974* (Jerusalem: Yad Vashem, 1977), 245–65.

Marrus, Michael. *The Unwanted: European Refugees in the Twentieth Century*. New York: Oxford University Press, 1985.

—— (ed.). *The Nazi Holocaust: Historical Articles on the Destruction of European Jews, Vol. 2. Pt. 6: The Victims of the Holocaust*. Westport, CT: Meckler, 1989.

Marshall, Oliver (ed.). *The Caribbean at War: 'British West Indians' in World War II*. London: The North Kensington Archive at The Notting Dale Urban Studies Centre, 1992.

Marshall, Trevor G. 'Bajans Come Back to Calypso', in Rachel Wilder (ed.), *Insight Guide: Barbados*. Singapore: APA, 1990.

Martin, Tony. 'Jews to Trinidad'. *Journal of Caribbean History* 28(2) (1994), 244–57.

'Max Markreich', in Fred Grubel et al. (eds), Catalog of the Archival Collections of the Leo Baeck Institute New York. Tübingen: Mohr Siebeck, 1990.

Medoff, Rafael. 'American Responses to the Holocaust: New Research, New Controversies'. *American Jewish History* 100(3) (2016), 379–409.

Mendelsohn, John, and Donald S. Detwiler (eds). *The Holocaust: Selected Documents in Eighteen Volumes. Vol. 5: Jewish Emigration from 1933 to the Evian Conference of 1938*. New York: Garland, 1982.

Menk, Lars. *Dictionary of German-Jewish Surnames*. Bergenfield: Avotaynu, 2005.

Mirvis, Stanley. 'Joshua Hezekiah Decordova and a Rabbinic Counter-Enlightenment from Colonial Jamaica', in Brian Smollett and Christian Wiese (eds), *Reappraisals and New Studies of the Modern Jewish Experience. Essays in Honor of Robert M. Seltzer* (Leiden: Brill, 2015), 104–233.

Mitchell, Sir Harold. *Europe in the Caribbean*. Edinburgh and London: W. and R. Chambers, 1963.

Klooster, W. 'The Jews in the Early Modern Caribbean and the Atlantic World', in J. Karp and A. Sutcliffe (eds), *The Cambridge History of Judaism* (Cambridge: Cambridge University Press, 2017), 972–996. doi:10.1017/9781139017169.038

Newman, Joanna. 'Refugees from Nazism in the British Caribbean', in Jane S. Gerber (ed.), *The Jews in the Caribbean* (Oxford: Littman Library of Jewish Civilization, 2014), 343–60.

Norman, Theodore. *An Outstretched Arm: A History of the Jewish Colonization Association*. London: Routledge & Kegan Paul, 1985.

Ogilvie, Sarah A., and Scott Miller. *Refuge Denied: The St. Louis Passengers and the Holocaust*. Madison: University of Wisconsin Press, 2006.

Omissi, David. 'Britain, the Assyrians and the Iraq Levies, 1919–1932'. *Journal of Imperial and Commonwealth History* 17(3) (1989), 301–22.

Orchard, Phil. *Refugees, States, and the Construction of International Cooperation*. Cambridge: Cambridge University Press, 2014.

Penkower, Monty. 'Dr. Nahum Goldmann and the Policy of International Jewish Organizations', in Selwyn Ilan Troen and Benjamin Pinkus (eds), *Organizing Rescue: National Jewish Solidarity in the Modern Period* (London: Frank Cass, 1992), 141–53.

Pitot, Geneviève. *The Mauritian Shekl: The Story of the Jewish Detainees in Mauritius 1940–1945*. Lanham, MD: Rowman & Littlefield, 2000.

Poole, Bernard L. *The Caribbean Commission: Background of Cooperation in the West Indies*. Columbia: University of South Carolina Press, 1951.

Post, Ken. *Strike the Iron, Vol. 1. A Colony At War: Jamaica, 1939–1945*. Atlantic Highlands, NJ: Humanities Press, 1981.

Potworowski, Tomasz. 'The Evacuation of Jewish Polish Citizens from Portugal to Jamaica, 1941–1943'. *Polin* 19 (2007), 155–82.

Prinz, Arthur. 'The Role of the Gestapo in Obstructing and Promoting Jewish Emigration'. *Yad Vashem Studies* 2 (1958), 205–18.

Roberts, George W., and Joycelin Byrne. 'Summary Statistics on Indenture and Associated Migration Affecting the West Indies, 1834–1918'. *Population Studies* 20(1) (1966), 125–34.

Robins, Steven. *Letters of Stone: From Nazi Germany to South Africa*. Cape Town: Penguin, 2016.

Rodrigo, Javier. 'Exploitation, Fascist Violence and Social Cleansing: A Study of Franco's Concentration Camps from a Comparative Perspective'. *European Review of History* 19(4) (2012), 553–73.

Rohlehr, Gordon. *Calypso and Society in Pre-Independence Trinidad*. Port of Spain: Gordon Rohlehr, 1990.

Rosenstock, Werner. 'Exodus 1933–1939: A Survey of Jewish Emigration from Germany', in *Leo Baeck Institute Year Book, Vol. 1* (1956), 373–90.

Rovit, Rebecca. 'Cultural Ghettoization and Theater during the Holocaust: Performance as a Link to Community'. *Holocaust and Genocide Studies* 19(3) (2005), 459–86.

———. *The Jewish Kulturbund Theatre Company in Nazi Berlin*. Iowa City: University of Iowa Press, 2012.

———. 'Jewish Theatre: Repertory and Censorship in the Jüdischer Kulturbund, Berlin', in John London (ed.), *Theatre under the Nazis* (Manchester: Manchester University Press, 2000), 187–221.

Samuel, Wilfred S. 'A Review of the Jewish Colonists in Barbados in the Year 1680', in *Transactions of the Jewish Historical Society of England, Vol. 13 (1932–1935)*, 1–111.

Sanders, Ronald. *Shores of Refuge: A Hundred Years of Jewish Emigration*. New York: Holt, 1988.

Schorsch, Jonathan. *Jews and Blacks in the Early Modern World*. New York: Cambridge University Press, 2004.

Segev, Zohar. *The World Jewish Congress during the Holocaust: Between Activism and Restraint*. Berlin: de Gruyter, 2014.

Sheramy, Rona. '"There Are Times When Silence Is a Sin": The Women's Division of the American Jewish Congress and the Anti-Nazi Boycott'. *American Jewish History* 89(1) (2001), 105–21.

Sherlock, Philip. *West Indies*. London: Thames & Hudson, 1966.

Sherman, Ari J. *Island Refuge: Britain and Refugees from the Third Reich, 1933–1939*. London: Elek, 1973.

Siegel, Alisa. 'An Unintended Haven: The Jews of Trinidad, 1937 to 2003'. PhD thesis, University of Toronto, 2003.

Sives, Amanda. 'Dwelling Separately: The Federation of the West Indies and the Challenge of Insularity', in Emilian Kavalski and Magdalena Żółkoś (eds), *Defunct Federalisms: Critical Perspectives on Federal Failure* (Aldershot: Ashgate, 2008), 17–30.

Skran, Claudia. *Refugees in Inter-War Europe: The Emergence of a Regime*. Oxford: Clarenden Press, 1995.

Snyder, Holly. 'English Markets, Jewish Merchants, and Atlantic Endeavors: Jews and the Making of British Transatlantic Commercial Culture,1650–1800', in Richard L. Kagan and Philp D. Morgan (eds), *Atlantic Diasporas: Jews, Conversos, and Crypto-Jews in the Age of Mercantilism, 1500–1800* (Baltimore, MD: Johns Hopkins University Press, 2009), 50–74.

Stent, Ronald. 'Jewish Refugee Organisations', in Werner E. Mosse et al. (eds), *Second Chance: Two Centuries of German-Speaking Jews in the United Kingdom* (Tübingen: Mohr Siebeck, 1991), 579–98.

Stern, Malcolm, and Bernard Postal. *Jews in the West Indies*. New York: American Airlines Guide, n.d.

Strauss, Herbert. 'Jewish Attitudes in the Jewish Press', in idem (ed.), *Jewish Immigrants of the Nazi Period in the USA. Vol. 6: Essays on the History, Persecution and Emigration of German Jews* (New York: Saur, 1987), 95–141.

————. 'Jewish Emigration from Germany: Nazi Policies and Jewish Responses (I)', in *Leo Baeck Institute Year Book, Vol. 25* (1980), 313–61.

————. 'Jewish Emigration from Germany: Nazi Policies and Jewish Responses (II)', in *Leo Baeck Institute Year Book, Vol. 26* (1981), 343–409.

Szajkowski, Zosa. 'Budgeting American Jewish Overseas Relief (1919–1939)'. *American Jewish Historical Quarterly* 59(1) (1970), 83–113.

————. 'Private American Jewish Overseas Relief, 1919–1938: Problems and Attempted Solutions'. *American Jewish Historical Quarterly* 57(3) (1968), 285–342, 347–50.

————. 'Private and Organized American Jewish Overseas Relief (1914–1938)'. *American Jewish Historical Quarterly* 57(1) (1967), 52–106.

Verteuil, Anthony de. *Edward Lanza Joseph and the Jews in Trinidad*. Port of Spain: Litho Press, 2014, 169–70.

Vincent, C. Paul. 'The Voyage of the *St. Louis* Revisited'. *Holocaust and Genocide Studies* 25(2) (2011), 252–89.

Wasserstein, Bernard. *Britain and the Jews of Europe* (2nd Revised Edition). Leicester: Leicester University Press, 1999.

Weber, Wolfgang. 'Gibraltar liegt in Amerika: Zur Geschichte des Internierungslagers Gibraltar in Kingston 1940–1948', in *Historisches Jahrbuch der Stadt Linz* (2003/2004).

Weis, Paul. *Nationality and Statelessness in International Law*. Dordrecht: Kluwer, 1979.

Weisgal, Meyer (ed.). *Chaim Weizmann: Statesman, Scientist, Builder of the Jewish Commonwealth*. New York: Dial Press, 1944.

Williams, Eric. *From Columbus to Castro*. London: André Deutsch, 1970.

Wischnitzer, Mark. *To Dwell in Safety: The Story of Jewish Migration since 1800*. Philadelphia: JPS, 1948.

————. *Visas to Freedom: The History of HIAS*. Cleveland, OH: World Publishing Co., 1956.

Wyman, David S. (ed.). *America and the Holocaust. Vol. 3: The Mock Rescue Conference, Bermuda*. New York: Garland, 1990.

———— (ed.). *America and the Holocaust. Vol. 5: American Jewish Disunity*. New York: Garland, 1990.

Yahil, Leni. *The Holocaust: The Fate of European Jewry*. New York: Oxford University Press, 1990.

————. 'Madagascar: Phantom of a Solution for the Jewish Question', in Bela Vago and George L. Mosse (eds), *Jews and Non-Jews in Eastern Europe, 1918–1945* (New York: Wiley, 1974), 315–34.

Zweig, Ronald. *Britain and Palestine during the Second World War*. Woodbridge, UK: Boydell, 1986.

INDEX